F

Encyclopedia of Modern Bodybuilding

BY
ARNOLD SCHWARZENEGGER

WITH BILL DOBBINS

A FIRESIDE BOOK
Published by Simon & Schuster
NEW YORK LONDON TORONTO SYDNEY TOKYO SINGAPORE

First Fireside Edition, 1987

Published by Simon & Schuster, Inc.
Simon & Schuster Building
Rockefeller Center
1230 Avenue of the Americas
New York, New York 10020

FIRESIDE and colophon are registered trademarks
of Simon & Schuster, Inc.

Designed by Irving Perkins Associates

Manufactured in the United States of America

10 9 8 7 6 5 4
20 19   Pbk.

Library of Congress Cataloging in Publication Data

Schwarzenegger, Arnold.
   Arnold Schwarzenegger encyclopedia of modern bodybuilding.

   Includes index.
   1. Bodybuilding. 2. Exercise. I. Dobbins, Bill.
II. Title. III. Title: Encyclopedia of modern
bodybuilding.
GV546.5.S383   1985   646.7'5   84-27545
ISBN: 0-671-42764-4
ISBN: 0-671-63381-3 Pbk.

Drawings by Bruce Algra
Drawing on page 103 by Lynn Marks

For my mother.

NOTE:

Before starting any new exercise program, it is important that you consult your physician. This is a must if you have any serious medical conditions or if you are taking medication. Get your doctor's consent before you begin.

ACKNOWLEDGMENTS

I would like to express my great appreciation to all of the bodybuilders included in this book, who I think are the greatest bodybuilders in history, and whose cooperation helped to make this book a reality.

Also, my gratitude to all the highly talented and hard-working photographers whose photographs you will find on these pages.

Special thanks to Susan Victor of Simon and Schuster for all of her good ideas; to Albert Busek for his unfailing support and encouragement; to Joe Weider for opening his archives to me and for providing valuable research material; to Franco Columbu, a true friend and great training partner; and to Jim Lorimer for consistently providing great advice.

Last but not least, thanks to my assistants Anita Lerner, Ronda Columb and Lynn Marks for working with me on the book over the last few years.

CONTENTS

Chapter 7   Mind Over Matter: The Mind, the Most Powerful Tool   201

BOOK THREE: Body Part Exercises

The Shoulders   219

Shoulder Exercises   242

Trapezius Exercises   265

The Chest   269

Chest Exercises   294

The Back   315

Back Exercises   334

The Thighs   446

Leg Exercises   464

The Calves   480

Calf Exercises   494

The Abdomen   501

BOOK FOUR: Competition

BOOK FIVE: Health, Nutrition, Diet, and Drugs

CHAPTER 1 Nutrition and Diet   668

CHAPTER 2 How to Gain or Lose Weight   686

CHAPTER 3 Contest Dieting   695

The more popular competition bodybuilding becomes, the more confusion there seems to be about how to actually do it. Basic training principles are debated—heavy training versus light training; whether to use free weights or machines; what kind of training schedule yields the best results; how to gain muscle mass; how to get ripped up; how to bring up slow-to-respond calves or develop the maximum sweep in the lats.

This confusion and debate was the primary reason I set out to write this "encyclopedia." With each of my other books, I had a definite purpose—to tell the story of my bodybuilding career, to introduce men to the benefits of bodybuilding training, and to make these same benefits available to women as well. Each of these books achieved its purpose, but none answered all the questions plaguing the hard-core competition bodybuilder, the athlete whose goals may include becoming Mr. America, Mr. Universe or even Mr. Olympia.

As a matter of fact, this kind of information has not been available in *any* book. Sure, plenty of bodybuilding books have been published, but each represents only one specific point of view, not an exhaustive reference manual covering every conceivable aspect of the sport. The beginning bodybuilder trying to learn what is necessary to master his sport is not in a much better position than I was the first day I walked into a bodybuilding gym.

In Austria, when I was fifteen years old and just getting started in bodybuilding, the only way I could learn was to listen to and copy the more advanced bodybuilders training in the gym. Looking back, I can see how little any of us knew at the time. All we had to go on were some basic principles that had been passed on from one bodybuilder to another and written about in bodybuilding magazines. We studied these magazines with such intensity it nearly burned the print right off the pages.

I had to learn about training, diet, nutrition, posing and all the other elements of competition training by observation and trial and error. It took a lot of effort and a very long time. However, my ambition to become a great bodybuilder has been the driving force in my life, and so I learned what I had to, whatever the cost. For example, I was massive when I went to my first Mr. Universe contest in 1966—the biggest man there. But I was beaten by Chet Yorton, a smaller man who had much better definition. He had learned how to reduce his body fat to show off his muscles to their best advantage. In 1968, the same thing happened when I went to Florida to compete against Frank Zane. It didn't take me long to figure out that I needed to master the principles of dieting.

I was to suffer yet a third defeat at the hands of a great body-builder—against Sergio Oliva in the 1969 Mr. Olympia contest—but by now I had acquired a lot more experience and knowledge about my own body and how to train and diet for both maximum muscle mass *and* definition. And I was determined never to be defeated again.

Experience is a great teacher, but you have to be willing to learn. Win or lose, I made sure I benefited from any contest I entered. I asked the judges to explain what qualities they believed were necessary to become a great bodybuilder. They told me about the importance of creating the right *kind* of physical shape in addition to simply building mass. They explained about proportion and balance—how a small waist accentuated a massive chest and flaring lats; how small knees and large calves perfectly complemented sweeping thighs. I began to understand the difference between mere size and a truly *quality* physique. Since my observations in the gym had, from the first, taught me the importance of using the mind in bodybuilding, I was a quick learner. I was hungry for knowledge, desperate for new information. And the outcome was that after 1969 I never again lost a contest, and I avenged my early losses by beating all three men who had handed me my defeats.

Yet, in some respects, this grasp of technique came almost too late. Perfection is obviously not attainable on this earth, but that was not an axiom I would have accepted when I was fifteen years old and first experiencing the thrill of cold iron in my hands. Yet certain assumptions that I and the other bodybuilders who trained with me were making were imperceptibly creating a barrier to the attainment of that perfection I so deeply desired.

For example, we knew nothing about triceps training. We believed that a man should have big, strong arms, but that the sign of a manly arm was a fully developed biceps. So we would blast our biceps with set after set of mind-boggling training, and then finish off the workout with some passing attention to triceps work. I later realized the error of this approach and began to give the triceps the attention they required. But my early years of training have continued to have their effect, and my biceps have remained more outstanding than my triceps.

Bench presses are another good example. How we loved to do bench presses. The champions we saw in the magazine photos all had massive chests, and they were the ones winning the competitions. So we continually strained against heavier and heavier barbells, drove each other to greater feats of strength. It never occurred to us that various parts of the pectoral muscles could be isolated and trained specifically to produce the most ideal contours. Nor did we think to train the upper pectorals in a different way than the inner pectorals, or to give attention to the serratus and the tie-ins to the deltoids.

In spite of my many victories and my string of titles, including my phenomenal seven Mr. Olympia championships, I believe that a more thorough education in the fundamentals during my early, formative years would have resulted in at least a 10 percent improvement in my absolute best Olympia form. However, whatever I may have been doing wrong that cost me that hypothetical 10 percent, I must have been doing a lot right to achieve that very real 90 percent.

One advantage I had going for me is that I did not overintellectualize my workouts. Oh, I thought about what I was doing—I thought a lot about it. But I used my mind to understand how my training was affecting my body and what specific results I was getting by using particular exercises and routines. I never got caught up in abstract training ideas or became distracted by bodybuilding principles which I didn't have the experience to properly interpret. I didn't agonize over ideas like "pre-exhaustion"; I went to the gym and exhausted myself by really hard training. As a result, I created a fundamentally sound muscle structure, the kind of mass that I could later sculpt into a world-champion-level physique.

I believe it was my willingness and ability to listen to what my own body was telling me that got me through my early years. I was able to substitute trial-and-error experience—however slow and inefficient—for access to the sophisticated knowledge that three decades of modern bodybuilders had created. In time, I began to travel and meet top champions like Reg Park, Paul Winter, Chet Yorton, Bill Pearl, and other stars of the day. Gradually I acquired the necessary knowledge to allow me to sculpt my body like an artist, choosing the exercises and creating the routines that would produce whatever physical responses I desired.

I became, in due time, exactly what I had set out to be: a bodybuilding champion, able to bring myself to a contest in the best possible shape—massive, yet cut and defined. I could do it *on purpose,* over and over if need be. I was the master of my physical structure. I was in control.

I can't say how much better I might have become if things had been different, if I had known more, if there had been books to read and world-class bodybuilders to consult. But when I look back on the time I wasted, on the blind alleys my curiosity led me into, I have to conclude I would have benefited immensely by better early instruction.

So it is very frustrating sometimes when young bodybuilders approach me in the gym, or at one of the many seminars I give all around the world, and I realize from their questions that they are going through the same kind of learning process as I did. I try to answer as best I can, but that kind of brief discussion, with no opportunity to go into complex details, is simply not adequate to communicate the kind of information I know they are hungry for. There is no way I can relate all they need to know to make it in this difficult but rewarding sport, no chance to impart to them enough of the hard-won knowledge I have spent most of my life accumulating.

The obvious solution was to include all this vital information in a book, a complete encyclopedia of bodybuilding containing everything a person needs to know about every possible aspect of the sport—from basic training techniques to the most advanced, from how to start training the first day you walk into a gym to how to deal with the demands of international-level championship competition.

I knew that putting together such an encyclopedia was a tall order. No matter how much I knew about bodybuilding, there was always more to be learned. I found that out en route to my seventh Mr. Olympia win in Australia in 1980, when I suddenly found it necessary to get in shape for the contest in only half the time I normally would have allowed myself, and in spite of a five-year layoff from competition to pursue my writing, business, and movie ambitions. In effect I had to start from scratch, abandon principles that had carried me through years of competition and go back to a trial-and-error kind of learning, listening to my body and letting it tell me what I had to do.

So it was obvious to me that, for any book to qualify as a genuine *encyclopedia* of bodybuilding, it could not deal with the sport on a superficial level. It would have to contain the widest possible range of information and up-to-date technical knowledge, and require the efforts and cooperation of a host of experts in the field.

One of the problems with "how-to" books or courses by champion bodybuilders is that they tend to tell you how that individual does things—which may or may not suit you and your particular personality and body type. Therefore, in writing this book I called upon a variety of individuals whose experience and expertise encompass virtually every aspect of bodybuilding. Who, for example, knows more about the art of posing and presentation than Ed Corney. He came along at a time when posing technique in bodybuilding contests had been languishing for years and turned everything around with his innovative ideas. And who is better able to advise on the role of strength training and power lifting than Franco Columbu, who is not only a Mr. Olympia titleholder and a doctor of chiropractic but whose legendary strength is such that when competing in the "World's Strongest Man" competition he has bested individuals in some events who outweighed him by a full 100 pounds.

When putting the biceps section together, I had help from Robby Robinson. Tom Platz sat down with me and explained his leg-training techniques in detail. Franco gave me a lot of ideas about chest training. In addition to consulting with all of these great competitors and others such as Samir Bannout, Mohamed Makkawy, Bertil Fox, Albert Beckles, Lee Haney, Danny Padilla, and Jusup Wilkosz, I have included photos of many of these physique stars in the training sections—because no bodybuilder has a perfect physique and the more examples of outstanding development I can include in the book, the more the reader can learn.

And, finally, I solicited the advice of physiologists, nutritionists, and medical scientists. I wanted to be certain that any question that may occur to the reader will be covered comprehensively.

In the beginning, I expected that putting this book together would be a lot of work, but I was unprepared for what a Herculean task it actually turned out to be. Instead of ending up with a 300-page manuscript, I watched the pages pile up until there were 500, 600 and, eventually, more than 700 pages stacked in front of me! The more I got into it, the more I realized how much there was to say and how much work it required. I had no idea that I would be spending hundreds of hours going through the Joe Weider photo archives—with the patient help of photo librarians Mandy Tanny and Susan Fry—to find just the right pictures: a shot of Reg Park's 20-inch calves, for example, or a Mr. Universe lineup from the 1960s.

And so the manuscript continued to grow: not only covering how to train each muscle, but how to deal with weak body parts or weak points within a given muscle group; how to pose; the psychology of training and competition; genetics, contest politics, nutrition, drugs, dealing with pressure; how, when, and where to compete.

There is so much to know and so many areas where you can make a mistake. For example, I remember the time I was pumping up backstage beside Freddy Ortiz in 1968 and, still very much a neophyte, watched as he indulged himself in smoking cigarettes and sipping whiskey. I didn't speak very much English, so I couldn't really ask him why he was doing this, but I figured it must give him some sort of edge, and I decided to try it.

It was a bad mistake. I was not used to cigarettes or hard liquor, and it didn't take much to make me so dizzy that I almost lost control. A friend took me aside, slapped me across the face, and yelled, "Arnold, what are you doing! You're asleep! Wake up, you're letting your stomach hang out!" I was able to recover enough to go on to win, but later I realized what a risk I had taken, and how unnecessary it had been. If I had had a little more guidance, from a coach or from an encyclopedia like this, I would never have put my victory in such jeopardy.

And there is more, and more, and more. It never ends. In fact, looking back, I can hardly believe I managed to thread my way through the maze of international bodybuilding with little more to guide me than simple trial and error. But the fact that I did it that way doesn't mean I would recommend it to you. I had to do it the hard way because I had no other choice.

All of this, of course, is in addition to the bottom line: how do you train, what kind of exercises, reps, and sets do you do to build a champion physique? You go to one gym and see a top bodybuilder lifting very heavy weights and doing forced reps with mind-boggling intensity. Then you read in a magazine that somebody else you respect trains with lighter weights but does set after endless set. Albert Beckles builds his chest one way, Serge Nubret another; will certain techniques build you up or tear you down? Should you run for its aerobic benefit while you are doing competition training, or will this interfere with your progress?

Whenever bodybuilders find themselves facing a situation that they have no easy answer for, whenever a question arises that seems to stand in the way of career development, or whenever a beginning bodybuilder simply needs a little guidance and information, my wish is that they will reach automatically for *Arnold's Encyclopedia of Modern Bodybuilding*. "Let's look it up," I want them to say, and know they will find the answers they are looking for. Anything and everything about bodybuilding:

- how to lose 30 pounds in eight weeks if that's what it takes to win a contest;
- how to put 2 inches on your thighs in a hurry to create the proportions it will take to achieve victory;

- when you should oil up prior to the contest and how much to pump up for each round of competition;
- what kind of posing routine will best suit your individual physique and how to practice your presentation.

You can't learn bodybuilding from a book. But then you can't drive from New York to Chicago by studying a road map, either. But taking a look at the map before heading for the Pennsylvania Turnpike can save you a lot of time in transit, and having the encyclopedia handy for reference will, I believe, make your journey on the way to bodybuilding achievement that much faster and easier.

And so, from me to you, best wishes for your own bodybuilding ambitions. *Viel Glück!*

BOOK ONE
Introduction
to
Bodybuilding

CHAPTER 1
Evolution and History

At the end of the nineteenth century a new interest in muscle-building arose, not muscle just as a means of survival or of defending oneself, but a return to the Greek ideal—muscular development as a celebration of the human body.

The ancient tradition of stone-lifting evolved into the modern sport of weightlifting. As the sport developed, it took on different aspects in different cultures. In Europe weightlifting was a form of entertainment from which the professional strongman emerged—men who made their living by how much weight they could lift or support. How their physiques looked didn't matter in the least, so they tended to develop beefy, ponderous bodies.

In America at this time, there developed a considerable interest in strength in relation to its effect on health. The adherents of "physical culture" stressed the need for eating natural, unprocessed foods—an idea that took root in response to the increasing use of new food-processing techniques. Americans were beginning to move from farms and small towns to the cities; the automobile provided a new mobility. But at the same time, life was becoming increasingly sedentary, and the health problems that arise when a population eats too much of the wrong food, doesn't get enough exercise, and exists in constant conditions of stress were just becoming apparent.

The physical culturists were battling this trend with a belief in overall health and physical conditioning, advocating moderation and balance in all aspects of life. The beer-drinking, pot-bellied strongmen were certainly not their ideal. What they needed was a model whose physique embodied the ideas they were trying to disseminate, someone who related more to the image of the ancient Greek athlete than the Bavarian beer hall. They found such a man in the person of Eugene Sandow—a turn-of-the-century physical culture superstar.

Sandow made his reputation in Europe as a professional strongman, successfully challenging other strongmen and outdoing

Eugene Sandow

them at their own stunts. He came to America in the 1890s and was promoted by Florenz Ziegfeld, who billed him as "The World's Strongest Man" and put him on tour. But what really set Sandow apart was the aesthetic quality of his physique.

Sandow was beautiful, no doubt about it. He was an exhibitionist, and enjoyed having people look at his body as well as admire his strongman stunts. He would step into a glass case and pose, wearing nothing but a fig leaf, while the audience stared and the women "oohed" and "aahed" at the beauty and symmetry of his muscular development. This celebration of the aesthetic qualities of the male physique was something very new. During the Victorian age, men had covered themselves in confining clothing, and very few artists used the male nude as a subject for their paintings. This is what made Sandow's appeal so amazing.

Due largely to Sandow's popularity, sales of barbells and dumbbells skyrocketed. Sandow earned thousands of dollars a week and created a whole industry around himself through the sale of books and magazines. Contests were held in which the physical measurements of the competitors were compared, then Sandow awarded a golden statue of himself to the winners. But, ultimately, he fell victim to his own macho mystique. It is said that one day his car ran off the road and he felt compelled to demonstrate his strength by single-handedly hauling it out of a ditch, resulting in a brain hemorrhage that ended the life of the man who King George of England had appointed "Professor of Scientific Physical Culture to His Majesty."

Eugene Sandow

NEW YORK, SATURDAY, JANUARY 27, 1894.

THE LADIES IDOLIZE SANDOW.

THE STRONG MAN EXHIBITS HIS FORM AT SELECT RECEPTIONS TO THE PRETTY CREATURES.

George Hackenschmidt

George Hackenschmidt earned the title "The Russian Lion" for his performance as a weightlifter, winning the Russian weightlifting championship in 1898 and various world wrestling championships, and eventually made a fortune after emigrating to Great Britain. He was also a fluent orator and a prolific writer, who turned out philosophical books such as *The Origins of Life*, debated intellectuals like George Bernard Shaw, and even challenged Albert Einstein to an exchange of ideas.

And there were many more—Professor Attila, Arthur Saxon, Herman Gomer, Oscar Hilgenfeldt, and W. A. Pullum, an illustrious tradition of men of strength that continues right up through Paul Anderson and Alexeev and other weightlifters of our day.

One of those for whom the pursuit of physical culture became practically a religion was the publisher-businessman Bernarr Macfadden, a man who could serve as the prototype "health nut" of all time. To promote the idea that physical weakness was actually *immoral*, he founded the magazine *Physical Culture*. Later he went on to publish the *New York Evening Graphic*—a newspaper aimed at an audience that possessed as little education as he did.

Macfadden also presented a series of contests at Madison Square Garden to select the "Most Perfectly Developed Man in

Arthur Saxon

Herman Gomer

America." The first one was held in 1903, with a prize of one thousand dollars (a small fortune in those days) along with the title. Both the contests and the magazine were successful for decades. And he continued to practice what he preached—walking barefoot every morning from his home on Riverside Drive in New York City to his office in midtown and appearing barechested in his own magazine, an example of health and fitness until well into his seventies.

Macfadden probably would not have approved of modern bodybuilding with its emphasis on the visual development of the body rather than athletic skill. However, Macfadden and other physical culturists played a big part in the evolution of bodybuilding. His contests helped to promote interest in how the body looked, rather than simply how strong the muscles were, and there emerged from these contests a superstar who was to become one of the most famous men in America for decades to come.

The winner of Macfadden's contest in 1921 was a young man named Angelo Siciliano. To capitalize on his growing fame, this magnificently developed man changed his name to Charles Atlas and acquired the rights to a mail-order physical fitness course called "dynamic tension." For more than fifty years boys have grown up seeing the ads for this course in magazines and comic

Louis Cyr

books—the one where the scrawny kid gets sand kicked in his face, sends away for a muscle-building course, then goes back to beat up the bully and reclaim his girl. "Hey skinny, your ribs are showing!" became the most memorable slogan of one of the most successful advertising campaigns in history.

The Transition to Bodybuilding

By the 1920s and '30s it had become evident that health and the development of the physique were closely connected, and that weight training was the best way to produce the greatest degree of muscular development in the shortest possible time. Charles Atlas, for example, used weights rather than the dynamic tension of isometrics to produce his outstanding body. Training knowledge was limited, but bodybuilders of that day were learning a great deal simply by comparing their physiques with those of the stars of the previous generation.

For example, there was a famous strongman at the turn of the century named Louis Cyr—300 massive pounds, thick, chubby, huge around the middle and every inch the barrel-shaped strongman. But by the '20s there appeared men like Sigmund Klein, who exhibited a physique with beautiful muscular shape, balance, and proportion, as well as low body fat and extreme definition. Klein became very influential as a gym owner and writer on training and nutrition. His physique, compared to Cyr's, was as day to night. Klein, along with the example of Sandow and the influence of physical culturists like Macfadden, gradually began to convince people that the look of a man's physique—not just his ability to perform feats of strength—was worthy of attention because the kind of training that produced the aesthetically muscular body also contributed to overall health. But the era in which the male physique would be judged purely on an aesthetic basis was still a few years away.

Strength developed by weight training was still somewhat suspect in the 1930s, as if weightlifters were not truly worthy to be called athletes. It was almost considered "cheating" to build up your body by training in a gym instead of participation in a variety of sports. John Grimek, the Olympic weightlifter who was to serve as the model for so many aspiring bodybuilders, recalls how he rarely volunteered the information that his magnificent muscles were created by weightlifting, although you'd think that anyone seeing that physique on a beach would have realized that no amount of hand-balancing or water polo could have led to such development.

However, the tradition of physique competition continued, and by the late '30s there were numerous shows that brought together boxers, gymnasts, swimmers, weightlifters, and other athletes. These contestants had to perform some sort of athletic feat as well as display their physiques, so it was common for weightlifters of the day to be able to do hand-balancing and other gymnastic moves.

In 1939, things started to change. A Mr. America contest was held in Madison Square Garden which competed with Macfadden's "Most Perfectly Developed Man in America" event. That same year, the Amateur Athletic Union (AAU) stepped in and created a Mr. America contest of its own. The participants were still not full-fledged bodybuilders, but came from all sorts of ath-

Sigmund Klein

John Grimek

letic backgrounds and posed in everything from boxer shorts to jock straps.

But as more and more emphasis was put on how the physique looked, the weightlifters began to enjoy a distinct advantage. Weightlifting changed the contours of the body more than any other kind of training, so they were able to make a very strong impression on the judges.

In 1940, the AAU produced the first real modern bodybuilding event. Mr. America that year and the next was John Grimek, who trained primarily by lifting weights in a gym. This served notice to anyone who wanted to compete against him that they would have to follow a similar training program. Grimek also put the lie to the idea that men who trained with weights were "muscle-bound" and unable to perform well athletically. His posing routines were legendary; he was able to stay on the stage for more than thirty minutes at a time doing poses that involved an extraordinary degree of strength, flexibility, and coordination.

Bodybuilding in the Forties and Fifties

The winner of the Mr. America title in 1943 was a man whom many believe to be the first truly modern bodybuilder. Clarence (Clancy) Ross's physique would not look out of place on any stage today—wide shoulders, flaring lats, narrow waist, good calves and abs. By this time the distinction between lifting weights purely for strength and training with weights to shape and proportion the body had been clearly made. The bodybuilder's physique, as opposed to other types of muscular development, was now recognized as something unique.

However, bodybuilding still remained an obscure sport. No champion was known to the general public—that is, until Steve

Clarence (Clancy) Ross

Steve Reeves

Reeves came along. Reeves was the right man in the right place at the right time. He was handsome, personable, and had a magnificent physique. Survivors from the Muscle Beach era recall how crowds used to follow Reeves when he walked along the beach, and how people who knew nothing about him would simply stop and stare, awestruck.

After winning Mr. America and Mr. Universe, Reeves made movies and became an international star with his portrayal of the

Reg Park in his early twenties

Reg Park at forty

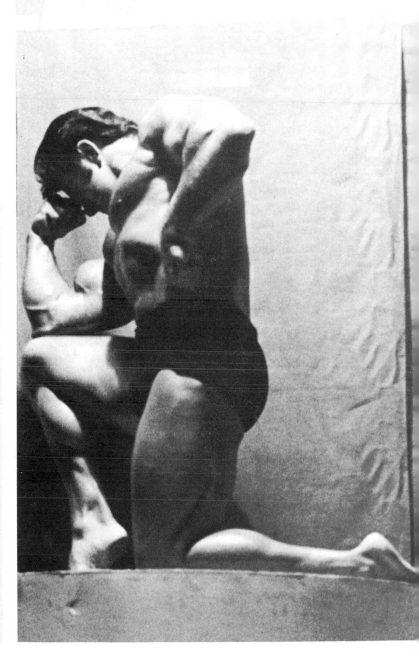

title roles in *Hercules* (a role that both Reg Park and I were later to undertake for the movies), *Morgan the Pirate*, and *The Thief of Baghdad*. As far as the general public was concerned, in the 1950s —except for the perennial Charles Atlas—there was only one famous bodybuilder: Steve Reeves.

Probably no human being in the history of the planet had ever achieved the level of development of men like Grimek, Ross, and Reeves. Bodybuilders began to learn things about the physical potential of the body that even medical scientists could not have predicted. Soon there were more and more great bodybuilders coming along every year—Bill Pearl, Chuck Sipes, Jack Delinger, George Eiferman, and one of my great idols, Reg Park.

I remember how incredible it seemed when I first met Reg Park in 1967. I was almost speechless with awe. One reason I have always admired him is that he is a big man, very strong, with a powerful-looking physique. When I was just getting started I knew I wanted to build the kind of mass and density that I had seen in his photos—big, rough, and Herculean. Reg was the next major champion to emerge when Reeves left competition for his movie career. He became Mr. Universe in 1951, won again in 1958, and became Professional Mr. Universe in 1965. At this point, everyone recognized that Reg was far above all other leading bodybuilders. He would dominate the bodybuilding scene for two decades.

Bodybuilding in the Sixties

I first came on the international bodybuilding scene in 1966. At that time most of the top bodybuilders I read about in magazines lived and trained in California.

Beating Dennis Tinerino (Mr. America of 1967) in the NABBA Mr. Universe in 1967 was my first big international victory, but that meant I would now have to go against the other champions of the day. There was certainly some fierce competition around —Frank Zane, a man who prepares as thoroughly for a contest as anyone in bodybuilding; my good friend Franco Columbu, who went from being a great power lifter to a Mr. Olympia practically by sheer determination of will; and, of course, Sergio Oliva.

Any time people discuss who might be the best bodybuilder of all time, the name Sergio Oliva inevitably comes up. He and I had some unbelievable confrontations on stage. The only way I could beat him was to be in absolutely perfect shape—massive, dense, and cut—and then not make any mistakes. Sergio was so

In 1967 Bill Pearl won the pro Mr. Universe title and I won amateur Mr. Universe

Joe Weider and Sergio Oliva —1967 Olympia

Larry Scott

good he could beat you in the dressing room if you weren't careful. His shirt would come off, and there would be that incredible mass. He would transfix you with a look, exhale with a kind of animal grunt, and suddenly the lats would begin to flare . . . and just when you thought they were the most unbelievable lats you ever saw, BOOM—out they would come, more and more, until you began to doubt that this was a human being you were looking at.

While I was battling for titles in Europe, I was very much aware of the competitions in the United States. Larry Scott had won the first two Mr. Olympia contests, and I knew I would eventually have to beat Larry and other top stars like Chuck Sipes. But one bodybuilder I was also impressed with, not just because of his outstanding physique but because of the image he was able to create, was Dave Draper.

Draper represented the epitome of California bodybuilders—big, blond, sun-tanned, with a personable manner and winning smile. Surrounded as I was by three feet of snow in the middle of an Austrian winter, the image of Dave Draper on a California beach was a very attractive one indeed. And Dave's roles in movies like *Don't Make Waves* with Tony Curtis and his appearances on television shows made me aware of the possibilities of bodybuilding beyond the competition arena.

In the 1960s there were two distinct worlds in bodybuilding: Europe and America. My Universe titles in '67 and '68 established me as the preeminent bodybuilder in Europe (Ricky Wayne wrote in an article, "If Hercules were to be born today his name

Dave Draper

Freddy Ortiz

Harold Poole

Rick Wayne

would be Arnold Schwarzenegger''), but the question still remained as to how well I would do against the American champions.

I looked across the ocean and saw Dave Draper, Sergio Oliva, Chet Yorton, Frank Zane, Bill Pearl, Freddy Ortiz, Harold Poole, Ricky Wayne, and others. My challenge was to compete against these great bodybuilders and defeat them.

My awareness of the world had expanded tremendously in just a few years. While training in Austria, I had considered winning the Mr. Universe contest in London to be the highest achieve-

With Roy Velasco at the 1968 Mr. International in Mexico

1968 Mr. Universe

ment I could aspire to. Now I found that taking that title *was only the beginning!* I still had a long journey ahead of me and many bodybuilders to defeat before I could consider myself the best. And that meant confronting the top American bodybuilders. So after winning my second Mr. Universe title in 1968, I set off for the States.

1969 Mr. Universe

In 1969, I devised a plan that involved winning three top titles in one year, the championships of all the important federations. I competed in the IFBB Mr. Universe contest in New York and then went immediately to London for the NABBA Universe—which gave me two titles in one week! But even with these victories I had not beaten everyone, so I planned to do even more the next year.

As the '60s drew to a close, six names emerged as dominant among the ranks of those who had been competing in the championship events: Dave Draper, Sergio Oliva, Bill Pearl, Franco Columbu, Frank Zane, and myself.

Bodybuilding in the Seventies

In 1970 I went all out—I won the AAU Mr. World, the NABBA Mr. Universe, and the IFBB Mr. Olympia titles. Finally, I had defeated *everybody*, and now felt I could justifiably call myself world champion.

1970 Mr. Universe posedown with Dave Draper and Reg Park

Bill Pearl

The year 1971 marked the high point of the remarkable career of Bill Pearl. Pearl first won Mr. America in 1952, then went on to victories in the Universe in 1953, 1961, and 1967. At the 1971 Mr. Universe, nineteen years after his Mr. America title, he came back to defeat the awesome Sergio Oliva and prove, once more, that he was one of the greatest bodybuilders of all time. Unfortunately, he did not continue on and enter the Mr. Olympia that year, so I never had a chance to compete against him, which prevented us from seeing who would come out as the top champion.

I won six Olympia titles between 1970 and 1975, but it was not without considerable opposition. In 1972, for example, the formidable Sergio gave me a battle that is still talked about today. Serge Nubret emerged as a potent force during this period, and at the 1973 Olympia he was amazing in his ability to create such size and definition on an essentially small frame.

In 1973, a new monster came on the scene. Lou Ferrigno won the Mr. Universe title and gave notice that a new force in bodybuilding was on the horizon. Lou went on to win the Universe

In 1970 Frank Zane won the amateur Mr. Universe and I won the pro Mr. Universe. Christine Zane won Ms. Bikini.

*1970 Mr. Olympia posedown
with Sergio Oliva*

1970 Mr. World

With Serge Nubret and Joe Weider at the 1971 Olympia

Sergio Oliva

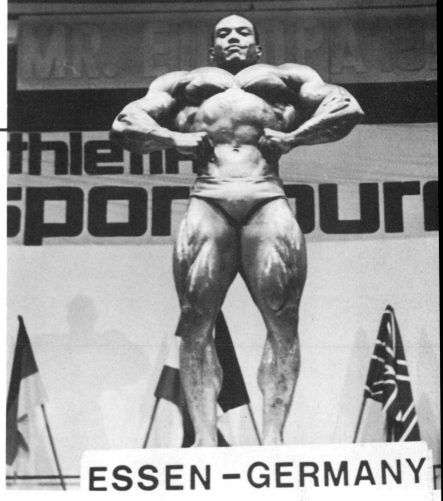

ESSEN – GERMANY

*Posedown at the 1972
Olympia with Serge Nubret
and Sergio Oliva*

Joe Weider handing out trophies to the 1973 winners —Ken Waller, Mr. World; Lou Ferrigno, Mr. America; and me, Mr. Olympia

1973 Olympia pose-off with Serge Nubret and Franco Columbu

The 1974 Olympia with Lou Ferrigno and Joe Weider

*The 1975 Olympia with Serge
Nubret, Ben Weider, and Lou
Ferrigno*

1975 Olympia with Franco Columbu

Franco Columbu

title again the next year and then entered the Olympia. He may have admitted he had always idolized me, but that did not keep him from doing his best to take the Olympia title away from me.

The 1975 Mr. Olympia was something of a high point in the history of this great event. Ferrigno returned, determined to achieve victory; Serge Nubret was also back and in top shape. For the first time, there were six or seven absolutely first-rate champions contending for the title, and I was especially proud of this victory, after which I retired from competition.

The next year saw a truly earth-shaking event in the history of bodybuilding: Franco Columbu won the 1976 Mr. Olympia title, the first small man to do so. Until this time, the big man always won, but from '76 on the small man came into his own. Muscularity and extremely low body fat became the winning factor, which required an almost scientific approach to training and diet to achieve.

Frank Zane

Robby Robinson

The late '70s saw Frank Zane hit his prime, winning three consecutive Olympia titles with his aesthetic physique. Robby Robinson also achieved world-class status and displayed both highly aesthetic and muscular qualities. In contrast, when Kal Szkalak won the 1976 Mr. Universe, it was more by virtue of an incredible development of mass than a Zane-like symmetry.

In 1980, I came out of retirement to win the Mr. Olympia contest in Sydney, Australia. I could hardly believe how competitive the sport had become by then, or that I would be pushed so hard by a bodybuilder as small as Chris Dickerson. All around me I saw examples of once unthinkable development, from Tom Platz's legs to Roy Callender's lats, unbelievable thickness, incredible density. My career has lasted a longer period of time than most (due, I believe, in part to the fact that I started competing so young), but in the 1970s the growing popularity of the sport meant that many of the stars of the '60s could stay active in competition to contend against the rising champions of the '70s.

The 1970s also saw the rise of the International Federation of Bodybuilders as the dominant bodybuilding organization. Under the guidance of its president, Ben Weider, the IFBB now consists of more than a hundred member countries and has become the

1980 Olympia pose-off with Boyer Coe and Frank Zane

sixth largest sports federation in the world. In addition, the Mr. Olympia title is now recognized as the top professional championship in bodybuilding—comparable to Wimbledon in tennis or the U.S. Open in golf.

Pumping Iron

One of the greatest influences on bodybuilding in the '70s was the book, and later the movie, *Pumping Iron.* Charles Gaines and George Butler took a subject most people knew virtually nothing about and made it one of the hot topics of the decade. It was the first time that anyone had given the general public insight into what bodybuilding was all about, and what bodybuilders were really like. Gaines and Butler were able to attract the public to a sport that had long been neglected and misunderstood, and the success of *Pumping Iron* has been one of the most important factors in the recent popularity of bodybuilding. The success of the book not only gave my career a big boost and helped bodybuilding find its way into network sports broadcasts and big-budget movies, but it was also influential in taking bodybuilding from the local high-school gym to culture palaces like the Sydney Opera House and New York's Whitney Museum, onto the covers of countless magazines and the subject of numerous best-selling books.

Bodybuilding in the Eighties and Beyond

Once, I could stand on the Olympia stage and be challenged by one or two other competitors. In 1980, the Olympia stage included Frank Zane, Chris Dickerson, Boyer Coe, Ken Waller, Mike Mentzer, Roger Walker, Tom Platz, Samir Bannout, and

1981 Olympia—Franco Columbu

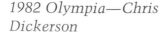

1982 Olympia—Chris Dickerson

Roy Callender among others. That lineup of talent would have been unthinkable in 1967, although a Sergio Oliva, Larry Scott, Reg Park, or Harold Poole in top shape would have been as impressive as ever in the 1980 Olympia. It isn't that the best are better, but that there are so many more top contenders than ever before.

As the '80s got fully under way, it was clear that this breadth of competition was here to stay. The 1981 and 1982 Olympia winners were experienced competitors—Franco Columbu and Chris Dickerson—but youth was clearly nipping at their heels: Tom Platz, Lee Haney, Mohamed Makkawy, Casey Viator, Samir Bannout, Bertil Fox, Johnny Fuller. With so many more contests and so many more top competitors, it seems clear that it will be really difficult for any one person to emerge as totally dominant in the future.

The Profession of Bodybuilding

As bodybuilding gained in popularity, the money to be made from the sport also increased. Whenever a lot of money suddenly becomes involved, everything starts to change. Professional bodybuilders had been making money at the sport since the days of Sandow, but very few were able to make a good living. Many opened gyms, manufactured equipment, got into movies, or supplemented their income through mail-order sales and posing exhibitions. But the prize money available in contests was minimal.

Now, with the Grand Prix events and so many other professional contests, and a total purse in the Olympia exceeding $100,000, there is enough money in bodybuilding competition to attract an increasing number of young athletes. And a larger proportion of established stars are staying active through their thirties and even into their forties.

The opportunities available in bodybuilding today are extraordinary. We can see from the proliferation of bodybuilding magazines, from the fact that the circulation of Joe Weider's *Muscle & Fitness* has more than quadrupled in the last few years, from the tremendous increase in the number of gyms around the country, and from the sale of gym and fitness equipment that bodybuilding has turned into big business.

Bodybuilding events are now televised as a matter of course. The Mr. America competition is held at Caesars Palace in Las Vegas; Manila and Cairo are the sites of Mr. Universe competitions; and the day is approaching when bodybuilding will be included in the Olympics.

Any discussion of bodybuilding would be incomplete without mention of the contribution of Joe Weider and his magazine *Muscle Builder* (now *Muscle & Fitness*). Joe has done more than simply provide good articles and photos detailing the lives and training methods of the top physique stars, he has also managed to gather and preserve enormous amounts of valuable training information.

Joe spent a lot of time going into gyms around the country and observing how the stars trained. For instance, he noticed that Larry Scott used a preacher bench to do Curls, and that Chuck Sipes continued to do set after set with great intensity by quickly taking weight off the bar between sets. He took note of these methods, wrote them down, then gave them names. Scott didn't call his technique "Scott Curls," and Sipes didn't realize he was using the "Stripping Method." But, through Joe, soon everyone had access to these particular training techniques.

In Austria, I trained in the morning and again in the evening because that's what my daily schedule demanded. Now, this is known as the "Weider Double-Split System," and is being used by bodybuilders all over the world.

Joe Weider with bodybuilders at the 1970 Olympia

The "Weider Training Principles" are a collection of the best bodybuilding techniques ever created. Joe Weider recognized these principles, tagged them with his own name (the Weider Instinctive Principle, the Weider Priority Principle, the Weider Peak-Contraction Principle, and so on), and promoted them in his magazine. A generation of bodybuilders has benefited from Joe's ideas on training, nutrition, diet, and anything else new in bodybuilding.

The Evolution of Modern Training Techniques

New information about training, diet, and nutrition has greatly influenced the evolution of bodybuilding. In the days of John Grimek, bodybuilders still trained largely as weightlifters and tended to work the whole body three times a week. Today body-builders, like modern athletes in most other sports, train better and harder than they did twenty or thirty years ago. They have learned that simply training with heavy weights would not by itself produce a championship physique. To achieve "quality" in a physique meant doing many sets of a great variety of exercises, so that every aspect and contour of a muscle could be brought out and developed; meant isolating not only individual muscles but specific areas within a muscle as well.

As bodybuilders developed new techniques, the tools used to shape their bodies also changed. Gyms in the '30s and '40s were primitive places by today's standards. Gym owners like Vic Tanny experimented with various types of cable and pulley devices to give their patrons a wider choice of exercises, but the barbell and dumbbell still dominated the gym. In the early '60s, the introduction of exercise machines made a greater variety of exercises possible. Today Universal, Nautilus, DynaCam, Corbin Gentry, Paramount, and many other manufacturers produce training equipment that can be used to supplement a body-builder's free-weight training. At World Gym, Joe Gold himself designs and builds equipment to suit his patrons. His designs have been widely copied and imitated around the world. The level of sophistication in training continually increases— with the use of Double-Split Training, Forced Reps, Forced Negatives, even to the use of oxygen during workouts!

Bodybuilders have also learned to master the principles of diet and nutrition. Lean muscularity was not always the important factor in bodybuilding competition that it is today; pure muscle mass was considered more important. But bodybuilders realized along the way that the bulk produced by body fat had no place in a quality physique, and that it was necessary to get rid of as much fat as possible in order to fully reveal their muscular development.

So bodybuilders stopped "bulking up." They learned to follow strict diets while still training very hard, and to take vitamin, mineral, and protein supplements to enhance their progress. They investigated the effect on the body of steroids, thyroid, and a whole range of biochemical agents. And they began using motivational techniques and even hypnosis to harness the power of the mind to force the body's development beyond previous limits. And, in doing so, bodybuilders began attracting the attention of doctors and medical scientists, who came to realize that the ability of these athletes to develop the human body represented a major breakthrough in our understanding of exercise and its effect on the body—leading to a revolution in exercise and fitness techniques available to the general public.

The Future of Bodybuilding

As I travel across the country and around the world, seeing more and more good bodybuilders develop in the United States and an increasing number of competitors from Europe winning international contests, I have great hope for the future of the sport. Bodybuilding is so specialized and so difficult that only a small percentage of people will ever want to do what it takes to become an international champion, but athletes who once would have been drawn to other sports are now beginning to consider a career in bodybuilding. This is one of the things that will ensure that the sport will continue to grow, that the level of competition will remain high, and that the public's interest will continue to increase.

Bodybuilding means so much more today than it did when I first fell in love with it. Then, there was only competition, but now it has developed a recreational side—bodybuilding for physical fitness, health, and developing confidence and a better self-image. Orthopedists are beginning to use it as a means of rehabilitation for patients with certain types of physical problems. It is being used by the elderly as a means of combating many of the debilitating effects of aging. It is also becoming more important in sports training as many athletes find that bodybuilding can greatly enhance their performance. Women, children, and even whole families are becoming involved in bodybuilding programs. This is not a fad; it is obviously here to stay.

But as the ranks of professional bodybuilders increase, and bigger cash prizes become available, it should not be forgotten that the primary reason for bodybuilding is a fundamental love for the sport. Without this love, the camaraderie between bodybuilders is lost and the athletes compete without joy or satisfaction. If you consider only the financial side, then when another bodybuilder beats you, he has not just bested you in a contest, he has taken away part of your living, and it is difficult for anyone in this position to have anything but negative feelings for other competitors, and eventually for bodybuilding itself.

But I would like to see bodybuilding introduced to many more people than just those who are considering competition. Bodybuilding training is one of the best methods of achieving physical fitness, and the more people who understand this and benefit from it the better. Organizations like the IFBB often forget there is a world out there beyond organized bodybuilding, and put restrictions on bodybuilders as to where, when, and for whom they can give bodybuilding seminars. My view is that bodybuilding should be energetically encouraged on any occasion and for any audience. Enhancing all aspects of life through better physical fitness is a need that takes priority over any jurisdictional considerations.

CHAPTER 2

The ABC's of Bodybuilding

Bodybuilding is the process of developing and shaping the muscles of the body by means of progressive-resistance weight training. It can be used to make the body stronger, to enhance sports performance, and to rehabilitate injured body parts. Competitive bodybuilders use bodybuilding techniques to develop their physiques to a degree human beings have never been able to achieve before, and then compete with one another on stage to determine who has reached the highest level of development.

Since you can only shape and develop your body in this manner by means of extremely difficult physical effort and precise exercise techniques, bodybuilding must be defined as a sport; but the aesthetic goal of achieving just the right blend of muscularity, symmetry, proportion, and muscle shape, and the need to show it off by a mastery of stage presentation, also makes bodybuilding a highly demanding art form.

The Training Effect

Any kind of exercise program depends on the "training effect" for its results. This merely means that, when the body is subjected to unusual stress over a period of time, it adapts itself so that it can deal more effectively with that stress. Dr. Lawrence Golding of the University of Nevada explains it this way: "If you have a 10-horsepower motor and you subject it to a 12-horsepower load, it will burn out. But when you have a human body that is the equivalent of a 10-horsepower motor and you subject it to a 12-horsepower load, it eventually becomes a 12-horsepower motor." However, the kind of increase in performance you get from the body depends on what kind of training you subject it to. A runner does not train like a weightlifter or vice versa. The need to do a particular kind of training for particular results is called "specificity of training."

The body doesn't care what you *think* you are telling it to do, it will respond to the specific message being sent through the nervous system. In bodybuilding, what you are trying to do is to make your muscles grow. As you do this, you get stronger, but strength is just a side effect. Weightlifters are primarily concerned with how much weight they can lift. For bodybuilders, the weight is simply a means to an end, resistance against which they can contract the muscles to cause them to change and develop. But this does not mean that bodybuilders aren't strong— the bigger your muscles get, the stronger you become and, therefore, the harder you are capable of training. Strength is very important to bodybuilding, it just doesn't represent the ultimate goal.

The Bodybuilding Physique

To be a really good bodybuilder, just creating mass is not enough. You need to create *muscle shape,* and this happens when you train every part of the muscle, at every angle possible, so that the entire muscle is stimulated and every possible bit of fiber is involved. Muscles are really aggregates of many smaller units— bundles of bundles of fiber—and every time you use the muscle in a slightly different way you stimulate different combinations of these bundles and activate additional fibers.

This is what sets the bodybuilder's physique apart from the kinds of muscle structure developed by weightlifters, swimmers, football players, and other athletes. The bodybuilder attempts to achieve *total* development of every muscle in the body, to create the fullest possible shape in each muscle, to have the muscles proportionate to one another, and to achieve an overall symmetry that is as aesthetically pleasing as possible.

Developing the body this way requires a complete knowledge of technique. You may want to change the shape of your pectoral muscles, peak the biceps more fully, or achieve a better balance between upper and lower body development, but these results do not come about by accident. So the best bodybuilders are those who understand how muscle tissue works, how training actually affects the body, and what sort of techniques lead to specific results.

How Bodybuilding Training Works

Imagine you have a barbell in your hands and you lift it up over your head. Several things happen at once: first, the muscles of the shoulder (the deltoids) lift your arms upward; then the muscles at the back of the upper arm (the triceps) contract and cause the arms to straighten. Any movement you make, whether pressing a weight overhead, walking, or simply breathing, is the result of any number of complex combinations of muscle contractions.

The action of individual muscle fibers, on the other hand, is quite simple—a fiber contracts when stimulated and relaxes when the stimulation ceases. Contraction of an entire muscle is the result of the contraction of many tiny, individual muscle fibers. Fibers contract on an all-or-nothing basis. That is, they always contract as hard as they can, or they don't contract at all. However, after a series of contractions a fiber begins to get tired and the amount of effort it can generate diminishes. When you lift a maximum amount of weight one time, you use only a fraction of the total amount of fiber in the muscle. The amount of weight you can lift is determined by three things: (1) how much fiber you are able to recruit; (2) how strong the individual fibers are; and (3) your lifting technique.

When you do only one or two repetitions of a lift, your body never gets a chance to recruit fresh fiber to replace that which is getting weak and tired. Weightlifters learn to recruit an unusually large number of fibers in one, maximal lift. But they put such an immense strain on those fibers that the body adapts and protects itself by making those fibers bigger and thicker. This is called fiber "hypertrophy."

No matter how many fibers the weightlifter involves in one, maximal lift, he still uses fewer than he would if he used less weight and did more repetitions. Therefore, he only trains and strengthens part of the muscle structure. Also, the weightlifter does a limited number of different kinds of lifts, so that there are many angles at which the muscle is never trained at all.

Bodybuilders have learned that you can create greater visual change in the body by a different kind of training. Instead of one, maximal lift, a bodybuilder uses less weight and does more repetitions, usually 8 to 12 for the upper body, 12 to 15 for legs, and does each set to failure—until the muscles are unable to do even one more repetition. Then he rests briefly and continues on to do more sets, perhaps as many as 15 or 20 sets of various exercises for any given body part.

Once a muscle has been strenuously exercised, it needs time to recover and to grow. Therefore, for maximum effect, it is necessary to avoid working the same muscles two days in a row.

It is not necessary to subject a muscle to maximum stress in order to get it to respond. A lesser degree of overload builds muscle just as well, and enables you to do a greater volume of training. The specific percentage of maximum stress necessary to do this is not precisely known—but if you do the correct number of reps and sets to failure, you will get as close to this level as necessary.

Bodybuilding training combines overload and volume to get its effect. That effect is not just visual. Muscle biopsies done on weightlifters and bodybuilders reveal a startling difference: the weightlifter, as we might expect, has a relatively small number of very thick and strong fibers; the bodybuilder, on the other hand, has normal-size fibers, *but a tremendously large number of them!* The question is, where did all that extra fiber come from?

One exciting new idea is the possibility that bodybuilding depends for its training effect to some degree on muscular hyperplasia—the actual creation of new muscle cells in response to the demands of training. When we are young we grow by means of cell multiplication, but when we reach adolescence this process ceases. It was previously thought that growing new muscle cells was impossible after the body matures. But if bodybuilding training does in fact restart this process, it has enormous implications for all other sports and for human life in general. Athletes are ultimately limited by the total amount of muscle fiber in their bodies. Suppose they could simply grow more? How much better might their performances become?

It is apparent that much of the muscular deterioration we think of as being an inevitable effect of aging is not inevitable at all. We can certainly slow down the atrophy of muscle tissue through proper training and, just conceivably, may actually be able to stimulate the formation of new muscle fiber.

Bodybuilding and Sports

Not many years ago, most coaches urged athletes to stay away from weight training. Lifting weights, it was thought, made you "muscle-bound," slowed your reflexes, and interfered with sports performance. Today, it is a rare athlete that does not do some form of weight training. If you examine the weight-training programs advocated by most coaches and trainers, you will find that what they are prescribing is, in reality, bodybuilding training.

Dwight Stones, one of the great high jumpers of all time, devotes several days a week to a training program which includes training with weights, and only short periods to practicing his sport. Why? Because, after all the years of effort he has put into perfecting his jumping technique, he has reached a point of diminishing returns. He is so close to his absolute potential in terms of technique and neuromuscular coordination that he cannot expect much improvement no matter how hard he tries.

Training, for someone like Stones, is a matter of learning to be more consistent, and to increase the strength and conditioning of his body so that he is at his best as much of the time as possible. This is the key to much of the improvement we see in modern athletics: while a world-class athlete cannot better his technique or neuromuscular coordination to any significant degree, he or she can, in many cases, double, triple, or even quadruple the absolute strength of the body, thereby greatly improving athletic performance.

When a muscle has been strengthened, it is capable of more intense effort. Intensity of effort manifests itself in two ways—ability to do more work (lift more weight, overcome more resistance) or do equal work in less time. This means that a trained muscle is not only stronger, it is also faster. For the athlete who is trying to maximize his performance, the fact that bodybuilding training can actually give him improvements in speed, dextcrity, and coordination (all of which come about when the muscle is able to function more efficiently and effectively) is extremely important.

A swimmer, for example, might spend endless hours in a pool performing strokes with his arms and shoulders, but each stroke is done against a relatively fixed resistance, so the increase in the strength of the muscles involved is limited. If, however, he trains with weights—as Diana Nyad did for her swim to Florida—he can vastly increase muscular strength, making each stroke relatively easier and therefore extending the ability of the body to continue performing that motion for a longer period of time.

High jumpers and pole vaulters cannot improve beyond a certain point in their sports by practicing only the specific techniques involved; but by doing exercises like Squats they can increase the strength of the leg muscles. Even runners, who are not usually thought of as strength athletes, are turning more and more to bodybuilding-type weight training. Recently, discussing this with a world-class skier, he said he was amazed how much the Austrian ski team had begun to use weights in their training. In Europe you'll also find other top athletes like soccer players adding work with barbells, dumbbells, and machines to their training programs.

Since traditional weightlifting strengthens only some of the muscles and at very specific angles of effort, it is relatively ineffective in enhancing sports performance. Bodybuilding training, on the other hand, strengthens the *entire* body, leaving no weak areas that could be prone to injury, and leads to increased levels of muscular endurance. It will never take the place of the "specificity of training" necessary to develop individual athletic skills, but it will enhance the development and performance of those skills like no other type of exercise possibly could.

It is now established by research that muscles developed by bodybuilding make you faster as well as stronger, enhance your coordination rather than make you awkward, add to your endurance in physically demanding situations, and make you less liable to injury. The Medical Committee of the International Federation of Bodybuilders states: "If you had no muscle, you could not move at all. With some muscle, you can move a little bit. With more muscle, you become better at movement. Up to the point where specific forms of body composition are necessary to succeed in a sport (a marathon runner can't carry any extra muscle weight, for example, and excessive size in baseball has rarely proved to be an advantage), the stronger you are, the better developed your muscles, the better your ability to perform well in athletics." In other words, when you have two athletes of equal skill, the stronger one will usually win out.

It is important, however, to emphasize that sheer muscle *size* is not necessarily an advantage in many sports. I find when I run, for example, that the size of my leg biceps works against me, and I have to work harder than I would if those muscles were not so developed. Also, when I did sword fighting in the movie *Conan the Barbarian*, my extra size and weight made me slightly less nimble than I would have been had I weighed thirty pounds less.

What counts in cases like this is your *strength-to-weight ratio*, and the more muscle weight you carry around that doesn't directly contribute to performing a particular athletic feat, the less strength-to-weight advantage you have. But bodybuilding training can often lead to an increase in overall strength without a huge increase in size. For example, if a boxer runs early in the morning, does bodybuilding training afterward, and then goes to the gym in the afternoon for a strenuous boxing workout, that volume of effort makes it very unlikely that his muscles will have a chance to grow a great deal, although they will get stronger.

After you have used bodybuilding training to develop a strong and balanced physique, there are specific kinds of resistance exercises that will work on the particular muscles used in various sports (I discovered weight training in the first place as part of a strengthening program for competition skiing). But these sophisticated programs should only be employed *after* all the muscles of the body have been developed proportionately and brought up to a certain level of minimal strength through bodybuilding. Skiers, for example, stand on the side of a long bench, put a 135-pound barbell on their shoulders, and then leap, feet together, from one side of the bench to the other with a sideways movement, moving forward from one end of the bench to the other, then doing the same back-and-forth jumping in reverse, this time backing up slowly along the length of the bench. This kind of training would hardly be in the repertoire of the average bodybuilder, but it does show how adaptable progressive-resistance training can be when it is applied to various sports by inventive and competent coaches.

Whatever system an athlete uses, the principle remains the same—the stronger the athlete, the better, and the kind of physical development achieved by bodybuilding training is the most beneficial.

Bodybuilding and Flexibility

In the past it was thought that resistance training often led to a condition called "muscle-bound," a nonmedical term that is used to indicate a body that lacks flexibility. However, this is not the case. All a muscle can do is contract; its function is that simple. This means that once you contract a muscle to move your body in one way, you need to use an opposite muscle or muscles to bring it back to where it was. This is why muscles are situated around the body in opposing pairs.

Bodybuilding training has its best effect when the exercises are done through *the longest range of motion possible.* This allows you to stimulate the maximum amount of muscle fiber. But it has another effect as well: when you fully contract one muscle, you are stretching its opposing muscle. Therefore bodybuilding, done correctly, leads to an increase in flexibility rather than a decrease.

However, *maximum* flexibility can only be achieved through a specific program of flexibility training. Modern bodybuilders are increasingly taking up some specific kind of stretching exercises (yoga, flexibility classes, etc.) to develop the most flexibility and longest range of motion of their muscles.

Bodybuilding and Aerobic Endurance

There are two fundamentally different kinds of endurance: muscular and cardiovascular. Muscular endurance is the ability of the

Frank and Christine Zane

muscle to engage a large number of muscle fibers during an exercise so that you can do numerous repetitions. For example, while doing heavy Squats, you fatigue muscle fibers in the leg so quickly that if you want to get through an entire set you need to be able to bring many additional fibers into play. Cardiovascular endurance is the ability of the heart, lungs, and circulatory system to deliver oxygen to the muscles to fuel further exercise.

If you are not used to running and you suddenly take off and do four or five miles, you'll soon find your lungs laboring and your leg muscles burning. But it will not be the actual muscle fibers of the leg that are failing; failure occurs because your inefficient aerobic system is unable to provide enough oxygen to rid your muscles of lactic acid buildup.

Because bodybuilding training relies on a certain volume of effort to achieve its effects, it leads to an increase in muscular endurance. But bodybuilders prove to have a high degree of cardiovascular endurance as well. This is because they train at a pace which is just below the threshold of cardiovascular failure —that is, they train as fast as they can without overwhelming the ability of the body to provide oxygen to the muscles. This doesn't necessarily make bodybuilders good runners, however; because of their size most bodybuilders have to work very hard trying to run carrying that weight. Good long-distance runners tend to be slender to the point of emaciation so as to increase their strength-to-weight ratio. But this does not mean that bodybuilders do not have highly developed cardiovascular systems or that they are not capable of other types of sustained effort.

Cardiovascular endurance is as important to a bodybuilder as muscular endurance. Hard training results in a buildup of lactic acid in the muscles being used. Lactic acid is a waste product of the process that produces the energy for muscular contraction. If the heart, lungs and circulatory system have been able to provide enough oxygen to the area, the lactic acid will be reprocessed by the body into a new source of energy; if not, the buildup will eventually prevent further contraction, leading to total muscular failure.

Every serious bodybuilder should do a substantial amount of aerobic training. I have always liked to run several miles a day. Some bodybuilders, however, find that running does not suit them and leads to problems with the legs and ankles, so they seek other ways of developing cardiovascular conditioning. Tom Platz, for example, after working his legs to exhaustion in the gym gets on a bicycle and rides for twenty miles. Bill Pearl used to do the same thing. A lot of bodybuilders are developing their aerobic systems using "Lifecycles" and other types of stationary bicycles. The fact is, the better conditioned your heart, lungs, and circulatory system, the more intense training you will be able to do in the gym and the more progress you will make as a bodybuilder.

Bodybuilding and Fitness

"Physical fitness," explains Dr. Ernst Jokl, "has tended to be defined too narrowly. There is more to being fit than developed cardiovascular ability and being able to run long distances. Muscular fitness is equally important."

When our muscles are exercised against adequate amounts of resistance, they become more efficient as well as stronger. They develop better tone and increased blood flow, and are less liable to suffer aches, pains, and injuries. Moreover, exercising the muscles tends to counteract the process of muscular atrophy that inevitably happens as one ages. "The average man," says Dr. Jokl, "loses fifty percent of his muscle mass between the ages of eighteen and sixty-five." But this loss of muscle is due as much to misuse of the body as it is to time; a comprehensive program of bodybuilding training will stimulate the muscle fibers and replace lost muscle mass.

Bodybuilding training also tends to stabilize or lower blood pressure over a period of time (using sustained, high-volume training, rather than heavy weightlifting), to strengthen the back and so reduce the chances of lower back pain and other back problems, and to increase the flow of blood to the skin, keeping it younger-looking and more flexible. Increasing numbers of doctors are now prescribing progressive-resistance training both as a preventive against physical deterioration and an efficient means of rehabilitation after deterioration has already taken place.

Obviously there are dangers associated with the lifting of excessively heavy weights, and Olympic power lifters are prone to any number of more or less serious physical problems due to the stresses of their sport. But bodybuilding involves the *controlled* use of weight training, with submaximum levels of resistance and a relatively high volume of training. Therefore, if properly done, with sufficient attention to technique, there is no reason why a bodybuilder should ever suffer a training-related injury beyond common muscle soreness or the occasional minor strain or sprain that any athlete comes to expect.

CHAPTER 3

The Training Experience

No bodybuilder ever succeeds without a lot of very hard, very disciplined work. First you have to assimilate the basic principles of bodybuilding, learn the exercises, how to put together routines, where and when to train. But there is more to success in bodybuilding than just being able to go through a workout; almost anybody can learn to do a Bench Press or put together a good shoulder routine. Once you get to the highest levels of competition, you have to go beyond accepted principles and techniques and find out *what really works for you*. What it takes to be a champion is to develop your own instincts, to learn to listen to your body, to feel what is happening almost down to the cellular level—and to involve your mind in your training to the point where you are actually willing your muscles to grow.

Experimenting in my own workouts I found that I could do many sets for chest or for lats, train these muscles with as much intensity as possible, but I still didn't get as good a result as when I supersetted back and chest—combined a pulling movement with a pressing movement. But this same technique does not necessarily apply to every muscle. You must learn all of the relevant techniques, and then study how each technique affects you as an individual. This is the true art of bodybuilding.

Mastering this process takes time. The first step is to understand exactly what you are doing in the gym, and to learn to interpret the feelings you experience from day to day as you go through your training routine. Remember, if you contemplate ever becoming a *competitive* bodybuilder, your opponents will probably know just as much about technique as you—what will make the difference is the degree to which you have been able to utilize your own instincts and feelings.

No matter how advanced a bodybuilder gets, there are still questions that arise. Even a Mr. Olympia can find himself dissatisfied with his progress in the gym, and begin to experiment with various training principles to find something that works better.

This is all the more reason to learn as much as possible about different principles and ways of training, so you will understand what alternatives are available to you.

The Pump

One of the first things you will experience when you start training is "the pump"—your muscles swell up well beyond their normal size, your veins stand out, you feel huge, powerful, and full of energy. The pump is usually felt after about four or five sets. Often you can keep this sensation throughout your workout, and then go on to experience an even better pump as more and more blood is forced into the area being exercised, bringing in fresh oxygen and nutrients for continued muscular contraction.

What causes the pump is blood rushing to the area faster than your circulatory system can carry it away. So the area becomes engorged with blood and swells to a noticeably larger size.

Bodybuilders traditionally associate the sensation of the pump with having a good workout. The feeling is so marvelous, so nearly sexual in nature, that it can enhance a workout tremendously and make you feel like training all that much harder.

The psychological aspect of the pump is very important. When you are pumped up, you feel better and stronger, and it is easier to motivate yourself to train hard, to achieve a high level of intensity. Of course, this feeling may differ from day to day. Sometimes, you will walk into the gym feeling tired and lazy but you will get a fantastic pump after a few minutes of work and suddenly feel strong and energetic; other days, nothing you do will bring this feeling.

Therefore, pay attention to the circumstances that give you the best pump—how often you are training, at what time of day, what combinations of exercise, what you eat before you go to the gym, and so on. These are all variables that can affect your training, and can affect you differently than somebody else. You still have to train correctly and with all the energy you can muster, but learning to be in touch with your instincts can give you that extra edge you need to become a champion.

One of the most common reasons for not being able to get a pump is lack of concentration. Keeping up interest in your training can be very difficult. Too many bodybuilders come into the gym and just go through the motions, doing their 20 sets for back or 30 sets for chest but not putting any real effort and concentration into it. "Be here now" is an important axiom in bodybuilding —it means pay attention to what you are doing, link your mind with your muscles so that you are aware of every rep of every set. In this way you can achieve the kind of quality training that will give you the satisfaction of a full pump.

Training Intensity

As with most things, you get out of bodybuilding what you put into it. The harder you work, the more results you will see, assuming that your training methods are as efficient as possible.

But at a certain point it becomes very difficult to escalate your workload: it seems you can't lift any more weight; you can't complete your reps; you can't train more frequently or you would not be able to recuperate; and you can't include any more sets or you would practically be living at the gym.

Working harder at this point is a matter of increasing your training *intensity*. You automatically increase intensity whenever you add weight to exercises in your routine—you are doing more work in the same amount of time. But you can also create more intensity by training faster, and cutting down your rest period between sets.

Cardiovascular endurance is the limiting factor in increasing intensity. If you outrun your ability to supply oxygen to the muscles, they will fail prematurely and you will not fully stimulate them. However, if you cut down on rest periods and speed up your training on a *gradual basis*, you will give your body time to adapt so that you will not fail aerobically.

Of course, there is a big difference in the intensity needed for beginning, intermediate, and competition bodybuilding. When you are first starting out, just getting through your workouts can be such a shock to the body that additional intensity is not required. Intermediate bodybuilders, however, may find that they have to give some thought as to how to shock the body into further growth. And competition bodybuilders, who are striving for the ultimate in physical development, must generate an unbelievable amount of intensity.

Suppose you are doing Bench Presses, eight reps with 400 pounds. For you, a ninth rep at that weight just isn't possible no matter how hard you try. But you can keep going if you have someone quickly remove a couple of small plates so that you can continue your reps with slightly less weight. The muscles may be too tired to lift 400 pounds but they can probably still lift 350 pounds. (There are computerized machines now that do this automatically, but all you really need is a training partner with quick hands.) Or your training partner could grab the bar and help you force out an additional series of repetitions, making the muscles involved work far beyond what they are accustomed to.

The more advanced you become, the harder it is to continue developing and the harder you have to train. Back in 1971 when I was doing 30 sets for shoulders and wanted to shock them into even more development, my training partner—a professional wrestler—told me I didn't have to add more reps, but just to follow him. We started with 100-pound Dumbbell Presses, then to 90 pounds, 80 pounds, and on down to the 40-pound weights —and then without resting we started doing Lateral Raises. After a one-minute rest we went back and did the whole thing over again. In one hour I did so many more repetitions and sets than normal that my shoulders felt as if they had been tortured!

"Forced reps," "burns," "forced negatives," "supersets," "giant sets," "partial reps," "rest/pause"—all of these are special techniques for generating intensity that I will explain later, in the exercise sections.

Pain

Every bodybuilder has heard the phrase "No pain, no gain," but it is important to be able to differentiate the (almost) enjoyable pain of an intense workout from pain resulting from actual physical injury.

Whenever you contract your muscles against heavy resistance, the energy produced tends to be "anaerobic," which means that energy is being produced without the benefit of available oxygen to help fuel the process. In the absence of oxygen, there is a buildup of a waste product called lactic acid. The presence of an excessive amount of lactic acid is what gives you the "burn" when you do a lot of hard repetitions. This pain is not the same kind of pain you get when you have injured yourself. When there is too much lactic acid present, you will simply not be able to contract your muscles, no matter how hard you try. However, in most cases, it is not harmful to continue a set in spite of this kind of pain sensation.

But pain can also be a warning that you have damaged yourself physically. The very real pain of a strain, sprain, or other stress-related injury is telling you to STOP—immediately! There is no "working through" this kind of pain. Anything you do that causes you to feel the pain is just going to make the injury worse. Your only recourse is to rest the area in question, and to seek medical help if the injury is serious or if it persists.

Eventually, you have to learn to tell the difference between "good" pain and the pain of injury if you want to succeed in bodybuilding. Because it is those last few reps that you perform after your muscles are burning and telling you to stop that often mean the difference between progress and the lack of it. That tenth or eleventh repetition of Barbell Curls, while your biceps are screaming in agony, may be the only way to develop championship arms. This phenomenon isn't something that happens just in bodybuilding: when Muhammad Ali was asked how many Sit-Ups he did in preparing for a championship fight he replied that he didn't know. "I don't start counting till it starts to hurt," he explained.

Soreness

Muscle soreness following a heavy workout is common among bodybuilders. This soreness is the result of minor damage to muscles, ligaments, or tendons. A certain amount of soreness is inevitable, a sign that you have really trained intensely. However, should you get so sore that it interferes with your training or other areas of your life, you should ease up for a while.

After my very first workout in a gym, I fell off my bicycle riding home because I was so numb. The next day I was so sore I could hardly lift a coffee cup or comb my hair. But I took pleasure in this feeling because it meant I had really gotten something out of my training. Many times I have deliberately bombed a certain body part—did Chin-Ups all day or countless sets of Squats—and ended up sore for a week! I never minded the inconvenience if it meant I had shocked my muscles into growth.

Actually, what we feel as muscle soreness is really pain originating in the tendons and ligaments. But even though you can't really feel the damage to the muscle cells, if you are sore you can be certain that the muscles have also been somewhat overstressed. Usually you will not feel soreness until the day after you have trained a particular area. In fact, it is often worse two days afterward.

Soreness seems to result more from "negative" repetitions (lowering a weight) than from positive repetitions (raising a weight). The reason for this is that eccentric contraction of a muscle—lowering a weight—puts a disproportionate amount of stress on the supporting tendons and ligaments.

In general, you can train despite soreness, and you will start to feel better when you pump more blood into the painful area. Saunas, massage, and other treatments can make you feel better, but ultimately you will have to wait several days for the injured tissue to heal before you fully recover.

Setbacks

Progress in bodybuilding usually does not come about in a smooth, upward curve. But when it does, the results can be very gratifying. I remember a time when I could count on seeing a ½-inch increase in the size of my arms every couple of months, regular as clockwork; those were the days I could count on putting on more than twenty pounds of muscle every year no matter what.

But I soon learned that events can conspire to get in the way of a regular training schedule, such as vacations, scheduling of classes, getting a job, losing a job, getting married, getting divorced, having a baby, or a death in the family. Such interruptions in your training simply have to be dealt with in the best way possible—for instance, I invented for myself a Double-Split training schedule during the time I served in the Austrian Army, and in Munich I trained late at night so that my afternoons would be free to lie in the sun and work on my tan. Life can get complicated, and you can't always expect to concentrate on training without interference.

There is also the matter of injuries. Many bodybuilders never experience a serious injury, but you have to consider the possibility. My worst injury did not happen while training, but occurred when a posing platform slipped out from under me during a competition in South Africa. My knee was so badly injured that it was feared for a while that my bodybuilding career was over. The first doctor I saw advised me not to continue training, but I soon realized that he did not understand athletes and sports injuries, so I simply went and found another doctor.

This was a very discouraging period. I had worked for five years to build my thighs up from 23 to 28 inches, but two months after the accident my thighs measured 23 inches again! I felt as if five years of sweat and sacrifice had been thrown out the window.

Luckily, I found a specialist, Dr. Vincent Carter, who was able to help me. He told me, "Don't you know that the body is stronger after an injury than before? That a broken bone heals stronger than before the break? We'll whip you into shape in no time!'' That positive attitude cheered me up right away. I had an operation, but when the cast came off I still had that 23-inch thigh.

Now I had to not only rehabilitate the injured knee but deal with the psychological setback as well. I found a therapist named Dave Berg who put me on a serious exercise program and wouldn't let me baby myself. In only three weeks I gained 1½ inches on my thigh and soon I was starting to do Squats again. When I went back to Dr. Carter, he asked me how much I was squatting with, and I told him 135 pounds. "Why?" he said. "What's wrong with you? The injury is healed, it's all finished with. You told me you could squat with 400 pounds, so it's time to get back into it."

My injury and operation had taken place in November 1971, and by March 1973 I was healed and ready to train seriously again. It was seven months until the Mr. Olympia contest, so I decided to forget about the injury and train for the competition, and this led to another Olympia title. However, if I had not kept a positive attitude, sought out the medical help I needed to completely recover, and fought against the discouragement that comes with any serious setback, my career might really have ended right then.

Coping with Adverse Conditions

Being a good bodybuilder means being adaptable, because you can never be sure in what conditions you will be training. Having to travel a great deal and having many demands made on your time are two factors that require you to be flexible and to be able to improvise in order to get your training done.

But there are environmental factors you will sometimes be faced with, too. For example, I remember being in Denver on a book promotion tour and going into the gym with a television crew. With the lights and camera on, I got all psyched up and I did lots of Bench Presses and other exercises, but at the end of twenty minutes I was so out of breath I could hardly stand up. The television producer told me, "Okay, we have enough," and all I could think of was, "I've had enough too!" I realized that my difficulty came from being over a mile above sea level and not being able to get enough oxygen. I knew I would have to pace myself carefully if I ever tried to really work out at that altitude before becoming fully adapted to the thinner air.

High humidity is another difficult environmental condition. Try training in Florida or Hawaii in the summer with no air conditioning and you will find you cannot hit your workouts nearly as hard as normal. I once went to South Africa to train with Reg Park—it was the middle of winter in Austria and the middle of a very hot and humid summer below the equator—and I found myself using 30 pounds less on most exercises, 50 pounds less on others, until I had been there for a week or two and my body became acclimatized to those very different conditions.

Cold does the same thing. During a break in the filming of *Conan* I flew from Spain to Austria at Christmastime, accompanied by Franco Columbu, and we trained every day. But training when it is very cold requires certain kinds of adaptation—you have to warm up more thoroughly, and keep your warm clothes on even after you start to sweat. You also have to be careful because it can get so cold that your hands will literally stick to the metal dumbbells and barbells. I adapted fairly quickly to these conditions because I had trained in this kind of cold so often before, but it still required an effort to get a good workout without the sunny California climate helping me along.

Overtraining

The way to make progress in bodybuilding is consistency, which means not missing too many workouts, and making sure you get as much out of each training session as possible. Training too hard, too long, and too often can be physically and psychologically debilitating. You can start to feel permanently fatigued, worn out, and discouraged. And what's more, on a physiological level, overtraining can cause you to tear your muscles down rather than build them up. Young bodybuilders, especially, tend to subscribe to the "more is better" philosophy of training. But there is also something called "too much," the risky business of trying to rush the process of physical development.

In the exercise programs, I have made recommendations as to how often and how long you should train at each level of your development and for a variety of individual goals. Take these recommendations seriously and you will avoid the setbacks that result from overtraining.

Your Training Partner

Franco Columbu is one of the best training partners I ever had. In the years Franco and I trained together, I know I made much more progress than I would have training alone.

Dave Draper was the original Golden Boy of the sport. To Europeans he represented the classic California-type bodybuilder.

There are many advantages to working with a training partner. For one, you have somebody on hand to spot you when you are lifting heavy poundages and someone to help when you feel like forcing out extra repetitions or doing additional negative repetitions.

But it is also a great advantage just to have somebody waiting in the gym expecting you to show up no matter what the weather is like, how much sleep you got the night before, or how you happen to be feeling. It is unlikely that both of you will have a down day at the same time, so if one of you is not feeling energetic, the other can put extra energy into the workout to inspire and motivate both of you. Franco and I used to compete constantly, each trying to lift more weight than the other and do more sets and reps. But we weren't competing in order to defeat each other—we simply used competition to create an atmosphere in which any incredible effort seemed possible.

But one word of warning: as great as it is to have a good training partner, having a bad one is sheer disaster. Don't train with anyone unless he really helps you. Training with some people will make you feel like you have been pumped full of energy; but with others, like your muscles have been shot with novocaine.

I have relied on different training partners for different results

My training was always first-rate when I had training partners like Franco Columbu and Ken Waller to push me.

Casey Viator was one of the most powerful training partners I've ever had.

Nobody in modern bodybuilding is more massively developed than England's Bertil Fox.

Training with Ed Corney got me in my best possible shape for the 1975 Mr. Olympia in South Africa.

Franco Columbu, Jusup Wilkosz, and I all started out as weightlifters, which gives us a muscle density that bodybuilders who have not done power training lack.

One of the biggest thrills of my life was when I actually got to train with and compete against my bodybuilding hero, Reg Park.

depending on their individual characteristics. I trained with Franco in the morning, since he only trained once a day, and we did mostly power training. I trained with Dave Draper for lats because I wanted extra sets for these muscles; Dave just loved working in the gym, and would train for hours doing endless sets. Frank Zane was a good training partner for isolating specific muscle groups. Each training partner has his own particular value, so you may want to train with more than one person in order to get a whole range of benefits.

But training-partner relationships don't always work. Like a marriage, you have to use a little care in choosing a partner. In 1975, when I was training for my sixth Olympia title, Franco was not available because he was going to chiropractic college. So I called various bodybuilders and asked them certain questions: Are you training for competition this year? Do you think you are going to win? How important is it for you to win, and how much time and energy are you willing to put into your training? Do you have a job, or are you going to concentrate fully on training?

When I talked to Ed Corney, I knew I had found my training

partner. Because when I asked him what he was doing that year he told me, "Winning the Olympia short-man class." How are you going to do that, I wanted to know. "Training twelve hours a day, if I have to," he said. And working on his posing every day when he wasn't in the gym training. This was great to hear, and he agreed to come and stay with me and we would train together for the Olympia. Ed didn't win, but he came in a close second and he was in the best shape of his life.

The important thing is to choose a partner who likes to train the way you do. How heavy or light doesn't matter—you can always adjust the weight—but how fast or slow, a lot of sets or a few, training early or training late, all of these things are vital elements to be considered when deciding whom to choose as a workout partner.

This is not just a matter for competition bodybuilders. A beginning bodybuilder might want to train with someone more advanced, but that advanced bodybuilder may be working on refining his physique rather than creating a basic, powerful muscle structure, and the beginner would not profit much from that kind of workout. A businessman who wants to train to stay in shape might find himself overtaxed trying to train with a full-time bodybuilder. It's all very simple: a training partner who helps you make faster and better progress is a good one; a partner who holds you back in any way is a poor one.

Bill Pearl never talked me into becoming a vegetarian, but he did convince me that a vegetarian could become a champion bodybuilder.

Scheduling Training

Young bodybuilders often complain that they can't make any progress because they aren't able to devote their full time and energies to training. They believe that only bodybuilders who don't have a regular job or other responsibilities can actually become champions. This is not true, and it never has been.

I made much of my best early progress when I was in the Austrian Army and had a lot of other demands on my time. When out on maneuvers for six weeks along the Czechoslovakian border and driving tanks fifteen hours a day, I had to pump in fuel with a hand pump, wrestle with huge fuel drums, change wheels, and do maintenance. We slept in trenches under the tanks until we were awakened each morning at six. But I had another idea—my buddy and I would get up at five, open the tool compartment of the tanks where we had stored our barbells, and exercise for an hour before everybody else woke up. After we finished maneuvers for the day, we would train for another hour. I can't imagine any more difficult circumstances in which to train, so I submit that finding the time and energy for your workouts is simply a matter of motivation plus imagination. Each bodybuilder has to find a time to train that suits his particular situation.

There are other considerations to be dealt with as well. For example, how supportive of your ambitions are your family, friends, or spouse? Negative vibes from the people around you can be difficult to handle. It takes extra effort to retain your confidence when those close to you don't accept your chosen goals.

People who care about you can be well-meaning but still get in your way. I am sure I am not the only bodybuilder who has had his girlfriend complain about his getting up at five o'clock in the morning to go to the gym. The same thing happens with friends who want you to go out with them and have a good time, but don't understand that you have to schedule your time to make your training possible. You can end up being called egotistic and self-centered by people who don't realize that *they* are the ones being self-centered by not appreciating how important training is to a bodybuilder and what it costs to pursue this kind of career.

Your diet regimen can create problems, too. Eating with friends is a very pleasant social ritual, but one you will have to forgo much of the time. When somebody who knows you are in training keeps offering you pizza, you know they don't have your best interests at heart.

Many bodybuilders who work take food with them to the job, or even keep a hotplate at the workplace so they can make meals during the day. Having a supportive boss who understands what you are trying to do can be very helpful. If you don't, then you will simply have to make whatever adjustment is necessary.

CHAPTER 4

The Gym

A gym is only as good as the equipment you find there, the atmosphere in which you train, and the people who share the gym with you and help to create that atmosphere. If you train in the local health spa, you may be the only serious bodybuilder using the facility, and it is pretty hard to really blast your muscles while the people around you are just going through the motions. That is why good bodybuilders tend to congregate in certain gyms. By having the example of other serious bodybuilders constantly in front of you, you will train that much harder. That is what made the original Gold's Gym such a great place—a small gym with just enough equipment, but where you would constantly be rubbing shoulders with the likes of Franco Columbu, Ed Corney, Dave Draper, Robby Robinson, Danny Padilla, Paul Grant, and Ken Waller. Joe Gold's World Gym is an updated version of the same thing, and that is why I train there. Seek out local bodybuilders and try to find a place you can all train in. You can turn whatever gym is available into a bodybuilding gym by filling it with bodybuilders.

In my seminars, I frequently make a comparison between how environment affects the development of a child and how the gym environment can affect the development of a bodybuilder. If you grow up among successful, motivated people, you yourself will tend to be successful and highly motivated; growing up in an impoverished environment, among people with little hope and little motivation, you are going to have to fight that influence all your life.

I remember coming to California in 1968 and training at Joe Gold's gym in Venice. I was already a two-time Mr. Universe, but training every day among bodybuilders like Frank Zane and Dave Draper—Mr. Americas and Mr. Universes all over the place—and bodybuilders like Sergio Oliva showing up from time to time, I practically had no choice but to become better.

In 1980, when training at World Gym for the Mr. Olympia

competition, I showed up at the gym at seven o'clock one morning to work out and stepped out on the sundeck for a moment. Suddenly the sun came through the clouds. It was so beautiful I lost all my motivation to train. I thought maybe I would go to the beach instead. I came up with every excuse in the book—the most persuasive being that I had trained hard the day before with Jusup Wilkosz, so I could lay back today—but then I heard weights being clanged together inside the gym and I saw Wilkosz working his abs, Ken Waller doing shoulders, veins standing out all over his upper body, Franco Columbu blasting away, benching more than 400 pounds, Samir Bannout punishing his biceps with heavy Curls.

Everywhere I looked there was some kind of hard, sweaty training going on, and I knew that I couldn't afford not to train if I was going to compete against these champions. Their example sucked me in, and now I was looking forward to working, anticipating the pleasure of pitting my muscles against heavy iron. By the end of that session I had the best pump I could imagine, and an almost wasted morning had turned into one of the best workouts of my life. If I hadn't been there at World Gym, with these other bodybuilders to inspire and motivate me, I doubt that day would have ended up being so productive.

Most of the top bodybuilders began their training somewhere else and migrated to places like World Gym after they had already begun to win titles. If you are a beginner, visiting a place like World can be a great experience; however, unless you are already quite advanced, training in a gym of this type is not absolutely necessary. But once you are no longer a beginner and are determined to become a champion, it is important to find someplace to train in which there is the right kind of equipment and the right kind of atmosphere.

You can pay to train in most bodybuilding gyms by the day, week, month, or year. Usually, the longer the time you sign up for, the cheaper it is per day. Gyms like World Gym and Gold's Gym in Los Angeles charge between $200 and $300 per year. Sometimes a gym will let you pay off your yearly fee in installments. Here are some of the things I recommend you look for when choosing a gym:

1. A gym should have a variety of equipment, including plenty of free weights. Nowadays a lot of gyms are equipped almost exclusively with machines and, while there is a place for a certain amount of machine training in any bodybuilder's program, there has never been a champion bodybuilder who did not create fundamental muscular quality by the use of dumbbells and barbells.

2. A gym should not be too big, or too small. If it is too small, you constantly have to wait for equipment and you can't keep up the rhythm of your training. But if it is huge, you can feel dwarfed by too much space, which makes it hard to keep up your concentration.

3. A gym should have the right training atmosphere. If it is too elegant, it can make you too careful, too reserved. Training, after all, is tough and sweaty, not refined like an afternoon tea party. After winning my second Universe in 1968 I trained for a while in a health spa in London—very elegant and posh—and I found I couldn't get a pump no matter how hard I tried. It felt like a living room, nice carpeting, chrome equipment, as antiseptic as a doctor's office. I was concentrating on training while trying to block out conversations going on around me about the stock market or what kind of car somebody was thinking of buying. I can accept that a spa with that kind of atmosphere was probably perfect for most of the people training there, who merely wanted to shape up their bodies and maybe lose a few inches around the waist. But it was not appropriate for what I wanted to do.

But even for the hard-core, competition bodybuilder, it is no fun training in a smelly dungeon either, so don't be afraid to call a dump a dump. (Although, personally, I have had some very good workouts in some very definite dumps!) Also, there is the matter of music—I like to train to really loud rock and roll, but others prefer different music or none at all. Check to see what kind of music is played in any gym you intend to train in.

Training at Home

Although there is really no substitute for training at a good gym, some training at home can be useful. You can do extra ab work, for example, with just an abdominal board. With a simple bench and a basic set of weights, you can do reps and sets whenever you feel like it. This can be very valuable if you occasionally have trouble getting to the gym or if you run out of time in the gym and can't get a full workout.

For those with more money to invest, there is quite a bit of good equipment available for the home. Most sporting goods stores carry benches and weight sets selling for around $100. Sears, Montgomery Ward, J. C. Penney, and other chain stores also sell weight-training equipment. Joe Weider has a multi-exercise bench, weights, and a whole home gym priced from $300 to $400.

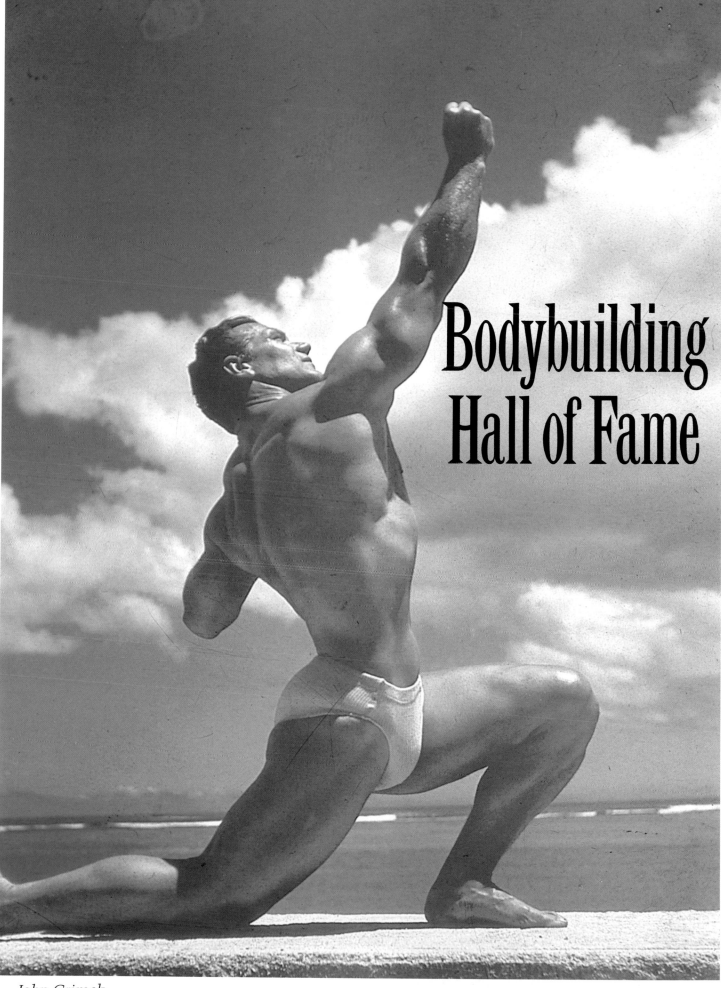

Bodybuilding
Hall of Fame

John Grimek

Steve Reeves

Reg Park

Bill Pearl

Larry Scott

Dave Draper

Sergio Oliva

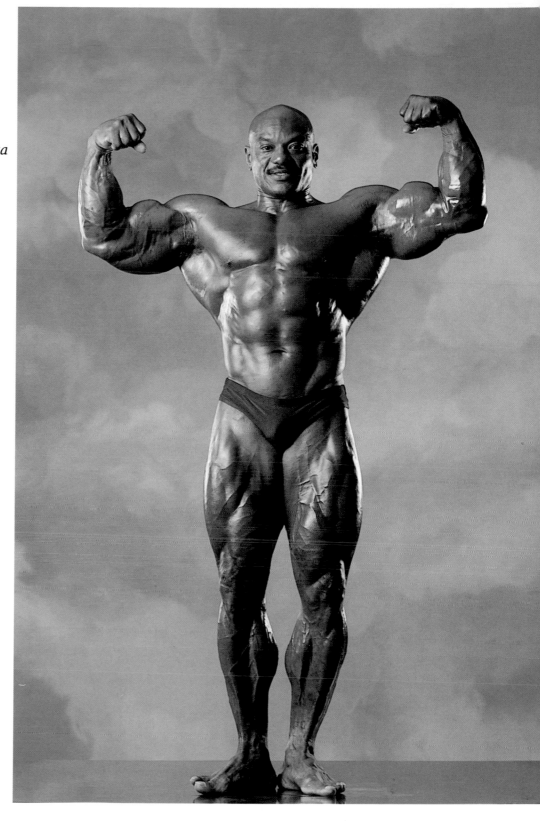

Franco Columbu

Frank Zane

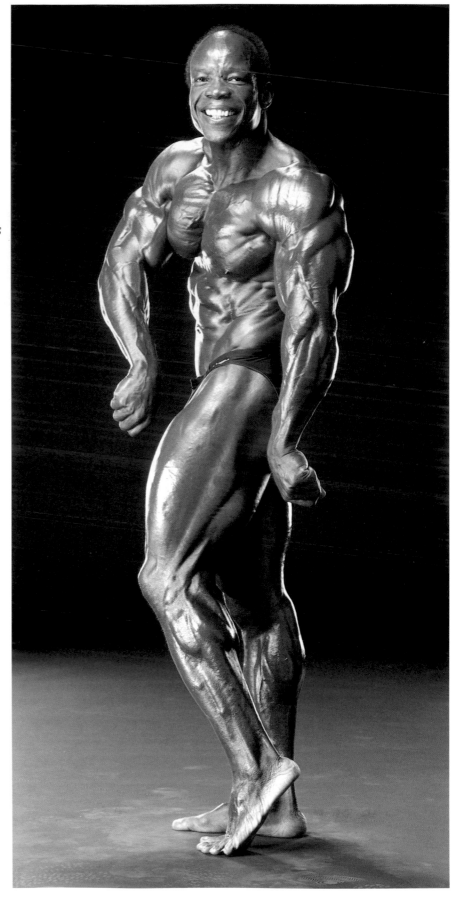

Albert Beckles

Lou Ferrigno

Chris Dickerson

Bertil Fox

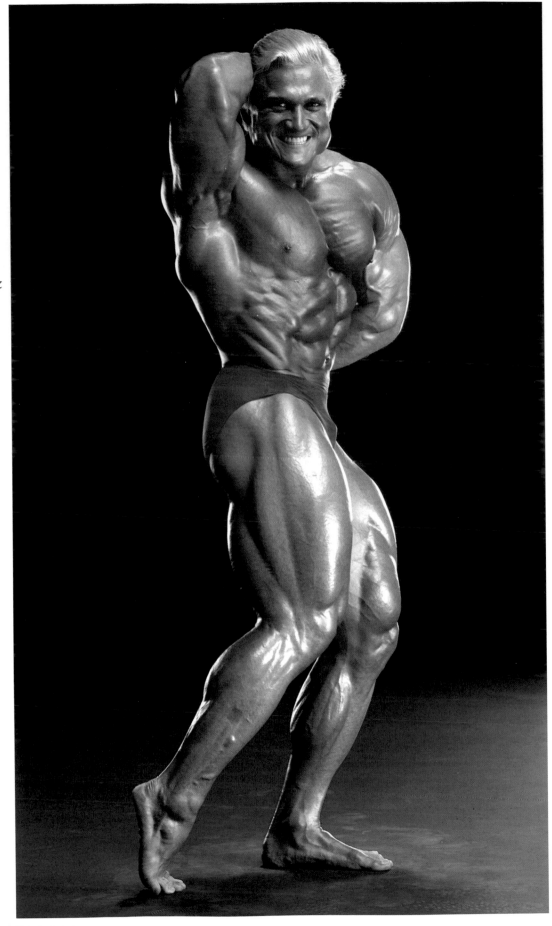

Tom Platz

Samir Bannout

Lee Haney

There are also many exercise machines available that are suitable for home training. Marcy sells a home exercise device for about $300. Universal's home equipment is more expensive at about $2,000, but this is still less than a full multi-station Universal installation at around $5,000.

But I would caution anyone who wants to train at home against using equipment that is less than he needs for a good workout. If you can bench-press 400 pounds, for example, then it does no good to bench at home with only 250 pounds.

Frank Zane has had good success training at home. Franco has a small home gym, and we have from time to time used it for working a specific body part. But I have always preferred the energy level of the gym, the excitement and interaction with the rest of the bodybuilders. In any event, even if you've made good progress by training at home, I recommend that you get thoroughly familiar with a gym and be able to make full use of the facilities you find there. There has never to my knowledge been a champion bodybuilder who developed his physique any place other than a good gym, and I recommend that you find one to train in if you have any serious aspirations.

CHAPTER 5
Getting Started

If you are just getting started in bodybuilding, remember the old saying "The longest journey begins with a single step." A bodybuilding career can be one of the longest in sports; you can keep getting better right through your thirties and forties.

The thing to do right at the start is to set a clear goal for yourself. Why is it that you want to train with weights? For competition? Health? To improve at sports? This helps to determine where you should train, how often and how hard, what kind of a training partner to have, and what famous bodybuilders to use as models.

I recommend that before you begin you have photographs taken that show your physique from all four sides. Write down all your important measurements (neck, chest, biceps, forearms, wrists, waist, thighs, and calves) as well as your weight. This way you can always check back to find out what kind of progress you have made.

To begin, you need to find a place to train that suits your goals, and to master the basic bodybuilding exercises in this book. Keep in mind that your first task is to create a solid, quality muscle structure. Advanced bodybuilders are concerned with improving muscle shape, achieving separation, tying in various muscle groups—none of which need concern the beginner.

When I was starting out, I found it very important to find somebody on whom to model myself. A businessman training for fitness would be wasting his time trying to create a physique to rival Sergio Oliva's; a serious bodybuilder with a frame and proportions like Frank Zane shouldn't spend his time studying posing photos of Danny Padilla or Mike Mentzer. In my case, it was Reg Park, with his great size and muscularity. I would put up photos of Reg all over the walls, then study them endlessly, picturing in my mind how that kind of development would look on my own frame. So much of bodybuilding is mental that you have to have a clear idea of what you want to be and where you are going if you want to achieve extraordinary results.

Too many young bodybuilders try to run before they learn to

walk. They copy my routine or pattern their workout on some other champion's example, and end up doing exercises that are inappropriate to their stage of development. However, if after six months or so of training the idea of competing begins to appeal to you, start to work toward that goal: learn your body, what makes it grow, its strengths and weaknesses; create a picture in your mind of what you eventually want to look like.

When I talk about sticking to the fundementals, I don't mean doing anything less than a real bodybuilding program—which you will see when you study the programs in this book. I only mean that you should limit your training to those exercises and methods that build the most mass in the shortest time, and then go on to carefully sculpt and shape that mass into championship quality. Even if you have no intention of becoming a competition bodybuilder, if you are only training for health and fitness, *there is never any reason to waste time by training in any but the most effective and efficient way possible.*

You build a basic structure, learn how to train correctly, acquire a knowledge of diet and nutrition, and then just give the body time to grow. In a year, maybe a little less or a little more, you will begin to see radical changes in your physique and will have enough experience so that you can begin to develop an individualized training program based on your own instincts of what is right or wrong for your particular body.

And, just as you write down your physical measurements and keep track of your development with photos, I would recommend that you write out your training program, noting how many sets of each movement you do and with how much weight, so that anytime in the future you can check back to find out how much you have really done and compare that with the actual progress you have made.

You should also learn to keep track of your eating habits, how many protein drinks you had during any given week, how long you dieted, and what kind of diet you followed. All of this will allow you, perhaps five years down the line, when memory no longer recalls these facts, to be certain exactly what you did or did not do in pursuing your bodybuilding development.

Fast and Slow Developers

Your genes have a lot to do with how your body will respond to training. I started training at fifteen, and photos taken after only a year reveal the beginnings of the physique that won me seven

Me at sixteen

Mr. Olympia titles. Every month or two I gained ½ inch on my arms, so people told me right away, "You should be a bodybuilder." Casey Viator turned from power lifting to bodybuilding at an early age and at nineteen became the first and only teenage Mr. America.

But not all great bodybuilders were early bloomers. Frank Zane was good enough to win his share of victories in the '60s, but it wasn't until the '70s that he achieved the perfection of development that allowed him to be victorious in three Mr. Olympia competitions. For slow developers, there is not as much immediate positive feedback to help keep up motivation. But bodybuilding is like the race between the hare and the tortoise: ultimately, determination and endurance over a long period of time wins the title, not a quick start and an all-out sprint for the finish line.

It is not how quickly you develop that will finally make the difference, but how far you are able to go. The judges don't look at competitors on stage and say, "That contestant has been training for eight years but the other one is better because he's only been training for three!" No, all that counts is how good you get, and you can't make your body develop any faster than your own biological makeup will allow.

But it is possible to develop *more slowly* than your biology would allow, simply by not believing that rapid gains are possible and not training to develop as far and as fast as you can. I remember watching Franco Columbu train for two years with only moderate gains. Then he saw me win Mr. Universe and he suddenly decided that he too wanted to win that title. After that, he trained really hard for two or three hours a day and began to make unbelievable gains in a very short time. His mind believed, so his body responded.

Free Weights versus Machines

I have to tell you straight out that I prefer barbells and dumbbells for most purposes. Free weights demand more of your body, and yet allow your joints and limbs to move in their natural planes, not just along lines dictated by the design of a machine. Franco tells me that in his chiropractic practice most of the muscle strains and joint injuries he sees come about as the result of using machines that put unnatural stresses on the body, that lock you into too rigid a position.

Also, most of the really good bodybuilders I know have also been power lifters—a subject I will explore in more detail elsewhere. Forcing the body to lift against gravity, to coordinate and balance masses of iron, gives it a structure and quality that high-repetition, relatively light training alone does not provide.

Free weights give the experienced bodybuilder the freedom to isolate certain muscles and to work the body in any number of creative ways. They also enable people of different heights, weights, physical proportions—long-armed, short-armed, long-legged, short-legged, etc.—to get a complete workout, while many machines seem to be designed only to satisfy those who represent the "average" customer of a commercial health spa.

But I am not against machines. Joe Gold, who is a master craftsman when it comes to building exercise equipment, has filled World Gym with many useful machines and devices. It is difficult to get full thigh development, for example, without a Leg Extension machine. But I believe that a good bodybuilding program should include no more than 30 percent to 40 percent training with machines. Certainly, a Curl gets better results done with dumbbells or a barbell because of the way you can isolate and stimulate the biceps—but it would be hard to really work the lats without a Lat Pulldown machine or to do Triceps Pushdowns without cables.

Machines keep the resistance working along one plane only, requiring the use of less muscle while doing the exercise. But the whole idea of bodybuilding and strength training is to use as much muscle as possible, so this is no real advantage at all!

It is true that a muscle doesn't "know" what kind of resistance it is working to overcome. In that sense resistance is resistance. But the muscle does indeed react differently if it is constantly subjected to resistance that comes from varying angles and different directions as opposed to that which is always along a predictable line.

If you are training somewhere that does not have the free weights you need for your workout, and there is nothing you can do about it, *use whatever you have to use in order to accomplish your training!* The bottom line is to get that workout, no matter how you have to do it. Whatever works, works—and, as a bodybuilder, that's all you need to worry about.

Gear

Bodybuilding is an inexpensive sport in the sense that you don't need a lot of training equipment beyond what is supplied by the gym. But there are a few basic items you might consider obtaining.

Shoes

I have trained wearing athletic shoes and I have gone through workouts barefoot. Either way is okay for some exercises, but there are those in which I think wearing shoes is essential. Doing heavy Squats, for example, or when you do power lifting exercises or very heavy Calf Raises, you need the extra support that shoes give you. In fact, high shoes that give you extra ankle support can really help to protect you. When you are doing Chin-Ups or

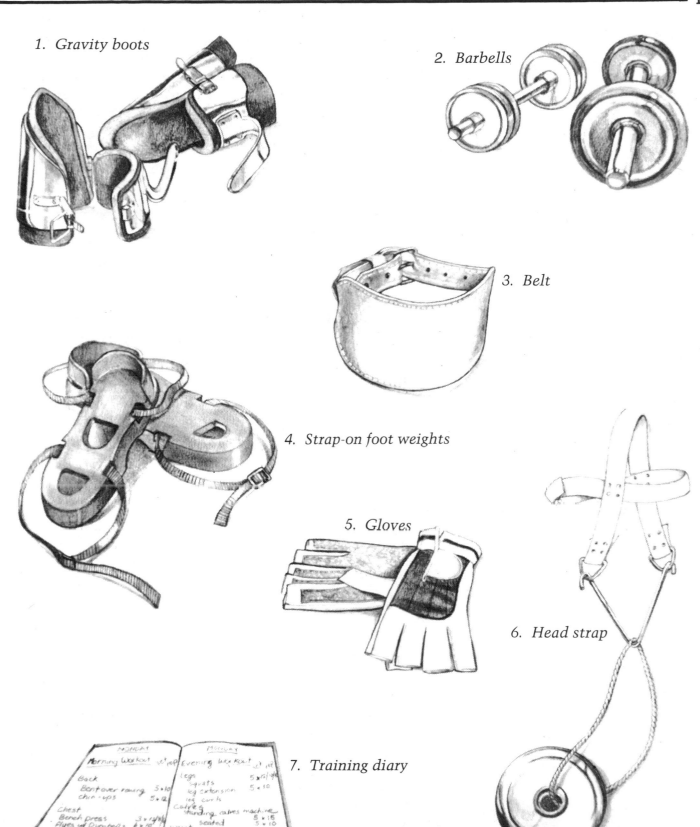

1. Gravity boots

2. Barbells

3. Belt

4. Strap-on foot weights

5. Gloves

6. Head strap

7. Training diary

Curls, shoes don't matter. Be aware that not all shoes are created equal. Many running shoes are made so soft and light—which are great qualities if you plan to run 10 miles or so—that they don't give you much support. However, you can also find athletic shoes that are thick-soled, solid, and with good arch support. Remember how much pressure is borne by the feet when you are doing exercises like heavy Squats, and how hard that can be on the arches. So choose the appropriate shoe for whatever kind of workout you have planned.

Gloves

Many good bodybuilders wear gloves while training to protect their hands. Others use pieces of rubber cut from inner tubes to improve their grip. This is okay, but I have always trained bare-handed and used chalk whenever my grip felt too slippery. Power lifters work with enormous amounts of weight and don't use any of these aids. If you have particularly sensitive skin, or if you are a chiropractor, concert pianist, or in some other profession which requires that you take special care of your hands, by all means wear gloves. However, I recommend most bodybuilders simply grip the weights with bare hands and let them toughen up and develop calluses. Don't worry about sponges, gloves, and other aids.

Straps

Straps are fastened around your wrist and then twisted around a bar to effectively strengthen your grip, although my personal feeling is that using aids like this keeps hand strength from fully developing naturally. Straps are used because with bare hands it is often difficult to hold on to a weight that will really challenge your back in a heavy workout. However, champion power lifters don't use straps, and they lift enormous amounts. Franco and I have always lifted heavy without the use of straps. If you lift without straps, your grip will gradually strengthen. If you continually use straps, you will never develop this kind of strength.

Belts

The purpose of wearing a heavy belt is to support the muscles of the lower back when you are lifting very heavy weights. The waist belt was originally used by weightlifters doing heavy Overhead Presses. However, they are often considered necessary by those doing heavy Squats, pressing heavy weight, or doing heavy standing Calf Raises. But too many bodybuilders wear belts all the time they are in the gym, which has the effect of binding the lower back muscles and preventing them from developing the strength they ought to have, which is a high price to pay for an illusory feeling of security. Use a belt only when you really need one, for very heavy lifts.

Wraps

Wraps are used to support weak or injured joints and muscles. You will occasionally see a bodybuilder who has wrapped one or both elbows due to some physical problem. More commonly, wraps are used around the knees when doing very heavy Squats, or around the elbows when doing heavy Bench Presses. Unless you have an injury or joint problem (for which you should seek medical attention), you will not need to wrap your knees until you have progressed to the point where you are using very heavy weights. Ace bandages are most frequently used, wrapped firmly, but not too tightly, around the area. Remember that whenever you wrap an area tight enough to give it additional support, you are also limiting its flexibility of movement.

Head Straps

Many bodybuilders use a kind of harness that fits around the head to which you can attach a dumbbell or weight plate so you can do progressive-resistance exercises for the neck. The "Barbarian Twins," David and Peter Paul, amaze people at Gold's Gym with the enormous amount of weight they can train their necks with —and sometimes they even attach the head strap to a car and pull the vehicle across the parking lot. If you feel your neck is too small, by all means find a way to train it. Some companies now make machines for this purpose. However, a complete workout routine tends to build the neck muscles along with everything else, so don't waste your time with these exercises unless you really see a need for them.

Gravity Boots

Gravity boots enable you to hang upside down and stretch out the spine. Those who advocate using this device point to the fact that our bodies are constantly being compressed by the force of gravity—the spine is compressed, the internal organs are pulled earthward. The effect of this over a lifetime is shown by the fact that most of us are an inch or two shorter at age sixty than at age twenty-five. Stretching out the spine by hanging upside down and taking the strain off the internal organs is supposed to help counteract this process, and I can tell you that it feels very relaxing. However, hanging upside down has no direct effect on building up your body, so this remains an adjunct to training rather than a fundamental part of bodybuilding. If you do use gravity boots, start out by hanging for only short periods—no more than a minute or so—until you get used to the unusual sensation of being upside down. Then gradually increase your suspension periods a little at a time as you feel necessary.

Rubber Suits

Rubber suits and various kinds of rubber belts are used by some bodybuilders to increase perspiration and accelerate water loss. I suppose they have their uses, but if you are training really hard you will sweat buckets, and should allow your pores to "breathe." The primary use a competition bodybuilder would have for these suits would be to help lose water weight just before a contest. However, wearing a suit like this on a hot day when you are training hard could lead to hyperthermia, a dangerous increase in body temperature, and therefore I don't really recommend it. Keep in mind that any water loss due to the use of a device like this is only temporary.

Training Diary

When I first began to train, I wrote everything down—training routines, sets and reps, diet, everything. And I kept this up right through my 1980 Mr. Olympia victory. I would come into the gym and put a line on the wall in chalk for every set I intended to do. I would always do five sets of each movement. So, for example, the marks / / / / / / / / / / on my chest day would stand for five sets of Bench Presses and five sets of Dumbbell Flys. I would reach up and cross each line as I did the set. So when I finished Benches the marks would look like X X X X X / / / / / and I would never think to myself, "Should I do three sets today, or four?" I always knew it was five and just went ahead and did them. Watching those marks march across the wall as I did my workout gave me a tremendous sense of satisfaction and accomplishment. They were like an invading army crushing all opposition in its path. This visual feedback helped me to keep my training goals clearly in mind, and reinforced my determination to push myself to the limit in every workout.

Totally by instinct, I stumbled onto a concept widely accepted by educators and psychologists: human beings work best and learn best when they are given the right kind of feedback. Knowing that you have accomplished something is one thing; *seeing* what you have accomplished is another. It makes your accomplishment all the more real and exciting, and therefore motivates you to try even harder the next time.

Feedback also lets you know when you are not on the right track. Memory can play tricks on you, but the information in the pages of a training diary is right there for you to see. If you are suddenly getting good results, you can look back to see what kind of exercise program and diet regimen helped you. If you begin to develop problems—your progress slows or you seem to be losing strength—you can check your records to try to determine where you might be making your mistake.

Continuing to keep a training diary over long periods helped my development tremendously. I would sit down at the beginning of the month and outline my program for the next thirty days—what days I would work out, what body parts I would train, and what exercises I would do. After a while, if a body part was lagging behind somewhat in development or I decided that certain muscles needed more training than I had been giving them, I would make an adjustment in my thirty-day plan and add the necessary exercises.

I also kept a careful record of my body weight and would take measurements every month—neck, shoulder width, biceps (hanging and flexed), forearms, waist (standing relaxed and in a vacuum), and so forth—so that I could make comparisons of how much I had progressed from one period to another.

I kept track of those days when I felt great or felt terrible, when I cancelled a training session, or when I had a particularly good workout. I wrote down what I ate, how many meals and protein drinks I had during the day.

So be sure to keep a training diary. Write down your entire program, make note of sets, reps, and weights, record your physical measurements, and take periodic photographs of your physique to keep track of your development. This way you will always know what your training program is supposed to be, and can always look back and check to see how you were training in the past and what kind of success that program brought you.

Age and the Sport of Bodybuilding

I don't like to see young children lifting weights. Their bodies are too unformed, their bones still too soft, to stand up to the stresses of weight training. I have seen boys five and nine years of age profiled on television, both of whom were supposed to be "bodybuilders," and there is a very young girl who can "lift" (that is, barely move) some 400 pounds on a Hack Squat machine at a body weight of only about 60 pounds, but, assuming that these children are not doing themselves injury by their training, they must be considered rare exceptions rather than the norm.

The youngest legitimate bodybuilder I have ever seen is Barbara Brown, who has competed in numerous women's contests since the age of twelve. However, in spite of her competent posing and good stage presence, it is obvious looking at her that she is still physically immature—and, while she uses a full bodybuilding program in her training, her parents are careful that she doesn't train with too much weight.

Pre-teen training, in my opinion, should rely on calisthenics or gymnastic exercises rather than weight training—exercises that use body weight resistance such as Push-Ups instead of Bench Presses, Knee Bends instead of Squats, and so on—with a lot of athletic activities to develop all of the body's physical potentials.

Once the body begins to mature—and you can usually tell this simply by how the body looks—weight training can begin. I began at fifteen, but this doesn't mean that every fifteen- or sixteen-year-old has to decide whether he wants to pursue competition bodybuilding right from the start. It takes a few months, maybe a year, simply to learn the exercises and begin to understand the experience of training. However, as in most other sports, the sooner you make up your mind to pursue serious training, the better chance you have of going all the way.

There have been bodybuilders who started much later in life and gone on to become great competitors (Ed Corney, for example), though your chances of becoming a Mr. Universe diminish with a late start. But once you have gotten into serious training, you can continue to improve almost indefinitely. Bodybuilding is a potentially long-lived career. When I competed in the 1980 Mr. Olympia contest, at age thirty-four I was one of the young guys. Bodybuilders like Chris Dickerson and Albert Beckles are showing us qualities once thought impossible in the over-forty bodybuilder. Bill Pearl, in his fifties, looks as if he could still compete in top-level bodybuilding competitions.

But certain obstacles do intrude as we get older. For one thing, after age twenty-five the metabolism tends to slow down (by about 10 calories a day per year), which means that an older bodybuilder has to diet more strenuously to stay lean. I know I had to watch what I ate much more carefully during my 1980 contest preparation than I did back in the 1960s. Also, older bodybuilders tend to have more on their minds—business, family, career, and so forth—while younger ones more often need only be concerned with eating, sleeping, and training.

However, if we tend to gain muscle more slowly, add fat more quickly, have more trouble concentrating, and recuperate more slowly as we get older, there is another side to the issue: since the body tends to deteriorate more quickly with age, the effect that bodybuilding has in building, shaping, and strengthening the body is even more pronounced in older bodybuilders than in younger ones.

"Am I too old to do bodybuilding?" I am frequently asked. My answer is always, "You're too old not to!" Certainly, a person who is fifty years old, or older, and just starting out is no threat to win the Mr. Universe contest. But when you realize how much age can take away from your muscle structure, and that bodybuilding training is the one sure way of offsetting this loss, the question simply answers itself. The basic principles of bodybuilding, the training effect that kind of workout provokes, remain the same at any age.

I am confident that there will be more and more competitions for older bodybuilders—over-40, over-50, or even over-60 events. I like this idea because it is much easier to make progress if you have firm goals, and having contests for older bodybuilders who would like to compete gives them the inspiration to train hard.

I was talking recently with John Grimek—Mr. America of 1940 and 1941 and a former Mr. Universe—who is now in his seventies and still keeps up his training. "I still get offers to pose and do exhibitions, but I turn them down," John told me. "I tell them that I stay in shape nowadays to feel better, not for publicity." He points out that too many men and women give up on keeping themselves fit by the end of their twenties or their thirties instead of staving off the aging process by exercising.

"I think we're only just beginning to understand how much bodybuilding can do for older people," he says. "An individual like Eugene Sandow, probably the best-built man of his day, was more of a weightlifter than bodybuilder. As a result, he was showing his age as he hit his fifties. If he had trained more like a modern bodybuilder, he would have developed that ageless quality that so many of today's bodybuilders have achieved. Just consider that Albert Beckles won the 1984 World Professional Championship at age fifty-two and I think you'll get the point."

John doesn't train with the amount of weight he used to—which was considerable, indeed—but he still does Squats regularly with about 415 pounds, and can go up to 500 if the occasion warrants. "I see lots of older men with bad hips and knees, so I do the Squats to keep my lower body in shape. I don't want any problems like that. I do too much dancing for that."

Making the Transition

Making the transition from training for fitness to training for competition is largely an evolution of consciousness: you begin to appreciate certain potentials of your body that you were not previously aware of and slowly your attitude toward your training begins to change and you have to make a decision—which way are you going to go? Are you going to keep this just a small part of your life, or will it gradually become the centerpiece of your existence?

I decided almost immediately that I wanted to be Mr. Universe. Franco competed for a while as a power lifter before making that decision. Mike Katz was a professional football player, Carlos Rodriguez a rodeo rider. You can decide early or late, but if you find yourself caught up in training, looking forward almost obsessively to your workouts in the gym, relishing every new plane and angle revealed as your physique grows and develops, this may be a decision that you, too, will have to make. There are many local amateur contests that will allow you to get your feet wet. There you can try competition and decide whether or not the rigors involved are to your liking.

There is so much more money in professional bodybuilding now than there was when I started that many athletes who might have concentrated on sports are deciding on a career in bodybuilding. But there are also more and more opportunities on the amateur level as well, and many bodybuilders continue to train and compete while pursuing careers as doctors, lawyers, chiropractors, or businessmen.

Most bodybuilders are highly competitive individuals, but there are those who are in the sport primarily for the meaning it gives their lives, regardless of whether or not they ever achieve a victory. Bodybuilding is more than a sport, it is also a way of life. It is an entire philosophy of how to live, a value system that gives specific answers to questions that concern so many of us these days—questions of what is worth doing and what value to give to excellence and achievement. It is a way of pursuing self-worth and personal validation, of finding satisfaction in your ability to set goals for yourself and working to reach them.

Of course, not everyone who takes up bodybuilding on a competitive level has the same experience, but no one goes very far in this sport without realizing the deeper meaning of physique competition.

I intend to do many things with my life besides competing in bodybuilding contests, but there will be no aspect of my life that will not be influenced or will not benefit from my having had the heady experience of competition. Bodybuilding training, I believe, is for everyone; but few are suited for the demands of competition. If the idea appeals to you even in the slightest, I urge you to give it some consideration. If you can share even a small part of what bodybuilding has given me, I know you will never regret your decision to try competition.

BOOK TWO
The
Training
Programs

CHAPTER 1

The Basic Training Principles

It takes hard, dedicated work to build a great physique, but hard work alone is not enough—you also need knowledge and a mastery of the principles that make bodybuilding training effective. These fundamental principles should be learned and mastered right from the beginning. It is much easier to learn the proper way to do something than it is to unlearn the wrong way and have to start over.

Progressive Resistance

Your muscles will grow only when they are subjected to an overload. They will not respond to anything less. As you grow stronger, the only way to make your muscles continue to grow is by increasing the amount of work you force them to do. This is most easily done by increasing the amount of weight you use in each exercise. By progressively adding on weight to keep pace with the growing strength of your body, you ensure that your muscles will always be working at their maximum capacity and therefore will grow as fast as possible.

Overtraining and Recuperation

"Intensity" is the measure of how hard you force the muscles to work in any training session. The more work you do in any given period of time, the more intensely you train. However, the more intense your workouts, the more recuperation time your body needs in order to rest and grow.

"Overtraining" occurs when you work a muscle too often to allow it to fully recuperate. You hear bodybuilders talk about "tearing the muscle down" and then letting it rebuild itself, but this is not really physiologically accurate. There can be small amounts of tissue damage during heavy exercise, and it is this damage that is associated with residual muscular soreness. But the soreness is a side effect and not the primary reason why the muscles need time to recuperate after heavy exercise.

There are a number of complex biochemical processes that accompany strenuous muscular contraction. The process of fueling muscular contraction results in the buildup of toxic waste products such as lactic acid. And during exercise the energy stored in the muscle in the form of glycogen is used up.

The body requires time to restore the chemical balance of the muscle cells, to clear out the residual waste products, and to restock the depleted stores of glycogen. But there is another factor that is even more important: time is needed for the cells themselves to adapt to the stimulus of the exercise and to grow. After all, that's what bodybuilding is all about, making muscles grow. So if you overtrain a muscle, forcing it to work too hard too quickly after the preceding exercise session, you will not give it a chance to grow and your progress will slow down.

Different muscles recover from exercise at different rates. The biceps, for example, recover the fastest. The lower back muscles recover the slowest, taking about a hundred hours to completely recuperate from a heavy workout. However, in most cases, giving each body part forty-eight hours' rest is sufficient, which means skipping a day after training a muscle before training it again.

Basic training involves only medium levels of intensity, so the time necessary for recuperation is shorter. Once you move on to more advanced training, higher levels of intensity will be needed in order to overcome the greater resistance of the body to change and growth. There is one other important factor, however: trained muscles recover from fatigue faster than untrained muscles. So the better you get at bodybuilding, the faster your recovery rate will be and the more intense your training program can become.

Full Range of Motion

Except for very specialized partial-range movements, bodybuilding exercises should take any muscle through its longest possible range of motion. You should take care to stretch out to full extension, and then come all the way back to a position of complete contraction. This is the only way to stimulate the entire muscle and every possible muscle fiber.

The Quality of Contraction

The bodybuilding training effect comes about by stimulating the muscle fibers with correctly performed exercises, *not* by trying to lift the heaviest weight possible by any means you can. To get the best results, therefore, concentrate on the muscles you are using in each exercise, feel the contraction, and don't get too involved with how much weight you are lifting. The weights are just a means to an end; how well you contract the muscles is what training is all about. When you finish a set, flex and pose the muscles involved to give them total stimulation.

"Cheating"

There are times when you do not have to do an exercise in the strictest manner possible in order to get the best results. "Cheating" is a specialized technique you can use to put maximum stress on your muscles. When you cheat, you use extraneous muscles to help out the ones directly involved in the exercise. But this is not done to make the exercise easier on those muscles, but to make it harder. For example, say you are doing a heavy Barbell Curl. You curl the weight up five or six times, and then find you are too tired to continue to do strict reps. At this point, you begin to use your shoulders and back to help in the lift slightly so that you can do another four or five reps. But you cheat just enough so that you can continue the set, and your biceps continue to work as hard as they can. By cheating, you have forced the biceps to do more reps than they could have done without the help from the other muscles, so you have put more stress on them, not less.

Warming Up

Often when people talk about "warming up," they don't understand how literally that should be taken. When you use a muscle, the temperature in the area actually rises, allowing you to contract the muscle much more forcefully. This makes it possible to train more intensely and to derive more benefit from your workout.

Warming up also pumps fresh, oxygenated blood to the area, raises the blood pressure, and increases the heart rate. This provides a maximum oxygen supply to the body and helps to eliminate the waste products of exercise from the working muscles.

Finally, warming up properly helps to protect the body from becoming overstressed, prepares it for the demands of heavy training, and reduces the chance of injury, such as a sprain or strain.

There are lots of ways to warm up. Some bodybuilders enjoy a short run before training, enough to get the heart going but not enough to deplete the body of energy. Calisthenics and other light exercises also give you a warm-up without putting any great stress on the body. But the most popular method of warming up is with the weights themselves. First spend some time stretching (see p. 125), and then do some moderately light movements with a barbell or dumbbells, hitting each body part in turn until the body is ready for something more strenuous.

Then, for each different exercise during your workout you begin with one light warm-up set in order to get those specific muscles ready to do that specific movement. When you do a set or two with higher reps and less than maximum weight, your muscles are then prepared to deal with the greater intensity generated by heavier weights and six-rep sets.

Warming up is even more important for power training because you are going to subject the body to still greater stress. The best idea is not to do power movements until your body gets into gear by doing the less stressful bodybuilding sets first.

The time of day is also a factor in determining how much warming up you need. If you are training at eight o'clock in the morning you are likely to be tighter and more in need of stretching and warming up than at eight at night, so adjust your preliminaries accordingly.

Always take care that you warm up thoroughly. If you are about to do heavy Shoulder Presses, for example, remember that you are going to involve more than the deltoids and triceps. The muscles of the neck and the trapezius will also contract intensely during the movement, and they should be given time to get ready as well.

Injuries in the gym happen for two primary reasons: either the person used sloppy technique (too much weight or failing to keep the weight totally under control) or didn't stretch and warm up properly.

Sets

Generally in the Basic Training Program I recommend doing 5 sets of each bodybuilding exercise, except where otherwise specified. I believe this is the best system for several reasons:

1. You need to do at least 5 sets in order to have the volume of

training necessary to fully stimulate all the available muscle fiber. If you do more sets per exercise, your total training volume will be so great that you risk overtraining.

2. Doing 5 sets per exercise, for a total of 15 sets per body part (for the larger muscle groups) in the Basic Training Program and 20 sets in Advanced Training, enables you to do a sufficient variety of exercises to work all the areas of a body part—upper and lower back, for example, the outside sweep of the lats, and the inner back.

3. The experience of four decades of bodybuilders has proven that the maximum amount of weight you can handle that allows you to just make it through 5 sets of an exercise will stimulate the muscles and make them grow.

For smaller muscle groups, such as the biceps and triceps, although I still recommend 5 sets per exercise, you actually need fewer total sets—around 10 per body part instead of 15 or 20. However, remember that arms get a lot of incidental training when you work the other areas of the upper body.

For power exercises, I have usually specified only 3 sets per exercise for the simple reason that you will be lifting heavier and won't need as much volume of training.

Reps

To get the most out of your training, unless otherwise specified, you should "train to failure" in each set. This simply means you should continue doing your repetitions until you are unable to lift the weight any more. This ensures that you have stimulated as much muscle fiber as possible.

But you don't go on indefinitely when training to failure; instead, you choose a weight for the exercise that will cause you to fail at or near a specific number of repetitions. For example:

First set. Choose a weight that causes you to fail at about 15 repetitions. This serves as a warm-up set.

Second set. Increase the weight so that you fail at about 10 repetitions.

Third set. Increase the weight again so that you fail at about 8 repetitions.

Fourth set. Add weight and aim at doing 6 repetitions.

Fifth set. Using the same weight, try to force out 6 reps.

Training this way gives you the best of all possible worlds: you start out relatively light, which gives your muscles time to fully warm up for that particular exercise; you go on to do slightly fewer reps with a heavier weight, which forces lots of blood into your muscles and gives you a great pump; and finally, you add on more weight so that you are training relatively heavy for strength.

Choosing the Right Weight

Occasionally you will use an amount of weight for an exercise that would normally make you fail at 10 repetitions, but you will feel exceptionally strong and be able to grind out 12 or 13 reps instead. That's fine, keep going as long as you can in any set. Don't stop simply because you have arrived at a certain number.

But the opposite will happen from time to time, and you will only be able to get 8 reps with a weight you could usually handle for 10. As long as you continue to go to failure, you are still getting the most out of your training, even though your body may not be as powerful on that particular day.

If, however, you are doing your set and you find yourself continuing on to do 13, 15, or more repetitions, you will know that you need to use more weight on that exercise. For the next set, increase the weight so that your repetitions return to the specified guidelines.

The idea of bodybuilding, unless you are doing heavy lifts or power training for special purposes, is not to lift too heavy or too light. Too heavy, and you tend to cheat—you don't work through a full range of motion and can't do enough repetitions; too light, and you do not put sufficient stress on the muscle to make it grow.

Resting Between Sets

It is important to pace yourself properly through a workout. If you try to train too fast, you risk cardiovascular failure before you have worked the muscles enough. Also, you may have a tendency to get sloppy and start throwing the weights around instead of executing each movement correctly.

However, training too slowly is bad too. If you take five minutes between each set, your heart rate slows down, you lose your pump, the muscles get cold, and your level of intensity drops down to nothing.

Try to keep your rest periods between sets down to a minute or less. In the first minute after a weight training exercise you recover 72 percent of your strength, and by three minutes you have recovered all you are going to recover without extended rest. But remember that the point of this training is to stimulate and fatigue the maximum amount of muscle fiber possible, and this only happens when the body is forced to recruit additional muscle fiber to replace that which is already fatigued. So you don't want to allow your muscles to recover too much between sets—just enough to be able to continue your workout and to keep forcing the body to innervate more and more muscle tissue.

There is one other factor to consider: physiologists have long noted the link between maximal muscle strength and muscular endurance. The stronger you are, the more times you can lift a submaximal amount of weight. This means that the more you press yourself to develop muscular (as opposed to cardiovascular) endurance, the stronger you become. So maintaining a regular pace in your training actually leads to an increase in overall strength.

Breathing

I am surprised how often I am asked how one should breathe during an exercise. This has always seemed automatic to me, and I am often tempted to say, "Just relax and let it happen. Don't think about it."

But now I know that there are people for whom this doesn't work very well, and for them I have a simple rule: "Breathe out with effort." For example, suppose you are doing a Squat—you take in a breath as you stand with the weight on your shoulders and squat down, and you expel your breath as you push yourself back up. And you breathe out, *you don't hold your breath.* There is a good reason for this.

Very hard contractions of the muscles usually involve a contraction of the diaphragm as well, especially when you are doing any kind of a Leg Press or Squat movement. This increases the pressure in your thoracic cavity (the space in which the lungs fit). If you try to hold your breath, you could injure yourself. For example, you could hurt your epiglottis, blocking the passage of air through your throat. Breathing out as you perform a maximal effort protects you from this and, some people think, it actually makes you a little stronger.

Power Training

There are various ways of assessing strength. If I can lift 300 pounds and you can lift only 250, I am stronger than you in one-rep strength. However, if you can lift 250 pounds ten times and I

Franco Columbu deadlifting 730 pounds

can only lift it eight times, that is a different kind of strength; you would be surpassing me in muscular endurance—the ability to continue to be strong over a series of movements.

To shape and develop the body, it is necessary to do a lot of the "endurance" kind of training—plenty of sets and reps. But I also believe that, unless you include low-rep, strength training, you will never achieve the hardness and density necessary to create a truly first-class physique.

In the days of John Grimek and Clancy Ross, virtually all bodybuilders trained for power. Although most of them lacked the total refinement that top bodybuilders have today, they were extremely strong, hard, and impressive physical specimens. Now, I feel, the pendulum has swung too far the other way and bodybuilders have been overlooking the benefits of including traditional power moves in their overall programs.

"If you don't do power moves," my friend Dr. Franco Columbu explains, "it shows immediately on stage. There is a soft look that shows itself clearly." Heavy power training puts tremendous strain on relatively few fibers at a time, causing them to become bigger and thicker (hypertrophy), and they also become packed much tighter together. This contributes enormously to that hard, dense look of the early champions.

Both Franco and I achieved a more Herculean look by power training. Jusup Wilkosz is another bodybuilder who has the hard, chiseled look that only power training can give you. Roger Walker of Australia is hard as a granite wall because of his early power training.

Including power training in your program also helps to make you stronger for the rest of your training. You will move up to using heavier weights more quickly, so your muscles will grow that much faster. It also toughens and strengthens your tendons as well as your muscles, so you will be much less likely to strain them while doing higher-repetition training with less weight, even if you should lose concentration at some point and handle the weights with less than perfect technique.

Heavy training strengthens the attachment of the tendon to bone. Separating the tendon from the bone is called an "avulsion fracture" (see Injuries, p. 704) and the right kind of power training minimizes the possibility of this occurring.

Muscle size and density created by a program including heavy training is easier to maintain for long periods of time, even with a minimum of maintenance training. With high-rep training only, much of the growth is the result of transient factors such as fluid retention and glycogen storage, but muscle created by

Jusup Wilkosz doing Lying Triceps Extensions using 255 pounds

With my long arms, bench-pressing 400-plus pounds eight times takes a lot of effort and concentration.

Heavy T-Bar Rows is one of the best power exercises for the back.

power training is due to an actual increase in muscle fiber size. Also, as Franco tells me, the muscle cell walls themselves grow thicker and tougher, so that they tend to resist shrinking.

When I was training in Austria, we put a lot of emphasis on strength. For example, we would have to clean the barbell in order to do Incline Barbell Presses because we didn't have a modern incline bench. I remember grabbing the weight, cleaning it, and falling back against an incline board before doing the incline movement. Pressing 315 pounds is one thing—cleaning it, believe me, is quite another. It is obvious that you have to use different muscles when doing the exercise this way.

Besides all this, when you do power training, you find out what the body can really do, how much weight you can really move, and this gives you a mental edge over someone who never does power training.

There are many sophisticated techniques that modern bodybuilders need to master. But you can't forget that the basis of bodybuilding is developing muscle mass by lifting heavy weights. This does not mean that I believe bodybuilders should train like weightlifters. I recommend a program of total development that includes a certain number of power moves to give you the advantage of *both* kinds of training.

Heavy Days

Even when you do power training, you do not necessarily go to your absolute maximum every time. Training moderately heavy one day and then to your limit the next is more likely to speed up your progress than maximum effort every time.

That is why I always scheduled "heavy days" in my training routine. Once a week or so, I would pick one body part and go to the maximum with a power move that worked that area. When training legs, for instance, I would try for a maximum Squat; for chest, a maximum-strength Bench Press, and so on. By doing it this way I would not tax my body to such an extent that it could not recuperate before my next workout. But by going to the maximum on a regular basis, I gained a very accurate perception of just how much progress I was making in developing my strength, and by forcing myself to go to the limit every so often, I counterbalanced the lighter-weight, higher-rep training that made up the majority of my workouts.

I recommend you try the same thing. Once or twice a week, pick one body part and test out your maximum strength. Have a training partner standing by to spot you so that you have no anxieties about handling a heavy weight. Stretch and warm up first to prepare your body for the effort. Keep track of your poundages in your training diary. You will feel a great deal of satisfaction watching the numbers climb as you grow stronger. Your ability to handle heavy weight will also contribute tremendously to increasing your confidence and mental commitment to your training.

Incidentally, because power training does work so many muscles at once, and you are using heavy weights, you will find you can use the Cheating Principle to great effect doing these movements.

Stretching

One of the most neglected areas of the workout, even among experienced bodybuilders, is stretching. If you watch a lion as he wakes from a nap and gets to his feet, you will see he immediately stretches his whole body to its full length, readying every muscle, tendon, and ligament for instant and brutal action. The lion knows instinctively that stretching primes his strength.

Muscle, tendon, ligament, and joint structures are flexible. They can stiffen, limiting your range of motion, or they can stretch, giving you a longer range of motion and the ability to contract additional muscle fiber. So stretching before you train actually allows you to train harder.

Stretching also makes your training safer. As you extend your muscles fully under the pull of a weight, they can easily be pulled too far if your range of motion is limited. Overextension of a tendon or ligament can result in a strain or sprain and seriously interfere with your workout schedule. But if you stretch the areas involved first, the body will adjust as heavy resistance pulls on the structures involved.

Flexibility will also increase if the various exercises are done properly. A muscle can contract, but it cannot stretch itself. It has to be stretched by the pull of an opposing muscle. When you train through a full range of motion, the muscle that is contracting automatically stretches its opposite. For example, when you do Curls, your biceps contract and your triceps stretch. When you do Triceps Extensions, the opposite happens. By using techniques that engage the full range of motion, you will increase your flexibility.

But that isn't enough. Muscles contracted against heavy resistance tend to shorten with the effort. Therefore, I recommend stretching before you train—to allow you to train harder and more safely—and stretching *after* you train as well, to stretch out those tight and tired muscles.

You can prepare for your workout by doing any number of the standard stretching exercises which follow. You might also consider taking a yoga or stretching class. Many bodybuilders feel that this extra effort devoted to flexibility is not necessary, but others, like Tom Platz, rely heavily on stretching to enhance their workouts. When Tom is limbering up for a workout, those gargantuan legs twisted like pretzels beneath him, it is almost unbelievable to watch. He spends the first part of his calf workout stretching his calves as far as possible, often using very heavy weights, because he realizes that the more they stretch, the more fiber becomes involved in the contraction.

But as important as stretching before and after the workout may be, I believe it is also essential to do certain kinds of stretching *during* your training. Just as I recommend flexing and posing the muscles between sets, I also believe in stretching certain muscles between one set and the next. The lats, for example, benefit from careful stretching interspersed with various Chinning and Pulldown movements. You will find I have included stretches in various exercises where I felt stretching to be particularly beneficial.

It is, after all, details like this—taking pains to leave nothing out that can enhance your development—that set champions apart, and the difference will be immediately visible when you pose on stage in competition. The difference will not only be in how you look—the utmost in separation and definition—but will also show in the grace and sureness of your presentation. Bodybuilders like Ed Corney, known as perhaps the best poser in modern bodybuilding, could never move with such beauty if their muscles, tendons, and ligaments were tight and constricted.

I don't recommend spending a lot of time and energy stretching unless you have a severe flexibility problem or are trying to rehabilitate an injured area. For most purposes, I think spending about ten minutes doing ten basic stretching exercises for the bigger muscles before and after you work out is enough.

Stretching requires slow, gentle movements rather than quick, bouncing ones. When you put sudden stress on a muscle or tendon, it contracts to protect itself, thereby defeating your purpose. On the other hand, if you stretch it out carefully and hold that position for thirty seconds or more, the tendon will gradually relax and you will gain flexibility.

I recommend spending about one minute on each of the following exercises. However, this should be considered the bare minimum. The more time you spend stretching, the more flexible you will become.

STRETCHING EXERCISES

Side Bends

Purpose of Exercise: TO STRETCH THE OBLIQUES AND OTHER MUSCLES AT THE SIDE OF THE TORSO.

Execution: Stand upright, feet slightly more than shoulder width apart, arms at sides. Raise your right arm over your head and bend slowly to the left, letting your left hand slide down your thigh. Bend as far as you can and hold this position for about 30 seconds. Return to starting position, then repeat to opposite side.

Ali Malla

Forward Bends

Purpose of Exercise: TO STRETCH THE HAMSTRINGS AND LOWER BACK.

Execution: Stand upright, feet together. Bend forward and take hold of the back of your legs as far down as possible—knees, calves, or ankles. Pull gently with your arms, bringing your head as close as possible to your legs in order to stretch the lower back and hamstrings to their limit. Hold this position for 30 to 60 seconds, then relax.

Hamstring Stretches

Purpose of Exercise: TO STRETCH THE HAMSTRINGS.

Execution: Place one foot or ankle on a bench or waist-high bar. Keeping your other leg straight, bend forward along the raised leg and take hold of it as far down as possible—knee, calf, ankle, or foot. Pull gently to get the maximum stretch in the hamstrings. Hold for about 30 seconds, relax, then repeat the movement using the other leg.

Lunges

Purpose of Exercise: TO STRETCH THE INNER THIGHS AND HAMSTRINGS.

Execution: (1) Stand upright, move one leg forward, then bend that knee, coming down so that the knee of your trailing leg touches the floor. Place your hands on either side of your front foot and lean forward to get the maximum possible stretch in the inner thighs. (2) From this position, straighten your forward leg and lock your knee, stretching the hamstrings at the back of the leg. Bend your forward knee and lower yourself to the floor again. Repeat this movement, first straightening the leg, then coming down to the floor again. Stand upright once more, step forward with opposite foot, and repeat the stretching procedure.

Feet Apart Seated Forward Bends

Purpose of Exercise: TO STRETCH THE HAMSTRINGS AND LOWER BACK.

Execution: (1) Sit on the floor, legs straight and wide apart. Bend forward and touch the floor with your hands as far in front of you as possible. (2) Hold this position for a few seconds, then "walk" your hands over to one leg and grasp it as far down as possible—knee, calf, ankle, or foot. Pull gently on your leg to get the maximum stretch in the hamstrings and lower back. Hold this position for about 30 seconds, then walk your hands over to the other leg and repeat.

Inner Thigh Stretches

Purpose of Exercise: TO STRETCH THE INNER THIGHS.

Execution: Sit on the floor and draw your feet up toward you so that the soles are touching. Take hold of your feet and pull them as close to the groin as possible. Relax your legs and drop your knees toward the floor, stretching the inner thighs. Press down on your knees with your elbows to get a more complete stretch. Hold for 30 to 60 seconds, then relax.

Quadriceps Stretches

Purpose of Exercise: TO STRETCH THE FRONT OF THE THIGHS.

Execution: Kneel on the floor. Separate your feet enough so that you can sit between them. Put your hands on the floor behind you and lean back as far as possible, feeling the stretch in the quadriceps. (Those who are less flexible will only be able to lean back a little; those who are very flexible will be able to lie back on the floor.) Hold this position for 30 to 60 seconds, then relax.

Hurdler's Stretches

Purpose of Exercise: TO STRETCH THE HAMSTRINGS AND INNER THIGHS.

Execution: Sit on the floor, extend one leg in front of you, and curl the other back beside you. Bend forward along the extended leg and take hold of it as far down as possible— knee, calf, ankle, or foot. Pull slightly to get the maximum stretch and hold for 30 seconds. Reverse the position of your legs and repeat the movement.

Spinal Twists

Purpose of Exercise: TO INCREASE THE ROTATIONAL RANGE OF MOTION OF THE TORSO.

Execution: Sit on the floor, legs extended in front of you. Bring your right knee up and twist around so that your left elbow rests on the outside of the upraised knee. Place your right hand on the floor behind you and continue to twist to the right as far as possible. Twist to the extreme of your range of motion and hold for 30 seconds. Lower your right knee, bring up your left, and repeat the motion to the other side.

Hanging Stretches

Purpose of Exercise: TO STRETCH THE SPINE AND UPPER BODY.

Execution: Take hold of a chinning bar and let your body hang beneath it. Hold for at least 30 seconds so your spine and upper body have a chance to let go and stretch. If you have gravity boots or some other appropriate piece of equipment available, try hanging upside down to increase the amount of spinal stretch.

CHAPTER 2

Learning Your Body Type

It is important to stick with the fundamentals until you see how your particular body type responds to training. Different body types respond very differently to training, and what works for one type will not necessarily work for another.

One method of categorizing body types recognizes three fundamentally different physical types, called "somatotypes":

The ectomorph: characterized by a short upper body, long arms and legs, long narrow feet and hands, and very little fat storage; narrow in the chest and shoulders, with generally long, thin muscles.

The mesomorph: large chest, long torso, solid muscle structure, and great strength.

The endomorph: soft musculature, round face, short neck, wide hips, and heavy fat storage.

Of course, no one is totally one type but rather a combination of all three types. This system of classification recognizes a total of eighty-eight subcategories, which are arrived at by examining the level of dominance of each basic category on a scale of 1 to 7. For example, someone whose body characteristics were scored as ectomorphic (2), mesomorphic (6), and endomorphic (5) would be an endo-mesomorph, basically a well-muscled jock type but inclined to carry a lot of fat.

Any body type can be developed by proper training and nutrition, but individuals with different body types will find it necessary to initially approach their training with different objectives, even though they may share the same long-term goals.

Ectomorph Training

The extreme ectomorph's first objective is gaining weight, preferably in the form of quality muscle mass. He will not have the strength and endurance for marathon training sessions, will find

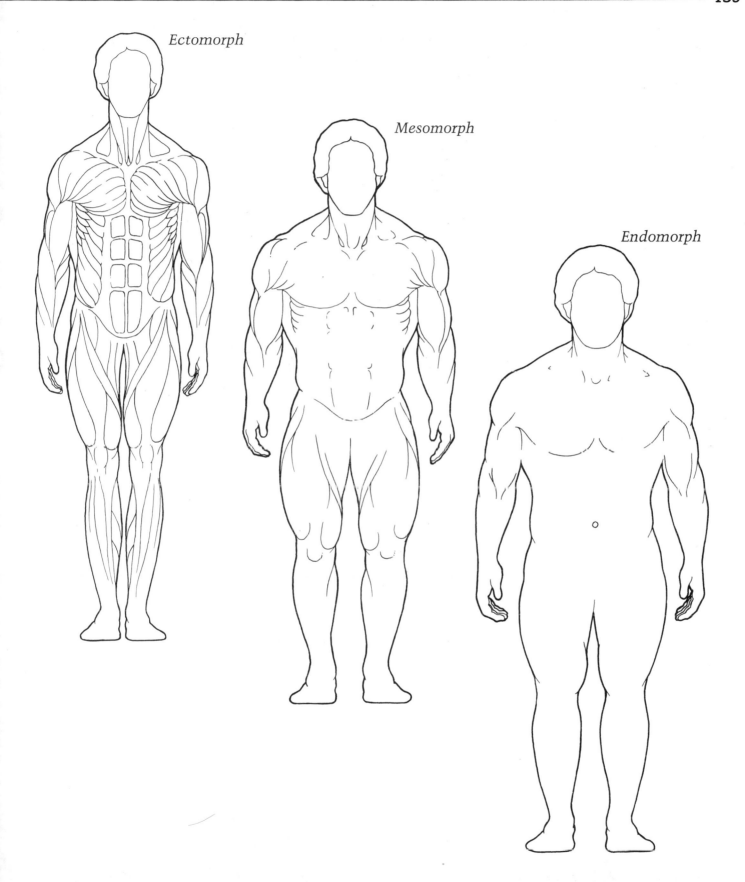

Ectomorph

Mesomorph

Endomorph

that muscle mass develops very slowly, and will often have to force himself to eat enough to ensure continued growth. Therefore, for the ectomorph I recommend:

1. Stay with the basic exercises, and include plenty of power moves for a program that builds maximum mass.
2. Do the entire Basic Training workout, but resort to longer rest periods, if necessary, to allow the body to cope with this level of effort.
3. Pay careful attention to nutrition; take in more calories than you are accustomed to, and if necessary, use weight-gain and protein drinks to supplement your food intake.
4. Keep outside activities—running, swimming, other sports—to a minimum so that you save calories for muscle building.

Mesomorph Training

The mesomorph will find it relatively easy to build muscle mass, but will have to be certain to include a sufficient variety of exercises in his program so that the muscles develop proportionately and well shaped rather than just thick and bulky. Therefore, for the mesomorph I recommend:

1. A combination of heavy power moves and a variety of shaping exercises. The more varied the program, the better the quality, proportion, and symmetry of the physique.
2. Relatively long workouts with short rest time. But remember that the mesomorphic physique responds so well to training that super-long sessions aren't needed.
3. A balanced diet with plenty of protein and maintaining a calorie level that keeps the physique within 10 or 15 pounds of contest weight all year long. No "bulking up" 30 or 40 pounds and then having to drop all of that useless weight for competition.

Endomorph Training

Generally the endomorph will not have too much difficulty building muscle, but will have to be concerned with losing fat weight and then being very careful with diet so as not to gain that weight back. Therefore, for the endomorph I recommend:

1. High-set, high-repetition training with very short rest periods so as to burn off as much fat as possible.

2. Additional aerobic exercise such as bicycle riding, running, or some other calorie-consuming activity.

3. A low-calorie diet that contains the necessary nutritional balance (see p. 681). Not "zero" anything, but the minimum amount of protein, carbohydrates, and fats, with vitamin and mineral supplements to be certain the body is not being deprived of any essential nutrients.

Understanding Your Body Type

There have been champions with every kind of body type. Steve Davis once weighed in at around 270 pounds, which means he tends heavily toward the endomorphic. Losing fat and replacing it with quality muscle was necessary before he could hope to win a bodybuilding title. Ken Passariello, lightweight Mr. Universe, came down from 250 pounds to win the title at 156 pounds, which puts him in the same category. Frank Zane, on the other

Here is a good example of how bodybuilding can change your body.

Steve Davis before, looking very endomorphic . . .

. . . and after, looking very mesomorphic

Ken Passariello, an
endo-mesomorph

Frank Zane, an
ecto-mesomorph

Dave Draper—classic
endomorphic mesomorph

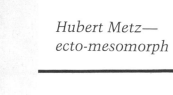
Hubert Metz—
ecto-mesomorph

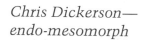
Chris Dickerson—
endo-mesomorph

Ken Waller—
endo-mesomorph

Ed Corney—endomorphic mesomorph

Casey Viator—almost pure mesomorph

hand, is much more ectomorphic. Muscle-mass gains have always taken Frank a long time to achieve, but this did not keep him from becoming Mr. Olympia three times. I am mesomorphic enough to be able to build muscle mass relatively easily, and at one point bulked up to 240 pounds, but my natural physique tended to be lean, which makes me more an ecto-mesomorph than an endo-mesomorph. Dave Draper is a classic endomorph, tending to get heavy and smooth easily, but able to stay lean and hard for competition by hard training and strict diet.

Really, though, no top bodybuilder is too much an ectomorph or an endomorph. Their bodies would lack proper proportion, symmetry, muscle mass, and definition. But you can see that bodybuilders like Hubert Metz tend to the ecto-mesomorphic, while others like Chris Dickerson and Ken Waller put on weight easily and are more endo-mesomorphic. Ed Corney is probably as endomorphic as anyone currently in competition. But despite the different body types, each of these men has held his own in competition against more totally mesomorphic types like Casey Viator or Tom Platz.

Understanding your own body type can save you a lot of time and frustration. An ectomorph who trains like an endomorph will overtrain and not grow. The endomorph who thinks he is more mesomorphic will grow, but will always have trouble keeping his body fat down. Certain principles of training are the same for everybody. But how you organize your training and how you integrate it with diet and nutrition can be profoundly different depending on what kind of body type nature has given you.

Tom Platz—another classic mesomorph

Body Composition Testing

Even though nature has given you a particular body type, when you add lean body mass and cut down on fat weight you are actually changing the composition of your body. It is often difficult to keep track of these changes just by using a scale and measuring tape. You can be on a diet and actually gain weight because your training is creating more muscle mass; you can go on a too strict diet and lose muscle tissue as well as fat; or you can train so hard that you are "overtraining" and forcing your body to burn up lean body mass in the process.

The best way to keep track of these physical changes—in addition to simply studying yourself in the mirror—is by some form of body composition testing. It is also useful in analyzing the benefits of one kind of training routine as opposed to another.

146

Tim Belknap, 1981 NPC
Mr. America, is an endo-
mesomorph, not as naturally
endomorphic as, say, Dave
Draper, but tending to put on
a lot of weight off-season if he
is not careful. In this photo,
Tim weighs 228 pounds.

This photo, taken only three
weeks later just prior to his
Mr. America victory, shows
him at a body weight of 196
pounds. By strict training and
dieting, Tim worked his body
composition toward a solid
mesomorph—all bone and
muscle, without an ounce of
extra fat on him.

The test will help show progress or lack of it in time for you to make some adjustments in your training program well in advance of a contest.

There are several ways of testing body composition. The most elaborate and expensive involves sitting in a vault while instruments record the potassium radiation from your body. This is impractical for most people. Another, more familiar method involves taking skinfold measurements all around the body, figuring out how much fat is trapped in the skin and then using a series of formulas to calculate overall body fat. But these formulas are based on "normal" body composition, so they don't apply to bodybuilders very well, making this method fairly inaccurate.

A more popular method, one that does work for bodybuilders, is the water-immersion test. The person is weighed out of the water, then in the water, and certain measurements such as the residual capacity of the lungs are taken and the numbers are applied to a formula to determine the ratio of fat to lean body mass—which is composed of muscle, bone, and internal organs.

The specific percentage you get indicating relative body fat is not that important. If you measure 6 percent in this test, you might really have 4 percent or 8 percent if measured using the potassium radiation method. The test is not that accurate in assessing actual fat percentage. But is fairly accurate when it comes to measuring *changes* in one's body composition, and that is very valuable to a bodybuilder. If you do two or three tests in a row and then find that most of the weight you are gaining is fat and not muscle, or when you are dieting, that you are losing more muscle tissue than fat, you can then alter your training and diet program accordingly.

The Basic Training Program

Me at nineteen

The first task facing the beginning bodybuilder is to build up a solid foundation of muscle mass—genuine muscular weight, not bulky fat. Later, you will try to shape this muscle into a balanced, quality physique.

You do this by basic, hard training using heavy weights—grinding it out week after week until your body begins to respond. And what I mean by "basic training" is not just a few exercises like Bench Presses, Bent-Over Rows, and Squats, but thirty or forty exercises all designed to stimulate and develop the major muscle groups of the body.

At the end of this period what you want is size, the raw material of a great physique. In my own, or Dave Draper's case, we had pretty much achieved this by the age of nineteen. I was huge, 240 pounds, but unfinished, like an enormous, gangling puppy who has not yet grown up to match the size of his feet. I had only a few cuts, but I had enough mass so that I was now ready to begin training for quality.

This initial period may last two, three, or even as long as five years. The length of the process depends on genetics, body type, and how much energy and motivation you are able to put into your training. But whether a bodybuilder develops faster or slower is no particular guarantee of ultimate quality. What counts is how far you are able to go, not how fast.

Dave Draper at nineteen

Split System Training

The harder you can work a muscle—using correct technique and giving it time to recuperate—the more it will grow. But this can present a dilemma: if you train the whole body as intensely as possible, trying to do as many as twenty sets for each of the larger body parts, you will probably drop from exhaustion before you finish your workout.

In the early days when champions like John Grimek and Clancy Ross reigned, bodybuilders usually attempted to train the entire body three times a week. They could train the entire body in one exercise session because they usually performed only three or four sets per body part. But as bodybuilding evolved it became evident that more precise training was needed to totally shape and develop the body. Different kinds of exercises were required so that the muscles could be worked from a variety of angles, and more sets of each exercise were necessary to stimulate the maximum amount of muscle fiber. But this meant that it was no longer possible to train the entire body in one workout. There was just too much effort involved, so the Split System of training was developed.

This system divides your training schedule so that you train only part of the body in each workout. There are different ways of doing this. Sometimes you can train only a third of the body each day, sometimes only half the body. This is determined by what you are specifically training for: whether you are concentrating on building strength and muscle mass, or trying to achieve optimum shape and definition for a contest.

The Basic Muscles

The human body has more than six hundred separate muscles, but in learning the fundamentals of bodybuilding we only need concern ourselves with a few of these.

Usually bodybuilders divide the body up into the following basic categories: back, shoulders, chest, arms, legs, and waist. But these categories are too general to guide your bodybuilding program. After all, when you talk about "legs," "arms," or "shoulders" you are not talking about single muscles but about very complex muscle groups that require a sophisticated program of training in order to develop them completely. Therefore, still keeping things as simple as possible, there are a number of subdivisions necessary in order to create useful bodybuilding routines:
Back (upper: latissimus dorsi; lower: spinal erectors)
Shoulders (deltoids: front, rear, side; trapezius)
Chest (pectorals; rib cage)
Arms (biceps; triceps; forearms)
Legs (quadriceps; biceps; calves)
Waist (upper, middle, and lower abdominals; obliques)
Actually I prefer to treat forearms and calves as separate body parts, since they respond best to intensive and specialized treatment. So I also include the following subdivisions: forearms (inside; outside) and calves (gastrocnemius; soleus).

If your Basic Training workout contains exercises designed to hit each of these important areas, you will be well on your way to creating a quality physique. Later on, as you move to Advanced Training and attempt to refine your development, you will find it valuable to subdivide even further and look at the muscles in an even subtler way.

The Two-Level Program

I recommend for the beginning bodybuilder a progressive two-level approach to a program of Split System Training. In the beginning when you are all fired up with enthusiasm it may seem as if you can train five hours a day, eight days a week without rest and recuperation. However, this initial optimism eventually comes up against fundamental physiological and biochemical limits, and you will find yourself overtrained.

But the body is amazingly adaptable if you just give it time. So if you are a beginning bodybuilder, or if *the workload you are currently undertaking in the gym is no greater than what you find in Level I of this Basic Training Program*, start at this level and stay with it for at least six weeks. At this stage, it is much more important to learn to do the exercises correctly and to fully condition the entire body than it is to rush ahead too quickly into more advanced forms of training.

For the Basic Training Program, I recommend the following split:

Level I: each body part 2 times a week

Level II: each body part 3 times a week

Abdominals: 6 times a week both levels

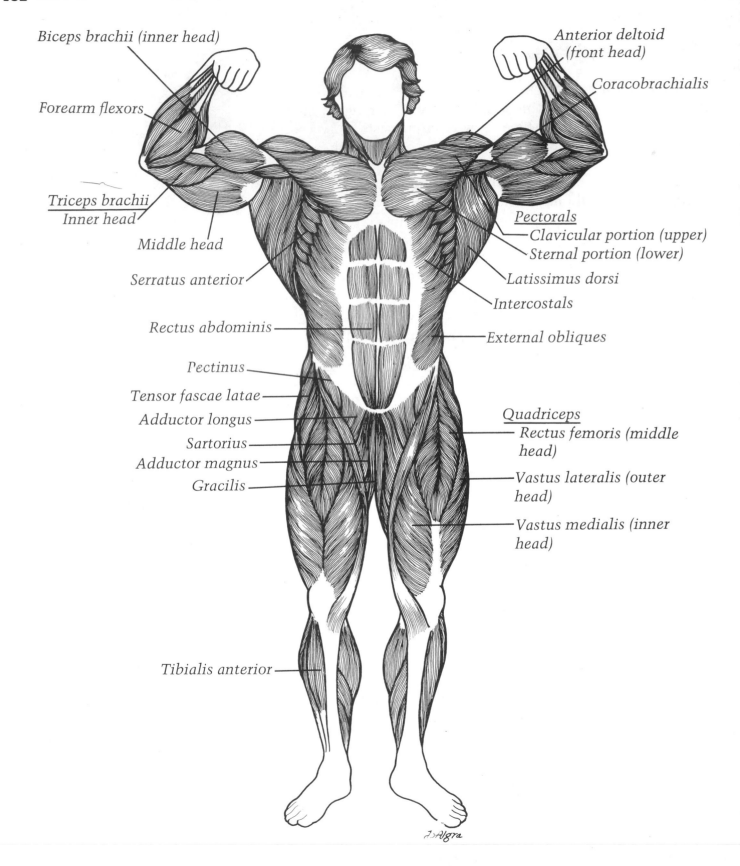

Biceps brachii (inner head)

Forearm flexors

Triceps brachii
Inner head

Middle head

Serratus anterior

Rectus abdominis

Pectinus

Tensor fascae latae

Adductor longus

Sartorius

Adductor magnus

Gracilis

Tibialis anterior

Anterior deltoid
(front head)

Coracobrachialis

Pectorals
Clavicular portion (upper)
Sternal portion (lower)

Latissimus dorsi

Intercostals

External obliques

Quadriceps
Rectus femoris (middle
head)

Vastus lateralis (outer
head)

Vastus medialis (inner
head)

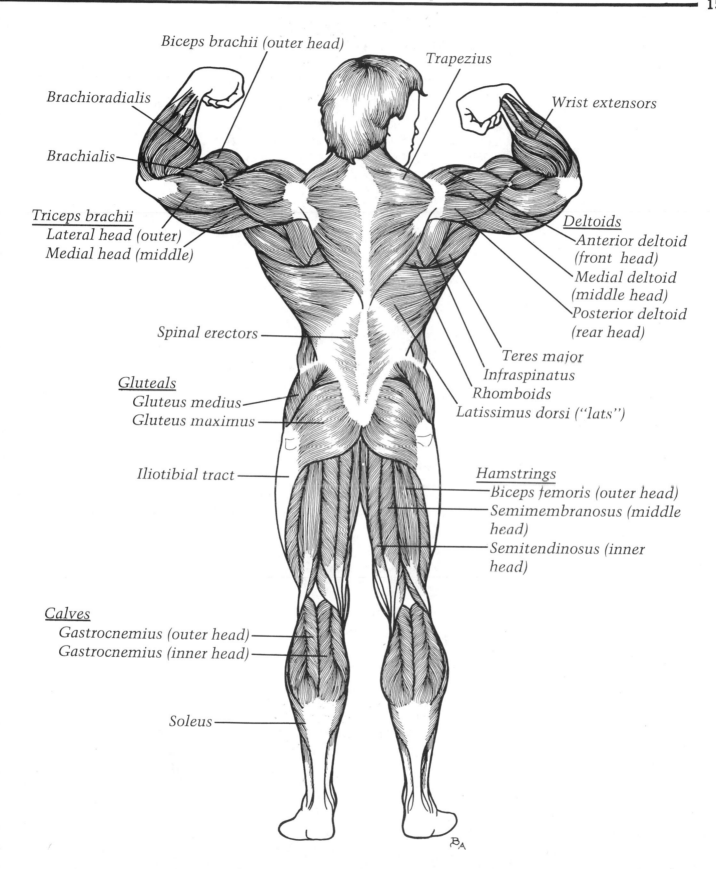

Biceps brachii (outer head)

Trapezius

Brachioradialis

Wrist extensors

Brachialis

Triceps brachii
Lateral head (outer)
Medial head (middle)

Deltoids
Anterior deltoid
(front head)
Medial deltoid
(middle head)
Posterior deltoid
(rear head)

Spinal erectors

Teres major
Infraspinatus
Rhomboids
Latissimus dorsi ("lats")

Gluteals
Gluteus medius
Gluteus maximus

Iliotibial tract

Hamstrings
Biceps femoris (outer head)
Semimembranosus (middle
head)
Semitendinosus (inner
head)

Calves
Gastrocnemius (outer head)
Gastrocnemius (inner head)

Soleus

LEVEL I EXERCISE PROGRAM

LEVEL I BASIC TRAINING

Mon	Tue	Wed	Thur	Fri	Sat
Chest	Shoulders	Thighs	Chest	Shoulders	Thighs
Back	Upper arms	Calves	Back	Upper arms	Calves
Abs	Forearms	Lower back	Abs	Forearms	Lower back
	Abs	Abs		Abs	Abs

NOTE ON SETS AND REPS: In the following program, always do 5 sets of 8 to 12 repetitions each unless otherwise specified.

Monday and Thursday

CHEST

Bench Press
Incline Press
Pullovers

BACK

Chin-Ups (do as many repetitions at a time as you can until you reach a total of 50 reps)
Bent-Over Rows

Power Training
Deadlifts, 3 sets of 10, 6, 4 reps to failure

ABDOMINALS

Leg Raises, 5 sets of 25 reps

Tuesday and Friday

SHOULDERS

Barbell Clean and Press
Dumbbell Lateral Raises

Power Training
Heavy Upright Rows, 3 sets of 10, 6, 4 reps to failure
Push Presses, 3 sets of 6, 4, 2 reps to failure

UPPER ARMS

Standing Barbell Curls
Seated Dumbbell Curls
Narrow-Grip Bench Press
Standing Triceps Extensions with Barbell

FOREARMS

Wrist Curls
Reverse Wrist Curls

ABDOMINALS

Incline Sit-Ups, 5 sets of 25 reps each

Wednesday and Saturday

THIGHS

Squats
Lunges
Leg Curls

CALVES

Standing Calf Raises, 5 sets of 15 reps each

LOWER BACK

Power Training
Straight-Leg Deadlifts, 3 sets of 10, 6, 4 reps to failure
Good Mornings, 3 sets of 10, 8, 6 reps to failure
> NOTE: Although these power movements work the lower
> back directly, they also involve the trapezius and the leg
> biceps and help to develop overall strength.

ABDOMINALS

Leg Raises, 5 sets of 25 repetitions each

LEVEL II EXERCISE PROGRAM

LEVEL II BASIC TRAINING

Mon	Tue	Wed	Thur	Fri	Sat
Chest	Shoulders	Chest	Shoulders	Chest	Shoulders
Back	Lower back	Back	Lower back	Back	Lower Back
Thighs	Upper arms	Thighs	Upper arms	Thighs	Upper arms
	Forearms		Forearms		Forearms
Calves	Abs	Calves	Abs	Calves	Abs
Abs		Abs		Abs	

NOTE ON SETS AND REPS: In the following program, always do 5 sets of 8 to 12 repetitions unless otherwise specified.

Monday/Wednesday/Friday

CHEST

Bench Presses
Incline Presses
Pullovers

BACK

Chin-Ups (do as many repetitions at a time as you can until you have reached a total of 50 reps)
Bent-Over Rows

Power Training
Deadlifts, 3 sets of 10, 6, 4 reps to failure

THIGHS

Squats
Lunges
Leg Curls

CALVES

Standing Calf Raises, 5 sets of 15 reps each

ABDOMINALS

Leg Raises, 5 sets of 25 reps each

Tuesday/Thursday/Saturday

SHOULDERS

Barbell Clean and Press
Dumbbell Lateral Raises

Power Training
Heavy Upright Rows, 3 sets of 10, 6, 4 reps to failure
Push Presses, 3 sets of 6, 4, 2 reps to failure

LOWER BACK

Power Training
Straight-Leg Deadlifts, 3 sets of 10, 6, 4 reps to failure
Good Mornings, 3 sets of 10, 8, 6 reps to failure
> NOTE: Although these power movements work the lower back directly, they also involve the trapezius and leg biceps and help to develop overall strength.

UPPER ARMS

Standing Barbell Curls
Seated Dumbbell Curls
Narrow-Grip Bench Press
Standing French Press

FOREARMS

Wrist Curls
Reverse Wrist Curls

ABDOMINALS

Incline Sit-Ups, 5 sets of 25 reps

CHAPTER 4

Advanced Training Principles

The whole idea of "progressive resistance" is based on the fact that you have to keep making the body work harder and harder if you want it to continue to grow. One way or another, you have to increase training "intensity."

Increasing Training Intensity

Increasing intensity in the beginning is not that difficult—you learn to do more exercises and to do them correctly; you get stronger and in better condition so you can work harder and longer and put more stress on your muscles. Once your body gets used to this effort, however, it becomes more difficult to continue to escalate intensity at the same rate.

Obviously, if you take long rest periods and train very slowly, so that it takes you half the day to get through your workout, the actual intensity of your efforts will be minimal. Time, therefore, is an important factor in increasing training intensity. By manipulating time, you can increase intensity in two basic ways: (1) by doing the same amount of work in less time; and (2) by doing an increased amount of work in the same time.

But the most obvious way to increase workload is simply to train with more weight. Another valuable method is to cut down on rest periods between sets and try doing two or three exercises in a row without stopping. This puts greater demand on your powers of endurance. Endurance, like strength, is something that can be developed in a progressive manner, a little at a time. You should also work at the fastest pace you are capable of without getting sloppy in your technique. This will help you to do the maximum amount of work in the minimum amount of time.

Advanced Training Principles

Beyond increasing intensity by manipulating time or adding weight, there are a number of special training techniques that can help ensure your progress in the Advanced Training and Competition Training Programs. These all involve methods of putting extra, unusual, or unexpected stress on the muscles, thereby forcing them to adapt to the increased demand.

Forced Reps

One method of forcing out extra reps is to have your workout partner supply a little extra lift to help you to keep going. However, I have never liked this method because your partner has no real way of knowing how much lift to supply, what you are really capable of doing on your own, and how much help you actually need. I prefer a kind of forced reps which is sometimes called "Rest/Pause" Training. You use a fairly heavy weight and go to failure in the set. Then you stop, let the weight hang for just a few seconds, and then force out an extra rep. Again, rest only a few seconds before forcing out another. This method depends on the fact that the muscles make a fast initial recovery from exercise, and you can use this recovery to force out several extra reps. If you rest too long, however, too many of the tired fibers recover and you end up using them again instead of stimulating new fiber. For ultimate rest/pause forced reps, you can actually put the weight down for a moment, pick it up again and force out additional reps. For exercises like Chin-Ups, you can do your reps, let go of the bar, rest momentarily, and then attempt to force out some more.

Isolation Training

Using heavy weights, especially with power training, is one way to increase intensity; another way is to train in such a way that smaller and more isolated muscles or parts of muscles are forced to do a majority of the work. For example, Bench Presses involve the chest, the front deltoids, and the triceps; Flys, on the other hand, work the pectorals more directly. And, depending on whether you do your Flys on a flat, incline, or decline bench, you can direct the stress to the middle of the chest, the upper chest, or the lower chest. In the same way, you can do various kinds of Curls that work the peak of the biceps, the width, or the upper or lower attachment. In combination with compound exercises and power training, isolation training can bring every part of your physique to complete development, bringing up any weak areas and helping to achieve the degree of muscle separation and definition necessary for that sculpted, champion look.

Negative Repetitions

Whenever you lift a weight using the contractile force of your muscles you perform what is defined as a "positive" movement; when you lower the weight, un-contracting the working muscle, you perform "negative" movement. Negative repetitions actually put more stress on the tendons and supportive structures than on the muscles themselves. This is beneficial because you want tendon strength to increase along with muscular strength. To get the full benefit of negatives in your normal workouts, always lower the weights slowly and under control, rather than letting them drop. To work harder at negatives, first try cheating a weight up that would otherwise be too heavy to lift strictly and then lower it slowly and deliberately. Your muscles can lower a weight under control that they could not actually lift in the first place. At the end of a set, when your muscles are very tired, you can have your workout partner give you a little assistance in lifting the weight, and then do strict negatives on your own.

Forced Negatives

To develop even more intensity in negative repetitions, have your workout partner press down on the weight as you lower it, forcing you to cope with greater resistance. This should always be done carefully and smoothly so that the muscles and tendons are not subjected to any sudden jerks. Forced negatives are more easily done with machines or cables than with free weights.

The Priority Principle

No matter how strong you are, you can't work as hard at the end of a workout as at the beginning. Therefore, if you have a particular area that is lagging behind and needs extra work, it makes sense to train those muscles at the beginning of a workout, when you are at your strongest. Giving particular body parts "priority" ensures that they will be trained with the maximum intensity you can generate. Tom Platz, for example, did not discover the benefits of the Priority Principle until after he had already won his Mr. Universe title, but he realized at that time that his lower body had become so superior to his upper body that he did not have the necessary balance to win a Mr. Olympia competition. Therefore, he began training his upper body first, especially his back and arms, and training his legs later in the day when he was rested but still not quite as fresh as for the first workout. Using the Priority Principle, he progressed so rapidly that he was able to place third in the 1981 Mr. Olympia, with some judges liking him enough to give him a first-place vote. In my own case, the Priority Principle meant putting my calf training first in my workouts—and ultimately seeing my calves develop from weak points to superior body parts.

Supersets

Supersets are two exercises performed in a row without stopping. For extra intensity, you can even do three exercises without stopping (tri-sets). It takes a while to build up the endurance necessary to do a lot of supersets, but this kind of conditioning develops in time if you keep working at it. You can use supersets to train two different body parts—Bench Presses combined with Chins, for example—or you can do a number of exercises in a row for the same body part. You will be surprised how a muscle which seems to be totally fatigued will still have a lot of strength remaining if you demand that it perform a slightly different movement. To do this, however, you need to start with the most difficult movement, with each succeeding exercise slightly less demanding—Bent-Over Rows, Seated Cable Rows, and One-Arm Rows are a good combination. Personally, I have always liked to use supersets to train opposite body parts simultaneously—chest and back, for example. This gives you a tremendous pump as you perform the alternating pushing and pulling movements, yet gives each muscle group involved the minimum chance to rest and recuperate.

Staggered Sets

Usually you do all your sets for a certain body part one right after another. However, when you want to put special emphasis on training certain muscles, you can include movements to work that area at intervals throughout your workout. If you want to train calves extra hard, for example, you can do a set of Calf Raises every three or four sets, so that by the end of your workout you will have already done around ten sets of calf work and will have only five more sets to go. If you find working calves, abs, or some other body part to be difficult or tedious, this is a relatively painless way to ensure that the muscle is adequately trained, and it helps to provide more variety in your workouts.

The Shocking Principle

The body is amazingly adaptable and can accustom itself to workloads that would fell a horse. However, if you always put the same kind of stress on the body, in the same way, it gets used to this and even very intense training will yield less response than you expected. The way to avoid this is by surprising the body with new workouts, unusual exercises, or exercises performed in a different way or order. You'd be surprised at how difficult a relatively easy training program becomes if you are not used to it. And once you do get accustomed to it, it is time to introduce another novelty or variation in your training to "shock" the muscles into continued response. Unusually heavy weight will tend to shock the muscle, but so will employing any number of specific intensity principles like the Stripping Method or the Isotension Principle (see below), or anything else that catches the muscle off guard, so to speak, that surprises the body and forces it to respond in a manner for which it is not prepared.

The Stripping Method

When I was first learning about bodybuilding training it was obvious to me that when you come to the end of a set and seemingly cannot do another repetition, that doesn't necessarily mean the muscles involved are totally fatigued, only that they are too tired to lift that amount of weight. If a plate or two is removed, you can do more repetitions. Take another plate off, and you can keep going even longer. Each time you do this, you are forcing the muscles to recruit more muscle fiber. This training principle is called the Stripping Method. (Actually, unknown to me, this same discovery was made in 1947 by Henry Atkins, editor of *Vigour* and *Body Culture* magazines. He called it the "multipoundage system.") You should never use the Stripping Method at the beginning of an exercise when you are fresh and strong, but only for your last set. Since the changes in weight must be made quickly so that the muscles don't have time to recuperate, it helps to have a workout partner ready to slip plates off the bar or move the pin in a machine weight stack. For example, you might do Bench Presses with the heaviest weight on the bar you can handle for six reps. Say that weight is 300 pounds. After you have failed, your partner would quickly strip off weight so that you could do more reps with 250 pounds. I don't recommend going too low, however, unless you are training for maximum definition, because you won't grow by handling weights that are too light. Many bodybuilders use this principle in a different way by working their way down a dumbbell rack as they do more sets of an exercise and get more and more tired (see Running the Rack, p. 164).

The Isotension Principle

During your one-minute rest period between sets, don't just sit around watching your training partner do his set. Continue to flex and contract the muscles you are training. This not only keeps them pumped and ready for more action, but is in itself a very beneficial kind of exercise. Flexing is a form of isometric exercise, and isometrics (although they do not usually apply to bodybuilding because they do not work your muscles through their entire range of motion) involve very intense muscle contractions. A bodybuilder who poses and flexes in the gym, watching himself in the mirror, is not doing so out of vanity. He is engaged in a very important part of his workout. You get the same kind of benefits from really hard sessions of posing, too, as we will discuss in another section.

Instinctive Principle

When you first begin bodybuilding training and are attempting to master the fundamental exercises and create a basically sound muscle structure, it pays to follow a set program. But after you have been training for a longer period, you will find that your progress will increase if you learn to perceive and understand your body's individual responses to training and vary your workouts accordingly. In my early years, I tended to go through my workouts in a rigid, set pattern, the same way every time. Then I started training with Dave Draper and he taught me another approach. Dave would come into the gym knowing which body parts he was going to train and which exercises he was going to do, but he would change the order of those exercises depending on how he felt on that particular day. If he usually began a back workout with Wide-Grip Chins, he might decide instead to begin with Bent-Over Rows and finish off with Chins. He had learned to trust his instincts to help guide him through his workouts.

Occasionally, he would abandon his normal workout and do something entirely different: 15 sets of Bench Presses, for example; fewer, very heavy sets or a lot of sets done rapidly. I learned from Dave that the body has its own rhythms, that it is different from day to day, and that the more advanced you become, the more you need to be aware of these variations and cycles. Let me caution you, however, that this awareness does not come overnight; a year or more of training is usually needed before you can begin to profit from making these occasional instinctive adjustments in your program.

Pre-Exhaust Training

The total bodybuilding effect comes about when you fully stimulate and innervate as many fibers in the muscle as possible. But some muscles are bigger than others and, when used in combination with smaller ones, will still have unused fiber available when the smaller muscles are totally exhausted. But you can plan your training so that you isolate and fatigue the big muscle first, before you train it in combination with smaller ones. When you do a Bench Press, for example, you are using your pectorals, front delts, and triceps in combination. The pectorals are by far the strongest of these muscles, and normally, when you press the weight up, the smaller delts and triceps fail long before the pectorals. To compensate for this, you can do Dumbbell Flys first, which isolate and "pre-exhaust" the pectorals. Then if you go on to do Bench Presses, the pectorals, which are already tired, will go to total fatigue at about the same time as the other muscles. Other pre-fatigue routines could involve doing Leg Extensions before Squats (pre-fatiguing the quadriceps), Dumbbell Laterals before Shoulder Presses (pre-fatiguing the deltoids), or fatiguing the lats in isolation on a Nautilus Pullback machine before doing Seated Rows, T-Bar Rows, or another rowing exercise involving the biceps.

Running the Rack

This is one of my favorite ways of using dumbbells to shock the body. It involves doing an exercise with a set of dumbbells, putting them down, picking up the next lighter weight, and doing another set without stopping. This is actually a dumbbell variation of the Stripping Method. For example, I would do Dumbbell Presses starting with 100-pound weights and going to failure, then immediately setting them down and continuing with 90-

pound dumbbells. My muscles were too tired at this point to press 100 pounds, but the remaining unused fiber could still lift the slightly lighter weight. Again, when the 90-pound weights got too heavy, I would go down to the 80s, then the 70s, and so on. Each time I went down the rack I reached a little deeper into the available muscle tissue to shock and innervate the muscle more thoroughly.

There are a number of ways of varying this technique; for example, using the dumbbells on a rest/pause basis—doing the exercise until exhausted, putting down the weights for ten seconds, then forcing out additional reps—or working your way up the rack as high as you can, then back down, doing fewer reps with the heavier weights and more reps with the lighter ones.

I Go/You Go

This is a method for increasing your training intensity and shocking your muscles with the help of your training partner. I often used this technique when doing Barbell Curls. I would do a set and immediately hand the bar to my partner. He would do his set and hand it back to me. Back and forth we would go, not really keeping track of reps but always conscious of equaling or bettering each other's reps in each set. The concentration and intensity we got training this way was fantastic, primarily because of the limited amount of rest time involved.

The I Go/You Go Method is more useful for training smaller muscles like the biceps or calves than it is for the big thigh and back muscles. Exercises like Squats and Bent-Over Rows demand so much energy that you run out of steam in a hurry even without this intensive kind of training.

The Flushing Method

This is a kind of isotension training used in conjunction with posing and flexing during your workout. It involves using a light weight and holding the weight steady at various points along the path of the exercise, forcing the muscle to tense isometrically. For example, after I have done as many Dumbbell Laterals as possible I hold my arms locked out by my sides and then lift them about five inches away from my thighs, feeling the deltoids tense and flex. I hold this position for about ten seconds as the "burn" accompanying the buildup of lactic acid gets stronger and stronger. This isometric tension applied at the end of an exercise causes an enormous increase in muscle separation, and can be done for many muscles in the body: for lats, hanging from the chinning bar and lifting the body only a few inches; doing Cable Crossovers, holding your hands crossed with chest fully contracted, flushing blood into the pectorals; holding a Curl steady at various angles of the total arc; or locking your legs out on a Leg Extension and holding as long as you can.

Partial Reps

Continuing to do partial reps when you are too tired to complete full-range-of-motion repetitions is a shock method I have always used, and it is a particular favorite of Tom Platz. I use partial reps for any muscle in the body, but Tom prefers using them for leg exercises. He will do a set of Leg Extensions until he can't do any more complete repetitions, and then will continue to do half reps, quarter reps, and on down until he is lying back on the bench, in agony from the burn, his thighs barely able to twitch. The important thing to remember is not to do partial reps until you are too tired to do any more full repetitions. Even though you are unable to lift the weight through a full range of motion, the fact you can move it at all proves there is still fiber there to be stimulated and trained.

Multi-Exercise Sets

Instead of doing five or six sets of a specific exercise for a body part, you do your sets using a different exercise for that body part each time. Multi-exercise sets are not done as supersets; you do them one at a time and rest in between, but you do only one set of each exercise and then go on to another. For example, you might do one set of Barbell Curls, rest for a minute, then do a set of Dumbbell Curls, Cable Curls, Incline Curls, and so on down the line until you have fully exhausted the biceps. The idea here is to make the stress of each set slightly different, attacking the body part from every possible angle to ensure that the entire muscle is trained and providing a shock which will force the maximum amount of response from the body.

The "One-and-a-Half" Method

Another way to vary the stress you put on your muscles in any set is to do a complete rep of a movement, followed by a half rep, and then alternating full and half reps until the set is finished. When you do this, make sure that the half rep is very slow and very strict. Hold the weight momentarily at the extreme point of the movement, then lower it slowly, totally under control.

The Platoon System (21's)

This system is more elaborate than one-and-a-halfs because you do a series of half reps in the lower range of motion, a series of half reps in the upper range of motion, and then a series of full reps. You can use any number of reps—I always did 10–10–10—as long as you do the same number for each of your half reps and full reps. Traditionally, many bodybuilders have used seven reps —hence the name "21's": 3 × 7. The extra stress generated by this kind of training comes about because you have to stop the movement right in the middle, and this forces the muscles to exert themselves in ways they are not used to.

1 to 10 System

In 1 to 10's, the muscles perform sets in a manner almost 180 degrees opposite from what they are accustomed to. Normally, you start out with a relatively light weight and increase the resistance set by set, doing fewer reps each time. Those first reps with the light weight don't really contribute to growth; it isn't until the muscle begins to get tired and fail that you are really getting to it. The 1 to 10 system bypasses all of this and makes you do hard reps with heavy weight right from the beginning, so from the very start you are shocking the muscle into growing. First you do a light warm-up, then you immediately go to a weight so heavy you can barely do one rep. As quickly as possible, you strip off some weight so that you can do two more reps. Again, you take off weight and this time do three reps. Keep taking off weight and increasing reps until you reach ten repetitions. The overall total of reps you do this way is fifty-five—which is a lot. And, unlike your normal sets, you do your heavy work first and the muscle gets a good pump at the end. This method doesn't work for every body part, but is especially good for Barbell Curls, Bench Presses, and Leg Extensions.

Progressive Workload

Nobody can go all out every workout. Using this training system, you plan your three-times-a-week body part sessions so that the first is intense, with relatively high reps and sets, but you don't use the heaviest weights possible; you increase the weight for the second session, but still stay short of going all out. For your third workout, however, you go very heavy, keeping your reps down to four to six maximum per set. By gradually building up each workout during the week, you prepare your body to handle the shock of very heavy weight.

Compounding Exercises

Sometimes, with similar exercises for the same body part, one is easier than the other. Therefore, when you get tired doing the tougher movement, you still have the strength to perform the easier one. Compounding exercises involves doing a set of the harder exercise, immediately followed by more repetitions of the easier one. A good example is Dumbbell Flys and Dumbbell Presses for the chest. The Flys involve just the pectorals. If you lie on a bench and go to failure with Flys, you will find you still have the strength to do Presses, which bring in the triceps and deltoids to help. Another example is Dumbbell Laterals and Dumbbell Shoulder Presses. If you do the Laterals to failure, you can still continue doing more reps by switching immediately to Presses, thereby shocking the deltoids by the extra effort.

Learning to Use Advanced Training Principles

Obviously you cannot just jump in and add a lot of these special training techniques to your workouts all at once. Everything in bodybuilding should be "progressive"—you gradually add exercises to your routine, add weight to each exercise, and include a variety of these special training principles.

As you go on to Advanced Training and then to Competition Training, you will find the programs include a number of these principles already. Also, in discussing specific body part training, training for special purposes, and "weak-point" training, I will recommend others wherever they might be useful.

Building a Quality Physique: The Advanced Training Program

The bodybuilder's physique is a carefully balanced combination of many factors, including shape, proportion, and symmetry. Bodybuilding has been compared to sculpture, with the bodybuilder creating and shaping a physique the way the artist sculpts a statue from marble or granite. For the bodybuilder, the only material he has to work with is muscle.

The exercises and training principles you learned in the Basic Training Program are not enough to give you the total control over your body that is needed to develop a sculpted, championship physique. You need more and different kinds of exercises, a knowledge of how to design your workouts to get very specific results, and an ability to generate sufficient intensity so your body will continue to grow and change.

Just as we broke down the body into specific muscle groups in order to understand how it should be trained, now we have to create even subtler categories. When your object is to build a quality physique, it is not enough to just train the chest and the lats; you need to develop each of the muscles totally and in every aspect. So you need to learn what exercises work each of these areas and incorporate them into your workouts. This will involve doing more exercises and therefore more total sets, and that requires higher levels of conditioning and endurance.

As your body continues to respond to the added work, you will begin to notice certain weaknesses and imbalances, areas that are not developing as quickly as others or parts of muscles that are not completely in proportion or lack the shape you are trying to create.

Setting these higher goals for yourself in Advanced Training will demand more time, more energy, more dedication and, therefore, more commitment. And it will be much more demanding mentally, requiring a steadfast awareness of purpose. But this step upward in effort and intensity comes after you have already developed both your body and mental attitude with a sufficient period of Basic Training, which has prepared you for the demands of Advanced Training.

Summing up, the specific goals you will be working toward in Advanced Training workouts include:

1. Developing extra mass and, therefore, muscle shape.
2. Working and developing every plane and contour of each muscle, muscle group, and body part.
3. Creating a physique with the aesthetic qualities of balance, proportion, and symmetry.
4. Bringing out the maximum degree of muscle separation.
5. Learning to totally control your physical development so that you are able to correct imbalances, weak points, and problem areas.

When to Move On to Advanced Training

Once you have gained 15 pounds or more of muscle mass, put about 3 inches on your arms, 5 inches on your chest and shoulders, 4 inches on your thighs, and 3 inches on your calves, you are then ready to begin adding a greater variety of exercises to your routine, to train for shape as well as size, for balance as well as mass.

But this is not accomplished in one sudden jump. You need time to learn new exercises, to begin to understand how specific exercises affect the body in different ways, and to learn to use these exercises and a wide range of new training principles so as to accelerate the response of your body to your workouts.

Since you gradually increase your workload, your transition from Basic to Advanced Training does not happen all at once. The point is that, sooner or later, if you want a championship body, you have to train with championship intensity, technique, and knowledge. It is a difficult task, but can be one of the most rewarding challenges of your life.

High-Set Training

There are training systems that claim you can make great progress by training with only a few sets per body part. Actually, this idea is not new; that was the way bodybuilders trained in the early days of the sport.

When Reg Park first began serious training, many bodybuilders still used the old-fashioned, low-set approach to working out. "Training strictly for power like a weightlifter," Reg says, "gave us certain advantages in the old days, a really solid foundation of muscle. But it wasn't until I learned to do fifteen or twenty sets per body part that I felt I was getting enough shape and definition in my physique. I'm sure that a lot of the bodybuilders from the very early days would have improved a lot if they had understood the need for high-set workouts the way we do today."

True. But it's also true that the more advanced you become as a bodybuilder, the more the body tends to resist further development. That means you have to work harder to create the necessary intensity in your workouts and be certain that you are training in the most efficient manner possible. To ensure that this continued development takes place, the Advanced Training Program requires performing a relatively high number of sets. This is not arbitrary or just a matter of personal preference; it is designed with specific physiological purposes in mind: (1) to recruit and innervate all the fiber available to each muscle, then work the muscle to exhaustion in any particular exercise; and (2) to do enough different exercises for every single body part so that each individual muscle is worked from every angle to create the fullest possible shape and development—and to be sure that no major muscle of the body escapes this complete stimulation.

You accomplish the first task by doing five sets of the movement. The fact that you can keep going for five sets, resting very little in between, proves that there is still fresh and unrecruited fiber available after the first few sets. The second task is sheer necessity, since no one exercise is enough to fully develop even the simplest muscle. Take, for example, a relatively small muscle like the biceps: you can train to develop the upper area (point of origin), the lower area (point of insertion), the thickness of the muscle, the inner and outer areas, or to create a really high peak. Once you start dealing with the larger muscle groups, the number of different ways you can train and shape them becomes really immense!

You don't have to be a mathematician to realize that a task of this size cannot be accomplished by doing three or five total sets per body part, or to realize how lacking in quality will be the physiques of those modern bodybuilders who are seduced into following an old-fashioned theory of training masquerading under the guise of a new, "scientific" approach to bodybuilding. It takes a minimum of four or five exercises to train each major body part, at least three for the smaller ones, and this adds up to a total of 20 to 25 sets.

With the right combination of exercises, you not only develop each individual muscle fully, but build definition, striations, and full separation between one muscle group and another.

Double-Split Training

One way to deal with the demands of Advanced Training is by following a program of Double-Split Training, which simply means breaking up each day's workout into two different sessions.

I discovered Double-Split Training on my own, strictly as a matter of necessity. After a year of training I really began trying to push my body to its ultimate limits. I wanted to train each body part as hard as possible and then come back the next time and train them even harder. One day I came into the gym and had a really dynamite chest and back workout. I felt great. Then I went on to do legs, but I noticed I was not training with the same intensity and enthusiasm as I had felt during my upper-body workout. Looking in the mirror at my developing teenage physique, I had to admit that my legs were not progressing as rapidly as my upper body. The next day, after training shoulders, biceps, triceps, forearms, and calves, I again took stock and realized that those last three muscle groups were also somewhat weak, that they obviously were lagging behind.

As I thought about it, it didn't seem to me that I lacked real potential to develop those weaker areas. So it had to be some fault in my approach to training. I experimented with nutrition, being much more careful of what I ate, trying to keep my blood sugar level up, but though this helped, it was not enough.

As I analyzed my training further, it became obvious that each of these body parts came toward the end of my workouts, when I was tired from doing numerous sets. Training chest, back, and legs in one day was very demanding, and it occurred to me that I could train each body part with more intensity if I trained chest and back in the morning, and then came back late in the afternoon, fresh and rested, to give my legs a really hard workout. Without knowing that any other bodybuilders trained this way and never having heard the name, I found myself doing Double-Split Training as the only means possible for training the entire body with the kind of intensity I knew had to be generated if I were to become Mr. Universe.

Advanced Training can often involve 75 to 100 total sets—25 sets for each of four body parts, or three body parts plus calves and abdominal training. Trying to do all of this work in one workout would be a killer—especially since some of the same muscles are involved in training different body parts, and if these muscles get too tired and don't have a chance to recuperate, your training can be severely hindered.

A 100-set session takes something like three or four hours to accomplish, and there is nobody who can train straight through for this long without running out of energy. Many bodybuilders try to cope with this workload by pacing themselves, not training the first and second hour as hard as possible, knowing that they could never make it if they did. But this lack of intensity means the body will not be forced to respond and grow. You have to go all out if you want maximum results.

With the Double-Split system, you train full out in the morning, recuperate during the day, and come back to the gym rested and ready to go the limit again. I've always preferred a good eight to ten hours between workouts to ensure full recovery. And that means making sure you actually get some rest. If you are too active during the day, that ten-hour rest period won't be enough.

Of course, scheduling a second training session in the late afternoon or evening creates yet another demand on your time, and you will have to make further adjustments in your schedule. An added advantage to this system is that you burn up a lot of additional calories in the course of your two workouts, which means you do not have to subject yourself to quite so demanding a diet as you would training only once a day.

The Two-Level Advanced Program

Just as in the Basic Training Program, I have created two levels for Advanced Training to provide a ready means of increasing workload and generating greater intensity on a progressive basis.

Both Level I and Level II in this program require that you train each body part three times a week. Level II, however, is a more demanding program, including a lot of supersets and a number of extra exercises.

Begin your training with Level I, and take the time to learn each new exercise thoroughly. Once you have been working at this level for six weeks or longer and feel your conditioning and recuperative powers will allow you to work even harder, go ahead and begin to add on new exercises to your routine until you have made the full transition to Level II.

ADVANCED TRAINING SPLIT

Mon	Tue	Wed	Thur	Fri	Sat
			Morning		
Chest	Shoulders	Chest	Shoulders	Chest	Shoulders
Back	Upper arms	Back	Upper arms	Back	Upper arms
	Forearms		Forearms		Forearms
	Calves		Calves		Calves
			Evening		
Thighs		Thighs		Thighs	
Calves		Calves		Calves	

Abdominals every day

LEVEL I EXERCISE PROGRAM

Monday/Wednesday/Friday

CHEST

Barbell Bench Press
5 sets: 1 set of 15 rep warm-up; sets of 10,8,6,4,4 reps—
   stripping last two sets
Incline Barbell Bench Press
5 sets: (same formula as Bench Presses)
   Every third workout, substitute Dumbbell Presses and Incline
   Dumbbell Presses for barbell exercises.

Dumbbell Flys	5 sets of 10,8,8,8,6 reps
Parallel Dips	5 sets of 15,10,8,8,8 reps
Pullovers	3 sets of 15,15,15 reps

BACK

Chin-Ups
5 sets: 10 reps minimum each set
   Use a dumbbell fastened around your waist for greater
   resistance; do chins to the rear one workout, to the front the
   next.

Close-Grip Chins	5 sets of 10 reps each
T-Bar Rows	5 sets of 15,12,10,8,6 reps
Bent-Over Barbell Rows	5 sets of 8 to 12 reps

THIGHS

Squats	6 sets of 20 rep warm-up; 10,8,6,4,4 reps
Front Squats	4 sets of 10,8,8,6 reps
Hack Squats	4 sets of 10 reps each
Lying Leg Curls	5 sets of 20,10,8,6,6 reps
Standing Leg Curls	5 sets of 10 reps each
Straight-Leg Deadlifts	3 sets of 10 reps each

CALVES

Donkey Calf Raises	5 sets of 10 reps each
Standing Calf Raises	5 sets of 15,10,8,8,8 reps

ABDOMINALS

Bent-Knee Leg Raises	100 reps
Bent-Over Twists	100 reps each side
Crunches	50 reps

Tuesday/Thursday/Saturday

SHOULDERS

Behind-the-Neck Barbell Presses	5 sets of 15 rep warm-up; 10,8,8,6 reps
Lateral Raises	5 sets of 8 reps each
Bent-Over Lateral Raises	5 sets of 8 reps each
Dumbbell Shrugs	3 sets of 10 reps each

UPPER ARMS

Standing Barbell Curls	5 sets of 15,10,8,6,4 reps
Incline Dumbbell Curls	5 sets of 8 reps each
Concentration Curls	3 sets of 8 reps each
Lying French Press	5 sets of 15,10,8,6,4 reps
Triceps Cable Pushdowns	5 sets of 8 reps each
One-Arm Triceps Extensions	5 sets of 10 reps each

FOREARMS

Barbell Wrist Curls	5 sets of 10 reps each
Reverse Wrist Curls	3 sets of 10 reps each

CALVES

Seated Calf Raises	5 sets of 10 reps each

ABDOMINALS

Bent-Knee Sit-Ups	100 reps
Incline Bench Leg Raises	100 reps

LEVEL II EXERCISE PROGRAM

Monday/Wednesday/Friday

ABDOMINALS Begin workout with 5 minutes of Roman Chair Sit-Ups.

CHEST AND BACK

Superset:	Bench Presses	1 set of 15 rep warm-up; 5 sets of 10,8,8,6,4 reps
	Wide-Grip Chins (to back)	5 sets of 10 reps
Superset:	Dumbbell Incline Presses	5 sets of 10,8,8,8,6 reps
	Close-Grip Chins	5 sets of 10 reps
	Dumbbell Flys	5 sets of 10,8,8,8,6 reps
	Parallel Dips	5 sets of 15,10,8,8,8 reps
	T-Bar Rows	5 sets of 15,10,8,8,8 reps
	Bent-Over Rows	5 sets of 10 reps
Superset:	Seated Cable Rows	5 sets of 10 reps
	Dumbbell Pullovers	5 sets of 15 reps

THIGHS

	Squats	6 sets of 15,10,8,8,6,4 reps
	Front Squats	4 sets of 10,8,8,6 reps
Superset:	Hack Squats	1 set of 15 rep warm-up; 5 sets of 10,8,8,8,8 reps
	Lying Leg Curls	1 set of 15 rep warm-up; 5 sets of 10,8,8,8,8 reps
Superset:	Standing Leg Curls	5 sets of 10 reps
	Straight-Leg Deadlifts	5 sets of 10 reps

CALVES

Donkey Calf Raises	5 sets of 10 reps
Standing Calf Raises	5 sets of 10 reps
Seated Calf Raises	5 sets of 10 reps

ABDOMINALS

Hanging Leg Raises (bent knees)	150 reps
Crunches	150 reps
Bent-Over Twists	100 reps each side

Tuesday/Thursday/Saturday

ABDOMINALS   Begin workout with 5 minutes of Roman Chair Sit-Ups.

SHOULDERS

Superset:	Behind-the-Neck Barbell Presses	1 set of 15 rep warm-up; 5 sets of 10,8,8,8,6 reps
	Dumbbell Laterals	5 sets of 8 reps
Superset:	Machine Front Press	5 sets of 8 reps
	Bent-Over Laterals	5 sets of 8 reps
Superset:	Upright Rows	5 sets of 10 reps
	One-Arm Seated Cable Laterals	5 sets of 10 reps each arm

UPPER ARMS

Superset:	Standing Barbell Curls	5 sets of 15,10,8,6,4 reps
	Lying French Presses	5 sets of 15,10,8,6,4 reps
Superset:	Alternate Dumbbell Curls	5 sets of 8 reps
	Triceps Cable Pushdowns	5 sets of 8 reps
Superset:	Concentration Curls	5 sets of 8 reps
	One-Arm Triceps Extensions	5 sets of 12 reps
Reverse Push-Ups		5 sets of 15 reps.

FOREARMS

Superset:	Wrist Curls	5 sets of 10 reps
	Reverse Curls	5 sets of 10 reps
One-Arm Wrist Curls		5 sets of 10 reps

CALVES

Standing Calf Raises	5 sets of 15,10,8,8,8 reps
Calf Raises on Leg Press Machine	5 sets of 10 reps

ABDOMINALS

Bent-Knee Sit-Ups	150 reps
Leg Raises	150 reps
Side Leg Raises	100 reps each side
Hyperextensions	3 sets of 10 reps

Going to the Limit

In Basic Training, we talked about the necessity of occasionally having "heavy days"—trying to go to your maximum on certain lifts. Heavy days are even more important when you get to Advanced Training.

I recommend that every so often you forget about your regular program and do an entire workout consisting of only power exercises. Remember that no amount of refinement, balance, and proportion looks exactly right unless it coexists with the kind of hard and dense muscle structure that comes from occasionally challenging your body to the maximum with heavy weights.

Varying Your Program

Advanced Training requires that you change your exercise program every three to six months, dropping certain exercises in favor of others. This is necessary in order to: (1) provide the variety of movements to develop every area of every single muscle and muscle group; (2) force the body to do new and unexpected movements to help shock it into further growth; and (3) help keep you from getting bored.

Exercises that seem fairly similar can feel very different. For example, if you are used to pressing a barbell over your head, doing the exercise with dumbbells instead feels totally different —although both are for the front deltoids. Having to balance and coordinate two weights instead of one puts very different demands on your muscles. Therefore, after a couple of months of an exercise like Behind-the-Neck Barbell Presses, it makes a lot of sense to switch to Dumbbell Presses for a while.

There are certain basic exercises that are so fundamental that they have to be included in any complete exercise program. However, exploring a whole range of different exercises like this gives you a much better idea as to which exercises work best for you and which don't really suit you. This will lead eventually to a much better understanding of your own body and of how to get the best results.

A Sample Alternate Workout

ABDOMINALS Begin workout with 5 minutes of Roman Chair Sit-Ups.

CHEST AND BACK

Superset:	Bench Press (on machine)	5 sets of 12,10,8,8,8 reps
	Wide-Grip Pulldowns	5 sets of 12,10,8,8,8 reps
Superset:	Incline Press (on machine)	5 sets of 12,10,8,8,8 reps
	Close-Grip Pulldowns	5 sets of 12,10,8,8,8 reps
Dumbbell Flys		5 sets of 8 reps
Decline Dumbbell Press		5 sets of 12,10,8,8,8 reps
Bent-Over Rows		5 sets of 8 reps
One-Arm Dumbbell Rows		5 sets of 10 reps each arm
Superset:	Seated Cable Rows	5 sets of 10 reps
	Nautilus Pullovers	5 sets of 10 reps

THIGHS

Squats		6 sets of 15,10,8,8,6,4 reps
Machine Front Squats		4 sets of 8 reps
Superset:	Vertical Leg Press	5 sets of 8 reps
	Lying Leg Curls	5 sets of 10 reps
Superset:	Standing Leg Curls	5 sets of 10 reps
	Good Mornings	5 sets of 10 reps

CALVES Donkey Calf Raises, Standing Calf Raises, Seated Calf
Raises as in regular workout

ABDOMINALS

Alternate Twisting Knee Raises	30 reps
Raised Leg Sit-Ups	30 reps
Toe-Touch Crunches	30 reps
Alternate Leg Raises	30 reps
Alternate Kickbacks	30 reps
Rear Scissors	30 reps

SHOULDERS

Superset:	Dumbbell Presses	5 sets of 10,8,8,8,6 reps
	One-Arm Cross Cable Laterals	5 sets of 10 reps each arm
Superset:	Front Dumbbell Raises	5 sets of 8 reps
	Cable Cross Laterals	5 sets of 8 reps
Superset:	Wide-Grip Upright Rows	5 sets of 8 reps (each side)
	Lying Side Laterals	5 sets of 10 reps (each side)

UPPER ARMS

Superset:	Standing Dumbbell Curls	5 sets of 8 reps
	Lying Dumbbell Extensions	5 sets of 10 reps

Superset:	Incline Curls	5 sets of 8 reps
	Standing Barbell Triceps Extensions	5 sets of 10 reps
Superset:	Preacher Curls	5 sets of 8 reps
	Dips	5 sets of 10 reps
	One-Arm Cable Reverse	5 sets of 10 reps
	Pressdowns	(each arm)
Dumbbell Kickbacks		5 sets of 12 reps

FOREARMS

Preacher Bench Reverse Curls	5 sets of 8 reps
Behind-the-Back Wrist Curls	5 sets of 10 reps
One-Arm Wrist Curls	5 sets of 10 reps

Weak Point Training

Once you have developed the necessary mass, you must then begin to seek quality. To do this, you need to study your body in the mirror or in photos and try to discover your weak points (although your friends at the gym will probably be all too happy to tell you exactly what they are). For me, my initial weak points were the thighs and calves, so I adjusted my training to put more emphasis on the legs, to bring them up and improve my lower body in proportion to my upper body.

A year later when I was ready to compete in the Mr. Europe and Mr. Universe contests, my thighs and calves had improved—not perfect, but a lot better. Now the criticism was that my muscle separation and definition weren't as good as they could be. So I had to add on more exercises. For example, I started doing a lot of Front Lateral Raises to separate the pectoral muscles from the deltoids, and a lot of Pullovers to separate the serratus from the lats.

But even this wasn't enough: people told me, "The center of your back isn't cut enough," so I started doing more Bent-Over and Cable Rowing. "Your leg biceps aren't as good as your quadriceps," "You could use some more rear deltoid development," and so on—and each time, when I realized where I needed improvement, I changed my program to try to overcome the deficiency.

Too many bodybuilders train to improve their strong points at the expense of their weak points. One bodybuilder who is famous for his tremendous arm development and equally infamous for his lack of leg development comes into the gym day after day and trains—arms! Endless repetitions of bicep and tricep work, set after set, yet anyone looking at him can tell that he should do nothing but basic maintenance training on his arms for the next year while he bombs and blasts his thighs and calves to bring them up to championship level. But he seems to lack that "sense of perfection," and it is doubtful he will ever learn to balance his physique.

Many bodybuilders do not start out with a sense of perfection, but acquire it later on. The truth is, it is possible to go quite far in competition—winning the amateur Mr. Universe title, for example—with glaring weaknesses in your physique. But frequently a Mr. Universe winner will go straight from the amateur championship to a professional contest and finish very poorly or even dead last! The fact that you have the outstanding physique of a Samir Bannout, Yorma Raty, or Tim Belknap is no guarantee that you will automatically be successful competing against the pros.

Stepping up from one level of competition to another—from state contests to the Mr. America, from the America to the Universe, from amateur bodybuilding to the pros and on to the Olympia—you will find that weak points in your physique become increasingly detrimental. Bodybuilders often find themselves unable to make the effort needed to correct them because it means, in a sense, starting over. After years of successful competition, you have to admit that you have a weakness that might take one or two years to totally correct. Making the decision to overcome a weak point, once you are advanced in a bodybuilding career, can take a great deal of moral courage.

When I first came to the United States I was criticized for my poor calf development, so I cut off the bottoms of my sweat pants to make sure my calves were visible at all times. That not only reminded me to train them harder, but let everyone else see how they looked—which *doubly* motivated me to train them even harder.

As another example, my left arm used to be slightly smaller than my right arm. I noticed that whenever I was asked to show my biceps, I would automatically flex the right arm. So I consciously made an effort to flex my left arm as much or more than my right, to work on that weak point instead of simply ignoring it, and eventually I was able to make my left biceps the equal of my right.

Actually, this stage of training, this pursuit of perfection, never really ends because there is no such thing as a perfect body and you can always improve your physique. Every year, as you train and compete, you learn more about your body and what kinds of diet and exercise programs benefit it the most. You never really stop doing the basics, you just add on new ways of doing things.

Training Weak Areas

Bodybuilding is as much an art as a science, so you can't always be governed by a rigid and unchanging program. From the first day you walk into a gym it may be apparent to you that one body part or another is much weaker than all the rest. One basic method of correcting such imbalances is by using the Priority Principle—work your weak areas first, when you are fresh and capable of generating the greatest amount of intensity. Or arrange your Double-Split schedule so that you are training only the weak body part in one of the sessions.

Another remedy is to increase the number of sets you do for the weaker area from five to seven sets. Continue doing this for as long as necessary, until you see an improvement, and then go back to a more balanced routine. This is a good time to use the Staggered System. Every third or fourth set, throw in one set of an exercise for the weak area in addition to the normal sets you do for that body part.

Of course, sometimes your weakness is in just a *part* of a body part—you biceps may have a great peak, but not enough width; your lats may be wide and sweeping enough, but you might lack density and mass in the middle back. The answer is to choose the particular exercises that work that specific area and arrange your training program to give those exercises special priority.

In the exercise section (beginning on p. 217) you will find a full analysis of each body part designed to help you spot your weak points and specific instructions as to which exercises or specific training techniques you can use to correct any weaknesses.

CHAPTER 6

The Competition Training Program

Today there are an enormous number of bodybuilders who are working out for two or three hours a day and dedicating themselves to building a bigger and better physique. Yet only a small percentage of these obviously motivated bodybuilders ever go on and take the next step—to competition training.

The barrier that has to be overcome in order to work toward competition is more mental than physical: you have to make up your mind that what you really want is to join the ranks of the competitive bodybuilders, pitting yourself against bodybuilders whom you have probably admired in the past and whose images have helped to inspire and motivate you to continue training.

Building a Competition Physique

Competition is a whole other ball game. Physically, you are not just trying to develop a massive, balanced, and defined physique —now you must reach for total perfection, every muscle and muscle group sculpted and chiseled into its ultimate form and a body fat percentage so low that every striation and muscle separation shows itself clearly.

You suddenly become concerned with things like skin tone, presentation, posing routines, and above all, learning to deal with a kind of pressure that simply does not exist in the gym and against which you may have developed no defenses.

When it comes to training for competition, there is no such thing as a beginning or advanced program—there is only demanding the utmost from your body and working hard to achieve ultimate quality. Competition training is aimed at producing complete "refinement," and that refinement is usually achieved at the cost of drastically slowing down muscular growth.

Competition training involves more sets, more reps, an across-the-board increase in volume of training—both in terms of what you do inside the gym with weights and the additional aerobic training outside the gym that helps supplement your overall program. This is all accomplished while you are cutting down your intake of food to the bare minimum in order to strip away as much body fat as possible.

To build a lot of muscle mass, it is necessary to overload your body with nutrients to some degree. But to attain maximum quality of muscularity, you cannot allow the body this over-abundance of nutrients, nor the extended periods of rest and recuperation it prefers in order to maximize muscle growth. So therefore your aim in competition training is to bring out as much muscularity as possible but at the same time minimize the loss of muscle tissue that can occur when the body is subjected to such a strict regimen.

Some bodybuilders are too strict with themselves and end up with "too much of a good thing." In the 1981 Olympia, Danny Padilla came into the competition cut to ribbons, his body fat lower than I have ever seen it, and his amazing symmetry superbly displayed. Yet he looked so drawn, and his physique so obviously lacked the tremendous density it is famous for, that it was evident his training and diet program had consumed enormous amounts of muscle tissue along with his body fat.

It is very probable that many of the top champions have actually slowed their progress in the last few years simply because of the opportunities which the rise in popularity of bodybuilding has afforded them. They participate in so many contests, so many exhibitions and seminars, that they spend most of their time at or close to competition shape. But competition training should be a sometime thing, a concentrated program you use for a short period in order to get ready for a specific contest, and not a program that you follow when you are trying to grow and develop muscle mass. In the days when bodybuilders entered only a few contests a year—which tended to be clustered together at a certain time of year—it was normal to use the "off-season" training hard for more mass and growth. So a bodybuilder would spend part of the year doing a lot of power training and eating well—then would shift gears totally for six months or three months, depending on the individual, into a competition mode of training in order to attain the quality and refinement necessary to win.

Because of the increase in opportunities, today's bodybuilders have had to alter their training methods drastically, picking their contests carefully and trying never to get too much out of shape between events. I of course have always been a believer in choosing particular contests rather than entering everything that came along, but many professional bodybuilders waste themselves entering one Grand Prix after another. This doesn't get them anywhere, nor does staying in shape for competition too long do them any good. I recommend competing in only the important contests. It's better to compete only once a year and win. Still, with so many more contests being held, deciding where and when to compete is more difficult than it used to be.

But if you are a beginniner or early intermediate at bodybuilding competition, you probably won't face that sort of problem until later in your career. For now, it is important simply to realize what competition training does and doesn't do: it does not build mass, it is not intended to make you bigger and stronger and, in fact, can sometimes do the opposite; but what it does do is to bring out the quality in the development you have created, strip away the unessentials, and reveal the diamond-like brilliance of each facet of your musculature.

The Fear of Smallness

One psychological block that many bodybuilders face when they attempt competition training has to do with their perception of their physical size. Whatever other motive bodybuilders may have for getting into training in the first place, part of it is always the desire to get big and strong. Therefore, anything which makes them feel smaller becomes a threat. That is why many bodybuilders are made very anxious by the effects of competition training.

The competition physique should be as much pure lean mass as possible, with any excess body fat stripped away. As the saying goes, "You can't flex fat." But fat on your body makes you feel bigger than you actually are, and this sense of being bigger is psychologically satisfying to most bodybuilders.

A person who weighs 240 pounds with 16 percent body fat would be lean for an average man, but not for a competition bodybuilder. When he starts to train and diet for competition he alters his body composition so that ultimately he gets down to 9 percent body fat. What does this change mean in practical terms?

At 240 pounds, he was originally carrying almost 38 pounds of fat. His lean body mass was therefore around 202 pounds. At 9 percent body fat he will find himself weighing about 222 pounds, assuming he has not lost any muscle mass. So, in terms of muscle he will be the same size, but he will *feel* a lot smaller. And this sense of smallness affects some individuals to the extent that they find themselves psychologically unable to keep to their program.

I have been through this experience myself. When I came to America in 1968 for the Mr. Universe contest, I weighed 245 pounds. I thought I had it made. Joe Weider took one look at me and declared me the biggest bodybuilder there was. Here I was in America to show everybody how great I was—and I lost! Frank Zane took the title with his smaller but cut-to-ribbons quality physique. And that taught me a valuable lesson.

A year later, at 230 pounds I completely dominated my competitors, winning both the NABBA and IFBB Universe contests. I had realized that sheer bulk alone was not the stuff of top champions. I didn't take off the extra fat weight in two months—it took a full year. Because I took this amount of time, I was able to get used to my new proportions, to realize that the lighter weight did not really make me smaller—my arms were still huge and so were my thighs. But all my clothes were loose around the waist, indicating a real loss of unwanted bulk. The result? By changing my body composition, *I won every contest I entered.*

Mass is vital to a bodybuilder's physique. But it is the *shape* and the *quality* of this mass that wins contests. Seeing big numbers on a tape measure or scale, or striving for the feeling of your clothes being tight all over your body, and not paying enough attention to stripping away fat, achieving ultimate definition and contest quality, will give you one inevitable result—you'll lose. And that I can tell you from experience.

The Elements of Competition Training

The Competition Training Program involves a number of new elements beyond Advanced Training:

1. An even higher volume of training
2. A faster training pace
3. An additional number of intensity training principles and a wider variety of exercises
4. A significant change in diet (see Contest Dieting, p. 695)

Analyzing and correcting your weak points becomes enormously important as you train for competition. Whereas you might previously have given weaker areas priority, now you must become a fanatic about correcting these imbalances. Of course, you have to realize that only so much can be done in a few weeks or months of training—totally correcting every weak area may take a year or two—but you do as much as humanly possible to produce the most nearly perfect physique to enter into competition.

Training for Maximum Muscularity

Attaining the highest possible quality for competition involves a change in workout style. You need to:

1. Cut down your rest time between sets. Instead of a one-minute interval, try to rest for only thirty seconds.

2. In addition to many supersets, you put further stress on your endurance capacity by doing tri-sets—three sets in a row done without stopping.

3. Do a lot more abdominal work. Hard, defined abs go a long way toward making strong visual impression on the judges.

4. Supplement your training in the gym with aerobic exercise outside the gym. (Running is one of the best ways to help you get cut up—both long distance and wind sprints. Aerobic exercise classes are also good, since they burn up a lot of calories and tend to include lots of ab work. Bicycle riding is a good calorie-consumer and won't put the strain on the joints that running can. But whatever supplementary exercise you do, remember to keep things in perspective. Running a mile or two a few times a week will help you get cut up and in shape, running ten miles will simply deplete your energy and tear down your muscle tissue. Ken Waller and I used to train and then immediately go out and run a fast mile or mile and a half. We'd come back exhausted, but knowing we had at least six or eight hours to rest and recuperate before we had to be back in the gym again.)

5. Make use of all of the intensity training principles to shock the body for ultimate progress.

THE COMPETITION TRAINING SPLIT

Mon	Tue	Wed	Thur	Fri	Sat
			Morning		
Chest	Shoulders	Chest	Shoulders	Chest	Shoulders
Back	Upper arms	Back	Upper arms	Back	Upper arms
	Forearms		Forearms		Forearms
			Evening		
Legs		Legs		Legs	

Calves and Abdominals every day in evening workout

COMPETITION EXERCISE PROGRAM

Monday/Wednesday/Friday

ABDOMINALS Begin workout with 10 minutes of Roman Chair Sit-Ups.

CHEST AND BACK

Deadlifts	3 sets of 10,8,6 reps	
Superset:	Weighted Chin-Ups —behind neck	4 sets of 10 reps
	Incline Barbell Press	4 sets of 15,12,8,6 reps
Superset:	Bench Press	4 sets of 15,12,8,6 reps
	Chin-Ups—to front	4 sets of 15 reps
Superset:	Dumbbell Flys	4 sets of 10 reps
	Wide-Grip Bent-Over Barbell Rows	4 sets of 12 reps, using Stripping Method
Tri-Set:	Nautilus Pullovers	4 sets of 15 reps, using Stripping Method
	Dips	4 sets, each to failure
	Cable Flys	4 sets of 12 to 15 reps
Tri-Set:	Seated Cable Rows	4 sets of 10 reps, using Stripping Method
	One-Arm Cable Rows	4 sets of 12 to 15 reps
	Dumbbell Pullovers	4 sets of 15 reps

THIGHS

Superset:	Leg Extensions	5 sets of 12 reps
	Squats	5 sets of 15 to 20 reps
Superset:	Front Squats	5 sets of 12 to 15 reps
	Leg Curls	5 sets of 12 reps
Superset:	Hack Squats	5 sets of 15 reps
	Leg Curls	1 to 10 Method
Straight-Leg Deadlifts	3 sets of 6 reps, standing on block or bench	

CALVES

(Alternate foot position: toes in, toes forward, toes out)

Donkey Calf Raises	5 sets of 15 reps
Standing Calf Raises	5 sets of 10 reps, as heavy as possible
Seated Calf Raises	5 sets of 15 reps
Front Calf Raises	5 sets of 15 reps

ABDOMINALS

(No rest between exercises)

Incline Bent-Knee Sit-Ups	30 reps
with twist	30 reps
Chinning Bar Leg Raises, straight leg	20 reps
bent leg	20 reps

Crunches	50 reps
Bent-Knee Leg Raises	50 reps
Alternate Leg Pulls	30 reps each side
Seated Leg Tucks	30 reps
Seated Twists	100 reps each side
Rear Leg Raises	50 reps each side
Side Leg Raises, straight leg	30 reps each side
bent leg	30 reps each side
Rear Scissors	50 reps

Tuesday/Thursday/Friday

ABDOMINALS Begin workout with 10 minutes of Roman Chair Sit-Ups.

SHOULDERS

Tri-Set:	Front Machine Presses	4 sets of 10 reps
	Dumbbell Lateral Raises	4 sets of 10 reps
	Bent-Over Lateral Raises	4 sets of 10 reps
Tri-Set:	Barbell Press, alternating front and back	4 sets of 12 reps
	Cable Side Laterals	4 sets of 10 reps
	Lying Incline Laterals	4 sets of 10 reps
Superset:	Front Barbell Raises	4 sets of 10 reps
	Seated Cable Rear Laterals	4 sets of 10 reps
	Dips	4 sets, each to failure
	Cable Flys	4 sets of 12 to 15 reps
Tri-Set:	Seated Cable Rows	4 sets of 10 reps, using Stripping Method
	One-Arm Cable Rows	4 sets of 12 to 15 reps
	Dumbbell Pullovers	4 sets of 15 reps

LEGS

Superset:	Leg Extensions	5 sets of 12 reps
	Squats	5 sets of 15 to 20 reps
Superset:	Front Squats	5 sets of 12 to 15 reps
	Leg Curls	5 sets of 12 reps
Superset:	Hack Squats	5 sets of 15 reps
	Leg Curls	1 to 10 Method
Straight-Leg Deadlifts		3 sets of 6 reps, standing on block or bench

CALVES

(Alternate foot position: toes in, toes forward, toes out)
Donkey Calf Raises   5 sets of 15 reps
Standing Calf Raises   5 sets of 10 reps, as heavy as possible

Seated Calf Raises	5 sets of 15 reps
Reverse Calf Raises	5 sets of 15 reps

ABDOMINALS

(No rest between exercises)

Incline Bent-Knee Sit-Ups	30 reps
with twist, arms behind neck	30 reps
Chinning Bar Leg Raises, straight leg	20 reps
bent leg	20 reps
Crunches	50 reps
Bent-Knee Leg Raises	50 reps
Alternate Leg Pulls	30 reps each side
Seated Leg Tucks	30 reps
Seated Twists	100 reps each side
Rear Leg Raises	50 reps each side
Side Leg Raises, straight leg	30 reps each side
bent leg	30 reps each side
Rear Scissors	50 reps

Tuesday/Thursday/Saturday

ABDOMINALS Begin workout with 10 minutes of Roman Chair Sit-Ups.

SHOULDERS

Tri-Set:	Front Machine Presses	4 sets of 10 reps
	Dumbbell Lateral Raises	4 sets of 10 reps
	Bent-Over Lateral Raises	4 sets of 10 reps
Tri-Set:	Barbell Press, alternating	
	front and back	4 sets of 12 reps
	Cable Side Laterals	4 sets of 10 reps
	Lying Incline Laterals	4 sets of 10 reps
Superset:	Front Barbell Raises	4 sets of 10 reps
	Seated Cable Rear Laterals	4 sets of 10 reps

UPPER ARMS

Superset:	Barbell Curls	4 sets 1–10 Method
	Standing Close-Grip Triceps Extensions with bar	4 sets of 10 reps
Tri-Set:	Barbell Preacher Bench Curls	4 sets of 10 reps
	Lying Barbell Triceps Extensions	4 sets of 10 reps
	Barbell Preacher Bench Reverse Curls	4 sets of 10 reps

Tri-Set: Lying Dumbbell Extensions   4 sets of 10 reps
          Incline Curls   4 sets of 10 reps
            (increase incline each set)
          Lying Reverse-Grip
            Barbell Extensions   4 sets of 10 reps
Superset: Concentration Curls   4 sets of 15 reps,
                                             using the "One-
                                             and-a-Half"
                                             Method

          Standing One-Arm
            Triceps Extensions   4 sets of 12 reps
Superset: Kneeling Cable Triceps Extensions 4 sets of 12 reps
          Kneeling Cable Triceps Extensions
            with rope   4 sets of 12 reps

FOREARMS

Superset: Barbell Reverse Wrist Curls   4 sets of 10 reps
           Barbell Wrist Curls   4 sets of 10 reps
One-Arm Dumbbell Wrist Curls   4 sets of 10 reps

CALVES

(Alternate foot position: toes in, toes forward, toes out)
Leg Press Calf Raises   4 sets of 12 reps
Standing Calf Raises   4 sets of 12 reps
One-Leg Donkey Calf Raises 4 sets of 12 reps

ABDOMINALS

(No rest between exercises)
Straight-Leg Raises, on floor   30 reps
Bent-Leg Raises, on floor   30 reps
Seated Leg Tuck, on floor   30 reps
Alternate Leg Pulls   30 reps each side
High-Leg Sit-Ups, feet together   15 reps
                  feet apart   15 reps
Side-Leg Raises, straight leg   30 reps each leg
                 bent leg   30 reps each leg
Rear Leg Raises   30 reps each side
Lying Side Leg Pulls   20 reps each side
Rear Leg Scissors   30 reps

Applying the Shocking Principle

Using the Shocking Principle is the best way of driving the body beyond its limits, and the only way of overcoming the barriers that stand between you and your total championship potential.

Shocking the body is how you get the extra cuts, extra hardness, veins, separation, definition, and other signs of quality development. Getting ready for competition is the time to really get serious and to use every method available for driving the body to the maximum.

A fundamental way of shocking the muscles is by making them work in unfamiliar ways. When I am trying to really blast my muscles, I sometimes alter the order of the exercises I would normally do for that workout. If I usually start training my chest with a certain movement, for example, I make sure I begin this workout with a different one. I also add new exercises to my routine, movements my body is not accustomed to. "It is always harder to do someone else's workout," Roger Callard has said. This is true. Forcing the muscles to work in unaccustomed ways, with unfamiliar workouts, subjects them to a greater than normal amount of shock.

The best way to make use of the Competition Program is this: Begin by doing the program just as it is outlined. Stay with it until it becomes totally familiar. Then, try varying your program to surprise and shock the muscles. It is important that you don't neglect the really fundamental exercises, and be sure to continue to put extra effort into training weak spots and problem areas.

Most of the training principles I mentioned earlier, such as the Stripping Method, Rest/Pause Training, staggered sets, tri-sets, and negatives, should be employed also.

Individualizing Competition Training

Because each individual has different strengths and weaknesses, there is no way I can give one routine that is perfect for everyone. I can outline general approaches, show you how to change your program so that you burn more calories, create more muscularity and definition—but it is you who must look in the mirror and determine where your weakness lies, whether in upper, lower, or middle pec development, biceps, triceps, or lat width.

Suppose your lower lats are not developing quite the way you want them to. It would make sense for you to add on about four extra sets for lower lats. But four sets in addition to everything else you are doing would probably be too much, so you could eliminate one set each of exercises like Close-Grip and Wide-Grip Chin-Ups, Seated Rows, and T-Bar Rows. You would still do these exercises, but with fewer sets of each, so the overall demand of your total workout would remain about the same.

The program as outlined above is only a starting point. However, if you are training for competition for the first time, you may want to follow this program closely until you strip away your body fat and see the effect of your training and diet. Otherwise you may have trouble assessing your weak points accurately.

If you are more experienced and have a clear perception of your weaker areas, then be certain you give those body parts the additional work needed to bring them into balance. Consult the exercise sections to find which movements are best for correcting the problems and make whatever alterations in your training routine you feel necessary.

All the top bodybuilders go through this process. I know when Franco and I used to train together I would do extra sets for certain areas and Franco would do extra for others. For instance, Franco had trouble getting his thighs really ripped, so he would do additional sets of an exercise like Front Squats on a Smith machine to help define his quadriceps. I didn't have this problem, so I would work harder on shoulders, triceps, abs, or whatever else I felt needed it the most.

As you make adjustments in your training, just be certain that you don't create new weaknesses trying to correct old ones. You must continue to give the rest of your body sufficient attention even while you work to correct problem areas.

Cardiovascular Demand

When you first begin competition training, with its much greater aerobic demand, you may find yourself running out of breath. Like the runner who is used to jogging three miles a day and suddenly tries for six, you may experience some cardiovascular failure. The remedy for this is not to slow down your training pace but to accelerate it. By forcing your heart, lungs, and circulatory system to adapt to this faster pace, you will find yourself getting into condition in a very short time.

PHA Training

PHA, or "peripheral heart action," training was invented by Bob Guida (Mr. America 1966). It is very useful for competition preparation, either on an occasional basis or more often, if it seems to suit you. PHA training involves a kind of circuit system—doing only one exercise for each body part in rotation. This helps to promote circulation throughout the body. PHA training is valuable because the heart itself is incapable of easily circulating enough blood throughout the body. There are one-way valves located in various areas to control the flow of blood so that, for instance, blood doesn't just sit and collect in the bottom of the legs because the heart can't pump it back up. Intense muscular contractions act as an auxiliary heart, "milking" the blood past each of these valves. The advantage of this for the bodybuilder is that the increased circulation creates certain chemicals in the blood that help to neutralize the toxins that occur as by-products of exercise. Once you get used to the cardiovascular demands of this kind of training, you can develop a much higher level of endurance.

Guida recommends a series of four to six exercises which do not work the same body part two exercises in a row, with minimum rest between each series. This kind of training, with its high endurance factor, allows you to burn up a lot of calories and get cut-up much more easily. Doing either of the following exercise groups satisfies the requirements of the PHA system:

Barbell Shoulder Presses	*or*	Leg Extensions
Lunges		Dumbbell Laterals
Dumbbell Flys		Triceps Extensions
Leg Extensions		Sit-Ups
Barbell Curls		Calf Raises

However, a group such as Seated Rows/Barbell Curls/Bench Presses/Triceps Extensions would not be acceptable since the first two exercises involve the biceps and the second two both work the triceps.

The examples shown above are just suggestions. You can put together your own workouts in a variety of different ways. Here are a few simple rules you can follow to get the most out of Guida's PHA training:

1. Put together several series of four to six exercises each and do them as fast as possible, with only a brief rest between series.

2. Construct your series so that each exercise works a different body part. Make certain that you include exercises for every body part, alternating between upper and lower body when possible.

3. Try to include exercises for each individual area of each muscle or muscle group. For example, your first series might include Dumbbell Laterals for the side deltoids, the next series Front Dumbbell Raises for the front deltoids, and your third se-

ries Bent-Over Dumbbell Laterals for the rear deltoids. Or you could include Dumbbell Flys, Incline Presses, and Dips in each succeeding series to work the middle, upper, and lower areas of the chest.

4. Once you have developed the endurance to go through a PHA workout with minimum rest, be sure to gradually increase the amount of weight you use. Remember, this is still progressive resistance training.

Muscle Separation

Muscle separation is a level of muscularity that goes far beyond simple definition. Training and diet can give you good definition, but it takes something more to become the walking anatomy chart that will win competitions.

The quality physique must show clear separation between each muscle group. For example, when you do a rear double-biceps shot, the borders between the biceps and triceps, shoulder, traps, and upper and lower back should leap out at the judges. Each individual muscle group itself should show clear internal distinctions: the two heads of the biceps, the three heads of the triceps. And each head should be further patterned with visible striations of individual bundles of muscle fiber.

Total muscle separation is the result of training each muscle so thoroughly that every plane, contour, and aspect is brought out and fully revealed once you have lowered your body fat sufficiently. To achieve this requires many different exercises for each muscle and a lot of sets and reps. But it takes specific technique as well:

1. It is necessary to totally isolate each muscle and then each specific area of every muscle in order to engage every fiber possible, thereby creating clear separation between each muscle and major body part. This is done by knowing exactly how each exercise affects the muscles and putting together a program that sculpts the body exactly as you intend.

2. The utmost muscle separation cannot be achieved without strictness of movement involving concentrated effort through the entire range of motion of the exercise, so that every engaged fiber is subjected to the maximum amount of stress. Any sloppiness of execution will defeat your purpose.

Unless you perform an isolation exercise in a totally strict manner, you will not be working the narrow and specific area for which the exercise was designed. When doing a Front Dumbbell Raise to get deltoid-pectoral separation, for example, if you swing the weight up instead of making the muscle do all the work you will not bring out the full shape of the muscles, nor will you get the kind of separation you are after. If you want to work a certain area, you have to do the movement strictly enough so that you *feel* the effort exactly where you want it.

3. Obviously, whatever separation you achieve will not show if the muscle is covered with body fat. So proper diet resulting in low body fat is also an important factor in achieving spectacular muscle separation.

Muscularity and Definition: Analyzing Your Progress

In the 1980 Mr. America contest, Ray Mentzer showed up to compete for a spot on the American team going to the Mr. Universe. For several months prior to the contest he had been going for body composition testing every three weeks. He came into the competition confident of victory because his last test had indicated that his body fat was below 4 percent.

Despite the results of the testing procedure, he failed in his bid to win a place on the Universe team because he looked smooth on stage. He lacked cuts and muscularity. He had failed to realize that how much he weighed, what his physical measurements were, or what his body composition testing had revealed had nothing directly to do with what bodybuilding competition is all about.

The only real way to know whether or not you are in shape is by how you look. After all, the judges are not going to use underwater weighing, a tape measure, or any other device to make their decision. They are going to go by what they see. And you have to do the same thing.

Of course, it helps to have some basis for comparison. It is easier to measure the difference between two things than it is to analyze a thing by itself. One good way to do this is to take photos periodically and compare how you look now with how you looked then. Another way is to stand alongside another bodybuilder in the gym, hit some poses, and see exactly how you stack up.

But the ultimate test is when you are actually on stage and either win or lose. That is why it is sometimes necessary to enter several contests before you can really judge your progress. How well you do from one contest to another can tell you very clearly whether or not your training methods are working.

In the short term, though, it is your mirror that will be your most honest critic—if you allow it to be. Body composition testing doesn't tell you anything about your muscle separation; the tape measure cannot analyze your muscularity and definition; and you cannot judge the proportion and balance of your physique by stepping on a scale. But looking into a mirror and seeing only what you want to see is not the way to become a champion. You have to see things as they are, no better and no worse.

Also remember to keep your training diary so you will have an accurate record of your progress. When I was training for the 1980 Olympia, I had Franco shoot photos of me every week, which I studied very carefully to see how hard, defined, and muscular I was becoming. Between the photos, my own ability to look at myself in the mirror, and Franco's insightful comments, I knew all the time just how fast I was making progress and was able to arrive in Australia in shape to win my seventh Olympia title.

Depending on Your Training Partner

At no time is having a dependable training partner more important than when you are preparing to compete. As the contest approaches, every workout counts and there is no time for any letdown in training intensity. Your training partner helps to provide the extra motivation you need to diet and train hard at the same time.

If you are a beginner at competition, you would do well to train with somebody who has more experience than you do. A knowledgeable training partner, who has been through it all before, can show you a lot of shortcuts and make your contest preparation that much easier and more effective.

When I was training at World Gym for the 1980 Olympia, I trained some days with two young bodybuilders getting ready for their first competition. They were both young and extremely strong, and they were able to push me hard in our workouts. On the other hand, because of my greater experience, I was able to show them training techniques they hadn't seen before and help them with their dieting and posing. We made a really fair trade: their energy and my knowledge. And we all got better because of it.

Outdoor Training

I have always enjoyed training outdoors in good weather. Training in the sun helps to give you a healthy look, tighter skin, and

Franco and I on Venice Beach

a good tan. Since the early Muscle Beach days, bodybuilders have taken advantage of sunny weather and trained outdoors.

You can certainly begin exercising outdoors right from the first day you start Basic Training, but outdoor training is almost essential prior to competition because of the finished look it helps to give the physique. When Franco and I trained on Venice Beach, we would work out, go lie on the beach for a while, and then return to the weight pit for more lifting. My tan became much deeper this way, and I benefited from training before an audience, because it helped to get me ready for the pressures of appearing on stage in a hall full of people.

When you train outdoors, I advocate a slower workout, but with very heavy weights. This can give you a nice break from your normal competition training and is another way of surprising and shocking the body.

Not everybody has a California beach right down the street, but when I lived in Austria and then later in Munich my friends and I would often go out to a local lake and spend the entire day training outdoors. You can go to a park, a recreation area, or even somebody's back yard and enjoy outdoor training yourself.

Mind Over Matter: The Mind, the Most Powerful Tool

The body will never fully respond to your workouts until you understand how to train the mind as well. The mind is a dynamo, a source of vital energy. That energy can be negative and work against you, or you can harness it to give yourself unbelievable workouts and build a physique that lives up to your wildest expectations.

"Where the mind goes, the body will follow" is a saying I have always believed in. If you want to be Mr. America or Mr. Universe, you have to have a clear vision of yourself achieving these goals. You have to have a picture in your mind of the kind of physique you need to build in order to win these titles. Focusing on such images gives your mind and body a clear-cut task, a well-defined goal to strive for.

One way to help you do this is to pick an idol, a champion whom you would like to emulate. A short bodybuilder might choose Franco Columbu or Danny Padilla. A medium-size, aesthetic type could choose Frank Zane. Since I was big and tall, my idol was Reg Park. He had the size and Herculean mass that I wanted to have. So I studied every photo of Reg I could find, cut them out of magazines and pinned them on the wall, and used his image to help define to myself what I was striving to become.

In this way you develop a single-mindedness of purpose that ultimately gives you the will to go into the gym for two to four hours a day and put yourself through the most punishing workouts possible. It makes the difference between just going through five sets of this and four sets of that and really pushing your body to the limit.

Beyond the act of visualizing the end product of your training, you also need to concentrate on how you want each individual muscle to develop. The key to success in your workouts is to get the mind into the muscle, not to think about the weight. When I am doing Barbell Curls, I am visualizing my biceps as mountains —not just big, but HUGE! And because I am thinking of the muscle, I can feel everything that is happening to it. I know whether or not I have fully stretched it at the bottom of the movement and whether I am getting a full, complete contraction on top.

When you think about the weight instead of the muscle, you can't really feel what the muscle is doing. You lose control. Instead of stretching and contracting the muscle with deep concentration, you are simply exerting brute strength. So you end up not working to the limits of your range of motion, not contracting and extending the muscle in a smooth, intense, controlled manner.

Concentration is vitally important while training. Not only does it allow you to achieve the best possible feel in any movement, but it allows the neuromuscular system to respond to the fullest. When you train, the changes in your muscle structure come about because you are reeducating the nervous system, stimulating it to multiply the number of muscle fibers and to protect the muscles from damage by causing the fibers to hypertrophy (increase in size).

The nervous system can inhibit muscular activity as well as stimulate it. In this way it protects you from putting too much stress on your body. It takes energy to overcome this inhibition, to overwhelm the protective mechanisms. The more intense the imagery you use, the more energy you can summon up. The more forcefully you pour this energy into your training and break through the limitations your mind is imposing, the more rapid your progress.

This intensity of mental concentration is why a champion can train with what appears to be a moderate weight and still get great results. I see bodybuilders all the time who think that just heaving weights around, psyching themselves up like weightlifters, and then doing all the movements any which way will give them great bodies. It won't. Watch a Chris Dickerson, Samir Bannout, or Tony Pearson in the gym and you will see how they wring every shred of benefit from each exercise—getting just the right feel for each movement, going from full extension, with the muscles totally stretched out, to full contraction, with every fiber in the muscles under complete control.

All of us have certain body parts that feel good to train and that respond easily, and others that we have to force ourselves to train and that respond reluctantly. In my case, training biceps has always been a piece of cake, while I never had the same great feel doing triceps movements. But a bodybuilder with competition ambitions can't afford to let this situation stand. He has to make use of the mind, concentrate on putting the mind into the muscle and establishing precise control of every muscle of every body part.

But there is only so much mental energy we can summon up on our own. Good bodybuilders have to be intelligent, but training is not an intellectual exercise. The training movements are sensual, and the deep motivation that excites you and keeps you going is emotional. You can't just sit down and feel those things any more than you can deliberately feel like you are in love. In both cases, something outside yourself has to inspire you.

Inspiration is vitally important to bodybuilding, and it is something you can go out and look for. Choosing an idol is one way to search for inspiration. So is picking the right kind of gym to train in, a place with positive energy and good vibes. Another is finding the right training partner.

I remember working out with Ed Corney before the 1975 Mr. Olympia and on one particular day I just couldn't get myself into training my back. Ed saw this and said to me, "Remember, you are going to be going up against Lou Ferrigno in South Africa, and his lats are so huge that if you stand behind him on stage the audience won't even be able to see you!"

Needless to say, when I started to think about competing against Lou, and how good his back was, I couldn't wait to do my Chins, Bent-Over Rows, and the rest of my back exercises. Corney's remark had inspired me, given me an energy I couldn't create all by myself.

The Power of the Mind

As long as I have been in bodybuilding I have heard this said, and it remains true: When the going gets tough, *it is always the mind that fails first, not the body.*

The best example of this I can think of occurred one day when Franco and I were doing Squats in the old Gold's Gym. Franco got under 500 pounds, squatted down, and couldn't get back up. We grabbed the bar and helped him get it back on the rack. Five hundred pounds for even one rep was apparently just too heavy for him that day.

Just then four or five Italian-American kids from New York came in. "Wow," they said, "there's Franco! Hey, Franco!" They were great fans, and were looking forward to watching him work out—only Franco had just failed in a lift and it seemed probable that he would miss it again next try.

I took Franco aside and told him, "Franco, these guys think you're the king. You can't get under 500 pounds again and fail." All of a sudden his face changed. He looked at me with big eyes, realizing he was on the spot. Then he went out onto the street and spent a while psyching himself up, taking deep breaths and concentrating on the lift.

He stalked back into the gym, grabbed the bar and, instead of the six reps he was supposed to do with 500 pounds, he did eight! Then he walked away coolly as if it were nothing.

Obviously Franco's muscles didn't get any stronger in that few minutes between sets, his tendons didn't get bigger—what did change was his mind, his drive and motivation, his desire for the goal. It was impossible to overlook how important the mind was in making the body do what he wanted.

Training the Mind

Following this fundamental program for training your mind will bring you that much closer to achieving bodybuilding success.

1. *Define your purpose.* You cannot achieve a goal until you define it clearly. Why are you training? To gain a little muscle size, or to become a bodybuilding champion? Are you trying to impress other people, or to overcome insecurity? If you decide that your purpose is purely and simply to become a great champion, this realization is the first step toward making the kind of total commitment that I spoke about earlier. Dedication to a goal cannot be done by halves.

2. *Keep in contact with your purpose.* Discipline is simply always being in contact with your purpose. If your goals are firmly in your mind, you never need to consider whether you should train or not, whether you are committing enough time and energy to your training, or whether or not to do all the sets and reps your program calls for. With your purpose always in mind, those questions simply disappear. When a bodybuilder is struggling through a set he may think, "Why am I going through all this? Why am I putting myself through all this effort?" This failure of will, this lack of push and drive, is a direct result of losing a clear vision of his purpose. When that purpose is firmly

in mind, when you know what you want to look like and why, this kind of failure cannot occur. In fact you'll find you cannot wait to do your next set, you'll look forward to your next workout, and training will become the major satisfaction in your life.

3. *Confidence comes from doing.* Much of what can intimidate you or cause you anxiety is simply fear of the unknown. Becoming a champion, packing on mountains of muscle mass, being able to handle huge weights can all seem hopelessly difficult to a beginning bodybuilder. But keeping your purpose firmly in mind, simply go into the gym and do *your* workout, do it well and don't worry about what other people are doing. They are not in the gym to pass judgment on you. Aspire to be like your heroes, fine. But continue on your own path and simply do each workout as well as you can. Your confidence will grow as it comes to rest on a foundation of solid achievement.

4. *Aim for the infinite—one step at a time.* The capacity for physical development is theoretically limitless. It is as if you are ascending an infinite staircase, spiraling up and up and never ending. But you must ascend that staircase one step at a time. Be certain in your mind that you want to be Mr. Universe or Mr. Olympia, look at the top champions and vow one day to blow them off the stage, but then get on with today's workout, this set and this repetition. Learn to "be here now," to master present-time consciousness. It is what you do today that will determine how well you perform tomorrow. So be realistic. If you can bench only 300 pounds while everyone around you is lifting 400 pounds, then accept this short-term limitation and aim at progressing just a few pounds a week. In fact, you can use this to your advantage, make it spur you on—after all, if everybody else is doing those lifts, obviously you can learn to do them too! Keep that up long enough, always aiming for progress but taking it one step at a time, and soon you will be pressing 500 or 600 pounds and working toward lifting even more!

5. *Learn the positive benefits of failure.* Failure can be a great learning tool. It defines limits for you, it instructs you as to which parts of your program are working and which aren't. It tells you what step of the staircase you are on and helps to motivate you to climb higher. Failure is not what hurts the aware bodybuilder—it is *fear of failure* that most often gets in the way. This prevents you from really trying hard, from releasing all of your energies, from summoning up total motivation. In fact, it often helps to seek out failure! Train as hard as possible, find out what your strength and endurance limitations really are. Push yourself until you run into a wall and can go no further. "You

*A little help from my friend—
Franco Columbu was always
my best training partner.*

*You and your training partner
should create your own little
world in which anything is
possible.*

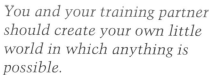

You and your training partner can feed off each other's energy, creating the kind of intensity that will push you beyond your limits.

don't know how much *enough* is until you know how much *too much* is" is a phrase I have often heard. Once you experience failure—failure to lift a weight, to get through a workout, to place well in a contest—you will know much more about yourself and can plan the next stage of your training more intelligently. Learn from it, benefit by it, but don't be intimidated and fail to dare. You may attempt a lift you are certain you cannot make, but make it anyway! The satisfaction and confidence that come from stepping over your supposed limit is enormous, but it never comes to those who fear to test their limits.

6. *Choose the right training partner.* When you and the right training partner go through a workout, you feed on each other's energy. The whole becomes greater than the sum of the parts, and

you can do things you never dreamed possible. Training together helps both of you focus your consciousness on what is going on right now—with this set, this rep. It helps you to create your own little world, a world in which any physical feat is possible and all challenges can be overcome. Conversely, the wrong training partner will sap your strength and drain you of motivation. Franco Columbu was a great training partner for me because of how he helped my workouts, not because we were best friends outside the gym. When it comes to training, what counts is the workout, not friendship. Franco and I trained well together because we cared about each other, wanted each other to succeed. Make sure

that your workout partner cares about your efforts and will be there, providing support, energy and motivation when you really need it.

7. *Use visualization and imagery to fuel your workouts.* Earlier I talked about the powerful effect of visualization (seeing yourself in your mind's eye lifting the weight before you actually attempt to lift it, for example) and imagery (imagining yourself as a mythic hero, a barbarian warrior, Conan!). These techniques create positive mental forces that help dispel doubts. They summon up energies from deep in your subconscious. You may not think of yourself as capable of unleashing these powers. But no matter how mellow, laid back, or even timid a person you are, these forces are present within you and can be evoked to push you to superhuman feats.

8. *Seek out circumstances that help your motivation.* Just as the right kind of training partner makes you work harder and the wrong kind can ruin your workouts, other factors often have a strong influence on how you feel during a workout and, therefore, how hard you train. Squats have never been my best movement, so I used to do legs with Ken Waller, who was phenomenal at Squats. He could use so much weight in this movement that I was compelled to try to lift as much as possible, and I usually found that I could. I remember one time I had a date after my workout and the girl came into the gym and watched while I trained. I felt as if she really cared how well I did, and I wanted to impress her, so I used 20 pounds more on the Squat than usual. She probably didn't know the difference, but I did. Her presence motivated me—and ever since, I've always tried to have someone watching me do Squats. I would go with Franco down to the weight pit at the beach, knowing I would have to do my absolute best while training in front of lots of people. Many things like this can help motivate you—where you train, when you train, with whom you train, and so on. Pay attention to what helps you and what gets in your way, and adjust your training accordingly.

9. *Learn to listen to your body.* Your body cannot be used like a machine. It is a living organism that has cycles, fluctuating levels of hormones, and a complicated biochemistry. It is affected by your mental state, the weather, fatigue, stress, nutrition, and countless other factors. Your body will not always perform on cue, doing just what you want it to when you want it to. Some days will be better than others; you will feel stronger or weaker, bigger or smaller depending on the circumstances. If you are aware of what is happening in your body, you can adapt yourself accordingly. You will not be disappointed on the down days. You

will be more sensitive as to how alterations in your training or diet make the body feel, which will motivate you to do everything you can to create the best program for yourself. When the mind is attuned to the body, the two work together in greater harmony, channeling the energy you need to pursue your purpose with drive and daring.

The mind must be trained and developed along with the body. Limits are often self-imposed. Just because things have been a certain way does not mean they have to stay that way. Positive thinking nourishes the mind the way food nourishes the body. If you think you can, then you can. In the gym or anywhere else, positive expectations will allow you to grow and develop; negative ones will hold back. To be a champion, you have to have the mind of a champion, and that mind is created step by step, just like the physique.

How Bodybuilding Affects the Mind

Up until now we have dealt extensively on the effect bodybuilding training has on the body. But the effect that bodybuilding has on the mind is also significant. Hard training causes the body to release endorphins (naturally occurring morphine-like substances), which leads to a mood elevation. There are many beneficial effects from the highly oxygenated blood that is pumped through your system. But bodybuilding can also have a profound effect on personality, life style, and success in dealing with the demands of the modern environment.

Discipline is all-important to success in bodybuilding. So is the ability to concentrate, to set yourself a goal and not let anything stand in your way. But as much as bodybuilding demands, it gives back a great deal more.

I have worked with thousands of youngsters who wanted to become bodybuilders. I have taught weight training to Special Olympics kids and to prison inmates, and discussed the role of weight training with physical therapists, medical scientists, and the experts at NASA. And in all my experience I have never seen a case in which an individual made progress in bodybuilding without experiencing an accompanying boost in self-esteem, self-confidence, and enjoyment of life.

A sense of self-worth should be based as much as possible on reality—you shouldn't just "believe" in yourself, but be able to point to real achievement. Educating your mind, sharpening your talents, and creating a physically superior body are all ways of realistically enhancing your self-esteem. When you have a superior body, it is not egotism to take pride in it; egotism is when you attempt to take credit for qualities you don't really have.

Bodybuilding changes you. It makes you feel better about yourself, and it changes the way people treat you. It is an avenue open to anybody. Man, woman, or child, you can improve your body through proper training and your self-confidence along with it. Bob Wieland, for example, is a Vietnam veteran who lost both legs in combat. Rather than treat himself as a cripple, he began training seriously in a gym and has since entered numerous power-lifting contests, breaking the world record for Bench Press in his weight class. Bob does not have to think of himself as handicapped; thanks to the benefits of training, he can rightfully claim the accolade of champion.

It has always seemed to me that bodybuilding is a good way to get in touch with reality. When you're working out, there is the reality of that cold iron in your hands . . . you can lift it, or you can't: reality. And then there is the progress you make. If you train correctly, you get results. Train incorrectly, or don't put enough intensity into your efforts, and you get little or nothing. You can't fake it. You have to face the facts.

The human body was never designed for a sedentary life style. It was created to hunt saber-toothed tigers and walk forty miles a day. When we have no physical outlet, tensions build up within us. The body reacts to minor frustrations, such as somebody cutting us off in traffic, as life-and-death situations—the "fight or flight" mechanism is tripped, adrenaline floods our system, our blood pressure skyrockets. Exercise in general and bodybuilding in particular give us an outlet for these tensions and satisfy the body's need for strenuous activity.

If this is true for most of us, it is particularly evident when you are dealing with people in extreme circumstances—prisoners serving time in penitentiaries, for example, and the Special Olympians.

In my work teaching bodybuilding to prisoners around the country I have been struck by what an effective system of rehabilitation training with weights can be. Many men in prison suffer from a poor self-image, have found themselves ignored and overlooked in life and felt trapped behind the bars of economic and social exclusion long before they found themselves behind real bars.

Many of these men have spent their lives blaming others for their own mistakes, rationalizing the behavior that has continually gotten them in trouble, failing to take responsibility for

Rick Wayne, Franco and I teaching bodybuilding techniques in the prison program.

their own actions. All of this can change when they begin seriously "pumping iron." That iron is very real, and failure can't be rationalized away. But the eventual achievement of getting through the set, building up the strength of the muscles, learning the discipline necessary to continue to make progress, has its effect on the mind and spirit of the individual. Whereas many of these men had sought attention through antisocial means, now, probably for the first time, they attract admiring attention, from people who respect their achievements. With this attention comes pride and self-confidence, and this is one reason why weight training has become so popular in prisons around the country.

Training with Special Olympians.

With the Special Olympians, the benefits are even more obvious. I remember working with some kids in Washington, D.C. One youngster was lying on a bench ready to do a bench press, while a line of others waited their turn. I handed him just the bar with no plates on it, and he freaked out—this kind of effort was more than he was used to or mentally prepared for. I didn't pressure him, but let him move off while I worked with the other boys. After a few minutes, I saw him edging nearer, watching the others closely. Finally, he indicated he wanted to try, and I helped him to press the bar three or four times, but he was still afraid and quickly got off the bench. But it wasn't long before he was back, this time with more confidence, and now he managed to do ten repetitions with very little help.

From that moment on, he was hooked. Not only did he join in the line of those waiting to try the exercise, he tried to push others out of the way so that he could have his turn sooner. In a world that contained so many frustrations and disappointments for him, this boy had found something to test his strength against, a physical barrier that could be approached and overcome, giving him a self-confidence usually denied him.

We are all a little bit like that youngster, only we possess enough ability and competence so that our needs are not always so obvious. But they are there. All of us run into limitations, have to deal with frustrations and disappointments, and most of us realize that few individuals ever really live up to the physical potential that evolution has built into the human body. But mind and body are interconnected, two facets of the same thing. As the body's health improves, so does the health and strength of the mind, and bodybuilding is the ideal vehicle for achieving this necessary balance.

BOOK THREE
Body Part
Exercises

As successful as I may have been in winning bodybuilding competitions, I would be the first to admit that nobody has a completely perfect physique. Certainly, when it came to body parts like chest and biceps, I felt I could stand up to a direct comparison with anyone. But what bodybuilder could say with confidence that he would be willing to compare lats with Franco Columbu, legs with Tom Platz, or shoulders with the massive Bertil Fox? It takes a great set of triceps to compare favorably with the huge arms of Jusup Wilkosz and fantastic stomach muscles to bear comparison with the washboard abdominals of Dennis Tinerino.

For this reason, and to make certain this book represented the absolute best in bodybuilding, I have selected a number of the top champions, known for their outstanding body part development, to help me illustrate the many different exercises in this section of the book.

For the photos of myself used as illustrations, I have selected from my files, and the photo library of Joe Weider, a variety of pictures dating from my earliest competitions right up through the present. This range of photographs shows my physique at every stage of its mature development, creating a picture album of my personal history as well as technically correct bodybuilding illustrations.

The Muscles of the Shoulders

The deltoid is a large, three-headed, thick, triangular muscle which originates from the clavicle and the scapula at the rear of the shoulder and extends down to its insertion in the upper arm.

> **BASIC FUNCTION:** To rotate and lift the arm. The anterior or front deltoid lifts the arm to the front; the medial or side deltoid lifts the arm to the side; the posterior or rear deltoid lifts the arm to the rear.

The trapezius

> **BASIC FUNCTION:** To lift the entire shoulder girdle, draw the scapula up, down, and to either side, and help turn the head

Deltoids

Looking at the Shoulders

In the 1940s men wore coats with huge, padded shoulders and pinched waists, giving them an exaggerated "V" shape (a style that seems to have come back into fashion recently). Coincidentally, that is the shape that bodybuilders work very hard to develop, and a significant part of this look is wide, fully developed shoulders.

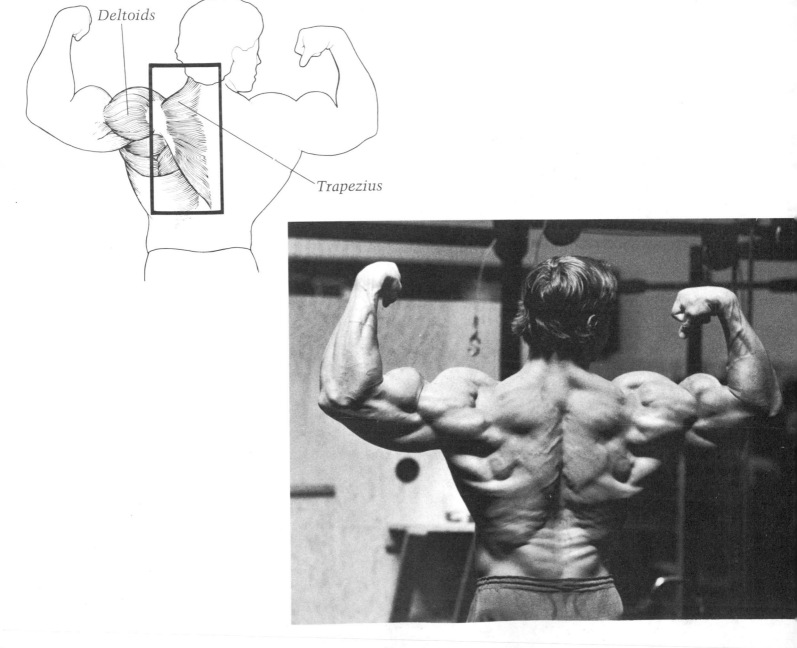

Deltoids

Trapezius

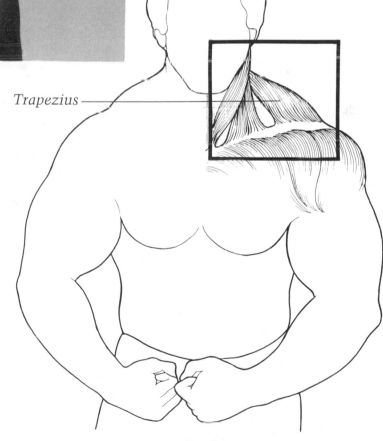

Trapezius

Steve Reeves was one of the first bodybuilders to develop the classic "V" shape. He was able to achieve this look because he had naturally wide shoulders and a small waist. Proportions like this help create the most aesthetic physiques in bodybuilding.

Shoulder width is, to a great extent, determined by skeletal structure. That is something you are born with. A bodybuilder like Reeves, with his very wide shoulder structure, has an enormous advantage, especially when he is standing relaxed. Don Howarth, Dave Draper, and Frank Zane are other good examples of this wide, square-shouldered look.

There is another type of physique which is characterized, not by narrowness through the shoulders, but by a "hanging" look. Reg Park was not narrow, but his traps and shoulders sloped downward. My own shoulders have this same sort of hanging look, so they look much narrower when I stand relaxed than when executing a pose like a lat spread, where the real width becomes apparent.

Steve Reeves

The other factor involved in a wide-shouldered look is the development of the side deltoids. When these muscles are fully developed, you get a very impressive display when they are flexed. Sergio Oliva and Tom Platz, for example, have tremendous shoulder development, yet do not look particularly wide and square when they are standing relaxed on stage. The ideal look for the competition bodybuilder is to have both a square bone structure *and* great side deltoid development. Samir Bannout is a good example.

Incidentally, these bodybuilders noted for fantastic deltoid development are also known for enormous shoulder strength—Behind-the-Neck Presses with 225 pounds and up; Front Presses with 315, as both Sergio and Franco used to do; Ken Waller, with his powerful front deltoids, doing Dumbbell Presses with 140-pound dumbbells.

But width—and the development of the side head of the deltoid—is only one aspect of the *total* development of the deltoid muscles. Shoulders also need to be thick, to show development in the front and the rear, to tie in properly to the pectorals and the biceps as well as the traps and rest of the back.

The deltoids are extremely versatile. They serve to move the arm forward, backward, to the side, up, and around—through a range of motion of nearly 360 degrees. To manage this, the deltoids have three distinct lobes of muscle called "heads": the anterior (front) head, the medial (side) head, and the posterior (rear) head.

The deltoids play a prominent part in virtually every body-

building pose. They add to your width and size in a front double-biceps pose; to your muscularity in a most-muscular pose. The thickness and development of all three heads play an important part in poses seen from the side, such as the side-chest shot or a triceps pose. From the rear, the effect of a pose like the rear double-biceps is highly dependent on how much shape, separation, and definition you have achieved in the rear delts.

Your deltoid development should show definition and striations no matter what movement you make—while hitting all of the above poses as well as when you are moving in transition

Here is Lee Haney displaying a lat spread pose. His square shoulders combined with great deltoid development turn a simple pose into an awesome look.

The square-shouldered look is also a matter of posing. Standing relaxed, I have a hanging-shoulder look . . .

. . . but when I do a front lat spread, you can see how much wider my shoulders appear.

Samir Bannout

Because the deltoids are evident from the front, back, and sides, they play an important part in virtually every pose. For example, Dennis Tinerino doing a side-chest shot . . .

. . . me executing a biceps pose . . .

. . . a most-muscular pose by Franco Columbu . . .

. . . and a fantastic back double-biceps pose by Roy Callender.

Franco Columbu

from one to another. There has to be an interconnection so that the three heads work together and with all the adjacent muscles, thereby giving you a hard, muscular look.

But having complete deltoid development is also important while standing relaxed. From the front and from the back, good side deltoid development makes you look wider. In front, you should have complete separation of the deltoids and pectorals. For some people, this separation is natural; for others, it requires a lot of specialized or "weak point" training. From the side, rear delt development gives you that "bump" in the back of the shoulder that Greg DeFerro and Franco Columbu show so clearly. The rear deltoid also contributes when you are seen from the back, as does the trapezius muscle. (When Greg DeFerro won the Mr.

Greg DeFerro

International Contest in Columbus, I remember taking one look at his massive deltoid development and thinking, "Talk about size and width—he's like an aircraft carrier. You could land airplanes on those deltoids!" And Franco Columbu's shoulders are probably as well developed as anyone's in bodybuilding.)

Of course, shoulder width and deltoid development are actually two different things. Steve Reeves, for example, was not particularly thick and massive through the delts, in spite of his great width. Conversely, Larry Scott, who in the 1960s won the first Mr. Olympia competition, exhibited thick, muscular deltoids, whose massive development offset his natural rather narrow proportions.

Many bodybuilders with comparatively narrow proportions have been saved by great deltoid development. My favorite example of this is Reg Park. Reg worked very hard to compensate for relatively narrow skeletal proportions, and he ended up with enormous shoulder development. He was the first bodybuilder to bench-press 500 pounds, and this was possible only because of the size and strength of his front deltoids, which along with the chest and triceps work very hard in that lift.

One additional thing worth mentioning is that all of these champions I have used as examples of great shoulder development trained very differently. Greg DeFerro, for example, has naturally well-developed rear deltoids but has had to work hard to bring up the front deltoids to the correct proportions. Franco has enormous front deltoids from all the pressing he has done, and so he has had to add a lot of rear deltoid training to his workouts to achieve the correct balance. Larry Scott got his best results in shoulder training using the Stripping Method, starting with heavy weights and going lighter set after set to really burn the deltoids—90-pound dumbbells on down to 30-pound dumbbells.

My point here is that no two individuals have bodies that are exactly alike or will end up training any body part exactly the same. There is not a bodybuilder alive who has never had to adjust his training to overcome weak points in order to create a well-proportioned and balanced physique.

Training the Deltoids

There are two basic kinds of exercises for the shoulders, Laterals and Presses.

Laterals involve lifting your extended arm upward in a wide

Larry Scott

arc. In order to work all three heads, you need to do Laterals to the front, to the side, and to the rear. When you do Laterals, you do not involve the triceps, but almost completely isolate the various heads of the deltoids. However, because you are isolating the deltoids, you cannot lift as much weight as with pressing movements.

In Shoulder Presses, you begin with your arms bent, the weight about shoulder height, and lift the barbell or dumbbells straight up over your head. Because you are straightening your arms as well as lifting upward, Presses involve both the deltoids and the triceps. You can vary the stress on your shoulders to direct it toward the different deltoid heads by doing different kinds of Presses—to the front or rear, using a barbell, dumbbells, or various machines.

Basic Training

I believe in doing a lot of power training to develop shoulders no matter how advanced you are. But power training is perhaps most valuable when you are first beginning. The deltoids respond well to working with heavy weights. This helps your overall development because so many other power exercises—from Bench Presses to Deadlifts to Bent-Over Rows—require a lot of shoulder strength.

Therefore, right from the beginning I recommend you do movements like the Clean and Press, heavy Upright Rows, and Push Presses in addition to Dumbbell Laterals. This kind of program will build up the shoulder mass and strength you need to enable you to go on to Advanced Training. Why I prefer to start beginners out with the Clean and Press exercise rather than just Shoulder Presses is because the extra movement—lifting the barbell off the floor, bringing it up to shoulder height, and tucking the arms in underneath to support it—works so many additional muscles besides the deltoids, specifically the back, traps, and triceps.

Advanced Training

When you get to the level of Advanced Training, you need more than just mass and strength. At this point, you have to work toward overall shoulder development—all three heads of the deltoids as well as the trapezius muscles. Therefore, in addition to exercises like Dumbbell Laterals, designed specifically for the side deltoids, I have included Behind-the-Neck Presses for the front delts, Bent-Over Laterals for the rear delts, and Shrugs to develop the traps. (Incidentally, for those who believe that the trapezius muscles are more associated with the back than the shoulders, just remember that once you have lifted your arm higher than the level of your head in any Lateral or Press movement the traps come heavily into play, pulling the shoulder up and in and allowing you to complete the full range of motion.)

You will also find a number of supersets in this part of the program, to further stress and shock the shoulders, and more specifically isolating exercises like Upright Rows (for the front delts and the traps), Machine Presses (to isolate the front delts and allow you to lower the weight farther than with a barbell), and One-Arm Cable Laterals (which isolate the outside and rear deltoids).

The Competition Program

The function of the deltoids is very complex, enabling your arm to move in virtually a 360-degree circle—and this means that there are many angles at which you can train your shoulders to bring out their full shape and development.

The Competition Program, therefore, introduces a few extra movements such as Lying Incline Laterals and Seated Cable Rear Laterals. There is also a great increase in time intensity, with every exercise done as part of a superset or a tri-set. This intense work is very effective in sculpting and defining the deltoid muscles, bringing in all the tie-ins and creating unbelievable muscular striations.

When training for competition, you have to pay close attention to detail. Not only must each head be developed in proportion, but each must be totally separated from the others, with all three heads clearly defined and visible. Additionally, the deltoid structure must be totally separated from the muscles of the upper arm

In this pose you can see how the front deltoids are clearly separated from the pectorals, a quality you can develop with specific exercises such as Front Dumbbell Raises and Barbell Upright Rows.

as well as from the trapezius and upper back muscles. The front delts also must be clear and distinct from the sweep of the pectoral muscles.

On top of all of this, you need the striations and cross-striations that give you the kind of quality that makes you competitive at the highest levels. Certainly, none of this comes easy. You can't just take any shoulder routine and expect to develop championship deltoids. It takes continually increasing intensity using techniques like supersets, tri-sets, the Stripping Method, and as many of the Shocking Principles as possible. If you find that despite your efforts you still have weak points in your deltoid development, intensive training is the only solution; you need to carefully study the weak point options listed below and decide how to reorganize your workouts to deal with these problems.

I remember training with Franco in 1971 when we did Dumbbell Presses down the rack starting with 100 pounds, then immediately went and punished our delts with Lateral Raises until we were unable to lift our arms. Or sometimes we would do tri-sets: first a front delt exercise, then one for side delts, and finally a set for rear delts. Believe me, after a couple of these our shoulders felt as if they were on fire, with every fiber screaming for mercy.

Training the Trapezius Muscles

The trapezius muscles are the visual center of the upper back, the diamondlike structure that ties together the neck, deltoid, and latissimus muscles. The traps play an important part in both front and rear poses. In shots like the back double-biceps, the traps help to produce that fantastic effect where your muscles ripple from elbow to elbow clear across the top of your back. In a rear lat pose, as your lats come forward and sweep out, the traps form a clear triangle of muscle in the middle of your back. Trap development also helps to separate the rear delts from the upper back. And in most front poses, the line of the traps, from neck to deltoids, is extremely important, especially if you want to be able to do an impressive most-muscular shot.

But the traps have to be developed in proportion to the rest of your body. If they stick up too high and slope down too abruptly, your deltoids will appear too small.

The traps work in opposition to the pulldown function of the lats—they raise the entire shoulder girdle. In the Basic Training Program, I included heavy Upright Rows as part of your power

The traps are important to both front and back poses. For example, see how they help tie the back together in a back double-biceps shot . . .

Bertil Fox

training so that your traps will build mass and strength right from the start. But the traps also benefit from the Barbell Clean and Press and from heavy Deadlifts, which are also included in the Basic Program.

Incidentally, you will get some trap development from Dumbbell Lateral Raises, provided you do them the way I have described in the exercise section, starting with the dumbbells in front of the thighs rather than hanging down by your sides.

In the Advanced Program, I have included Dumbbell Shrugs as part of your trapezius training. These work the traps directly, and you can build up to a tremendous amount of weight in this exercise. You will also find in the Advanced and Competition Programs a number of exercises that train the traps though they are not specifically designed to do so: almost any rowing exercise (Bent-Over Barbell Rows, for example) or Shoulder Press (barbell or dumbbell) involves a lifting motion of the traps as well as other muscle functions. And strong traps help you to use heavier weight in all of these other movements.

Weak Point Training

If shoulders are a weak point in your physique, adjust your training so that you do more sets and more exercises for shoulders, and use as many of the Shocking Principles as possible to work that area with maximum intensity.

I like to use the Stripping Method for shoulders. With dumbbells, you start with heavy weights and move on down the rack; with Machine Presses or Cable Laterals, you just keep moving the pin one plate lighter each set.

Another way of accelerating deltoid development is by supersetting Presses and Lateral Raises—for example, a Barbell Press followed by Front Dumbbell Raises (or Upright Rows) in order to completely blitz the front delts. For a really intense delt workout, try doing a 3-Pump Set: Presses, Front Dumbbell Raises, *and* Upright Rows. But be prepared to bear the pain.

To get the best results from Laterals, remember two things:

1. Keep your palm turned downward throughout the movement; or, even better, turn the hand a little farther so that the little finger is higher than the thumb (like pouring water out of a pitcher). This helps to isolate the deltoids and make them fully contract during the movement.

2. Be as strict as possible. Raise the weight without any cheating, and lower it fully under control. The stricter you are, the more intense the effect on the deltoids.

Another way of increasing the intensity of your deltoid training is, after each set of Dumbbell Raises, go over to the rack, take a heavier set of weights, and just lift them out to the side as far as possible and hold them there as long as you can. This "isometric lateral" will help to fully exhaust the deltoids and bring out maximum striations.

As a way of getting extra development in the rear deltoids, I used to leave a light dumbbell—usually 20 pounds—under my bed and, first thing in the morning, would do five sets of Lying Dumbbell Raises with each hand without stopping. However, I never counted this as part of my regular shoulder workout. I also did a 2-Pump Set, starting with face-down Incline Lateral Raises and, when I was too tired to continue the set, changing to a kind of Dumbbell Rowing motion to fully exhaust the rear delts.

Following are extra exercises and techniques you can use to develop a specific area that you have identified as a weak point.

Front deltoids

Machine Presses, because you can lower the weight farther with machines than with barbells or dumbbells, thereby stretching the front deltoids to the maximum and getting a longer range of motion

Do not lock out on top in any press movement.

Use dumbbells whenever possible to stress each individual front deltoid in isolation.

Arnold Press—my favorite front delt exercise—especially using techniques like Running the Rack (p. 164) or the Stripping Method (p. 162)

Front Dumbbell Raises for maximum front deltoid and pectoral separation
Front Barbell Presses
Upright Rows
Incline Barbell and Dumbbell Presses
Incline Dumbbell Flys

Many bodybuilders forget that front deltoids are also important to back poses. Franco Columbu demonstrates how the front deltoids are visible in a back double-biceps shot.

You can see in this semi-relaxed pose how the front deltoids, besides having mass and separation, can also be extremely defined and striated.

In all Presses, the forearms should be held straight, not out to the side, which overinvolves triceps.

The side deltoids help to create a very wide look, even in this pose by Serge Nubret that is basically an abdominal pose.

Seen from the side, the development of the side deltoid creates separation from the trapezius above and from the triceps and biceps below.

Side deltoids	Dumbbell Laterals—beginning with the dumbbells held beside the thighs instead of in front while standing straight or sitting on a bench with your back straight
	Cable Laterals, raising your arm from the side of the body, not across the front
	Do super-strict Laterals (not letting the weight rise above your head, to ensure that the delts do the work instead of the trapezius).
	Do "burns" after your Lateral Raises (taking very heavy dumbbells and holding them out with totally straight arms about 10 inches from your thighs for as long as possible—but at least 30 seconds).

*Shoulder width from good
side deltoid development
increases the effectiveness of
a front lat spread.*

This three-quarter back pose by Franco Columbu demonstrates the necessity of having good rear deltoid development.

Total shoulder development —the traps, the front, side, and rear deltoids, and the separation and definition of all the muscles involved—is extremely important in a most-muscular shot.

Rear deltoids

Use the Priority Principle (p. 160), beginning your deltoid training with rear delt movements.

Add extra rear delt sets: Bent-Over Laterals, Bent-Over Cable Laterals, Bent-Over Barbell Rows, Seated Cable Rear Laterals, Incline Bench Lateral Raises (face down), or Lying Side Laterals—try 10 sets for each arm done continuously without stopping (I used to do this every day, whether it was a shoulder day or not).

Take extra care to work the rear delts with the strictest technique possible, since any cheating will allow other muscle groups to do too much of the work.

In all Rear Laterals, twist the wrist as if pouring water from a pitcher in order to increase rear delt development.

Trapezius	Shrugs
	Upright Rows
	Deadlifts
	Clean and Press
	Reverse Laterals (very popular with British bodybuilders, these work the traps from an unusual angle as well as hitting the front delts)
	Rowing exercises, such as T-Bar Rows and Cable Rows
	Cable and Dumbbell Laterals

This twisting back pose is one that does not work at all unless you have well-developed rear deltoids along with all the other important back muscles.

Arnold Press

Purpose of Exercise: TO DEVELOP THE FRONT HEAD OF THE DELTOIDS. This is the very best deltoid exercise I know, and I always include it in my shoulder routine. By using dumbbells in this manner—lowering them well down in front— you get a tremendous range of motion.

Execution: (1) In a standing position, elbows at sides, grasp two dumbbells and raise them to your shoulders, palms turned toward you. (2) In one smooth motion, press the weights up overhead—not quite to the point where they are locked out—and at the same time rotate your hands, thumbs turning inward, so that your palms face forward at the top of the movement. (3) Hold here for a moment, then reverse the movement, lowering the weights and rotating your hands back to the starting position. Don't get so concerned with pressing the weight overhead that you begin to sway and cheat; this movement should be done strictly, keeping the dumbbells fully under control. By not locking the arms out when you press the weight overhead, you keep the stress on the deltoids the whole time. This exercise is half Lateral Raise and half Dumbbell Press, and works both the anterior and medial heads of the deltoids thoroughly.

Press Behind the Neck

Purpose of Exercise: TO TRAIN THE FRONT AND SIDE DELTOIDS.
Any pressing movement also involves the triceps, as well.

Execution: You can do these Presses standing, but I prefer doing them sitting, since it makes the movement stricter. (1) Either lift the barbell overhead and set it down on your shoulders behind your head, or lift it off the rack of a seated press bench. (I personally prefer to hold the bar with a thumbless grip.) (2) Press the weight straight up and then lower it again, keeping it under control, and keeping your elbows as far back as possible during the movement.

Bertil Fox

Dumbbell Presses

Purpose of Exercise: TO TRAIN THE FRONT DELTOIDS.

This exercise may seem to be similar to Barbell Presses of various kinds, but there are important differences, the most significant being the greater range of motion you get using the dumbbells.

Execution: (1) Hold the dumbbells at shoulder height, elbows out to the sides, palms facing forward. (2) Lift the dumbbells straight up until they touch at the top, then lower them again as far as possible. You will find that you are able to both raise and lower the dumbbells farther than you can a barbell, although the need to control two weights independently means that you are lifting slightly less poundage.

Military Press

Purpose of Exercise: TO TRAIN THE FRONT DELTOIDS.

This is the granddaddy of shoulder exercises. When done from a seated position the movement will be stricter than when standing.

Execution. (1) From a sitting or standing position, grasp a barbell with an overhand grip and hold it at shoulder level, palms underneath for support, hands about shoulder-width apart, elbows tucked in and under. (2) From a position about even with the collarbone, lift the bar straight up overhead until your arms are locked out, being careful to keep the weight balanced and under control. Lower the weight back to the starting position.

Clean and Press

Purpose of Exercise: TO TRAIN THE FRONT DELTOIDS AND BUILD UPPER-BODY DENSITY AND POWER.
"Cleaning" a weight is a method of lifting a barbell from the floor to the starting position of the Military Press. The Clean and Press is an important exercise that starts off with a lot of leg movement to get the weight moving, then involves the traps, arms, and back as well as the shoulders to help you develop a truly Herculean look.

Execution: (1) Squat down, lean forward, and take hold of the bar with an overhand grip, hands about shoulder width apart. (2) Driving with the legs, lift the bar straight up to about shoulder height, then tuck the elbows in and under to support the weight in the starting position of the Military Press. (3) Then, using your shoulders and arms, press the weight up overhead, bring it back down to shoulder height, then reverse the cleaning motion by bending your knees and setting the weight back onto the floor.

Machine Presses

Purpose of Exercise: TO
TRAIN THE SHOULDERS.
Doing Presses on a machine
helps you to do the
movements very strictly, and
allows you to avoid cleaning a
weight if you have some sort
of physical problem. Also, you
can let the weight come down
much lower, which gives you
extra stretch in your front
delts. There are any number of
machines on which you can
do a Shoulder Press
movement (Universal,
Nautilus, Smith), but the
principle remains the same.

Execution: (1) Grasp the bar or
handles at shoulder level and
(2) press upward until your
arms are locked out, then
come back down slowly to the
starting position, going
through the longest range of
motion possible. You can also
use machines to do Front
Presses or Behind-the-Neck
Presses; both will work the
front deltoids.

*Behind-the-Neck Machine
Press*

Push Press

Purpose of Exercise: TO USE A HEAVIER THAN NORMAL WEIGHT, OR TO CONTINUE TO DO REPETITIONS OF SHOULDER PRESSES AFTER REACHING A POINT OF FAILURE; TO DEVELOP ADDITIONAL DELTOID STRENGTH.

This is a "Cheating Principle" exercise. You can use it in power training to lift a barbell that you would normally find too heavy to use for strict Shoulder Presses. You can also use the Push Press to do forced reps at the end of a set, when you are too tired to continue to do strict Shoulder Press reps.

Execution: (1) Taking hold of a barbell with an overhand grip, hands slightly wider than shoulder width apart, clean the weight up to shoulder height. Bend your knees slightly and then press up with your legs to get the bar moving. Use this additional impetus to press the bar up overhead. Lock it out, then slowly lower once more to shoulder position.

Standing Lateral Raises

Purpose of Exercise: TO DEVELOP THE OUTSIDE HEAD OF THE DELTOID, WITH SOME BENEFIT TO THE REAR HEAD.

Execution: (1) Take a dumbbell in each hand, bend forward slightly, and bring the weights together in front of you at arm's length. Start each repetition from a dead stop to keep yourself from swinging the weight up. (2) Lift the weights out and up to either side, turning your wrists slightly (as if pouring water out of a pitcher) so that the rear of the dumbbell is higher than the front (this helps to involve the rear head of the deltoid). Lift the weights to a point slightly higher than your shoulders, then lower them slowly, resisting all the way down. (A common mistake with this movement is to rock back and forth and swing the weights up instead of lifting them with the deltoids. Doing this cuts down on the effectiveness of the movement and should be avoided.)

VARIATION: You may have a tendency to cheat a little when doing Standing Lateral Raises. However, this can be avoided if the same exercise is done in a seated position.

Seated Lateral Raises

Bertil Fox doing Standing Lateral Raises as a power movement with very heavy weights.

One-Arm Cross Cable Laterals

Purpose of Exercise: TO WORK THE OUTSIDE HEAD OF THE DELTOID AND BENEFIT THE REAR HEAD IN ISOLATION.

Doing One-Arm Laterals with a cable and floor pulley gives you two advantages: it allows you to isolate first one side of the body, then the other; and the cable provides constant tension unaffected by your motion relative to the pull of gravity.

Execution: (1) Grab the handle and stand with your arm down and across your body, your free hand on your hip. (2) With a steady motion, pull outward and upward until your hand is just slightly higher than your shoulder. Twist your wrist as you raise your arm as if you were pouring a pitcher of water. Do your reps with one hand, then an equal number with the other. Don't lift the weight by raising up with your body—use the deltoids.

VARIATION: Try doing the movement with the cable running behind your back instead of in front.

One-Arm Cable Laterals done from the rear will give you more separation between the delts and the upper arm.

If you have a weak point in the rear delts, bending forward slightly while doing Cable Laterals works this area in addition to the side delts.

One-Arm Side Cable Laterals

Purpose of Exercise: TO ISOLATE THE SIDE HEAD OF THE DELTOID.
This movement, which was a favorite of Sergio Oliva, helps bring out definition in the shoulders, and works the side and rear deltoid heads together.

Execution: (1) Stand upright, with your arm down beside you holding on to a handle attached to a floor-level pulley. Place your other hand on your hip. (2) Keeping your arm straight, lift it up in an arc in one smooth motion until it is higher than your head. Lower your arm back to your thigh. Finish your repetitions, then repeat using the other arm.

Seated One-Arm Cross Cable Laterals

Purpose of Exercise: TO DEVELOP THE REAR DELTOIDS.

Execution: (1) Sitting on a stool or low bench, take hold of a handle attached to a floor-level pulley in such a way that your arm is fully extended across the front of your body. (2) Keeping your body as still as possible, pull the handle across and up until your arm is fully extended to the side at about shoulder height. (3) At the top of the movement flex your rear deltoid to get a really full contraction. Lower the weight back to the starting position. Finish your repetitions, then repeat with the other arm.

Isolating and flexing the rear deltoid when reaching the top position of the Cable Lateral

Reverse Overhead Dumbbell Laterals

Purpose of Exercise: TO DEVELOP THE FRONT DELTOIDS.

This exercise, a favorite of British bodybuilders, also helps to develop the traps.

Execution: (1) Take a dumbbell in each hand, then extend your arms straight out to either side, palms turned up. (2) Slowly lift your arms up and bring them together over your head. Your arms do not have to be locked out on top. Keep your body steady during the entire movement. From the top, lower the dumbbells slowly down to the starting position.

MACHINE LATERALS
Various machines have been developed that attempt to duplicate the lateral movement of the deltoids, yet not involve any appreciable stress on the wrists, elbows, or upper arms. When using these machines, either with one arm at a time or both together, concentrate on feeling the deltoids lift the arm from a position at your side all the way up through the entire range of motion of the machine and then back down again under control, resisting the pull of gravity from the weight stack at all times.

Front Dumbbell Raises

Purpose of Exercise: TO DEVELOP THE FRONT HEAD OF THE DELTOIDS.

This exercise not only works the front head of the deltoids through its entire range of motion, but helps to create separation between the deltoids and the pectoral muscles. It can be done either standing or sitting.

Execution: Stand with a dumbbell in each hand, held slightly away from you against the front of the thighs. (1) Lift one weight out and up in a wide arc until it is higher than the top of your head. (2) Lower the weight under control while simultaneously lifting the other weight, so that both arms are in motion at the same time and the dumbbells pass each other at a point in front of your face. In order to work the front head of the deltoids directly, make certain that the dumbbells pass in front of your face rather than out to the side. To do this same movement with a barbell, grasp the bar with an overhand grip, let it hang down at arm's length in front of you, and with arms kept locked, lift it to a point just higher than your head, staying as strict as possible, then lower it again under control.

VARIATION: Do Front Raises in a seated position for a stricter movement, since you can't use your body to cheat on the lifts.

Seated Front Dumbbell Raises

Seated Bent-Over Dumbbell Laterals

Purpose of Exercise: TO ISOLATE AND WORK THE REAR HEAD OF THE DELTOIDS.

By bending over while executing a Lateral, you force the posterior head of the deltoids to work more directly. Doing them seated allows you to do a stricter movement than when standing.

Execution: (1) Sit on the end of a bench, knees together, and take a dumbbell in each hand. Bend forward from the waist and bring the dumbbells together behind your calves. Turn your hands so that your palms face one another. (2) Keeping your body steady, lift the weights out to either side, turning your wrists so that the thumbs are lower than the little fingers. Be careful not to lift up your body as you lift the weights. With your arms just slightly bent, lift the dumbbells to a point just higher than your head, then, keeping your knees together, lower them again slowly to behind your calves, resisting all the way down. Try not to cheat doing this exercise. And be sure you are lifting straight out to either side; the tendency doing this exercise is to let the weights drift back behind your shoulders.

Standing Bent-Over Dumbbell Laterals

Purpose of Exercise: TO DEVELOP THE REAR DELTOIDS.

Execution: (1) Stand with a dumbbell in either hand. Bend forward from the waist about 45 degrees, letting the dumbbells hang at arm's length below you, palms facing one another. (2) Without raising your body, lift the weights out to the side, turning your wrists so that the thumb ends up lower than the little finger. (Don't allow your arms to drift back behind your shoulders.) Lower the weights again under control, resisting all the way down.

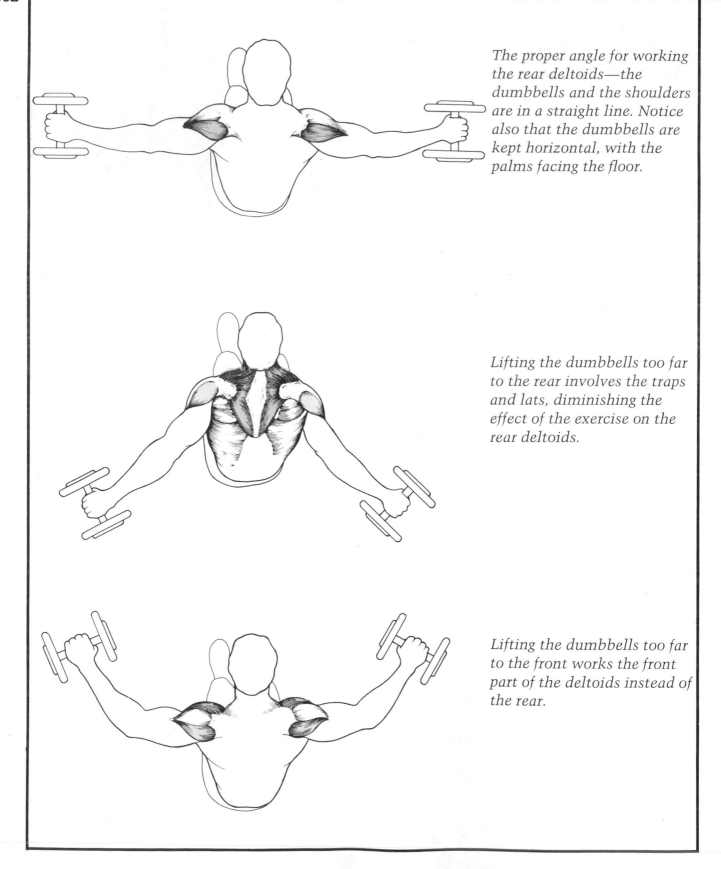

The proper angle for working the rear deltoids—the dumbbells and the shoulders are in a straight line. Notice also that the dumbbells are kept horizontal, with the palms facing the floor.

Lifting the dumbbells too far to the rear involves the traps and lats, diminishing the effect of the exercise on the rear deltoids.

Lifting the dumbbells too far to the front works the front part of the deltoids instead of the rear.

Bent-Over Cable Laterals

Purpose of Exercise: TO WORK THE REAR HEAD OF THE DELTOIDS.

By using cables, you get a slightly longer range of motion with continuous resistance throughout the movement. This is one of Franco Columbu's favorite rear deltoid exercises, and his rear delts are fantastic.

Execution: (1) Using two floor-level pulleys, take a handle in each hand with your arms crossed in front of your body (left hand holding right-side cable, right hand the left-side cable). Keeping your back straight, bend over until your torso is about parallel to the floor. (2) With a smooth pull, draw the handles across your body and extend your arms straight out to either side, turning your wrists slightly, thumbs down, as if pouring a pitcher of water. Stretch as far as possible, then release and let your arms come back slowly across your body as far as they can.

Lying Side Laterals

Purpose of Exercise: TO ISOLATE EACH REAR DELTOID.

This exercise is recommended by Serge Nubret, and will work wonders for both your rear and side deltoids. It should be done only with a moderate weight, and performed very strictly.

Execution: Preferably, you should use an abdominal board set at an angle. You can do the movement without a board, but it shortens the range of motion when you do. (1) Lie on your side, with your head raised. Holding a dumbbell in one hand, lower it almost to the floor. (2) Then raise it up all the way over your head. Remember to twist your hand slightly while lifting, turning the thumb down, to further contract the rear deltoid. When you have done the reps with one arm, turn over and do an equal number for the other side.

Upright Rows

Purpose of Exercise: TO DEVELOP THE TRAPEZIUS AND THE FRONT DELTOIDS, AND CREATE SEPARATION BETWEEN DELTOIDS AND PECTORALS.

Execution: (1) Stand grasping a barbell with an overhand grip, hands a few inches apart. Let the bar hang straight down in front of you. (2) Lift it straight up, keeping it close to your body, until the bar just about touches your chin. Keep your back straight and feel the traps contract as you do the movement. Your whole shoulder girdle should rise as you lift the weight. From the top, lower it once more under control to the starting position.

  This is an exercise that you should do strictly, not cheating or swinging the weight up, keeping your body still, and making sure that you feel the traps working as well as the biceps and front delts. (You can substitute a short bar and cable for the barbell and use Cable Upright Rows as a variation. The constant resistance of the cable helps you to do the movement as strictly as possible.)

Heavy Upright Rows

Purpose of Exercise: A HEAVY CHEATING MOVEMENT TO STRENGTHEN THE ENTIRE SHOULDER GIRDLE AND UPPER BACK.

Execution: (1) Choose a heavy barbell and grasp it with an overhand grip, hands about 12 inches apart. Let the bar hang down at arm's length in front of you. (2) Lift the bar straight up to a point just below your chin, allowing yourself to cheat by swaying with the back, pushing with the legs, and even helping with the calves. As you lift, keep your elbows out and up higher than the bar. Then lower the bar back to the starting position. Remember, this is a power movement in which cheating plays a vital part. This makes Heavy Upright Rows quite a different exercise from standard Upright Rows, which must be done very strictly.

Dumbbell Shrugs

Purpose of Exercise: TO DEVELOP THE TRAPEZIUS MUSCLES.

This exercise can be done extremely heavy to thicken the traps, which really helps you in doing back poses.

Execution: Stand upright, arms at sides, a heavy dumbbell in each hand. Raise your shoulders up as high as you can, as if trying to touch them to your ears. Hold at the top for a moment, then release and return to the starting position. Try not to move anything but your shoulders.

Barbell Shrugs

Purpose of Exercise: TO DEVELOP THE TRAPEZIUS MUSCLES.

Execution: Stand upright holding a barbell at arm's length using an overhand grip. Raise your shoulders as high as you can, as if trying to touch them to your ears. Hold for a moment at the top, then lower them back to the starting position.

Instead of a barbell, you can also do this exercise by holding on to the handles of a Universal Bench Press machine.

THE CHEST

The Muscles of the Chest

The **pectorals** consist of two parts, the clavicular (upper) portion and the sternal (lower) portion. The upper part is attached to the clavicle (collarbone). Along the mid-body line, it attaches to the sternum (breastbone) and the cartilage of several ribs. The largest mass of the pectorals starts at the upper arm bone (humerus), fastened at a point under and just above where the deltoids attach to the humerus. The pectorals spread out like a fan and cover the rib cage like armor plates. Attached to the rib cage in the center and across to the shoulder, this muscle lets you perform such motions as pitching a ball underhanded, doing a wide-arm Bench Press, twisting a cap off a bottle, swimming with the crawl stroke, and doing parallel bar Dips. In addition, because of its attachment to the humerus, it plays a large role in movements like Chinning. There is, in fact, a prominent interdependence between chest and back muscles. The chest will not reach its full potential size unless the latissimus dorsi muscles of the upper back are fully developed.

> **BASIC FUNCTION**: To pull the arm and shoulder across the front of the body

The **subclavicus,** a small cylindrical muscle between the clavicle and the first rib

> **BASIC FUNCTION**: To draw the shoulder forward

The **serratus anterior,** a thin muscular sheet between the ribs and the scapula

> **BASIC FUNCTION**: To rotate the scapula, raising the point of the shoulder and drawing the scapula forward and downward

Total Chest Development

A really deep, well-shaped chest is one of most important qualities in a bodybuilding physique. To achieve this requires training with a variety of exercises—to develop the upper and lower pectorals, the inside and outside pectorals, and the tie-ins to the deltoids, and to expand the entire rib cage to show off the pectoral muscles to their best advantage.

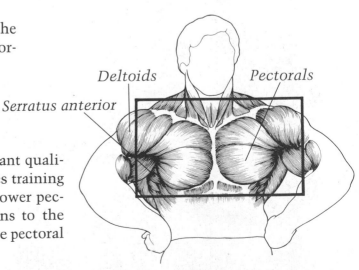

Deltoids   *Pectorals*

Serratus anterior

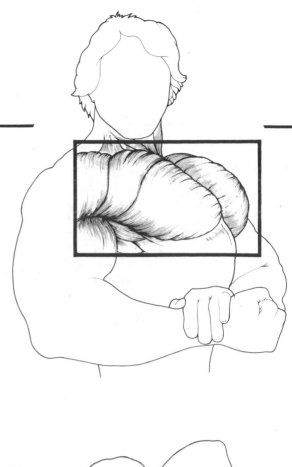

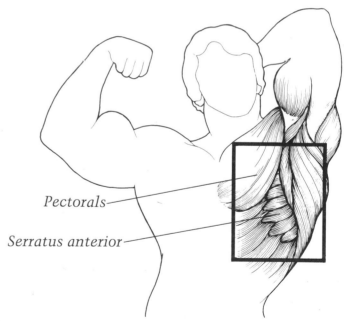

Pectorals

Serratus anterior

But perfecting the chest is more difficult than many body-builders believe. You can have a huge rib cage and huge, thick pectoral muscles, but this will not guarantee a perfect chest. Chest perfection, especially if you are interested in competition, involves *all* of the following:

1. A great rib cage
2. Thick pectoral muscles
3. Development of the inside, outside, upper and lower areas of the pectorals

This is what you need to make a side-chest pose really effective: a great rib cage under big, fully developed pectoral muscles.

Thick pectoral muscles complement deltoid and upper-arm muscularity in a straight-arm side pose.

When Franco Columbu hits a chest pose you can see every area of the chest clearly delineated—the upper and lower chest, the separation of upper chest from deltoids, the inner pectorals, and the tie-in of the chest to the serratus.

4. Visible striations when the pectorals are flexed, such as in a most-muscular shot, with the striations showing from the middle of the rib cage all the way across and from top to bottom
5. A clear separation of upper and lower pectorals
6. A shape that gives a nice square look, achieved by a lot of upper pectoral development, rather than one in which the muscle seems simply to be hanging down
7. Sufficient development so that the pectorals don't totally disappear when you lift your arms over your head or do a front double-biceps shot

The chest program I have included in this book is specifically designed to help you to achieve complete pectoral development as outlined above.

Of course, some bodybuilders are extremely lucky in their genetic potential for chest development. Sergio Oliva used to do only one kind of exercise for the chest—Bench Presses—and his chest muscles would rise like a loaf of bread. Reg Park is gifted with an enormous rib cage, making his pectoral development all the more impressive. John Grimek also displayed a wonderful rib cage that made his chest poses look terrific. As a former power lifter, Franco Columbu has developed his chest so that the split

The chest is the centerpiece of the most-muscular pose. Notice how the striations of the pectorals hold together all the other elements: the traps, front delts, arms, and abdominals.

Franco Columbu probably has the most separation of upper and lower chest of anyone in bodybuilding.

Serge Nubret's chest development is complete, including upper and lower, inner and outer pectorals. That's what gives him the desired "square" shape.

between upper and lower pecs is awesome. Sometimes we used to jokingly refer to this vast chasm as the "Grand Canyon."

But, genetically gifted or not, if you want to be a complete bodybuilder you need to develop your chest properly, and this means making up with skill, effort, and technique for what nature may have neglected to hand you on a silver platter.

As Steve Reeves demonstrates, with proper chest development your pectorals will not disappear when you lift your arms above your head.

Mike Katz's most outstanding body part is his chest, with a huge rib cage under massively developed pectorals.

Really thick pectorals allow a bodybuilder to hit a lot of very impressive poses. Casey Viator has always been known for his massive, Herculean chest development.

Training the Chest

There are two basic kinds of exercises for the chest: Flys, in which the extended arms are drawn together across the chest in a kind of "hugging" motion; and Presses, in which the weight is pressed upward off the chest with the involvement of the front deltoids and triceps in addition to a primary effort from the pectorals. The basic Bench Press is done with a barbell on a flat bench and is an all-time favorite exercise of bodybuilders as well as one of the three movements used in power lifting competition. If you do Bench Presses correctly—using the proper grip and getting the fullest range of motion possible—you will be able to develop the overall mass of the chest.

However, changing the angle of the Bench Press—by doing it on an incline, for example—you transfer more of the effort from the middle pectorals to the upper pectorals and front deltoids. I believe in including Incline Presses in your program right from the beginning so that you don't find your upper pecs are underdeveloped relative to the middle and lower portions of your chest. Also, doing a lot of Incline Presses will help you to create that split between upper and lower chest that is so impressive in most-muscular poses.

As with training other muscles, the greater the range of motion you get in chest exercises, the more intense the muscle contraction you achieve—which ultimately leads to the maximum amount of muscle growth. Therefore, especially when you are doing Flys, it is very important to stretch the pectorals as much as you can. This helps to develop maximum flexibility, and increased flexibility results in more development. This is why so many of the top bodybuilders, as massive as you can imagine, are also flexible enough to twist themselves into pretzels.

But simply having large pectoral muscles is not enough if they are hung on a small, unimpressive rib cage. And so you need to find a way to expand the rib cage as much as possible. This is accomplished by very strictly performed Dumbbell Pullovers. Be aware, however, that Pullovers performed on machines do not have the same effect. When you are locked into a machine the latissimus muscles bear most of the stress, so you do not get as much expansion of the rib cage.

As you progress in your training, you need to build on the basics and pay more attention to details. That is when I recommend including in your program a lot of Dumbbell Flys, Cable Crossovers, Dips, and other pectoral exercises—so that *every* area is reached for complete pectoral development.

Also, as you become more advanced, the program is designed so that you superset chest training with back movements, because I believe that the pectorals, like the lats, need to be stretched as much as possible as well as developed by resistance exercise. Therefore, after you do an exercise like a Bench Press, you should immediately go to something like Chins, which stretch the pecs to the fullest. This is also a highly time-efficient way to train, since you can work a different set of muscles while the first group is recuperating, making your workouts go much faster and burning off extra calories.

In the Advanced Program you also need to concern yourself with the serratus muscles, which are just below and to the side of the chest. The serratus will be dealt with in a special section, along with the intercostals. Development of these muscles shows the judges that you have achieved a high degree of quality as well as mass.

Beginning and Advanced Programs

In my own early training, I practiced what I am now preaching: I started with the basics—Bench and Incline Presses, Dumbbell Flys, Dips, and Pullovers. After three years I was still doing only these five basic chest exercises.

When I moved to Munich after having been training for about four years, my pectorals were huge and I had certain weaknesses —upper pecs, for example. There I began training with my friend Reinhard Smolana, who showed me a very different kind of pectoral training. We would begin by doing Incline Presses standing and leaning back against a bench—which meant we had to clean the weight, fall back against the bench, do the set, then manage to stand upright again and put the weight back down. Only after we finished our Incline Press sets would we go on and do Bench Presses and Flys.

Even at age twenty, after only about five years of training, my concentration on heavy chest exercises gave me a huge rib cage and massive, powerful pectoral muscles.

This emphasis on Incline Presses had its effect—after a while my upper pecs grew enormously until I could literally stand a glass of water on the upper part of my chest when I hit a side-chest shot. This was an important lesson for me as to how a change in one's training program can overcome a weak point.

Incidentally, this particular way of doing Incline Presses, having to clean the weight and handle the bar as I was falling back against the bench, gave me a secondary benefit—it enabled me to develop enormous strength, and with that strength came the added thickness and density that results from power training with heavy weights.

By increasing the development of my upper pecs, I was learning two important lessons about how to sculpt the body and train for physical perfection: (1) It pays to put special emphasis on weak areas, especially to train them first when you are strong and fresh (Priority Principle); and (2) changing your training routine so that the body has to perform in unexpected ways accelerates development (Shocking Principle).

I also discovered how much the training ideas in any gym affect those who train there: in Austria, where the first exercise bodybuilders wanted to do was Curls, everyone had great biceps; in Munich, where we all used the same chest routine, everyone had good upper pecs; in Reg Park's gym, everyone had terrific calves and deltoids, just like Reg, but relatively less developed pecs because Reg himself believes excessive pec development interferes with the impressiveness of shoulder width.

It was also in the early days that I discovered the advantages of stretching the pectoral muscles while training them. Doing Dumbbell Flys or cable exercises, I would always stretch the chest muscles to their limit and then frequently include some back movements to further stretch the pecs.

One's particular anatomy can make certain exercises more or less effective. Bodybuilders like Greg DeFerro, with huge, barrel-like chests and short arms, get very little out of doing regular Bench Presses unless they use an extraordinary amount of weight. When DeFerro lowers the bar down to his massive chest and then lifts the bar back up, because of his relatively short arms he has limited range of motion, so the pectorals never get the kind of workout they need. People with this body type usually need to include more Incline Presses in their workouts or do Presses with dumbbells instead of a barbell so that they can lower the weights down past the top of the chest. This doesn't mean they shouldn't do Barbell Bench Presses at all, just that they must also include exercises with a greater range of motion. (I have also seen a bar used that has a curve in the middle, allowing you to drop your hands much lower when doing a Bench Press and thereby extending the range of motion considerably.)

Ken Waller has enormously strong front deltoids. When he does a Bench Press, his delts get a tremendous pump and his pectorals seem hardly to work at all. So Ken has always relied a lot on Incline Dumbbell Presses instead and done a lot of Decline Presses, which don't allow the participation of the front delts.

In all matters involving your genetic inheritance and your natural leverage advantages and disadvantages, you are going to have to learn to adjust your training accordingly.

Competition Program

When I first came to the United States I already had plenty of size, so I began to concentrate on detail training. I developed a more sophisticated program with additional exercises which included a lot of isolation movements for each of the important pectoral areas. Experts like Vince Gironda gave me a lot of ideas, and so I went from simply having huge pecs to having a first-rate, quality chest development.

Each time I competed I learned something more. Gradually, I mastered all of the training principles outlined in this book—from the Stripping Method to forced reps and so on. And I learned from competitors like Serge Nubret, Frank Zane, and Franco Columbu that it takes a lot of dieting and, especially, endless hours of posing to give the chest the totally finished, muscular and defined look.

I have always gotten good results finishing off my chest workout with a tri-set—for example, a set of Cable Flys, then Dips, followed by Cable Crossovers. This pumps an enormous amount of blood into the area and forces you to go all out at the end—rather than pacing yourself and taking it easy—to make you hard, defined, and competition-ready.

As you prepare for competition, you need to concern yourself with even more specific details—things that you would hardly notice at other times suddenly become major weak points. For example, I have seen bodybuilders hitting a side-chest pose and showing striations in the inner pecs, but not farther up on the chest. This kind of detail can make a big difference in a close contest. Therefore, I would advise these bodybuilders to superset Incline Presses (with barbell or dumbbells) with Cable Crossovers to rectify this weakness.

Serge Nubret has developed one of the most balanced chests in the world, with every one of the pectoral areas in complete proportion to the rest.

Sergio Oliva used to force his muscles to work in harder and unexpected ways by only doing three-quarter movements, lifting the bar off his chest in a Bench Press, for example, but not going all the way up, so that the triceps never came into play in the movement and his chest never got any rest at all. After using this method of training for just a few months, I found my chest became much harder-looking and more defined—which shows you how relatively small alterations in your training technique can make very substantial differences in your physique.

The Competition Program for chest is designed on a "push-pull" basis, combining movements for chest and back done as supersets and tri-sets. Combining these exercises gives you a tremendous pump, and will really blast your chest muscles and give them the size, shape, definition and tie-ins you need for successful competition.

Supersets like Weighted Chins plus Incline Bench Presses, flat Bench Presses plus Wide-Grip Chins, and Dumbbell Flys plus Bent-Over Barbell Rows keep the back and chest pumped at the same time and allow you to train pectorals and lats each in turn—muscles which work in opposition to one another—so that one has a chance to rest while the other does a set. And, since you are dealing with opposing muscles, every set for back helps to stretch the pectorals while they are recuperating for the next chest set.

Weak Point Training

As with any other body part, once you have been training for a while you are likely to notice that some areas of the chest are developing better and more rapidly than others. To correct this imbalance, you will have to alter your program and include more exercises to stimulate the areas that are lagging behind.

Following is a list of exercises for improving each area of the chest.

Upper pectorals	Incline Presses with barbell or dumbbells or Smith machine
	Incline Flys
Lower pectorals	Decline Presses with barbell or dumbbells or machines
	Dips
	Decline Flys
	Cable Flys

Inner chest	Cable Crossovers Presses or Flys holding contraction at top for several seconds Bench Presses done with narrow grip
Outer chest	Dumbbell Flys concentrating on full stretch and lower range of motion Dips Incline Presses and Bench Presses done with wide grip and lower ¾ movement Dumbbell Flys Dumbbell Bench Presses stretching at bottom, coming up only three-quarters of the way and not letting dumbbells touch Incline Presses with bar
Rib cage	Dumbbell and Barbell Pullovers

When you have a weak point in chest development, train your pectorals according to the Priority Principle, doing the exercise for that weak area first, when you are fresh and at your strongest. In the early stages of my career, I always felt I suffered from a comparative lack of upper pectoral development. So I would begin my chest training with Barbell Incline Presses followed by Dumbbell Incline Presses to really hit this area. Only then would I go on to regular Bench Presses and the rest of my chest routine.

But there are times when this kind of specialized weak point training is not justified. For example, if you have problems with the inner chest, I would not recommend starting out your routine with an exercise like Cable Crossovers. Instead, try to work on this area as you are doing the rest of your chest workout—perhaps locking out all of your pressing movements, and really tensing and contracting the inner pecs. Then, at the end of your workout, you could add on some extra Cable Crossovers or other exercises specifically designed to hit the inner chest.

The same thing can be done for outer chest development. You can emphasize this area during your routine by lowering the weights a few inches farther when doing Dumbbell Flys and also by getting the fullest possible stretch with other pectoral exercises. You don't have to schedule specific outer pec movements at the top of your routine in order to deal with this weak point the way you would if your problem was the upper, lower, or middle chest. The most adjustment I would recommend for inner

This is the proper way to do Narrow-Grip Bench Presses: Keeping the elbows out and away from the body at the bottom of the movement . . .

. . . allows a full contraction of the pectorals at the top, which helps to develop the inner part of the chest.

This shot of Roy Callender shows clearly the sharp and defined development of his inner chest.

Taking a wide grip on the bar . . .

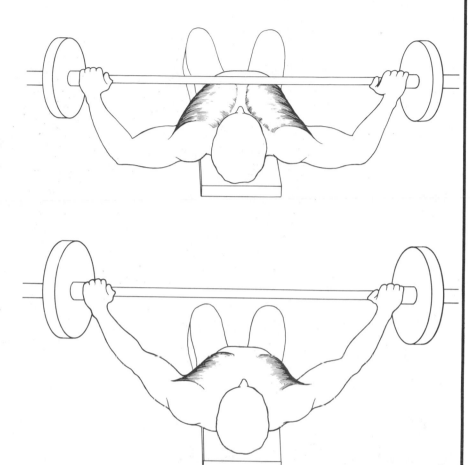

. . . allows you to get a tremendous stretch in the pectoral muscles as you lower the weight. This is very effective in developing the outer pectorals.

The development of the outer chest is what gives the pectorals a really full look when seen from the front. In this photo I am standing relaxed, but my outer pecs and biceps are almost touching.

This picture shows how important a good rib cage is for executing a side-chest pose.

or outer pectoral weak points would be to widen your grip doing Bench Presses in order to hit the outer pecs or bring in your hands to a narrow grip to work the inside pecs harder.

When doing Presses the area of the pecs you work hardest is determined by the angle at which you do the exercise. For example, in training the upper chest I used to start out doing three sets of Dumbbell Incline Presses at an angle of only 15 degrees. Then I would go to 25 degrees, 35 degrees, 50 degrees, and so on, doing three sets at each angle. At the end of a workout like that, I could feel I had really blasted the entire upper chest and that no part of that area had escaped attention.

Barbell exercises normally allow you to use more weight, so you develop maximum mass and strength. Dumbbell exercises give you a longer range of motion, so you get more extension and contraction. Cables allow you to work at a variety of angles, so you get more shaping for a better finished look. A disadvantage of machine training for the chest is that the apparatus only lets you work at very specific angles—but you can turn that to an advantage if you want to work the muscle at that angle to develop a weak area.

Dumbbell Flys are ideal for developing the outer pecs, but you need to employ a particular technique to get the most out of this movement. Lie on a bench and let the dumbbells down just as far as you can, almost to the floor. Then when you come up, stop about three-quarters of the way up. This puts all the effort on the outer pecs and never lets them disengage from the exercise.

But you can use Dumbbell Flys to work the inner pectorals as well, by bringing the weights all the way up, squeezing the muscles together at the top, and even crossing the dumbbells over slightly to get a full contraction of the inner pectorals.

Inner pectoral development in general comes about by working the top range of pectoral movements—a Bench Press with a narrower grip, for example, with the bar pushed all the way up; or Cable Crossovers, letting the arms cross over each other, which really contracts the inner pecs.

Decline exercises work the lower pecs. These include Decline Presses, Decline Flys, Decline Cable movements, and Dips. I like Dips because, by bending farther forward or holding yourself straighter, you can change the way the stress hits the muscle—even right in the middle of a set.

If your pectorals just seem to disappear when you raise your arms over your head, I recommend for this problem doing a series of Incline Dumbbell Presses at a variety of angles, starting out almost flat and going up until you are almost doing a Shoulder Press. This will produce the kind of total development that gives you impressive pecs even when your arms are raised or when doing a front double-biceps shot.

There are exercises you might do for weak point training that you would never do in a normal workout if you weren't trying to overcome a problem. This is why I caution young bodybuilders against simply copying what they see a champion doing in the gym. He may be doing some sort of One-Arm Cable Crossover motion at a special angle in order to deal with a weak point. If you assume that exercise is a standard one and include it in your regular routine you might end up wasting a lot of time and energy and holding back your overall progress.

Remember, even when doing weak point training, don't totally neglect any area of the muscle group. However, you can cut down on the number of exercises that work a strong area while adding extra movements to work a weak point.

Some experts say that you can't develop the size of your rib cage once you reach a certain age—about the early twenties. It is certainly true that the cartilage binding the rib cage stretches more easily at a younger age, but I have seen too many older bodybuilders improve their rib cage size to believe that this cannot be done. It is just a matter of time, effort, and patience—like so much else in the discipline of bodybuilding.

Finally, remember that the best way to force a weak body part to develop is by using a variety of Shocking Principles to increase training intensity. Chuck Sipes always liked to do Bench Presses using the Stripping Method. He would start off pressing around 400 pounds, would do as many reps as he could, and then have his training partner strip plates off the bar so that he could keep going and really blast his pectorals. You can also use techniques like Forced Reps, Rest/Pause, Three-quarter Movements, Staggered Sets, or anything else that will force the kind of development you need.

I especially like the idea of "heavy days" for maximum chest development. Once a week I usually trained my chest with extra heavy weight: five or six reps at the most, 100-pound Flys, Incline Presses using 365 pounds for six to eight reps, superheavy 450-pound Bench Presses to produce the maximum pectoral mass and thickness.

Power Training

To develop maximum power, mass, and strength in the chest, I recommend a program in which you:

1. Begin with Bench Presses. Do 20 reps the first set, then 10 reps. At this point, raise the weight so you go immediately down to 5 reps, 3 reps, and 1 rep.

2. Continue doing as many sets as you can (at least 5) with a weight that allows you only 1 or 2 repetitions.

3. Perform the last set with a lighter weight that allows you to go back up to high repetitions.

4. Go on to Incline Presses and do them the same way. Afterward, follow the same program with Dumbbell Flys.

Posing and Flexing

On heavy days especially, I always include a great deal of posing and flexing along with heavy weight training. Hitting a lot of side-chest shots and most-muscular poses along with intense training is the best way I know of to bring out pectoral striations. I've seen a lot of bodybuilders try to create these striations by artificial means—dehydrating themselves with diuretics, for example—but it just never looks as good as the results you get from hard training, posing, and flexing.

Learning to pose the chest properly takes a lot of practice. When you do a side-chest shot, a front double-biceps, a most-muscular, or a front-lat shot, in each shot the chest is posed differently and you need to practice each of these poses separately to get the effect you want. For a front double-biceps, you need to pose with your shoulders forward to create that sweeping line of the chest from sternum to deltoid; in the side-chest shot, you need to keep the shoulder down and lift the chest to make it look high and full. Flexing the chest as you train it is the only way to create maximum pectoral definition—and endless hours of posing practice is the only method that will give you total control of your physique for presentation.

Not only do you constantly need to pose and flex your pectoral muscles, you also need to practice a variety of ways of showing off the chest. Here, I am doing a side-chest shot.

Franco Columbu checks out his inner pectoral development.

The front double-biceps shot is one of the most difficult in bodybuilding. Any faults you have become immediately visible, especially if your chest tends to disappear when you lift your arms.

Sometimes you don't need to pose at all—just flex your pecs as hard as possible, hold it, and see what happens.

Upper and outer pec development is particularly important when you hit a front-lat spread.

When you hit a most-muscular pose, the chest should look like an anatomy chart—every area developed, defined, separated, and striated.

Steve Reeves at fifteen

Steve Reeves at twenty-three as Mr. Universe

The Serratus Muscles

The serratus muscles lie parallel to the ribs, coming out from under the lats and forward to tie into the pectorals and the intercostals and downward to the external obliques. When they are properly developed, these muscles look like "fingers," with each digitation clearly defined and separated from the others. The serratus muscles are not like other muscles, in that you don't measure their level of development with a tape measure; it is their visual impact that makes the difference.

Complete serratus development is important for a variety of reasons: for one, it announces clearly that this bodybuilder has achieved real quality detail training; for another, the serratus helps to separate the lats from the chest and the obliques, and aids in making them appear much larger when seen from the front. Good serratus development also helps to make you look more symmetrical and athletic.

Some people are naturally gifted with great serratus development. There is a photo of Steve Reeves doing a front lat spread when he was fifteen years old and had only been training for a year—and sure enough, you can see the serratus already several fingers deep. Later, when he went on to win the Mr. Universe contest, his serratus development was really spectacular.

Bill Pearl was able to combine impressive size with aesthetic qualities like highly defined serratus muscles, proving that you can achieve both mass and quality without compromising either. Pearl was able to hit a variety of overhead and front poses because of this outstanding serratus development, and this made him a much more formidable opponent on the competition stage.

However, if you weren't born with great serratus development you can train for it, by making a conscious effort to bring out these muscles. Frank Zane worked very hard at serratus training, and this helped to establish him as a model for the complete bodybuilder and to win three Mr. Olympia titles. Like Bill Pearl, Zane has found that his superior serratus development allows him to do a greater number of poses effectively, especially the aesthetic hands-over-the-head shots. (I recall standing on stage next to Zane in 1968, outweighing him by 50 pounds, and discovering that his lat spread was more effective than mine because of the tremendous lat separation his serratus development gave him. You can bet I started training the serratus extra hard after that!)

Reeves, Zane, and Pearl were my inspiration for developing the serratus. When they hit poses—especially ones in which the arms are raised—they demonstrated to me exactly what the serratus should look like.

Training the Serratus

Since a basic function of the serratus is to pull the shoulder forward and down, you train these muscles whenever you do movements like Chins, Narrow-Grip Pulldowns, various kinds of Dumbbell and Barbell Pullovers, and when you use the Nautilus Pullover machine. (When I do Dumbbell Pullovers, the structure of my body is such that this exercise becomes a rib cage expander. For others with different proportions—like Frank Zane and Bill Pearl—Dumbbell Pullovers tend to hit them more in the serratus.) There are, however, two exercises that work these muscles more specifically and that you can use if you have a weak point in this area: Rope Pulls and One-Arm Cable Pulls. In both cases, you have to do the movement as strictly as possible to get the maximum effect.

Working chest and back with Chins and Pullovers, you will have already done some serratus work. This is the time to consciously isolate the serratus, to concentrate on making these muscles burn. It is not enough just to throw in a few sets for the serratus, any more than for abs, calves, or intercostals. You need to train each muscle with maximum intensity if you want a complete and quality physique.

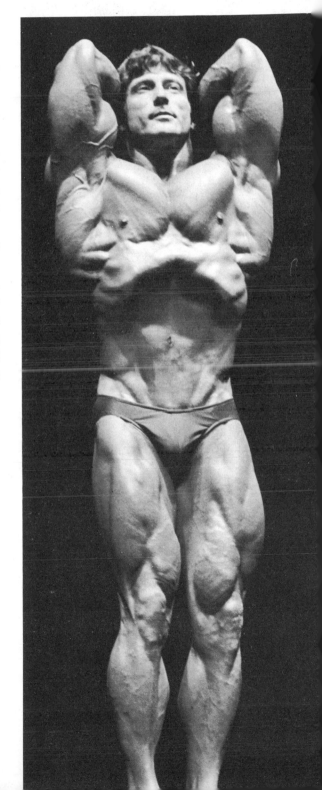

The combination of outstanding serratus development and an impressive vacuum make this hands-over-the-head pose one of Frank Zane's best.

CHEST EXERCISES

Barbell Flat Bench Presses

Purpose of Exercise: TO BUILD MASS AND STRENGTH IN THE PECTORALS, FRONT DELTS, AND TRICEPS.

The Bench Press is a fundamental compound exercise for the upper body. It produces growth, strength, and muscle density, not only for the chest muscles but for the front deltoids and triceps as well.

Execution: (1) Lie on a flat bench, your feet on the floor for balance. Your grip should be medium-wide (which means that, as you lower the bar to your chest, your hands should be wide enough apart so that your forearms point straight up, perpendicular to the floor). Lift the bar off the rack and hold it at arm's length above you. (2) Lower the bar slowly and under control until it touches just below the pectoral muscles. Keep the elbows pointed outward in order to fully involve the chest. The bar should come to a complete stop at this point. Press the bar upward once more until your arms are fully locked out. Always go through a full range of motion unless instructed specifically to do otherwise.

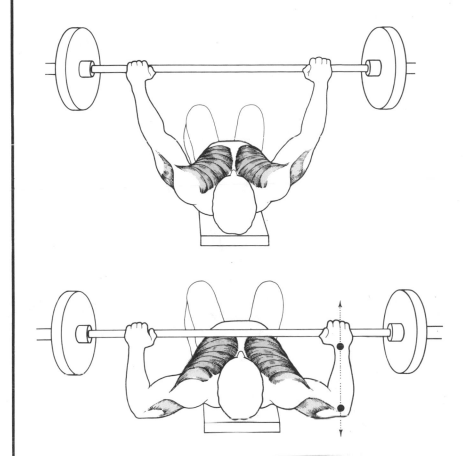

The classic Bench Press starting position: the hands are positioned on the bar slightly wider than shoulder width. This distributes the stress so that the pectorals do a major part of the work, with minimal front deltoid and triceps involvement.

Notice that as the weight is lowered to the chest, the hand position is such that the forearms end up perpendicular to the floor. This hand position gives the best overall results, developing the complete pectoral muscle—inner, outer, and through the middle.

I frequently did my heavy chest training on Sundays at Venice Beach. I got extra motivation for doing reps with 450 pounds because so many people were standing around watching me.

Barbell Incline Bench Presses

Purpose of Exercise: TO DEVELOP THE MASS AND STRENGTH OF THE UPPER PECTORAL MUSCLES AND FRONT DELTOIDS.

Changing the angle of the movement so you are pressing at an incline tends to put extra stress on the upper chest muscles and makes the deltoids work harder. But you will find you can't lift as much weight as you can when doing a flat bench press.

Execution: (1) Lie back on an incline bench. Reach up and

grasp the bar with a medium-wide grip. Lift the bar off the rack and hold it straight up overhead, arms locked.

(2) Lower the weight down to the upper chest, stop for a moment, then press it back up to the starting position. When working at an incline, it is extremely important to find the right "groove" or you are liable to find the bar drifting too far forward. It is useful to have a training partner to spot you while you are getting used to this movement.

Dumbbell Flat Bench Presses

Purpose of Exercise: TO DEVELOP THE MASS AND STRENGTH OF THE OUTER PECTORAL MUSCLES.

By using dumbbells rather than barbells, you can work the chest muscles through a greater range of motion, and the need to balance and coordinate two separate weights forces the muscles to deal with new and unexpected resistance.

Execution: (1) Lie on a flat bench, knees bent, feet flat on the bench. Take a dumbbell in each hand and hold them straight up overhead. Turn the dumbbells so that your palms face forward. (2) Lower the weights toward your chest, concentrating on keeping them fully balanced and under control. Lower them as far as you can, feeling a complete stretch in the pectoral muscles. Press the weights back up and lock your arms straight overhead.

Incline Dumbbell Presses

Purpose of Exercise: TO DEVELOP THE UPPER PECTORAL MUSCLES. You can vary the angle of the incline bench from almost flat to almost upright; the more upright the bench, the more you work the upper pecs.

Execution: Take a dumbbell in each hand and lie back on an incline bench. (1) Clean the dumbbells and hold them at shoulder height, palms facing forward. (2) Lift them simultaneously straight up overhead, then lower them back to the starting position. As a variation, you can begin with palms facing one another and twist your wrists as you lift so that the palms face forward at the top, then twist them back to the starting position as you lower the dumbbells. You can vary the angle at which you train from workout to workout, or from set to set in the same workout. If you do the latter, begin at a steep incline and work downward toward a flatter angle, rather than increasing the angle set to set.

Roy Callender

Decline Dumbbell Presses

Purpose of Exercise: TO DEVELOP THE LOWER PECTORAL MUSCLES.

Execution: Lie on a decline bench. Take a dumbbell in each hand and hold them at shoulder height, palms facing forward. Lift the dumbbells simultaneously straight up overhead, then lower them slowly back to the starting position.

Bertil Fox

Parallel Dips

Purpose of Exercise: TO DEVELOP THE PECTORAL MUSCLES.

Dips are a chest and triceps exercise that have a similar effect on the body as Decline Presses. However, with Dips you begin training with your own body weight, but can continue to progressively increase the resistance by holding a dumbbell between your legs or hooking a weight to the appropriate kind of belt. You can get a very long range of motion with this exercise.

Execution: (1) Hold yourself at arm's length above the bars, (2) then lower yourself slowly as far as you can. From the bottom, press back up to the starting position, tensing the pectorals at the top. In this movement, the farther forward you lean, the more chest you involve, so try hooking your feet toward the front, throwing your hips backward, which will shift your center of gravity forward and hit the pectorals harder.

Roy Callender

Machine Presses

Purpose of Exercise: TO ISOLATE THE PECTORAL MUSCLES.

One of the advantages of doing presses on a machine is that the machine stays in a certain groove, precluding any need for spending energy on balance and coordination. This is especially beneficial for people with a shoulder injury or other physical problem. Also, using a machine, your workout partner can push down on the mechanism to allow you to do heavy forced negative repetitions. However, being forced to stay in that groove limits the stimulation to the muscles and will slow down your muscular development, so I don't recommend an overreliance on Machine Presses except when you are working around injuries or are trying to shock the muscles with a totally unfamiliar exercise. Machine presses can be done at various angles:

Flat Bench Machine Presses. The pectoral station of the standard Universal machine is constructed to give you a flat Bench Press movement.

Incline Machine Presses. Using an incline bench and a Smith machine, you can isolate certain angles of the pressing movement in a very strict manner.

Decline Machine Presses. The standard Nautilus dual chest machine is designed to allow you to press at a decline angle.

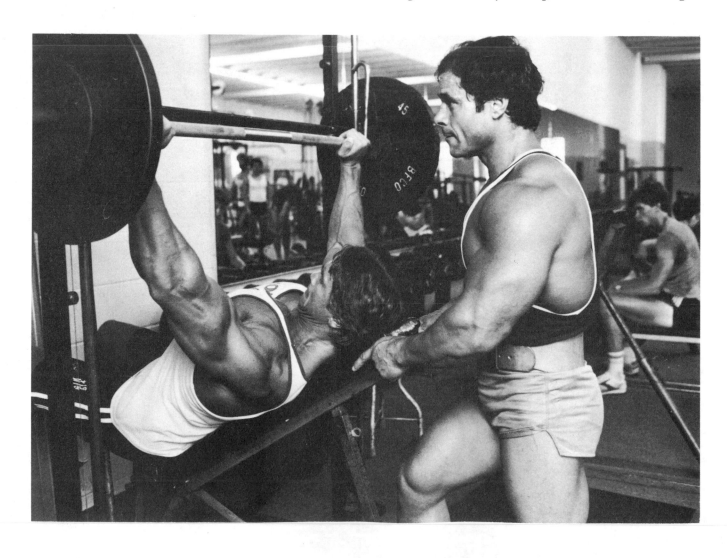

Dumbbell Flys

Purpose of Exercise: TO DEVELOP THE MASS OF THE PECTORALS.

The function of the pectorals is basically to pull the arms and shoulders inward across the body, and this is exactly what you do using a Dumbbell Fly movement.

Execution: (1) Lie on a bench holding dumbbells at arm's length above you, palms facing one another. (2) Lower the weights out and down to either side in a wide arc as far as you can, feeling the pectoral muscles stretch to their maximum. The palms should remain facing each other throughout the movement. Bend the arms slightly as you do the movement to reduce the stress on the elbows. Bring the weights to a complete stop at a point lower than the bench, your pectorals stretched as much as possible, then lift them back up along the same wide arc, as if giving somebody a big bear hug, rather than coming in and pressing the weights up. Bring the weights back up to the starting position and then contract the pectorals further, giving a little extra flex to make the muscle work that much harder.

Incline Dumbbell Flys

Purpose of Exercise: TO BUILD THE MASS OF THE UPPER PECTORALS.

Execution: These Flys are done like normal Dumbbell Flys, except you lie on an incline bench, with your head higher than your hips. (1) Lie on the bench with the dumbbells held straight overhead, palms facing one another. (2) Lower them out and down to either side in a wide, sweeping arc, keeping the palms facing one another and bending the elbows slightly. Lower the weights until they are below the level of the bench, your pectorals fully stretched. Come back up through that same wide arc, as if giving a big hug. Avoid bringing the weights in and pressing them straight up. At the top, flex the pectoral muscles to ensure a full contraction.

Standing Cable Flys

Purpose of Exercise: TO DEVELOP THE INSIDE OF THE PECTORAL MUSCLE.

Doing a flying motion using cables to provide resistance is a specialized exercise that works the center of the pecs and brings out those impressive cross striations, and also develops the lower pectorals as well.

Execution: (1) To do this movement from a standing position, take hold of handles attached by cables to overhead pulleys, step slightly forward of the line directly between the pulleys, and extend your arms almost straight out to either side. (2) Bend forward slightly from the waist, then bring your hands around and forward in a big hugging motion, elbows slightly bent, feeling the pectoral muscles contracting. When your hands come together in the center don't stop—cross one hand over the other and contract your chest muscles as much as you can. On each repetition of this movement, alternate which hand crosses over the other.

Bent-Forward Cable Crossovers

Purpose of Exercise: TO WORK THE INSIDE OF THE MIDDLE AND LOWER PECTORAL MUSCLES.

Execution: Using two floor-level pulleys, grasp a handle in each hand and bend forward, extending your arms out to either side. Draw your hands toward one another, allow them to cross, and continue pulling until you feel your pectorals contract to the maximum. Hold for a moment and flex for extra contraction, then release and let your arms be pulled back to the starting position.

Flat Bench Cable Crossovers

Purpose of Exercise: TO DEVELOP AND DEFINE THE INNER PECTORAL MUSCLES.

Execution: Lie on a flat bench between two floor-level pulleys. Take a handle in each hand and bring your hands together at arm's length above you, palms facing one another. With your elbows slightly bent, lower your hands out to either side in a wide arc until your pectorals are fully stretched. Bring your arms back toward the starting position, passing through the same sweeping arc as if giving a big hug. You can stop at the top or continue on and cross your arms over slightly to create the fullest possible contraction of the pectorals.

Bertil Fox

Machine Flys

Purpose of Exercise: TO BUILD DEFINITION AND STRIATIONS IN THE PECTORAL MUSCLES.

Fly machines are not for building mass, but are very useful in creating definition.

Execution: Many gyms are equipped with a variety of "pec decks" that approximate the flying motion. When using these in your training, work toward getting the fullest possible range of motion, stretching the pectorals to the maximum at full extension, then giving the muscles an extra, isometric contraction once you've brought your arms as close together as possible.

Roy Callender

Straight-Arm Pullovers

Purpose of Exercise: TO DEVELOP THE PECTORALS AND EXPAND THE RIB CAGE.

This is the best movement for expanding the thorax, as well as working the pectorals and building up the serratus anterior muscles.

Execution: (1) Place a dumbbell on a bench, then turn and lie across the bench with only your shoulders on its surface, your feet flat on the floor. Grasp the dumbbell with both hands and hold it straight up over your chest, with both palms pressing against the underside of the top plate. (2) Keeping your arms straight, lower the weight slowly down in an arc behind your head, feeling the chest and rib cage stretch. Drop the hips toward the floor at the same time to increase this stretch. When you have lowered the dumbbell as far as possible, raise it back to the starting position through the same arc. Don't let your hips come back up as you lift the weight. Keep them low throughout the movement to ensure the maximum possible stretch and therefore the greatest expansion of the rib cage.

Rope Pulls

Purpose of Exercise: TO DEVELOP THE SERRATUS MUSCLES.

Execution: (1) Kneel on the floor holding on to ropes attached to a cable and overhead pulley. (2) Keeping your arms extended above you, curl your body forward and down, pulling with the lats. Continue this motion until your head is almost touching your thighs. Bring your elbows down to the floor, pulling with the elbows. Release, uncurl, and come back up to the starting position, straightening your arms and feeling the stretch in your lats. You need to be very strict with Rope Pulls, not try for maximum weight. Try to make the serratus really burn by the end of the set.

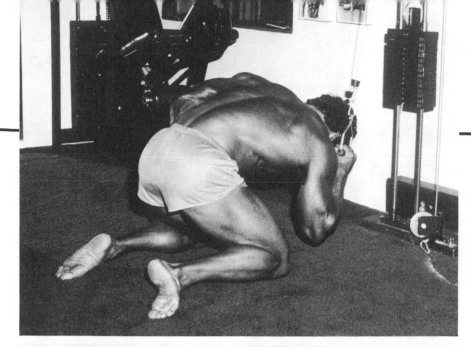

One-Arm Cable Pulls

Purpose of Exercise: TO ISOLATE THE INDIVIDUAL SERRATUS MUSCLES.

Execution: Kneeling on the floor, grasp a handle attached to a cable and overhead pulley with an underhand grip. Pulling with the lat, bring your elbow down to your knee. Consciously "crunch" the serratus and lat, getting a full contraction. Release and come slowly back to the starting position. The key to this exercise is absolute strictness. Do the movement slowly and under control, concentrating on feeling the contraction in the lats and serratus. Repeat using other arm.

Frank Zane

Pullovers

Pullovers (illustrated below) can be used to develop the serratus as well as the pectorals. For serratus, do the regular Pullover movement, but concentrate on making the serratus muscles do a maximum amount of the pulling.

Machine Pullovers
(see p. 349)

Machine Pullovers can be used to develop the serratus as well as the lats. Learn to feel when the serratus muscles are working the hardest, and adjust the position of your body and the movement of your elbows until you feel them contracting to the maximum.

Close-Grip Chins
(see p. 337)

By concentrating on contracting the serratus during this movement, you can change it from a lat exercise to one that gives you a very good serratus workout.

Hanging Serratus Crunches

Purpose of Exercise: TO ISOLATE AND DEVELOP THE SERRATUS.

Execution: Hold on to a chinning bar with a palms-forward grip. (Using lifting straps will take some of the strain off your hands and wrists.) Slowly swing your legs up and to one side, feeling the serratus muscles stretch fully on one side and contract to the maximum on the other. Slowly come back to the center, then repeat the movement to the other side. Concentrate on trying to get the maximum stretch possible and to execute the movement just with the serratus, isolating these muscles as much as possible. This exercise calls for complete control and strict technique. Bring your legs deliberately to each side, do not swing them back and forth like a pendulum.

Frank Zane

Hanging Dumbbell Rows

Purpose of Exercise: TO ISOLATE AND DEVELOP THE SERRATUS.

Execution: (1) Using a pair of gravity boots, hang upside down from a chinning bar. Take a dumbbell in each hand and let them hang down below you, feeling the serratus muscles stretch to their maximum. (2) Concentrating on using the serratus in isolation as much as possible, lift the dumbbells up in front of you. As you lift, your elbows come toward the front, not out to the side. Hold at the point of maximum serratus contraction, then lower the dumbbells slowly back to the starting position, feeling the serratus stretch once more. During the movement, be sure to keep your elbows, and the dumbbells, as close to your body as possible.

The Muscles of the Back

The **trapezius,** the flat, triangular muscle that extends out and down from the neck and then down between the shoulder blades.

    BASIC FUNCTION: To raise the entire shoulder girdle

The **latissimus dorsi,** the large triangular muscles that extend from under the shoulders down to the small of the back on both sides. These are the largest muscles of the upper body.

    BASIC FUNCTION: To pull the shoulders downward and to the back

The **spinal erectors,** several muscles in the lower back that guard the nerve channels and help keep the spine erect. They are also the slowest muscles in the body to recuperate from heavy exercise.

    BASIC FUNCTION: To hold the spine erect

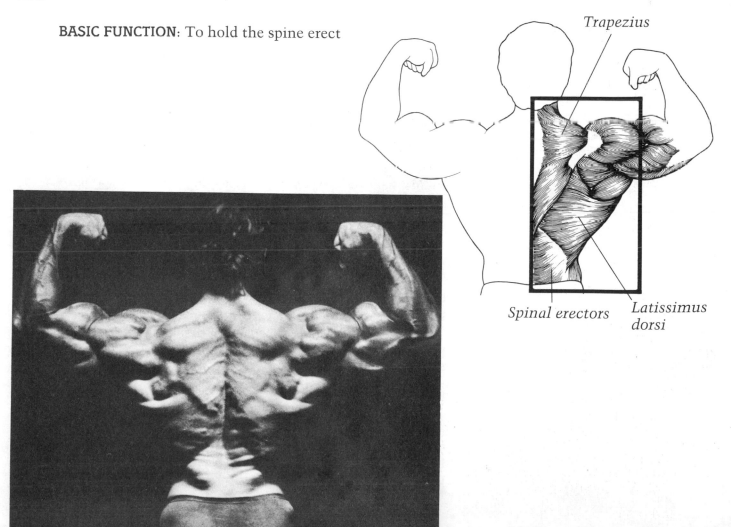

Trapezius

Spinal erectors

Latissimus dorsi

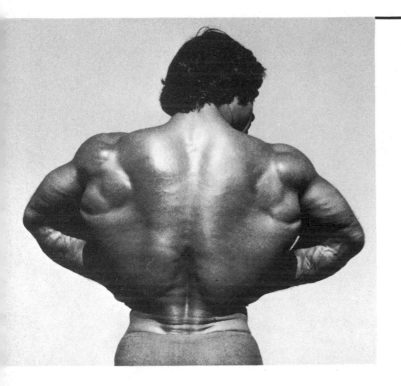

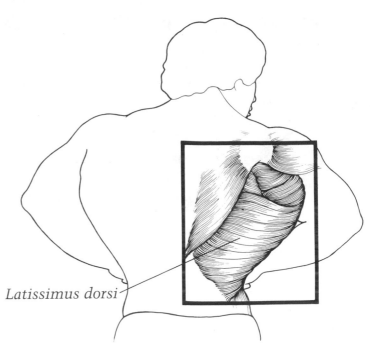

Latissimus dorsi

Training the Back

Developing a broad, thick, and massive back is absolutely necessary in the creation of a quality bodybuilding physique. Strong back muscles are essential for lifting and carrying heavy weight, and a highly muscular back has always been considered the measure of a man's strength.

"My back is a weapon I use to destroy my opponents," says two-time Mr. Olympia winner Franco Columbu. "I place my thumbs in the small of my back and begin to spread my lats. It doesn't all come on at once—first I flex them a few times and then begin to let them extend their widest. Each time the audience and the judges think that is all, I flex harder and they come out farther. And just when everyone is gasping with surprise that a human being could achieve such development, I lift my arms into a powerful double-biceps shot displaying enormous muscularity, thickness, and separation. Only the very best of bodybuilders can stand beside me when I do this without being blown off stage by the shock wave."

When a bodybuilding judge looks at a competitor's back, there are three things he is especially interested in: (1) the thickness and muscularity of the upper back; (2) the sweep and width of the lats; and (3) the definition and development of the lower back and lower lats.

The Upper Back

Upper back development involves more than just the back muscles themselves. When you hit a rear double-biceps pose, the traps and the muscles of the upper and middle back are dominant, but *all* the muscles from elbow to elbow play their part, including the biceps and the rear delts.

The central muscle of the upper back is the trapezius, a triangular muscle that extends down to the shoulders from either side of the neck, then comes together over the spine about halfway down the back. In a highly developed back the trapezius will be full and massive, balancing off the lats on either side and clearly separated from them in back poses. Exercises that specifically work the traps include anything which involves lifting the shoulders—Shrugs and Upright Rows, primarily, but also Rowing in certain positions and some kinds of Presses—and are covered in the Trapezius training program (p. 265).

In a twisting back shot, you need a thick and muscular upper back to balance off the development of the shoulders, biceps, triceps, and forearms.

Sergio Oliva is a perfect example of how impressive a thick upper back can be.

The Lats

The most impressive area of a fully developed back is the sweep of the lats. It is this muscular width that declares to the world that you are really a bodybuilder. And it is the lats that are likely to first attract the judges' attention, even when standing relaxed in the first round. The traditional V-shape of the bodybuilder, wide shoulders descending to a firm, tight waistline, is dependent on the right kind of lat development. A friend of mine once told me that when he did a lat shot on stage, he imagined his lats were so wide that the audience would think the curtains were closing!

The width of the lats is developed by any kind of pulldown movement, such as Cable Pulldowns or Chins. The precise way that the pulldown movement affects the lats is determined by the angle you are working at, how wide apart your arms are, and whether you are pulling down in front or to the rear. So I have included a variety of close-grip and wide-grip movements as well as front and rear Chins and Pulldowns in the back program to encourage total lat development.

The lats are also evident from the front view, complementing the chest by widening the torso with the line of the back muscles acting as a frame for the pectorals. They contribute to any number of poses, including front and rear double-biceps and a variety of twisting shots.

Franco Columbu

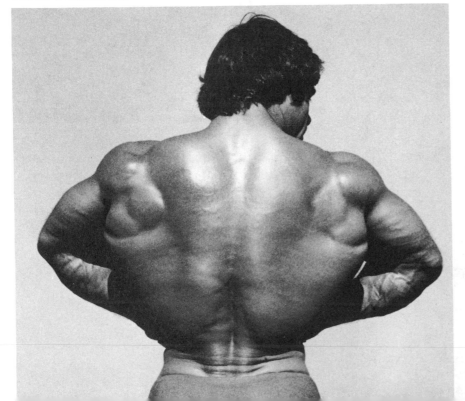

Franco Columbu, Robby Robinson, and Sergio Oliva are three great bodybuilders who are known for the V-shape of their torsos—from the back and from the front—which is the result of outstanding lat development.

Sergio Oliva

Robby Robinson

Lower Lats

When you see a Franco Columbu or Frank Zane do a twisting back shot you can't help being impressed by the way their lower lats sweep all the way down and insert into the waistline. This gives the lats a terrifically aesthetic look.

To develop the lower lats, you need to do your back exercises with a very narrow grip—Narrow-Grip Chins and Narrow-Grip Pulldowns, for example—as well as One-Arm Cable Rowing and One-Arm Dumbbell Rows. It is also important to do stretches between sets, grabbing hold of something with one hand at a time and really pulling until you can feel the lower lat almost down to the hip.

Well-developed lower lats will also help you in rear back poses because they come down at an angle and form a kind of frame that shows off a well-striated lower back.

Frank Zane

Franco Columbu

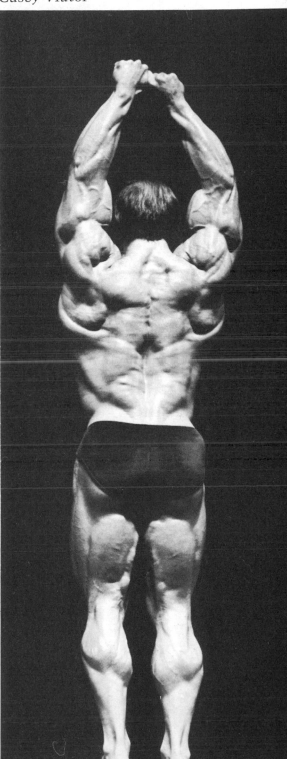

Roy Callender

Casey Viator

Middle Back Thickness

Not only should the lats be wide and sweeping, but they should look thick and powerful where they come together in the middle back. There are many bodybuilders who have wide backs with sweeping lats but who fail to look their best in back poses because the center of the back lacks that strong, thick look that a really great bodybuilder has to have.

When you look at Casey Viator, for example, you are immediately struck by the solid thickness of his back muscles. At the 1982 Olympia in London, Casey's back showed thickness and striations all the way down even when he was standing relaxed. Roy Callender is another bodybuilder who has trained his back properly and created a solid middle back structure.

The back can be posed in a number of different ways, but as you can see, total back development is necessary to make each one effective. Serge Nubret, Franco, and I all show thick upper and lower back development, lots of lat width, and good muscularity.

Thickness in the back is achieved primarily by doing rowing exercises—Barbell Rows, Cable Rows, T-Bar Rows, and so forth. However, if you want to target the middle back, do rowing that gives you a longer range of motion so that you can fully contract that area—Cable Rows with separate cables or a wide grip, One-Arm Rows, or Barbell Rows with a wider grip.

Lower Back

Many top bodybuilders have a great upper back but have never developed the lower back to the degree that they should. A really great lower back has two columns of muscle that stand out on either side of the spine, an indication of years of heavy Deadlifts, Bent-Over Rows, and other power exercises. When you see Boyer Coe on stage you notice the tremendous sweep of his lats, but when he stands next to someone like Danny Padilla, with his thick and powerful lower back, you can see he is weak in this particular area.

A truly Herculean physique needs that lower back development and thickness. Look at a Sergio Oliva, Casey Viator, Franco Columbu, Danny Padilla, or Ken Waller and you will see magnificent lower back development. Frank Zane at one time was very weak in the lower back. I recommended to him that he begin doing Bent-Over Rows, starting out with a relatively low weight and gradually increasing his poundages as his back developed. Zane is such a dedicated bodybuilder that within a relatively short time his lower back development increased enormously, and within a year you could see striations across the lower back.

Because we tend to store a disproportionate amount of fat around the waistline, leanness and definition in the lower back are visible proof that a bodybuilder has worked hard to get in shape. When he hits a back double-biceps shot and the judges see a clearly defined, sculpted lower back they know instantly that he has done an enormous amount of work, not just for the lats but for the entire back.

I have included exercises for the lower back right from the beginning so that bodybuilders following my training program will not find themselves with a weak lower back a year or so down the line. Heavy power exercises like Deadlifts are ideal because they not only develop the lower back but strengthen it, so you are able to do a variety of other exercises like Bent-Over Rows without having your lower back give out before your upper back.

These poses executed by Franco Columbu, Danny Padilla, and me illustrate the importance of a well-developed lower back, whether you are hitting a back pose or simply standing relaxed.

Back Muscle Functions

The lats have two basic functions as far as bodybuilding is concerned: they pull the shoulder back (a rowing motion) and pull the shoulders down (a pulldown or chinning motion). A common mistake when doing these movements is to use too much biceps effort and not enough back, or to involve the muscles of the lower back in a swaying motion instead of making the lats do most of the work. You have to make an effort when training lats to isolate them so that only these muscles are involved in the movement.

The lower back muscles function differently than most other muscles in the body. They are stabilizers, holding the body steady rather than constantly contracting and relaxing through a full range of motion like, say, the biceps. Therefore, when you do full-range exercises like Hyperextensions or Straight-Leg Deadlifts you put so much strain on the lower back that it can take up to a week to fully recuperate. This means that total-effort lower back training using power exercises and maximum weights is only necessary once a week. On the other days, do your sets with non-power exercises and less than maximum poundages.

Designing a Back Program

To plan a comprehensive program of back training you need to consider how each of the important back muscles functions so that you include exercises for each and every vital area. If you don't properly appreciate the complexity of the back and how many different movements it takes to get full back development, you will end up with serious weak points in this part of your physique.

For example, it doesn't do any good to do five sets of Chins to the front, five sets to the back, five sets of Wide-Grip Pulldowns, and five sets of Narrow-Grip Pulldowns and then figure you have worked your back adequately. Every one of those exercises works the pulldown function of the back, which develops the width of the lats, but a complete back program also has to develop the thickness of the back, the lower lats, and the strength and definition of the lower back.

The Basic Training Program starts out with simple exercises like Deadlifts and Chin-Ups. Later, to Deadlifts you'll add other back exercises such as Hyperextensions and Good Mornings. Similarly, chinning movements can be supplemented by various kinds of pulldown exercises and two-handed rowing exercises can be replaced occasionally by One-Arm Rows, and so forth. In the Advanced and Competition Training Programs, I have included an even greater variety of back exercises, so that by the time you are ready to compete you will be doing several movements for each of the important areas of the back.

Weak Point Training

The most common problem of today's competition bodybuilders is incomplete back development. One reason for this may simply be that they do not get to study their backs as clearly as they can a front view, and so are not as motivated to train their backs as diligently as chest or arms. One other reason, however, is poor back training technique. Back training is more subtle and more difficult than most people realize. For one thing, the basic function of the lats and other back muscles is to pull the shoulder girdle down and back. Many bodybuilders don't understand this and get confused as to which muscles they are supposed to be using. If they lurch back during the exercises and use the lower back or shoulders themselves, then the back muscles never get to work through a full range of motion.

Early in life you learned to coordinate your muscular efforts to make lifting easier. You learned to bend your knees when lifting something, to take as much strain as possible off the back muscles and distribute it more evenly to allow adjacent muscles to help. This is the opposite of what you try to accomplish as a bodybuilder. The trick to effective back training is to learn to isolate the various areas of the back, then make it *harder* on each individual area of the back instead of easier.

I have watched bodybuilders do Bent-Over Rows with an impossible amount of weight, so that they had to heave the bar into the air using every muscle in the body. This kind of cheating will never build a quality back. When doing Seated Rows, many bodybuilders add weight to the stack as if lifting heavy weights is all that matters and then sway way back, using too much lower back, in an effort to finish off the movement.

Also, many bodybuilders allow the biceps to do too much pulling when they are doing pulldown or rowing exercises, which results in some powerful arm development but doesn't do much for the lower back. They need to concentrate on using the arms simply as a link between the back and the bar or handle, and not as a primary means of lifting the weight.

But even if you learn absolutely correct back training tech-

What a difference three years can make! At age eighteen, I realized I needed more upper back thickness . . .

nique, the back consists of a number of complex and interrelated muscles and they do not necessarily all develop at the same rate in all individuals. As you become more advanced in bodybuilding and you begin to see which areas of the back have responded more quickly than others, you will want to alter your program to include more work for the muscles that are lagging behind.

Outer Back Development. The outer back responds to Rows done with a narrow grip, because with a narrow grip the handles or bar allows you to go back no farther than the front of the torso and shortens the range of motion. One of my favorite outer back exercises is T-Bar Rows, done as strictly as possible.

Upper Back Development. The primary exercise I recommend for developing the upper back is heavy Bent-Over Barbell Rows. Additionally, you can do Seated Wide-Grip Rowing, using a long bar instead of handles. If one side of the upper back is more developed than the other, try doing One-Arm Dumbbell Rows to work each side in isolation.

. . . by age twenty-one, after concentrated weak point training, this area had become my strong point.

Franco Columbu

Lat Width. The lats are extremely important for both front and back poses. Franco Columbu has truly Olympian lats, and they look good no matter what pose he hits or what angle they are viewed from. The sweep and width of the lats is accentuated by doing exercises which pull the lats out to the side as far as possible. Wide-Grip Chins and Wide-Grip Pulldowns are the primary exercises for achieving this.

Sergio Oliva displays perfect middle and lower back thickness.

Lower Lat Development. The sweep of the lats is less effective if the lats do not extend all the way down to the waistline. Exercises to help you train the lower lats include One-Arm Cable Rows and close-grip movements such as Close-Grip Chins and Close-Grip Pulldowns.

Middle Back Thickness. The middle back receives the greatest amount of work when you extend the range of motion as far as possible. Therefore, Seated Rowing done with separate handles, allowing you to bring your elbows farther back, puts more stress on the middle back. Rowing done with a fairly wide grip or T-Bar Rowing done on a machine allowing a wider grip creates the same effect.

Lower Back Development. Many bodybuilders forget that the lower back is an essential element in making any back shot really effective. Heavy Deadlifts force the lower back to work to the maximum. But you can also use exercises like Good Mornings and Hyperextensions to isolate and develop this area.

Overall Back Development. Remember that other muscle groups contribute to your back poses, especially straight-on back shots like the rear double-biceps and rear lat sread. Therefore, you need to be concerned with muscles like the rear deltoids, the trapezius, and even the biceps and triceps. Everything ties in with everything else, and judges may watch you pose and give you low marks for back when in reality it was some other aspect of your development that was at fault.

Stretching and Flexing

I am a firm believer in flexing and posing the muscles between each set. This is especially true for the back. You have to keep posing and flexing your back in order to gain full control over the muscles needed to show it off effectively in competition. Continually stretching the lats also helps to achieve that long sweep and low tie-in at the waistline that makes the champions' backs so impressive.

Flex the back or hit poses like a back double-biceps shot between sets of Rows and Pullovers. If you pose while your training partner is doing his set, you will keep the muscles pumped and warm and ready to really hit the next set.

When you are training lats with Chins and Pulldowns, between sets grab hold of something solid and really stretch them out one at a time, or both at once as pictured here. Also, all the serratus exercises (beginning on p. 310) can be used to stretch the lats. This lengthens the muscles, helps you to get a fuller range of motion and a deeper contraction, and develops the lower area of the lats as they extend down to the waist.

Dave Draper

Ken Waller

This series of poses demonstrates the number of different ways the complex muscle system of the back can be presented, and why it is necessary for the aspiring bodybuilder to achieve total back development in order to ensure success.

BACK EXERCISES

Wide-Grip Chins Behind the Neck

Purpose of Exercise: TO WIDEN THE UPPER BACK AND CREATE A FULL SWEEP IN THE LATS.

Wide-Grip Chins widen the lats and develop the entire shoulder girdle. It is an exercise primarily for the upper and outer regions of the lats and also spreads the scapula, making it easier to flare the lats.

Execution: Take hold of the chinning bar with an overhand grip, hands as wide apart as practicable. Hang from the bar, then pull yourself up so that the back of

Franco Columbu

your neck touches the bar. This is a strict exercise, so try not to help your back by kicking up with the legs. At the top of the movement hold for a brief moment, then lower yourself slowly back to the starting position. Chins involve your entire body weight, so some beginners may not be able to do the requisite number of repetitions for each set. I recommend they do what I used to do: instead of trying to do 5 sets of 10 reps each, do as many reps as possible at a time—maybe only 3 or 4—until a total of 50 reps is achieved. The stronger you get, the fewer sets it will take to get to 50 reps and the shorter the time it will take to do it.

Wide-Grip Chins to the Front (Optional)

Purpose of Exercise: TO WIDEN THE UPPER BACK AND CREATE A FULL SWEEP IN THE LATS.

Chinning yourself so that you touch your chest to the bar rather than the back of the neck gives you a slightly longer range of motion and is less strict, allowing you to cheat slightly so you can continue your reps even after you are tired.

Execution: Take hold of the chinning bar with an overhand grip, hands as wide apart as practicable. Hang from the bar, then pull yourself up, trying to touch the top of your chest to the bar. At the top of the movement, hold for a brief moment, then lower yourself back to the starting position.

Close-Grip Chins

Purpose of Exercise: TO WIDEN THE LOWER LATS AND DEVELOP THE SERRATUS.

This exercise is great for widening and lengthening the appearance of the lats. It also develops the serratus anterior, those little fingers of muscle which lie under the outside of the pecs, which add so much to front poses such as double biceps or any other overhead pose.

Execution: (1) Take hold of the chinning bar (or close-grip triangle device found in many gyms) with your hands close together, one hand on either side of the bar. Hang below the bar. (2) Then pull yourself up while leaning your head back slightly so that the chest touches (or nearly touches) your hands; lower the body slowly for a full stretch of the lats. Work for the fullest range of motion.

Close-Grip Chins (optional) pulling on a straight bar instead of a double-handle

Lat Machine Pulldowns

Purpose of Exercise: TO WIDEN THE UPPER LATS.

This exercise allows you to do Chins with less than your total body weight, so you can do a lot of extra reps for the upper back if you feel you need more work in that area (but should not replace Chins as the standard exercise for widening the upper lats).

Execution: (1) Using a long bar, grasp it with a wide, overhand grip and sit on the seat with your knees hooked under the support. (2) Pull the bar down smoothly until it touches the top of your chest, making the upper back do the work, and not swaying back to involve the lower back. Release, extend the arms again, and feel the lats fully stretch.

Lat Machine Pulldowns (optional)

For variation, you can do Lat Pulldowns behind the neck.

Close- or Medium-Grip Pulldowns

Purpose of Exercise: TO WIDEN THE LOWER LATS.

Again, working with an overhead cable and weight stack allows you to do the chinning movement with less than body weight.

Execution: Grasp the handles or a bar using a narrow or medium-close grip and pull down to your upper chest. Don't sway backwards, but try to concentrate on using the lats to do the movement. Draw the shoulders down and back and stick the chest out. Let the handles go upward again until your lats are fully stretched out.

Bent-Over Barbell Rows

Purpose of Exercise: TO THICKEN THE UPPER BACK.

This exercise also helps to widen the upper back and, to a lesser degree, add density to the lower back.

Execution: (1) Standing with feet a few inches apart, grasp the bar with a wide, overhand grip. With your knees slightly bent, bend forward until your upper body is about parallel to the floor. Keep your back straight and let the bar hang at arm's length below you, almost touching the shinbone. (2) Using primarily the muscles of the back, lift the bar upward until it touches the upper abdominals, then lower it again, under control, back to the starting position; then immediately start your next rep. It is important to make the back work so as not to make this a biceps exercise. Think of the arms and hands as hooks, a way of transmitting the contraction

of the lats to the bar. Don't bring the bar up to the chest area itself; bringing it only to the abdomen reduces the role of the arms. Make sure your first rep of any rowing exercise is relatively light to let your back get warmed up. By the time you get to your last set, a little bit of cheating is all right to get you through it, but keep it to a minimum.

In Bent-Over Barbell Rows, you pull with the lats but don't lift with the lower back. Keep your upper body parallel to the floor all through the exercise. Notice how the bar is pulled up to the abdomen rather than up toward the chest.

This drawing illustrates two major mistakes: If you don't hold your body steady when doing Bent-Over Barbell Rows, you involve the lower back muscles rather than isolating the lats. And if you lift the bar up toward the chest instead of the abdomen, you involve the arms, so that the biceps are doing a lot of the work you are trying to get the lats to do.

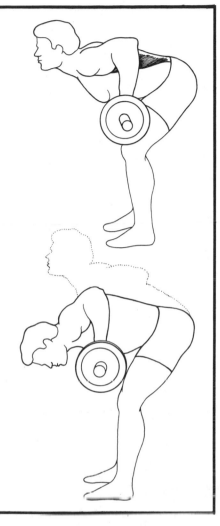

When you do Rows with an Olympic barbell set with its larger plates you need to stand on a block or a bench so that you can lower the bar all the way down without the plates touching the floor. With your head up, back straight, and knees flexed, you are in a position similar to an Olympic lifter about to clean a heavy barbell.

Bent-Over Dumbbell Rows

Purpose of Exercise: TO WORK EACH SIDE OF THE UPPER BACK IN ISOLATION.

You can still work heavy and give your back a good workout using dumbbells, but by using them you force each side of the body to work up to its own capacity, rather than running the risk of having the stronger side help out the weaker one. This is a good weak point exercise for anyone lacking upper back symmetry.

Execution (1) Grasp a dumbbell in each hand, bend your knees slightly, then bend forward from the waist, keeping your head up and your back straight. Let the weights hang at arm's length below the shoulders.
(2) Simultaneously lift both weights up as far as possible to your sides, holding your upper body steady to avoid involving the lower back (the weights should come up to your sides, not your chest, in order to keep biceps involvement to a minimum). Then lower the weights again, slowly.

T-Bar Rows

Purpose of Exercise: TO THICKEN THE OUTER BACK.

Execution: (1) Standing on a block with your feet close together, knees slightly bent, bend down and grasp the handles of the T-Bar machine with an overhand grip. Straighten your legs slightly and lift up until your body is at about a 45-degree angle. Without changing this angle, lift the weight up until it touches your chest, (2) then lower it again to arm's length, keeping the weight off the floor.

Remember that this is an upper back exercise—you are not supposed to do much lifting with the lower back or legs. If you find you are not able to do this lift without swaying and lifting up with your back to an excessive degree, you are simply using too much weight and should take off a plate or two. However, a small amount of movement is inevitable. But be certain to keep your back straight or even slightly arched and never to bend over hunchback-fashion, which could result in injury. By using a narrow grip, this exercise will work mostly the outer lats because you cannot get the range of motion to fully involve the inner back muscles. However, this limited range of motion means that you will eventually be able to lift more weight than when doing Barbell Rows, which makes this a good power movement.

One-Arm Dumbbell Rows

Purpose of Exercise: TO ISOLATE EACH SIDE OF THE BACK.

Rowing one side at a time with a dumbbell has two unique advantages over Barbell Rows: it isolates the latissimus muscles on each side, and it allows you to lift the weight higher and therefore get a more complete contraction. Using heavy weight in this exercise is less important than getting the fullest range of movement, which will help develop and define the center of the back.

Execution: (1) Taking a dumbbell in one hand, bend forward from the waist until your upper body is nearly parallel to the floor. Place your free hand on the bench for support. Begin with the weight hanging down at arm's length, feeling the fullest possible stretch. Turn your hand so that the palm faces toward your body. (2) Keeping your body steady, lift the weight up to your side, concentrating on doing the work with the back rather than the arm. Lower the weight, keeping it under control. Finish your repetitions with this arm, then repeat with the other arm.

One-Arm Cable Rows

Purpose of Exercise: TO DEVELOP THE LOWER LATS.

This is an especially good movement for tying in the lower lats to the waist.

Execution: (1) Using a floor-level pulley, take hold of a handle with one hand. If done standing, assume a balanced stance, the leg opposite the arm you will be using in the exercise forward, other leg back. (This can also be done while seated.) Begin with your arm fully extended in front of you, your hand twisted inward so that the thumb is lower than the little finger to create the fullest possible stretch. (2) Pull the handle back by your side as far as you can, twisting your hand outward so that the thumb ends up on the outside, feeling the back muscles contract. Release and extend your arm and twist your wrist back to the starting position. Complete your repetitions, then repeat the exercise using the other arm.

The secret to success doing One-Arm Cable Rows is range of motion. When you pull the cable, bring your elbow as far back as possible—which is a lot farther than you can go doing regular Cable Rows. Also, as you release and lower the weight again, make sure you stretch your arm and lats as far as possible.

Seated Cable Rows

Purpose of Exercise: TO DEVELOP THE THICKNESS OF THE BACK AND THE LOWER LATS.
This movement also works the lower sections of the lats.

Execution: (1) Take hold of the handles and sit with your feet braced against the crossbar or a wooden block, knees slightly bent. Extend your arms and bend forward slightly, feeling the lats stretch. You should be situated far enough away from the weight stack so that you can stretch like this without the weight touching bottom. (2) From this beginning position, pull the handles back toward your body and touch them to your abdomen, feeling the back muscles doing most of the work. Your back should arch, your chest stick out, and try to touch the shoulder blades together as you draw the weight toward you. Don't involve the lower back muscles by swaying forward and back. When the handles touch your abdomen you should be sitting upright, not leaning backward. Keeping the weight under control, release and let the handles go forward again, once more stretching out the lats.

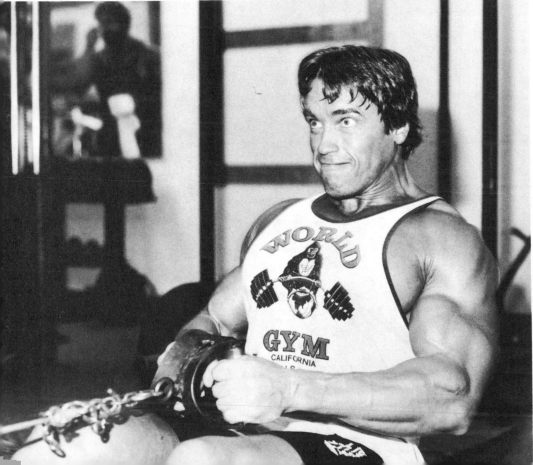

Seated Cable Rows (optional)

Using separate handles as pictured here allows you to get your hands and elbows farther back, putting more of the stress on the center of your back.

Machine Rows

Many gyms are equipped with a variety of specialized rowing machines. Some duplicate the effect of Seated Rows, while others allow you to do a rowing motion by pushing back with the elbows and not involving the contraction of the biceps. Each of these hits the back a little differently, and all are useful devices to include occasionally in your workouts to provide variety and to surprise the muscles.

Bent-Arm Pullovers with Barbell

Purpose of Exercise: TO WORK THE LOWER LATS AND THE SERRATUS.
It also stretches the pectorals and helps to widen the rib cage.

Execution: (1) Lie on your back along a flat bench. Place a barbell (or an E-Z curl bar) on the floor behind your head. Reach back and grasp the bar. (2) Keeping your arms bent, raise the bar and bring it just over your head to your chest. Lower the bar slowly back to the starting position without touching the floor, feeling the lats stretch out to their fullest. When using a heavy weight for this movement, I have someone sit on my knees to stabilize me, so that I can put all my effort into lifting the bar.

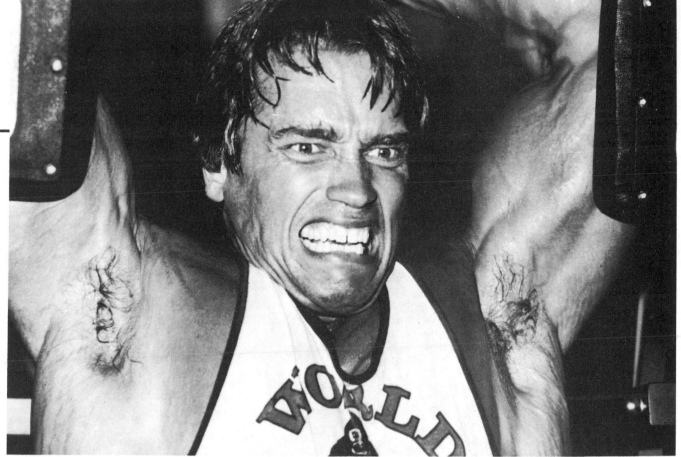

Machine Pullovers

The Pullover is actually a
circular motion, and it is
often difficult to work the
muscles through a full range
of motion using free weights
(although advanced
bodybuilders learn to do this
purely by experience).
Pullover machines are
valuable in that they allow
you to work against circular
resistance, and some also
provide for training one arm
at a time, giving you the
opportunity for additional
isolation. In fact in my
opinion Pullover machines are
among the most valuable
exercise machines you will
find in a gym.

(1) Grasp the bar over your
head, and (2) drive it down,
feeling the lats contract. At
the end of the movement the
bar should be jammed against
your abdomen.

Deadlifts

Purpose of Exercise: TO WORK THE LOWER BACK. Deadlifts are an overall power exercise that involve more muscles than any other exercise in your routine, including the lower back, upper back, and trapezius muscles, the buttocks, and the legs. A strong lower back is especially important when doing movements like Bent-Over Rows and T-Bar Rows, which put a lot of strain on this area.

Execution: (1) Place a barbell on the floor in front of you. Bend your knees, lean forward, and grasp the bar in a medium-wide grip, one hand in an overhand grip, the other in an underhand grip. Keep your back fairly straight to protect it from strain. If you curve your back you risk injury. (2) Begin the lift by driving with the legs. Straighten up until you are standing upright, then throw the chest out and shoulders back as if coming to attention. To lower the weight, bend the knees, lean forward from the waist, and touch the weight to the floor before beginning your next repetition.

Franco Columbu

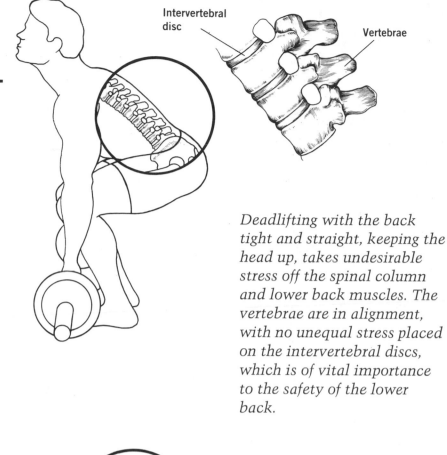

Intervertebral disc

Vertebrae

Deadlifting with the back tight and straight, keeping the head up, takes undesirable stress off the spinal column and lower back muscles. The vertebrae are in alignment, with no unequal stress placed on the intervertebral discs, which is of vital importance to the safety of the lower back.

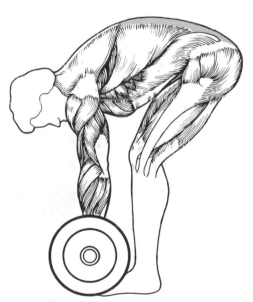

When you begin the Deadlift with your head up and back straight, you allow the glutei, leg muscles, and lower back to drive the bar upward with maximum force.

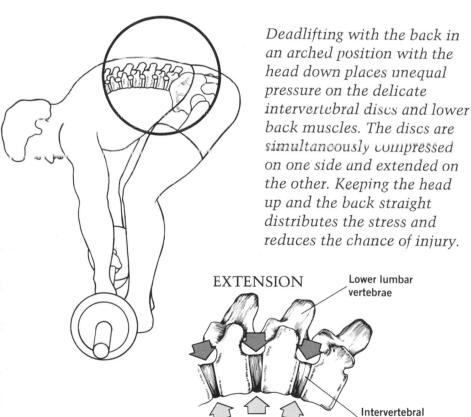

Deadlifting with the back in an arched position with the head down places unequal pressure on the delicate intervertebral discs and lower back muscles. The discs are simultaneously compressed on one side and extended on the other. Keeping the head up and the back straight distributes the stress and reduces the chance of injury.

EXTENSION

Lower lumbar vertebrae

COMPRESSION

Intervertebral disc

Starting a Deadlift with your back bent forward means that the lower back is going to have to do most of the initial work to get the bar moving. This is not only dangerous, but it turns the exercise into a lower back movement, which is not what it is supposed to be.

Good Mornings

Purpose of Exercise: TO WORK THE LOWER BACK IN ISOLATION.
Good Mornings are similar to Straight-Leg Deadlifts (see p. 479).

Execution: (1) Standing with feet a few inches apart, hold a barbell across the back of your shoulders as for Squats. (2) Keeping your legs locked and your back straight, bend forward from the waist, head up, until your torso is about parallel to the floor. Hold for a moment, then come back up to the starting position.

Hyperextensions

Purpose of Exercise: TO DEVELOP THE SPINAL ERECTORS OF THE LOWER BACK.

Execution: (1) Position yourself face down across a hyperextension bench, with your heels hooked under the rear supports. Clasp your hands across your chest or behind your head and bend forward and down as far as possible, feeling the lower back muscles stretch. (2) From this position, come back up until your torso is just above parallel. Don't lift up any higher than this or you will be using the hip flexor muscles rather than the spinal erectors.

Mike Christian

THE ARMS

The Muscles of the Arm

There are three major muscle groups in the arms:

The **biceps brachii,** a two-headed muscle with point of origin under the deltoid and point of insertion below the elbow

> BASIC FUNCTION: To lift and curl the arm, to pronate (twist downward) the wrist

The **triceps brachii,** a three-headed muscle which works in opposition to the biceps, also attaching under the deltoid and below the elbow

> BASIC FUNCTION: To straighten the arm and supinate (twist upward) the wrist

The **forearm,** involving a variety of muscles on the outside and inside of the lower arm that control the actions of hand and wrist.

> BASIC FUNCTION: The forearm flexor muscles curl the palm down and forward; the forearm extensor muscles curl the knuckles back and up.

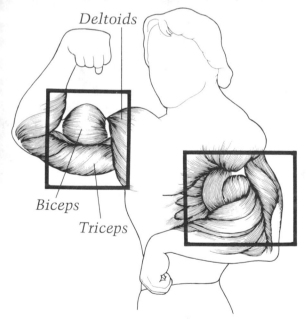

Deltoids

Biceps

Triceps

Jusup Wilkosz

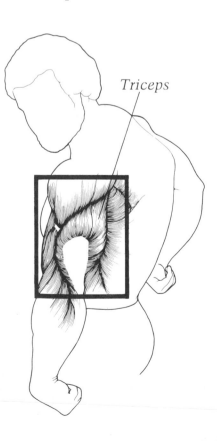

Triceps

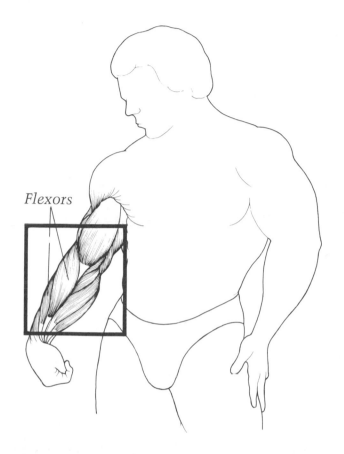

Flexors

Casey Viator

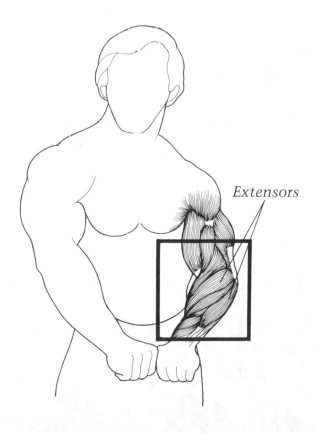

Extensors

Training the Arms

Along with the chest and back, bodybuilders have always considered massive arms the most impressive body part, an indicator of truly outstanding size and strength. When I first began training I would study photographs of bodybuilders, and what drew my attention most were the huge biceps. Leroy Colbert, for example, could hit fantastic biceps poses. Reg Park, Bill Pearl, and Serge Nubret were all known for tremendous arm development. I would go through the magazines page by page looking for examples of outstanding biceps and vow that someday my arms would look like that too.

Eventually, I did become known for my huge, high-peaked biceps. My arms measured over 20 inches when I was still only nineteen years old, and continued to develop until, at their largest, they measured 22¼ inches pumped. There are few things as thrilling on a bodybuilding stage as true 19- or 20-inch arms.

There is one great advantage when it comes to training arms: because muscles and big arms are so closely associated, it is not difficult to get yourself mentally into arm training. If you go into any serious gym around the country you will probably see young bodybuilders who are just beginning to show overall signs of competition potential, but will already have made great strides in arm development.

Leroy Colbert

Me at nineteen

One of the reasons this happens is that bodybuilders, especially when first starting out, train the arms according to the Priority Principle, whether they know it or not. They train arms first, with great concentration and energy. They flex and pose them all the time, measuring them constantly to see if they have made any progress—and so naturally they grow. If they thought the same way about their other body parts, we no doubt would see a lot of them walking around with 20-inch calves as well as huge arms!

But developing top-quality arms for competition is more than just a matter of size. They need to look good in a lot of poses and from a number of different angles. This means that every part of the arm muscles, every contour and angle, must be fully brought out. This takes a lot of thought and planning. You don't develop championship-level arms simply by throwing around a heavy barbell doing Curls and blasting out some reps for triceps.

Front double-biceps pose

Back double-biceps pose

Two aspects of the biceps. In the right arm, a high peak, great shape, and clear definition and separation; in the left, the biceps provides the mass and separation that helps make the arm look huge.

For a front double-biceps pose, for example, you need high-peaked biceps, triceps that hang impressively below the arm, and a well-defined separation between biceps and triceps. For the same pose from the back, you need brachialis forearm development at the elbow, good development of the outside head of the biceps, and a clear, visible tie-in between the deltoid and the muscles of the upper arm.

Along with biceps and triceps development, you also need to build and shape your forearms so that they are in proportion to the muscles of the upper arm. When you look at the arms of Casey Viator, Frank Zane, Dave Draper, Bill Pearl, Larry Scott, Sergio Oliva, or Chuck Sipes you see biceps, triceps, and forearms all developed in proportion to one another.

These various aspects of development do not come about by accident. You need to work at it, which means breaking the muscles of the arms down into separate categories and making sure that each gets its share of hard training.

Sergio Oliva in a straight-arm pose

Side-chest pose

Another straight-arm pose

Dave Draper, the California golden boy, used to blow away competition with his near-perfect arm development.

Sergio Oliva's arms are not only beautifully proportioned but so massive that he has to slit the sleeves of his shirts all the way to the shoulder to get his arms into them.

Larry Scott, the first Mr. Olympia, was one of the first modern bodybuilders with what I would call perfect arms.

Developing Perfect Arms

Though we tend to think of giant, bulging biceps when we think of well-developed arms, in point of fact the triceps are the larger, more complex muscle group. The biceps have two heads, the triceps have three. The ideally proportioned arm is usually one-third biceps and two-thirds triceps.

A few bodybuilders have been known for having almost perfect arm development. Ricky Wayne was one of these, as were Larry Scott, Serge Nubret, and Freddy Ortiz. Nowadays, I would also include Bertil Fox, Albert Beckles, Danny Padilla, and Casey Viator in that category. Sergio Oliva had massive arms, but the triceps tended to overly dominate. As impressive as I was able to make my arms, I would have preferred to have larger triceps.

The front double-biceps pose is one of the hardest to do well. Freddy Ortiz carries it off because he has everything: proper forearm proportion, good biceps, triceps, deltoids, and pecs, a full rib cage, impressive lats, and a small waist.

Ricky Wayne comes as close to possessing perfect arm development as any bodybuilder I can think of.

Larry Scott demonstrates the qualities necessary for a great biceps shot—peak, full biceps, triceps developed in proportion, and a distinct separation between upper and lower arms.

Bertil Fox is one of the most massively developed of today's bodybuilders, as this impressive arm shot demonstrates.

Albert Beckles displays one of the best peaked biceps in bodybuilding history.

Danny Padilla shows the importance of proportion. Although his 19-inch arms are smaller than the 21-inch arms of some of his competitors, in proportion to his small frame they are incredibly huge.

Achieving arm perfection means knowing which muscles to train, with which exercises, and what amount of effort to give to each. There are different ways of approaching arm training. You can train the whole arm in one workout, either finishing each muscle group before going on to the next or alternating sets for biceps and triceps, getting the whole arm pumped at one time. Or you can break up your training so that you train triceps one day, biceps the next, and forearms whenever it suits you.

As with other body parts, total development only comes about when you are able to shock the arms into responding no matter how big they become. Employing variety, change, and as many of the Shocking Principles as possible will all help to give you the kind of quality arms you are training for.

Casey Viator's forearm development is among the best in all of bodybuilding.

BICEPS TRAINING

Biceps have always been one of my best body parts. When I was young, building up my biceps was especially important to me, so I worked very hard and soon they blew up like balloons.

However, as hard as I may have worked, I now realize that my outstanding biceps development is largely hereditary. My biceps are like Tom Platz's thighs—once subjected to the hard work to make them develop, they possessed the genetic potential to be among the best in the world.

Hard work and proper training technique will bring out the full potential of any muscle, but not everybody has the same degree of potential. Some bodybuilders have longer biceps, some shorter; some with a higher or lower peak; some that develop enormous thickness and others that do not. You can work on each of these aspects of your development, bring up weak points with intelligent planning, but it certainly helps if you have a predisposition to great shape and proportion in the first place.

Actually, there are many different-shaped biceps that can still be considered first-rate. Larry Scott has long biceps that are thick and full at the same time. My own are noted for an extremely high peak. Franco Columbu's biceps are high, but short. Sergio Oliva has long biceps, but not particularly high. Boyer Coe has high, long biceps, but they are narrow. Yet each of these bodybuilders has been an outstanding champion, so it is obvious that there is no one way an arm has to be shaped in order to win contests.

The underlying bone structure and physical proportions have a lot to do with how the arm will ultimately look. Because Franco has short arms, it was not difficult for him to develop biceps that looked proportionately massive. But Lou Ferrigno, with his very long arms, needs 22-inch biceps just to have them look in proportion to his 260-pound body. If he had 20-inch arms, even though they might be the biggest on stage, he would look proportionately underdeveloped.

Proportion and relative strength of various other muscles can also make a difference in how the biceps are trained and developed. For example, when watching Franco Columbu and Ken Waller doing Barbell Curls, it seemed to me that because their front delts were so powerful, these muscles were taking over a lot of the lifting effort from the biceps. Therefore, they had to make a special effort to isolate the biceps, or else they would never get the training they required. One way they did this was by using the "Arm Blaster" to lock their elbows in place while doing Curls. Another was by doing a lot of biceps training using a preacher bench to further isolate the arm muscles.

If you have a similar problem but don't have this kind of specialized equipment, you can simply do your Curls standing with your back against a wall in order to minimize cheating.

Since my front delts were not so proportionately strong, I didn't have that problem. Therefore, I found doing regular Barbell Curls very beneficial. I did not have to make the special effort to isolate the biceps—which was just as well, since I didn't know that much about the physiology of training in my early years.

Nonetheless, you can't use other muscles to help with the lift and expect to develop great biceps. You also need to find the right groove—doing any Curl movement through the longest range of motion. When you do a Curl, you must bring your hand directly up to your shoulder. If you change that line an inch to the inside or the outside, you are taking stress off the biceps and you won't get the same results.

Another mistake I see all the time—Sergio Oliva used to do this—is starting off a Curl movement with a Wrist Curl—bending the wrist back, then curling it up just before engaging the biceps. All this does is to take stress away from the biceps by using forearm strength rather than biceps strength, and the result will be huge forearms and mediocre biceps.

But one Curl movement is not enough to work the entire biceps. The biceps not only lift and curl the arm, they also rotate the wrist. Lifting with a bar produces biceps mass, but it locks the wrists and keeps them from moving. So I always include a number of dumbbell exercises that let me twist the wrist to the outside as I lift the weight, giving me a more complete biceps contraction. Working with dumbbells, I'm able to get a better brachialis development (at the elbow), and that creates a much sharper separation between the biceps and triceps in a rear double-biceps pose.

Biceps length is also important. Many people do Reverse Curls as a forearm exercise, but I have noticed that this exercise also increases the length of the biceps. The muscle should extend all the way down almost to the elbow and then swoop into a full and powerful-looking curve.

I also like to change my hand position as much as possible when doing Curls in order to completely stimulate all the different areas of the biceps. The Barbell Curl locks the hand, the Dumbbell Curl lets you rotate the hand, the Reverse Curl brings the hand up in a palm-down position, and lifting a dumbbell with the thumb on top, a kind of Hammer Curl, hits the brachialis directly and is necessary for complete biceps development. And I add variety to my biceps workouts by using different kinds of

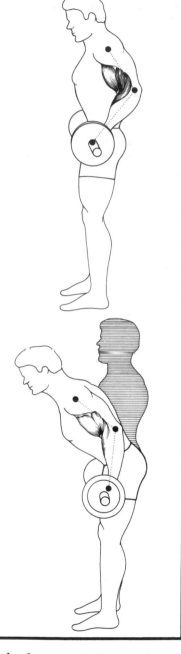

This is an incorrect beginning position for Barbell Curls. The arms are bent and elbows back, which prevents the biceps from being fully extended and drastically shortens the range of motion. Since the arms never get stretched out using this technique, you never develop the lower part of the biceps.

Starting the lift from a bent-over position is one of the most common mistakes made when doing Barbell Curls. If you begin the lift and straighten up at the same time, the lower back becomes involved. This produces extra momentum during the movement that causes you to swing the weight up instead of lifting it with an intense contraction of the biceps, so the lower part of the biceps never gets properly stimulated. For the correct approach to this exercise, see page 398.

equipment—the Arm Blaster, a straight bar, an E-Z curl bar, a preacher bench, a prone bench, barbells, dumbbells, cables, and machines.

Again, the major mistake I see in biceps training is lack of a full movement. There is probably no body part in which training for a full range of motion is so important. You will restrict the range of motion if you do things like lifting your elbows up or holding them too far back and therefore not getting a wide enough arc in the exercise.

Some bodybuilders don't want to lower the weight to full extension, with their arms locked out, because they can't lift as much weight that way. But they forget that it is this lower area of the range of motion that creates the real thickness in the lower biceps and makes the muscle appear to come right out of the forearm—an important look when you do poses with your arms extended. This part of the muscle also rolls up and helps to create height when you flex.

You see bodybuilders locking out their arms on Curls, but then they ruin the movement by not doing a strict curling motion right from the beginning. Instead, they lift the weight up, using a little shoulders and some back, so the first few inches of the movement are wasted because the biceps are simply not involved.

Another mistake is to bring the weight all the way up and then neglect to flex and contract the muscle. When the weight is up at your chin, the bones and joints are taking most of the strain. To keep the muscle working, you have to really flex it hard or it remains soft because you are not keeping it under stress. You are never going to have full, hard, and thick biceps with which to impress judges if you get lazy at the top of your Curl movements.

Cheat Curls

Curls are one of the exercises where "cheating" can be used effectively. Curls are essentially a rotary movement, yet the resistance of the weight works vertically. In other words, you are lifting with a circular motion but gravity continues to pull the weight straight down. Sometimes during the movement you are lifting out, other times lifting up, but the resistance is always up and down. So you are not continuously lifting in direct opposition to the weight. This makes the exercise less effective in certain parts of the movement.

The designers of Curl machines state that their equipment, which acts with a rotary rather than linear motion, is better for doing Curls than barbells or dumbbells. However, you don't need a complicated machine to overcome this difficulty. Instead, you can do some of your Curls using a weight that is too heavy for a strict movement. So even though you are using your back and shoulders to help "force" the weight up, you are also forcing the biceps to work to the maximum at every point along the movement.

The barbell or dumbbell is harder to lift at the point where your forearms are straight out than at the beginning of a Curl when your arms are pointed more toward the floor. Doing Cheat Curls, you can use a weight that feels very heavy in the "easy" part of the movement and then cheat a little to get you past the "hard" part where the resistance is too great to overcome using strict technique.

I remember doing exhibitions for Reg Park in South Africa in which I would do five repetitions of Barbell Cheat Curls with 275 pounds. Handling this amount of weight does not help to create great biceps shape or give the muscle a high peak, but it certainly is effective as a mass builder. However, Cheat Curls should be no more than 25 or 30 percent of your biceps program. You also need a variety of strict movements to develop the complete quality of the muscle.

Beginning Program

The Barbell Curl, done strictly or with cheating, is the fundamental exercise for building mass in the biceps. The Barbell Curl remains in the program all the way through, from beginning to competition training. This is the only way to continue to build and maintain maximum muscle mass and thickness. But I also recommend including Dumbbell Curls from the very start because this exercise allows you to supinate (twist) your wrist, which gives you a more complete contraction and helps to develop the full shape of the muscles.

I also recommend One-Arm Curls almost from the beginning. When doing these, I hold on to something with one hand to steady myself, lean a little to the side to give me a free range of motion, and concentrate totally on each biceps in turn—something you can't do when you are working both arms at the same time.

Advanced Program

When you get into Advanced Training, you continue trying to build additional mass, but you must also be concerned with creating separation and shaping the entire biceps structure. If your biceps lacks length, begin to lengthen it; if it lacks a peak, work on height. If not thick enough, make it thick.

Incline Dumbbell Curls are the best exercise for developing the shape and quality of the biceps and getting an even greater stretch in the muscle. Along with this, the Concentration Curl is specifically designed to create biceps height.

As you progress, you will begin to superset your exercises, creating more intensity by cutting down the time interval. I like the idea of supersetting biceps and triceps, which gives an enormous pump to your arms and makes you feel gigantic. Also, you can handle heavier weights for triceps when your biceps are pumped like a pillow, giving you a kind of cushion you can bounce off of with each triceps repetition.

Supersetting different muscles is also valuable in preparing you for competition, when you will need to pump your whole body at the same time. If you aren't used to this, you will not be able to show yourself at your best when you step out on stage.

The closer you get to competition, the more you have to be certain that you do enough additional exercises to fully develop every aspect of the biceps. Besides the mass-building Barbell Curls, you need to do more Incline Curls, which helps to develop the lower part of the muscle. I often would go even further and actually lie on a flat bench to do Dumbbell Curls, stretching the biceps even more. You also need additional cable and dumbbell work which allows you to twist your wrist and more fully shape the muscle.

Competition Program

At each level, you are required to do something extra, to continue to overload and demand more of the muscles. This principle is even more important when you are training your arms for competition. One good way of increasing the intensity of your training is by doing Alternate Dumbbell Curls instead of Barbell Curls. In this way you are able to isolate each biceps, and concentrate all your energy on each arm in turn. Because of the way this exercise is done—with one arm coming up as the other is going down—you are able to achieve a much stricter movement with very little cheating. You can increase intensity by going farther and locking in the elbows by doing Preacher Curls, which forces you to work in a stricter manner while hitting the lower biceps to a greater degree.

The degree of time-intensive training you need for competition preparation is greater than ever before, involving tri-sets—three exercises in a row without any stopping to rest in between. This will be difficult at first, but as your conditioning increases you will find this accelerated program gives you a tremendous pump and allows you to do an enormous amount of training in a very short time.

Above all, you need to employ as many techniques as possible to shock the biceps into further development. I always liked, for example, to do Barbell Curls with a partner: I would do a set, hand the weight immediately to him to do his set, have him hand it back to me immediately for my next set, and so on until exhaustion.

For total competition development, I made sure I did a lot of single sets, supersets, and tri-sets with a large variety of exercises —a set of biceps once an hour every hour the day before a contest; cheating reps; partial reps; forced reps; negative reps; Curls to the inside, Curls to the outside—nothing left out, nothing left to chance.

I attacked my biceps for competition with the Stripping Method, but also with "21s," combining a lot of partial reps and full reps, and supersetting one biceps exercise with another as well as supersetting biceps with biceps, biceps with triceps, or biceps with whatever.

I also used a lot of visualization in biceps training. In my mind I saw my biceps as mountains, enormously huge, and I pictured myself lifting tremendous amounts of weight with these super-human masses of muscle.

This kind of intense training will ensure that you build enough mass in the biceps, that you gain biceps length, thickness, and height, that you develop the inside and outside of the biceps and the separation between biceps and deltoids and between biceps and triceps—all of which you have to have if you want to build a championship physique.

Weak Point Training

But even if you do everything I have outlined above, and more, you may still find that certain areas of the biceps are relatively less well developed than others.

In general, when you are trying to build up a weak area of the biceps, the best technique you can employ is one-arm dumbbell exercises. Doing an entire set with just one arm at a time allows for maximum concentration and intensity, and ensures that each arm works to its maximum. This keeps a stronger biceps from overshadowing the weaker, which can result in asymmetrical arm development. Also, be sure to twist the wrist during the movement for total biceps contraction.

However, I believe one major reason why bodybuilders show weak points in the biceps is that they do the exercises incorrectly. You need to master proper technique—keeping the elbows steady, lowering the weight rather than dropping it, employing as many Shocking Principles as possible—and then you will be much less likely to have problems in this area.

For example, I see a lot of bodybuilders using their forearms when they do Curls, starting the motion with a kind of Wrist Curl which takes away from the effectiveness of the exercise. Or they will do a Curl and, at the top, instead of flexing their biceps —to create a high peak—they will just throw the weight back toward their shoulders, leaving the biceps loose and not working at all. I recommend instead using the Peak Contraction Principle —flexing the biceps as hard as possible when you get to the top of the Curl.

But sometimes biceps development lags behind simply because they aren't being trained hard enough, the bodybuilder feeling that five sets of biceps is plenty and ending up with big but relatively shapeless masses of muscle where he should have beautifully sculpted biceps.

This photo shows my arms at their most massive, when I weighed 245 pounds and relied heavily on Barbell and Cheat Curls using very heavy poundage. Notice how thick and huge the unflexed arm looks.

To correct specific weak points in the biceps, I recommend the following exercises:

For mass	Heavy Barbell Curls and Cheat Curls. Muscle size comes from lifting heavy weights. If you can curl 110 pounds and you train up to the point where you can curl 130 pounds, your biceps are going to get bigger. Try using my visualization technique to imagine your biceps growing to superhuman size.
For length and lower thickness	Curls that concentrate on the lower third of the range of motion.
	Incline or Prone Curls to stretch the biceps to their maximum.
	Strict movements, like Preacher Curls or Curls with the Arm Blaster, to lock your elbows and allow you to get the fullest extension of the biceps.
	After completion of each set of any Dumbbell Curl exercise, rotate the wrists 180 degrees five or six times.

The longer and thicker your biceps, the better they will look when you hold your arm straight out, and the bigger and higher they will be when you curl and flex your arm in a biceps shot.

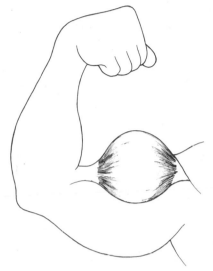

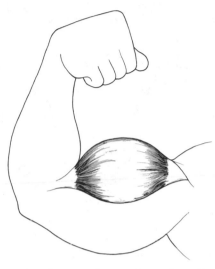

This is a biceps with a high peak but a short head. The muscle belly does not extend completely down to the elbow, which leaves a gap.

This biceps has a long head, but it lacks height.

Many bodybuilders don't realize that the function of the biceps is to twist the wrist as well as lift and curl. This is why I always started a curling movement as shown in pictures 1 and 2.

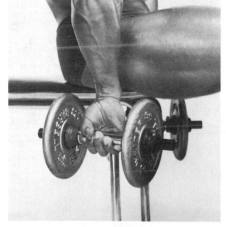

The hand positions in pictures 3 and 4 are good if you want to concentrate on the lower biceps while doing Dumbbell Curls.

Thickness in the biceps is important, but height is a quality that is often overlooked. I have always worked hard on developing peaks, and I feel that I won a lot of competitions because of my high biceps.

For height

Concentration Curls with a dumbbell or cable.

Dumbbell movements emphasizing a twist of the wrist (turning the thumbs outward) as you raise the weight—making certain you concentrate on the top third of the range of motion.

Use the Peak Contraction Principle—flexing the biceps as hard as possible at the top of the movement—and do a series of contractions and relaxations. Keep going until you get a tremendous pump.

Include "burns" in your workout—finishing off by bringing up the weight and fully contracting the biceps, then bringing the weight a third of the way, then back up to another full contraction. Do three or four reps of this movement and then put the weight down and pose and flex your biceps.

For outside biceps

Curls done inward toward the center of the body such as Narrow-Grip Barbell Curls or Narrow-Grip Preacher Bench Curls.

Concentration Curls that bring the weight into your chest.

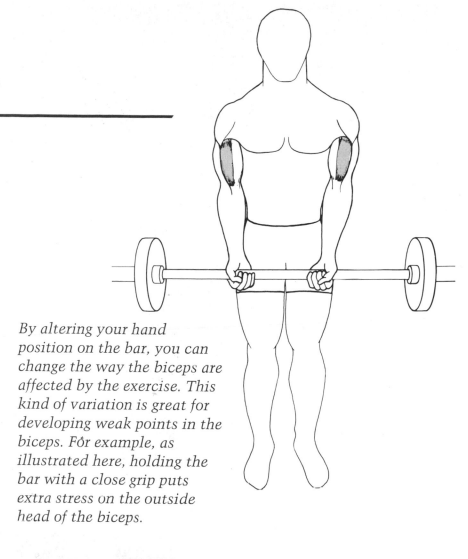

Well-developed outer biceps allow you to hit a number of poses effectively. For example, one of my favorite biceps poses is where I simply flex my arm and show the judges the outer biceps. But to get this kind of development you need to do the specific exercises for it that I recommend in my arm training program.

By altering your hand position on the bar, you can change the way the biceps are affected by the exercise. This kind of variation is great for developing weak points in the biceps. For example, as illustrated here, holding the bar with a close grip puts extra stress on the outside head of the biceps.

In order to make back poses like this twisting three-quarters back shot work, you have to have good outer biceps and brachialis development (at the elbow) in order to separate the biceps and triceps.

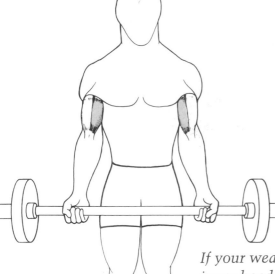

For inner biceps

If your weak point is the inner head of the biceps, you can put more stress on this area by holding your hands in a wide grip for Barbell Curls.

Hold dumbbells in a "hammer" position—palm turned toward the inside rather than facing upward. You will feel how this forces the outside of the biceps to do more of the work.

Standing Barbell Curls
Barbell Preacher Curls done with a wide grip
Seated or Standing Dumbbell Curls

Incline Dumbbell Curls

Standing Alternate Dumbbell Curls in which your arms are kept wide, outside the line of the shoulder biceps. If you curl out and downward and turn your wrists slightly outward, dropping your thumbs slightly, you will feel the exercise much more specifically in the inner biceps.

Inner biceps development helps create the necessary separation between biceps and triceps and between biceps and forearms, and Albert Beckles is a perfect example of how effective this can be.

For separation and definition

High set training, supersets and tri-sets. Try to use as many different bi-ceps exercises as possible, especially dumbbell movements that allow you to train at the greatest variety of angles and lots of one-arm movements to cre-ate maximum isolation.

Reverse Curls, to develop that little "bump" on the biceps that looks so good when you do a rear double-biceps shot. Remember to keep your elbows steady as a pivot point and keep your wrists steady throughout the move-ment.

Robby Robinson's arms are one of the best examples of biceps definition and separation. Looking at Robby is like examining an anatomy chart.

TRICEPS TRAINING

Serge Nubret has full, thick triceps, so his arms still look massive even when he is standing relaxed.

The triceps is a larger muscle mass than the biceps, and it needs more training. Like the biceps, the triceps have to look good from many angles. But unlike the biceps, the triceps need to make your arm look big, massive, and impressive when your arms are not flexed as well. When somebody says, "Wow, look at the size of that guy's arms!" you can be sure it is the triceps that are creating that effect. They are visible 90 percent of the time you are on stage whether you are standing relaxed or hitting poses.

Bill Pearl, Serge Nubret, Sergio Oliva, Albert Beckles, Freddy Ortiz, Casey Viator, Jusup Wilkosz, and Frank Zane are all good examples of bodybuilders who have great triceps. The triceps need to be developed in such a way that they look good when you do a side triceps shot, a front or rear biceps shot, or pose with your arms raised overhead or held straight out (a pose Larry Scott, Dave Draper, and I were noted for and which requires outstanding triceps). Imagine doing a rear lat shot and how effective good triceps can be from that angle. Or a most-muscular pose, with the triceps sticking out right from the elbow and continuing on to the rear deltoid. Or a front abdominal shot where your hands are behind your back.

While it is possible to hide weak biceps to some extent, weak triceps are obvious in almost any pose. When the judges look at you standing relaxed in round one they will know immediately if you have good triceps or not. Sergio Oliva, for example, could just stand there, his triceps looking huge and powerful, and make an impression on the judges, even though his biceps were not that outstanding.

However, just as with other body parts, there is a difference between big triceps and good triceps. Each and every part of this relatively complex muscle needs to be fully developed. When your arms hang, the triceps need to be evident all the way from the elbow to the rear deltoid. When they are flexed, each of the heads must be fully shaped, separated, and distinct.

Beginning and Advanced Programs

The first step in training triceps is to build up the mass and strength of the muscle structure. This means doing the basic triceps press and extension movements, gradually adding more and more weight until the area begins to respond. Different kinds of presses and extensions are designed to develop specific areas of the triceps. But there are also techniques you can use to maximize your triceps training. Remember that any time you

This triceps pose by Casey Viator shows tremendous separation of triceps from deltoid and the kind of quality detail—look at how clearly the outer triceps stands out—you can develop with proper training.

Casey Viator shows what total triceps development really means. The triceps of the straight arm shows each head clearly separated, while that of the flexed arm has the mass necessary to achieve a balance with the biceps.

The mass of the flexed triceps and the great shape of the triceps of the straight arm blend in perfectly with the outstanding muscularity of Albert Beckles' back.

Triceps are just as important in any back double-biceps shot as when you are doing specific triceps poses. Here you can see the way the triceps hang below the arm, and the separation between triceps, deltoids, biceps, and forearms.

straighten your arm against resistance—whether you are specifically doing triceps training or not—you will involve the triceps muscles.

In most cases, muscle mass and strength are enhanced by employing a cheating technique, but you don't need to cheat in order to put extra stress on the triceps. With all the effort you expend doing power training with Bench Presses, Dumbbell Presses, and Shoulder Presses, you are already putting an enormous strain on the triceps area.

Even though triceps are involved in a wide range of different exercises, it is also necessary, especially as you become more advanced, to isolate them and put the stress on each part directly to make certain you get full development of the muscle structure. For this, I recommend a number of different Triceps Extension movements, using barbells, dumbbells, and cables, each of which tends to hit a different area of the triceps.

Proportions and bone structure of individual bodybuilders will make it easier for some to develop good triceps. When doing Triceps Pressdowns, for example, it is easy for some to isolate the triceps, while others with different proportions and muscle attachments will find themselves involving the pectorals or even the lats instead of just the triceps. You see this a lot when some bodybuilders try to do Triceps Pressdowns and end up with a good chest pump. In a case like this, learning to totally isolate the triceps becomes extremely important, and can be accomplished by doing One-Arm Dumbbell Extensions or Barbell Triceps Extensions.

Lying Triceps Extensions work the muscle from the elbow to the rear deltoid, and are also great for developing the triceps for straight-arm poses. One-Arm Triceps Extensions help to develop the triceps so that they look good when you are doing biceps shots, with the fullness of the triceps offsetting the peak of the biceps. Lying Dumbbell Extensions work the outer head of the triceps to a much greater degree, giving you the shape and thickness you need for total triceps development.

Your hand position makes a difference in how an exercise affects the triceps. If you hold your hand so that the thumb is up, palm facing the inside, you work the outside of the triceps—as when doing Triceps Pressdowns holding on to a rope rather than pressing down on a bar or performing Dumbbell Kickbacks. If you turn your hand so that the palm faces straight, as in a French Press or Triceps Pressdown, you put more stress on the inner part of the triceps. If you twist your wrist, thumbs in and down—which is easiest when doing One-Arm Cable Triceps Pressdowns—you really hit the inside of the muscle.

Bill Pearl is the king of this particular triceps pose, which is a great way of showing the development of the upper triceps.

Advanced training also involves supersetting, hitting the muscle with one exercise after another to develop size, strength, shape, and endurance. You need to work the upper and lower, inner and outer triceps. Adding on exercises is important, but only if you pursue them with the kind of intensity that forces the muscles to continue to grow no matter how advanced you become.

Competition Program

Until you have seen a top-rated bodybuilder in shape for competition hitting a triceps shot, you probably have no idea what that muscle structure is supposed to look like. It is, in fact, almost like a horseshoe that curves up from the elbow behind the arm, striated and cross-striated, separated clearly from the deltoids above it and the biceps on the other side of the arm. In a great bodybuilder, this muscle can be awesome.

The Competition Program, which will help you to achieve this kind of look in your own physique, uses additional exercises besides those you have already learned, and a lot of time-intensive supersets to create the maximum training intensity.

Exercises like Cable Pressdowns, Kickbacks, Narrow-Grip Presses, and Dips tend to work the upper area of the triceps. Almost any triceps exercise will help develop the lower part of the muscle if you work only the lower range of motion. Take hold of the weight and bend your elbows, stretching the triceps as fully as possible. Then start to straighten out your arms, but stop after going through only about a third of the range of motion. Go back and forth just through this partial range and you will effectively work the lower area.

The opposite is true for upper triceps. For this area, completely lock out your arms on any triceps exercise and hold this contraction for three or four seconds, tensing the muscle isometrically. Following your set, pose and tense the muscle while your training partner does his set and you will get even more response from the upper triceps.

Remember, too, that the triceps rotates the wrist in opposition to the biceps. Just as you twisted the wrist outward in biceps exercises, you should do some triceps exercises in which you twist the wrist in the opposite direction. This will give you more complete contraction of the triceps muscle. Behind-the-Neck Dumbbell Extensions and One-Arm Cable Pressdowns are good exercises for this purpose.

Jusup Wilkosz

Weak Point Training

If you have a real problem with the triceps, I recommend training them according to the Priority Principle, working them first, when you are fresh. I did this myself years ago when I realized that my biceps had developed out of proportion to my triceps. I began to concentrate on this area, using the Priority Principle, and soon they began to respond so that I had an Olympia-quality arm rather than just Olympia-quality biceps.

I also found that supersetting triceps exercises, going right from one to the other, was another way of getting extra triceps development. I would first do a few sets to pump up the biceps, which creates a "cushioning" effect, and then really blast the triceps. After the superset, I would continue to flex and pose the triceps, never giving them any relief.

If triceps are an especially weak point for you, I recommend changing your program so that you train them by themselves from time to time, allowing you to concentrate only on the back of the arms to totally shock and stimulate the triceps. To overcome specific weak points, I recommend the following exercises.

For mass

Use the maximum weight possible in each exercise:

Narrow-Grip Bench Presses

Weighted Dips

Dips Behind the Back

Standing Triceps and French Presses (the heavy Bench Presses you use in your chest training will also help to build triceps mass)

Albert Beckles displays the ultimate in triceps mass. He doesn't have to squeeze his arm in against his lats to make the triceps appear huge; all he has to do is to extend the arm downward and flex.

For upper triceps   Cable Pressdowns and One-Arm Cable Pressdowns (regular and reverse grip)

Kickbacks

Dips

Do all triceps exercises strictly so that you really flex them totally, concentrating on locking out on each movement. Using the Peak Contraction Principle—holding the full contraction for a few moments at the top of each repetition.

Chris Dickerson is not known for having huge arms, but his triceps—particulary his upper triceps—are so well developed that his arms look really massive in this pose. Notice also the kind of superb separation between triceps and deltoid that helped Chris win the 1982 Mr. Olympia title.

Roy Callender is known for having perfect arms. One reason is the extremely thick development he has achieved of both the lower triceps and lower biceps.

For lower triceps	Weighted Dips
	Dips Behind the Back—doing partial reps in which you go all the way down, but only come up about three-quarters of the way (and not locking out) to keep the lower area of the triceps under stress the whole time (the more your arm is bent, the more your lower triceps takes up the stress)
For outer triceps	Movements with the hands in a thumbs-up position:
	Triceps Pressdowns using a rope
	Behind-the-Neck Dumbbell Triceps Extensions
	Dips
	Dumbbell Kickbacks
	One-Arm Cable Pressdowns with reverse grip (palm up)
	Behind-the-Neck Cable Extensions with a rope
	Lying Triceps Extensions in which the dumbbell comes down across the body
For inner triceps	Movements in which the thumb is turned inward:
	French Presses
	Triceps Pressdowns with a bar
	One-Arm Cable Pressdowns (palm downward)
	Close-Grip Barbell Presses

Here Jusup Wilkosz displays a very defined, separated, and well-developed triceps. This particular pose shows off more of the outer triceps.

This is a great illustration of how specific exercises work specific areas of the body, in this case how Triceps Pressdowns develop the inside of the triceps.

FOREARM TRAINING

Forearms should be taken just as seriously as any other body part if you want to develop a truly quality physique. They are involved in nearly every exercise for the upper body, either by helping you to grip a piece of equipment or by being a part of all pushing and pulling actions. So they get a lot of incidental training even when you are not specifically doing forearm exercises. In fact, any time you flex the elbows or wrists, you put stress on the forearm muscles.

Good forearm development is necessary to create a champion physique, but forearm strength is just as important. Strong forearms allow you to train with heavier weights and, in exercises such as Chins and Cable Rows, in which the hand and wrist are generally the "weak link," give you the capacity to train harder and put more stress on other muscles.

As with other muscles, genetic structure is a factor in determining the potential size and strength of the forearms. The reason some forearm muscles seem to extend all the way to the hand, with almost no tendon intervening, is because that person has an extremely long "muscle belly"—the actual contractile part of the muscle-tendon structure. Muscle size is affected by the length of the muscle belly because mass is a product of *volume*—that is, three dimensions rather than just one. So having two inches more length in the forearm actually translates into a lot of extra potential when you consider what the increase in cubic measurement can be. Casey Viator, Sergio Oliva, and the Mentzer brothers all have this type of forearm. Many bodybuilders constructed like this claim they do not need to do forearm training but get adequate results with exercises like heavy Barbell Curls. However, when I trained with Casey I saw him doing Barbell Wrist Curls with 155 pounds and Reverse Curls with 135 pounds. Sergio did endless sets of Reverse Curls on the preacher bench to get that enormous upper forearm development. Dave Draper, Chuck Sipes, and others with great forearms also did a lot of forearm training. So, even if you are genetically gifted with good forearms, this doesn't mean you don't have to train them.

Sergio Oliva is a good example of a bodybuilder with an extremely long forearm muscle, running from the elbow all the way down to the hand.

It is also possible to have "high" forearms, that is, to have a relatively short muscle belly and a long tendon, limiting the cubic volume of the muscle mass. Most bodybuilders, myself included, are somewhere in between, with neither the full forearm structure of a Sergio or impossibly high forearms. With this kind of forearm, it is possible to build the muscles up to where they are proportionate to the upper arm, but you have to train them hard to do so.

Beginning Program

Forearm training should be included as a part of your regular workout schedule right from the beginning, but these workouts will differ somewhat from those for other body parts. Because forearms are involved in so many other exercises you will not need very many forearm exercises to start with—Barbell Wrist Curls and Reverse Wrist Curls will suffice. I do not recommend doing as many sets for forearms as for legs, back, or other body parts—but I have found that doing sets of relatively high reps gives the best results.

Casey Viator demonstrates a basic forearm pose.

This pose by Dave Draper requires great forearm development to balance off the mass and separation of the upper arm.

One mistake many bodybuilders make with forearm training is that they don't use enough weight. Forearms are somewhat like calves in that they are accustomed to continuous use and heavy stress. So you need to use as much weight as possible in order to really stimulate the muscles.

Strict technique is also necessary to totally isolate the forearms and not let the biceps do the work. This is done by laying your forearms firmly on a bench, elbows close together and locked in between your knees.

It may seem to some that concentrating on forearms right from the beginning is not that important, but I disagree—forearm and grip strength are so essential to being able to train hard and heavy that you need to develop the forearms right from day one. And since forearm growth comes slowly to some people, the sooner you get started working on it the better.

Advanced Program

In the Advanced Training Program I have added One-Arm Wrist Curls to isolate and increase the intensity on each forearm in turn, and constructed the workout so that you superset Wrist Curls and Reverse Wrist Curls, giving you a total forearm pump.

Of course, just the fact that you are training the rest of the body so much more intensely at this point will in itself force the forearms to work harder. Your total workout will tend to exhaust the forearms so that, once you get to training them specifically, it will take a great deal of concentration and dedication to work these tired and worn-out muscles.

Remember that forearm size, more than almost any other body part, depends on genetics. If you have a short forearm muscle, and therefore have trouble gaining the kind of size you would like to have, begin thinking about extra forearm work early on. Because forearms gain in size slowly, you need time to make the changes you are looking for.

But you might be surprised just how quickly you can develop forearms if you really make the effort. Often, the reason bodybuilders have problems developing forearms is simply because they don't train them hard enough. They tack forearm training onto the end of their workout and do a few halfhearted sets. Believe me, if you want any body part to develop to its maximum, you have to take it seriously. Forearm training is no less important than training chest or biceps—not if you truly want to become a champion.

Competition Program

Once you begin training for competition, I recommend that you make sure you have hit every one of the fourteen forearm muscles by adding Preacher Bench Reverse Curls and Behind-the-Back Wrist Curls to your forearm program.

When you do Reverse Curls for the upper part of the forearms, use a straight bar rather than an E-Z curl bar. As you lift the bar in an upward arc from the area of your thighs, you curl the wrists back and fully involve the upper forearms. Incidentally, many bodybuilders lean back as they do Reverse Curls, but you should actually lean slightly forward. This further isolates the arms, puts continuous stress on the forearms, and gives you a much stricter movement.

Reverse Curls also work well on certain kinds of curl machines and when you use a preacher bench. But no matter which way you do this exercise, remember always to get a full range of movement, all the way down, all the way up, and keep it slow and under control. Remember, too, that your wrists and forearms will also be affected by heavy Barbell Curls and Cheat Curls, Triceps Extensions, and a number of other exercises throughout all the various levels of training.

I recommend doing forearm training at the end of your workout. If you try doing other upper body exercises when your wrists and forearms are already fatigued, you will severely limit your ability to train intensely.

One good method for totally stimulating your forearms is after you do your Wrist Curls—when you are too tired to do any more reps—simply let the bar hang in your fingers and then flex your fingers by opening and closing your hands and getting to those last few available muscle fibers.

Posing the Forearms

There are two different kinds of forearm poses: direct, in which you are deliberately calling attention to these muscles, and indirect, in which you are primarily posing other body parts but the forearms play a part nonetheless. Often when you hit a pose, people watching don't specifically notice forearm development—but they would certainly notice if it weren't there.

Since forearms are a third of the total arm, without proper forearm development the whole arm looks out of proportion. In a front double-biceps pose, the forearm must be full enough to

Dave Draper showing a direct forearm pose

balance off the development of the biceps. From the rear, in a back double-biceps, the muscularity of the forearm is part of the total effect.

Impressive forearms help you in every pose from side-chest to most-muscular and are extremely important when you have your arms extended, as in the classic javelin-thrower pose in which one arm is flexed, the other extended.

Certain poses are virtually impossible to carry off without exceptional forearm development. One that comes to mind is Sergio Oliva's famous pose where he lifts both hands overhead, flexes his forearms, and flares out his fantastic lats. In spite of Sergio's enormous back, if he didn't have such large and powerful forearms this pose would be much less impressive.

Some bodybuilders have such well-developed forearms that they can turn non-forearm poses into forearm showcases. Casey Viator is one of these. When he stands on stage and simply lifts his arms out to either side, it is impossible not to notice those huge forearms sticking out below the massive upper arms.

Another pose in which good forearms are absolutely essential is one Dave Draper and I both liked so much, in which the arms are held straight out and parallel to the floor. It takes both fully developed biceps and forearms to do this pose effectively.

Larry Scott was another bodybuilder who was able to pose his

Casey Viator and I demonstrate poses in which the back and the biceps are featured but well-developed forearms are necessary to make the pose complete.

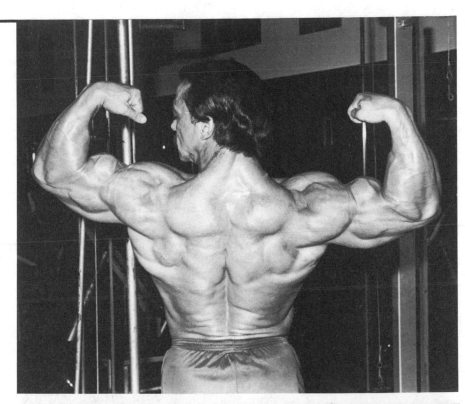

forearms to great advantage. When he won the very first Mr. Olympia contest in 1965, he had a thickness and muscularity that very few bodybuilders had ever attained. But he had also spent a lot of time in detail training, so his forearm development matched the rest of his physique, making many of his other poses that much more effective.

Weak Point Training

Many bodybuilders end up with a weakness in forearm development simply because they don't train forearms right from the beginning. Another reason for forearms lagging behind, aside from the obvious one of bone structure, is failing to execute the exercises correctly and in a strict enough manner. The more you isolate the forearms and force them to do the movements without any help from the upper arms, the more they will respond. This means being very, very strict in your execution.

It is also important to work the forearms through a long range of motion. You need to lower the weight as far as possible, getting the maximum stretch, then come all the way back up to get a total contraction of the muscles. Working through only three-quarters of the range of motion is not that beneficial because you already use this part of the muscle in a variety of other exercises.

If you want to drastically increase your forearm development, you can use the Priority Principle in a special way: train forearms by themselves when you are rested and strong, or train your forearms on leg days when your arms are rested. You can also keep a barbell or dumbbells at home and do a couple of sets of Wrist Curls and Reverse Wrist Curls as often as you like, even once an hour every hour.

Many bodybuilders forget that you can use the Shocking Principle to help develop your forearms, just as you can other body parts. Every shock method that works with Curls will also work for Wrist Curls—forced reps, supersets, the Stripping Method, partial reps, and so on.

An important technique for bringing up lagging forearms is one-arm training. Forearms that are used to working together to curl a barbell will often be shocked into accelerated development when you force them to lift and control a weight on their own. Dumbbell Wrist Curls and Dumbbell Reverse Wrist Curls are two of the primary exercises for accomplishing this. Additionally, doing cable work one arm at a time not only forces each forearm to work independently, but to work against a different

kind of resistance as well. For this kind of movement, I recommend One-Arm Cable Reverse Curls.

It is also necessary to pose and flex your forearms as often as possible—not just when you are training them, but between sets of arms, chest, back, and shoulders as well. Your forearms will have to be flexed every time you hit any kind of pose in competition, so you might as well get them used to it. And the effort of contracting them like this will also accelerate their development.

To sum up, the exercises I recommend for forearm weak point training are:

For upper forearms	Reverse Curls with a barbell, dumbbells, and on a preacher bench One-Arm Cable Reverse Curls Hammer Curls Reverse Wrist Curls
For inner forearms	One-Arm Wrist Curls Barbell Wrist Curls Behind-the-Back Wrist Curls
For lengthening the forearm muscle	Wrist Curls—letting the bar or dumbbells roll all the way down into the fingers, then opening and closing the hands without moving the wrist Reverse Curls with wrists kept bent downward and no Wrist Curl movement included at all

Here is a pose by Dave Draper in which inner forearm development is extremely important.

In this side-chest shot, Casey Viator shows the importance of good upper forearm development as well as long forearm muscles which insert all the way at the wrist.

ARM EXERCISES

Standing Barbell Curls

Purpose of Exercise: TO DEVELOP THE OVERALL SIZE OF THE BICEPS.

This is the most basic and popular of biceps exercises.

Execution: (1) Stand with feet a few inches apart and grasp the bar with an underhand grip, hands about shoulder width apart. Let the bar hang down at arm's length in front of you. (2) Curl the bar out and up in a wide arc and bring it up as high as you can, your elbows close to the body and stationary. Keep the arc wide and long, rather than bringing the bar straight up and making the movement too easy. Get a full flex of biceps at the top. Lower the weight again, following the same arc, and resisting the weight all the way down until your arms are fully extended. A small amount of body movement in this exercise is acceptable, because it is a mass-building movement, but this is to be kept to a minimum unless you are doing deliberate Cheat Curls. Bending forward and leaning back cut down on the range of motion.

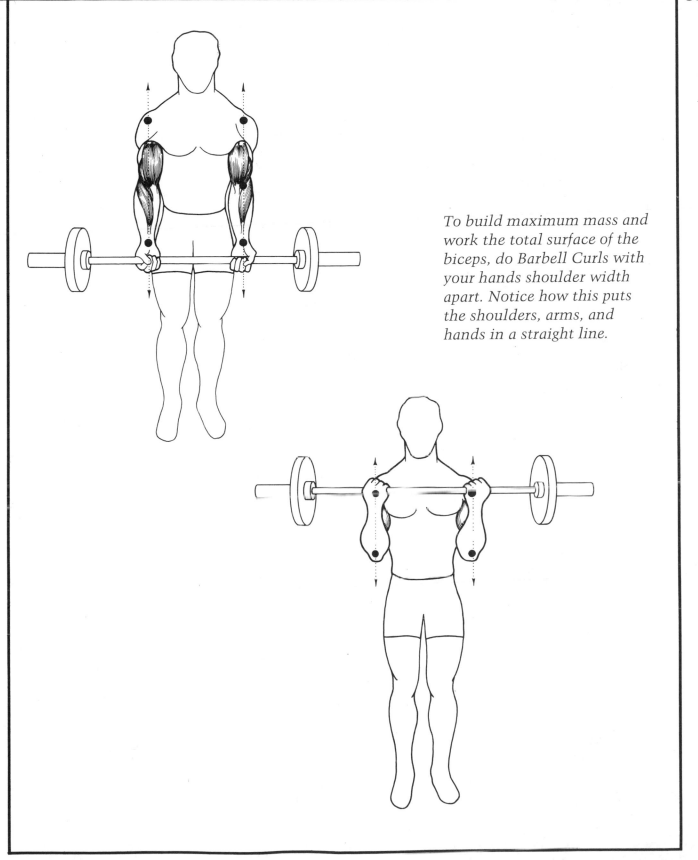

To build maximum mass and
work the total surface of the
biceps, do Barbell Curls with
your hands shoulder width
apart. Notice how this puts
the shoulders, arms, and
hands in a straight line.

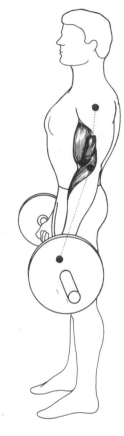

The correct beginning position for Barbell Curls: standing upright, elbows at sides, arms fully extended to stretch out the biceps

The correct finishing position for Barbell Curls: the body upright without swaying, the elbows fixed at the sides. This strict form forces the biceps to do all the work, without any help from the back or the shoulders. Notice too that when you hold your elbows steady your arms are still at an angle at the top of the movement rather than straight up and down. This means that the biceps are still doing the work of supporting the weight, instead of resting while the bones and joints do the work.

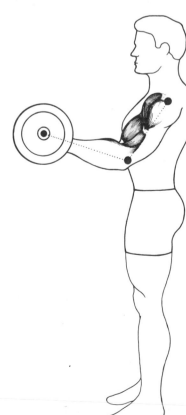

Notice what happens when you lift the elbows during the Barbell Curl. Instead of isolating and really working the biceps, you are involving the front deltoids, which defeats the purpose of the exercise.

Another problem that develops when you lift your elbows during the Barbell Curl instead of keeping them fixed by your sides: at the end position of the movement, the forearms are straight up and down, meaning that the bones are bearing the weight of the bar and the biceps are not doing any work at all.

Arm Blaster Curls (optional)

Doing Curls with an Arm Blaster is a very strict way of working the biceps that tends to develop the lower part of the muscle close to the forearm. By using the Arm Blaster, you get the same kind of effect as with a preacher bench—no elbow movement at all and strict isolation of the biceps.

Cheat Curls

Purpose of Exercise: TO DEVELOP EXTRA MASS AND POWER IN THE BICEPS.

Execution: Stand and hold the bar as for Barbell Curls, but use enough weight so that it becomes difficult to do more than just a few strict repetitions. At this point, you begin to swing the weight up using your back and shoulders to help your arms. The trick is to keep your biceps working as hard as they can, and cheat only enough to keep the set going. Keep the elbows stationary at the waist. I like to combine Barbell Curls and Cheat Curls, doing a normal set of Curls and, when my arms are too tired to do any more strict repetitions, loading on extra weight and doing some Cheat Curls to really blast the biceps.

Preacher Curls

Purpose of Exercise: TO DEVELOP THE LOWER AREA OF THE BICEPS AND TO LENGTHEN THE BICEPS MUSCLE.

This is especially good for anyone who has space between the lower biceps and the elbow joint, to fill in and shape this area and help to create thickness throughout the biceps.

Execution: Preacher Curls are an even stricter movement than regular Barbell Curls. (1) Position yourself with your chest against the bench, your arms extending over it. This puts the arms at an angle, which transfers additional stress to the lower area of the muscle. Take hold of a barbell with an underhand grip. (2) Holding your body steady, curl the bar all the way up and then lower it again to full extension, resisting the weight on the way down. You can use an E-Z curl bar for this movement, or even use the bench for One-Arm Dumbbell Curls. Don't lean back as you lift the bar, and deliberately flex the muscle extra hard as you come to the top of the movement, where there is little actual stress on the biceps muscles.

Preacher Curls can also be done with an E-Z curl bar.

Doing Preacher Curls with dumbbells forces each arm to work independently.

Doing this exercise with the dumbbells together works the outer biceps . . .

. . . and done with the dumbbells apart works the inner biceps.

Robby Robinson

3-Part Curls ("21s")

Purpose of exercise: TO DEVELOP AND SHAPE THE ENTIRE BICEPS AREA.

This exercise, a combination of partial-range and full-range movements, is a great test of endurance. Because of the combination of 3 sets of 7 repetitions each, this exercise is also known as "21s."

Execution: (1) From a seated or standing position, take a dumbbell in each hand, holding them at arm's length down at your sides. (2) Curl the weights upward but stop halfway, when your forearms are about parallel to the floor, then lower them again to the starting position. Do 7 repetitions of this movement and then without stopping, (3) curl the weights all the way up but stop halfway down and do 7 repetitions of this partial movement. At this point, even though exhaustion will be setting in, finish off the set by doing 7 full-range Dumbbell Curls. I like to do this exercise in front of a mirror so that I can really be sure of lifting in exactly the proper range.

Incline Dumbbell Curls

Purpose of Exercise: TO STRETCH THE BICEPS AND FOR OVERALL BICEPS DEVELOPMENT.

This exercise develops mass and biceps peak at the same time. If you do the movement to the front, it is a general biceps exercise. If you do it to the outside, it becomes a specialized exercise for the inner part of the biceps.

Execution: (1) Sit back on an incline bench holding a dumbbell in each hand. (2) Keeping your elbows well forward throughout the movement, curl the weights forward and up to shoulder level. Lower the weights again, fully under control, and pause at the bottom to keep from using momentum to swing the weights up on the next repetition. I find I get the best results with this exercise by pronating and supinating my wrists during the movement—turning the wrists so that the palms face one another at the bottom, then twisting the weights as I lift so that the palms turn upward, then outward, with the little finger higher than the thumb at the top.

Dumbbell Curls to the outside work the inner biceps and are an important part of weak point training.

Seated Dumbbell Curls

Purpose of Exercise: TO BUILD, SHAPE, AND DEFINE THE BICEPS.

Doing a standard curl with dumbbells rather than a barbell means you will use slightly less weight, but the arms are left free to move through their natural range of motion and you can achieve an even greater degree of contraction. As with Barbell Curls, you can cheat a little with this exercise, but keep it to a minimum.

Execution: (1) Sit on the end of a flat bench, or against the back support of an incline bench adjusted to an upright position, a dumbbell in each hand held straight down at arm's length, palms turned toward your body. (2) Holding your elbows steady as unmoving pivot points, curl the weights forward and up, twisting your palms forward as you lift so that the thumbs turn to the outside and the palms are facing up. Lift the weights as high as you can and then give an extra flex of the biceps to achieve maximum contraction. Lower the dumbbells down through the same arc, resisting the weight all the way down, until your arms are fully extended, the biceps stretched as far as possible. Twisting the wrists as you lift and lower the dumbbells causes a fuller contraction of the biceps and develops the inner biceps and separation between biceps and triceps. You can also do this exercise standing instead of seated, which will allow you to use a little more weight, although the movement will not be as strict.

Hammer Curls (optional)

This is done the same way as regular Dumbbell Curls except the palms face inward and stay that way throughout the movement. This way you train the forearms as well as the biceps.

Alternate Dumbbell Curls

Purpose of Exercise: TO ISOLATE THE BICEPS OF EACH ARM.

This is a variation of a Dumbbell Curl in which you curl the dumbbells alternately, first one arm and then the other, to give you that extra bit of isolation, allowing you to concentrate your energy on one arm at a time and to minimize cheating.

Execution: Stand upright, a dumbbell in each hand hanging at arm's length. Curl one weight forward and up, holding your elbow steady at your waist and twisting your wrist slightly, bringing the

thumb down and little finger up, to get maximum biceps contraction. Curl the weight as high as you can, then bring it back down under control through the same arc, simultaneously curling the other weight up so that both dumbbells are in motion, and twisting the wrist of the other hand as you bring it up. Continue these alternate Curls until you have done the required repetitions with both arms. Make sure you fully extend and contract the arm to get the fullest possible range of motion.

Using the Arm Blaster you get the strictness of a Preacher Curl, with the elbows fixed solidly in place, which is especially good for training the lower biceps.

You can do Alternate Dumbbell Curls in a sitting position as well.

Concentration Curls

Purpose of Exercise: TO CREATE MAXIMUM HEIGHT IN THE BICEPS, ESPECIALLY THE OUTSIDE OF THE BICEPS.

I like to do this exercise at the end of my biceps training because it is one of the best means of peaking the muscle. This is a very strict movement but it is for height, not definition, so use as much weight as you can handle. The name "Concentration Curl" is significant: you really need to concentrate on the biceps contraction and on being strict to make this exercise effective.

Execution: (1) In a standing position, bend over slightly and take a dumbbell in one hand. Rest your free arm on your knee or other stationary object to stabilize you. (2) Curl the weight up to the deltoid without moving the upper arm or the elbow and make certain you don't allow your elbow to rest against your thigh. As you lift, twist the wrist so that the little finger ends up higher than the thumb. Tense the muscle fully at the top of the Curl, then lower the weight slowly, resisting it all the way down to full extension. At the top of the Curl, the biceps are taking the full stress of the weight. Don't curl the weight to the chest—it must be curled to the shoulder in order to work the high outside biceps.

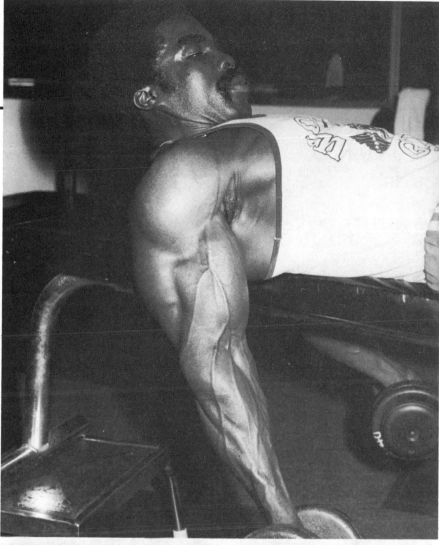

Lying Dumbbell Curls

Purpose of Exercise: TO BUILD THE ENTIRE BICEPS AND ESPECIALLY TO CREATE A HIGHER PEAK.

This is an exercise I learned from Reg Park, and it is particularly effective because it gives you a great biceps stretch and helps to lengthen the muscle. Also, due to the angle, the biceps must contract fully to offset the pull of gravity.

Execution: Use an exercise bench and, if necessary, place it on blocks to raise it higher off the ground. (1) Lie on your back on the bench, a dumbbell in each hand, your knees bent and feet flat on the bench. Let the dumbbells hang down (but not touching the floor) and turn your palms forward. (2) Keeping your elbows steady, curl the weights up toward the shoulders, keeping the movement very strict. Then lower the dumbbells back toward the floor, resisting the weight all the way down.

Two-Hand Cable Curls

Purpose of Exercise: TO DEVELOP AND SHAPE THE BICEPS, PARTICULARLY THE HEIGHT OF THE BICEPS PEAK.

Execution: Attach a bar to a floor-level cable and pulley. (1) Grasp the bar with an underhand grip, hands about shoulder width apart. Keeping your elbows fixed at your sides, extend your arms out and down until your biceps are fully stretched. (2) Curl the bar upward, not letting your elbows move, to a postion just under your chin. Contract your biceps as hard as possible on top, then lower the bar slowly back down until your arms are fully extended, biceps stretched. This is a shaping rather than a mass exercise, so the key to doing it properly is a slow, smooth, controlled motion.

Mike Christian

Cable Curls with Preacher Bench (optional)

To do this movement with a preacher bench, (1) sit down and place your arms over the bench to hold them steady as you (2) curl the weight up and slowly lower it again, resisting the weight all the way down.

Preacher Cable Curls combine the strictness of the preacher bench with the strictness that comes from the steady resistance provided by a cable.

Doing Preacher Curls with a cable gives the biceps resistance even on the top. (With dumbbells or barbells, the resistance is mostly on the bottom.) Therefore, doing the exercise with a cable helps you to add height to your biceps.

Reverse Curls

Purpose of Exercise: TO DEVELOP THE OUTSIDE OF THE BICEPS.

This exercise is also good for forearm development.

Execution: (1) Standing with your feet a few inches apart, grasp a barbell with an overhand grip and hold it down in front of you at arm's length. (2) Keeping your elbows steady, curl the weight out and up to a position about even with your chin. Lower the weight through the same arc, resisting all the way down. Gripping the bar this way, you put the biceps in a position of mechanical disadvantage, so you will not be able to curl as much weight. The reverse grip makes the top of the forearm work very hard. Reverse Curls for the biceps rather than the forearms do not begin with any kind of Reverse Wrist Curl. Keep the wrists steady as you curl the weight up. Notice that the thumb is kept on top of the bar. This will help to work the outside brachialis.

Machine Curls

A lot of equipment companies make Curl machines designed to allow you to subject your biceps to full-range rotary resistance. One advantage of these machines is that they allow you to do heavy forced negatives, your workout partner pressing down on the weight as you resist during the downward part of the movement. Another is that you can often get a longer range of motion, giving you more stretch and total contraction. However, machines lock you into one narrow range of motion, which will not allow for a really full development of the biceps. Use machines as a method of getting more variety in your workouts in addition to, but not instead of, free weight Curls.

Reverse Preacher Bench Curls

Purpose of Exercise: TO DEVELOP THE OUTSIDE OF THE BICEPS AND THE TOP OF THE FOREARM.

Using a preacher bench, the movement is done very strictly.

Execution: Grasp a bar with an overhand grip, hands about shoulder width apart. Lean across a preacher bench and extend your arms fully. Let your arms hang toward the floor, then curl the weight up, curling back with the wrists as well, and keeping the elbows firmly anchored. Curl the weight as far as possible, then lower it again, keeping it under control and resisting all the way down. Keep your body steady throughout the movement and avoid rocking back and forth.

Triceps Cable Pressdowns (or Lat Machine Pressdowns)

Purpose of Exercise: TO WORK THE TRICEPS THROUGH A FULL RANGE OF MOTION.

Hook a short bar to an overhead cable and pulley, (1) stand close to the bar and grasp it with an overhand grip, hands about 10 inches apart. Keep your elbows tucked in close to your body and stationary. Keep your whole body steady—don't lean forward to press down with your body weight. (2) Press the bar down as far as possible, locking out your arms and feeling the triceps contract fully. Release and let the bar come up as far as possible without moving your elbows. For variety, you can vary your grip, the type of bar you use, how close you stand to the bar, or the width between your hands; or you can do a three-quarter movement, going from all the way up to three-quarters of the way down in order to work the lower triceps more directly.

Jusup Wilkosz

Arm Blaster Pressdowns . . . I frequently do Pressdowns using an Arm Blaster to keep the elbows from moving and so create a superstrict movement.

When doing Pressdowns with incline board, you force the triceps to work at an unfamiliar angle, and you can't cheat. This is one of Jusup Wilkosz's favorite exercises.

With a normal grip, Pressdowns tend to work more of the outer triceps. Reverse-Grip Pressdowns put more stress on the inner triceps, and also help give you that "horseshoe" effect.

One-Arm Cable Reverse Pressdowns

Purpose of Exercise: TO ISOLATE THE TRICEPS AND DEVELOP THE HORSESHOE SHAPE OF THE MUSCLE.

This exercise is especially good for contest or weak point training, because by using a cable you can work each arm separately in isolation.

Execution: (1) Using an overhead cable and pulley, take hold of the handle with a reverse grip, palm up.
(2) Keeping your elbow fixed and unmoving, straighten your arm until it is locked out and extended straight down. Flex the triceps in this position for extra contraction. Still not moving the elbow, let your hand come up as far as possible until the forearm touches the biceps, feeling a complete stretch in the triceps. Finish your repetitions, then repeat with the other arm.

Seated Triceps Presses

Purpose of Exercise: TO DEVELOP THE INSIDE AND REAR HEADS OF THE TRICEPS.
This exercise gives you extra stretch to hit the inside of the triceps more directly.

Execution: Grasp a barbell with an overhand grip, hands close together. (1) Sit on a bench and raise the bar straight up overhead, arms locked out. (2) Keeping your elbows stationary and close to your head, lower the weight down in an arc behind your head until your triceps are as stretched as possible. Only the forearms should move in this exercise. From this position, using only your triceps, press the weight back up overhead to full extension. Lock your arms out and flex your triceps. You might prefer doing this exercise using an E-Z curl bar, or on an incline bench.

Standing Triceps Presses

Purpose of Exercise: TO DEVELOP THE FULL SWEEP OF THE TRICEPS.

Doing this movement gives your triceps a full look to complement the biceps when doing a double-biceps pose. Performing Triceps Presses standing instead of seated changes the angle at which the triceps are forced to work and, in addition, allows you to do a cheating movement and thus to use more weight. This exercise can also be done with a cable and rope through a floor-level pulley, which hits the outer arm of the triceps.

Execution: Grip a straight or E-Z curl bar with an overhand grip, hands about 10 inches apart. Stand upright and hold the bar extended straight overhead. Keeping your elbows stationary and close to your head, lower the weight down behind your head as far as possible, then press it back up to the starting position through a semicircular arc.

Lying Triceps Extensions

Purpose of Exercise: TO WORK THE TRICEPS ALL THE WAY FROM THE ELBOW DOWN TO THE LATS.

Execution: (1) Lie along a bench, your head just off the end with knees bent and feet flat on the bench. Take hold of a barbell (preferably an E-Z curl bar) with an overhand grip, hands about 10 inches apart. (2) Press the weight up until your arms are locked out, but not straight up over your face. Instead, the weight should be back behind the top of your head, with your triceps doing the work of holding it there. Keeping your elbows stationary, lower the weight down toward your forehead, then press it back up to the starting position, stopping short of the vertical to keep the triceps under constant tension. Keep control of the weight at all times in this movement to avoid banging yourself on the head with the bar. When you can't do another rep, you can still force the triceps to keep working by repping out with some Close-Grip Extensions.

If you keep your head up as you do a Lying Triceps Extension, you will not be able to lower the bar far enough to stretch the triceps completely.

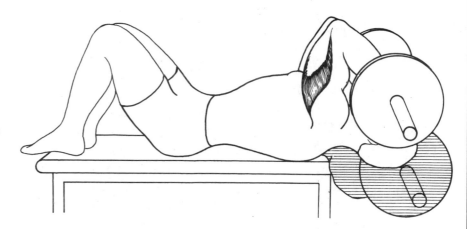

Letting your head drop slightly over the end of the bench gives you room to lower the bar far enough to get full extension of the triceps.

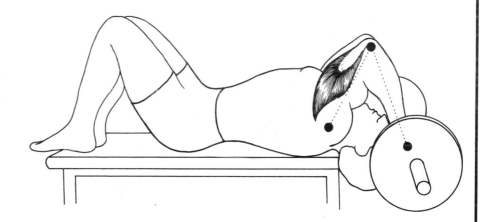

A common mistake when doing Lying Triceps Extensions is to lift the weight up so that you hold it straight overhead, which means the bones and joints are doing the work rather than the triceps. This illustration shows the right way to do it—positioning yourself so that your arms are still at an angle when you lock out. This angle ensures that the triceps can't rest on top but still have to fight gravity to support the weight.

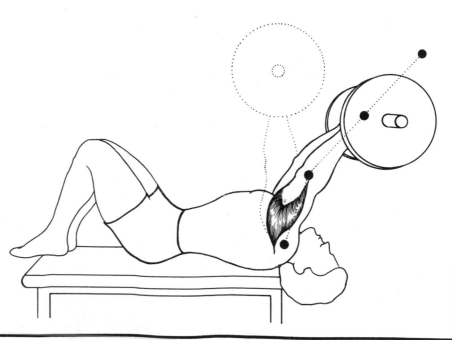

*Close-Grip Extension—
starting position*

*Close-Grip Extension—
end position*

Lying Dumbbell Extensions

Purpose of Exercise: TO WORK THE OUTER TRICEPS.

Execution: (1) Lie on a bench, head even with the end, knees bent, feet flat on bench. Hold two dumbbells overhead, arms straight, palms facing one another. (2) Hold your elbows stationary and lower the dumbbells down on either side of your head until your triceps are fully stretched and the weights touch your shoulders. Press them back up through a sweeping arc, but lock your elbows out before your arms are pointed straight up overhead and flex your triceps.

Lying Cross Face Triceps Extensions (optional)

Lying Dumbbell Extensions also can be done with one dumbbell at a time by bringing the dumbbell across your body to the opposite shoulder. When you finish your reps with one arm, repeat with the opposite one. Changing the angle like this hits the outer triceps.

Dumbbell Kickbacks

Purpose of Exercise: TO DEVELOP THE UPPER TRICEPS.

Execution: (1) Stand with knees bent, one foot in front of the other, putting your hand on the leading knee or a low bench for balance. Take a dumbbell in the opposite hand, bend your arm and raise your elbow back and up to about shoulder height, elbow close to your side and letting the dumbbell hang straight down below it.

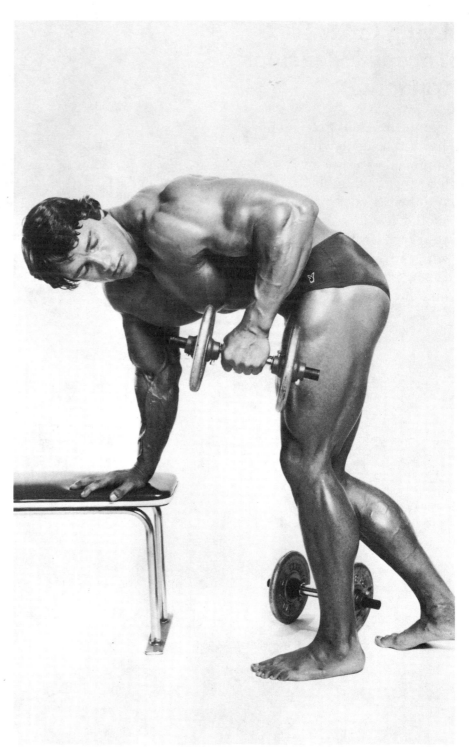

1

(2) Keeping your elbow stationary, press the weight back until your forearm is about parallel to the floor. Hold here for a moment and give the triceps an extra flex, then slowly come back to the starting position. For added triceps development, twist your hand slightly as you lift the weight, bringing the thumb up, and twist back the other way as you come down. Finish your set, then repeat the movement using the other arm. Make sure that only your forearm moves in this exercise, not the upper arm. This exercise can also be done with cable pulleys.

MACHINE TRICEPS EXTENSIONS

Various machines allow you to do Triceps Extensions with one arm at a time or both together, and many give the opportunity to work the full range of motion of the triceps under constant resistance. Use these machines for variety in your workout or to allow your training partner to help you with forced reps and forced negatives when you feel like working extra heavy.

432

One-Arm Triceps Extensions

Purpose of Exercise: TO WORK THE ENTIRE TRICEPS AND TO SEPARATE THE THREE TRICEPS HEADS.

Execution: (1) Sitting on a bench, take a dumbbell in one hand and hold it extended overhead. (2) Keeping your elbow stationary and close to your head, lower the dumbbell down in an arc behind your head (not behind the shoulder) as far as you can. Feel the triceps stretch to their fullest, then press the weight back up to the starting position. It is essential to do this as strictly as possible (looking in the mirror helps you to check your form). Finish your set, then repeat the movement with the other arm. Be sure to go back and forth from one hand to the other without stopping to rest in between.

One-Arm Triceps Extensions can also be done standing up—just balance yourself by holding on to something with your free hand.

Dips

Purpose of Exercise: TO DEVELOP THE THICKNESS OF THE TRICEPS, ESPECIALLY AROUND THE ELBOW.

Dips are often thought of as only a chest exercise, but they can be done in such a way as to hit the triceps really hard as well.

Execution: (1) Taking hold of the parallel bars, raise yourself up and lock out your arms. (2) As you bend your elbows and lower yourself between the bars, try to stay as upright as possible—the more you lean back, the more you work the triceps; the more you bend forward, the more you work the pectorals. From the bottom of the movement, press yourself back up until your arms are locked out, and then give an extra flex of the triceps to increase the contraction. You can also increase the effort involved in this exercise by using a weight hooked around your waist and by coming up only about three-quarters of the way rather than locking out the movement and taking the tension off the triceps.

Mike Christian

Dips Behind Back

Purpose of Exercise: TO DEVELOP THE THICKNESS OF THE TRICEPS, ESPECIALLY AROUND THE ELBOW.

This movement is also known as "Bench Dips" or "Reverse Push-Ups."

Execution: (1) Place a bench or bar behind your back and hold on to the bench at its edge, hands about shoulder width apart. Place your heels on a bar or another bench, preferably at a level higher than the bench you are holding on to. Bending your elbows, lower your body as far as you can toward the floor. (2) Then push back up, locking out your arms to work the upper triceps. To work the lower triceps, stop just short of locking out. If your own body weight is not enough, try doing the movement by having a training partner place a barbell or Olympic plate on your lap.

Fixed Bar Triceps Extensions

Purpose of Exercise: TO FULLY STRETCH AND DEVELOP THE LOWER AREA OF THE TRICEPS.

Using this movement, you can completely stretch the triceps more safely than with any other exercise.

Execution: (1) Using a fixed horizontal bar positioned at about waist height, grasp the bar with an overhand grip, hands about shoulder width apart. Lock your arms out to support your weight, then move your feet back until you are in a semi "push-up" position above the bar.
(2) Bend your arms and lower your body so that your head comes down below and under the bar as far as possible. When you feel the maximum stretch in your triceps, press forward with your arms and raise yourself back to the starting position, arms locked out.

Ali Malla

Barbell Wrist Curls

Purpose of Exercise: TO DEVELOP THE INSIDE (FLEXOR MUSCLES) OF THE FOREARMS.

Heavy Barbell Curls make the forearms work very hard, but Wrist Curls allow you to more fully isolate these muscles.

Execution: (1) Take hold of a barbell with an underhand grip, hands close together. Straddle a bench with your forearms resting on the bench but with your wrists and hands hanging over the end, elbows and wrists the same distance apart. Lock your knees in against your elbows to stabilize them. (2) Bend your wrists and lower the weight toward the floor. When you can't lower the bar any further, carefully open your fingers a little bit and let the weight roll down out of the palms of your hands. Roll the weight back up into your hands, contract the forearms, and lift the weight as high as you can without letting your forearms come up off the bench. Forearms, like calves, need a lot of stimulation to grow, so don't be afraid to make them really burn.

Dumbbell One-Arm Wrist Curls

Purpose of Exercise: TO ISOLATE AND DEVELOP THE FOREARMS.

This is a variation of Wrist Curls that allows you to isolate one forearm at a time.

Execution: (1) Take hold of a dumbbell and sit on a bench. Lean forward and place your forearm on your thigh so that your wrist and the weight extend out over the knee, with your palm and the inside of your forearm facing upward. Bend forward, reach over with your free hand, and take hold of the elbow of the working arm to stabilize it. Bend your wrist and lower the weight as far as possible toward the floor, opening your fingers slightly to let the dumbbell roll down out of your palm. (2) Close your fingers again and, keeping the effort in your wrist, rather than the biceps, curl the weight up as high as you can. Finish your repetitions, then repeat using the other wrist. Leaning the upper body slightly out to the side enables you to develop the inside of the forearm.

Casey Viator

Behind-the-Back Wrist Curls

Purpose of Exercise: TO DEVELOP THE FLEXOR MUSCLES OF THE FOREARM.
This is a real power exercise for the forearm flexors, and you can go for the heaviest possible weight.

Execution: (1) Back up to a barbell rack and grasp a bar. Lift it off the rack and hold it down at arm's length behind you, hands about shoulder width apart, palms facing toward the rear. Keeping your arms steady, open your fingers and let the bar roll down out of your palms. Close your fingers, roll the bar back up into your hands, and then lift it up and back behind you as far as possible, flexing your forearms. Make sure only the wrist moves in this exercise.

Reverse Wrist Curls with Barbell

Purpose of Exercise: TO DEVELOP THE OUTSIDE (EXTENSOR MUSCLES) OF THE FOREARMS.

Execution: (1) Grasp a barbell with an overhand grip, hands about 10 inches apart. Lay your forearms on top of your thighs so that they are parallel to the floor and your wrists and hands are free and unsupported. Bend your wrists forward and lower the bar as far as you can. (2) Then bring them back up and lift the bar as far as possible, trying not to let the forearms move during the exercise.

Reverse Barbell Wrist Curls with Preacher Bench (optional)

This movement can also be done with your forearms across a preacher bench.

Reverse Wrist Curls can also be done with your forearms across a preacher bench.

Reverse Wrist Curls with Dumbbells

Reverse Curls work the forearm extensors. Using dumbbells, you ensure that each side of the body will work up to its own capacity, with no help from the other.

Reverse Wrist Curls with Dumbbells—starting position

Reverse Wrist Curls with Dumbbells—end position

Reverse Barbell Curls

Purpose of Exercise: TO DEVELOP THE OUTSIDE HEAD OF THE BICEPS AND THE FOREARM EXTENSORS.

Execution: (1) Grasp a barbell with an overhand grip, hands about shoulder width apart. Let the bar hang down at arm's length in front of you. (2) Keeping your elbows fixed in position at your sides, curl the bar upward, beginning the movement with a curling motion of the wrist. (3) Bring the bar up to a position just under the chin, contract the biceps as fully as possible on top, then lower the weight slowly back down to the starting position.

By stabilizing the elbows on a preacher bench, you isolate the forearms and make them work a lot stricter. Notice that you begin a Reverse Preacher Bench Barbell Curl with the wrists bent down, so that the first part of the movement is actually a Reverse Wrist Curl.

Reverse Preacher Bench Barbell Curls

Purpose of Exercise: TO ISOLATE AND DEVELOP THE OUTSIDE HEAD OF THE BICEPS AND FOREARM EXTENSORS.

As with any Preacher Bench Curl, this exercise is designed to be done strictly to create shape rather than mass.

Execution: (1) Position yourself with your arms extended over a preacher bench. Grasp a barbell with an overhand grip, hands about shoulder width apart. Let the bar hang so that your arms are fully extended. (2) Curl the bar upward, beginning the movement with a curling motion of the wrist, and bring it up as far as possible toward your chin. Your position on the bench should be such that, at the top of the movement, your forearms have not come up completely to a perpendicular angle. From the top of the movement, lower the weight slowly back down to the starting position.

Reverse Curls on a Machine

Purpose of Exercise: TO DEVELOP THE FOREARM EXTENSORS.

This movement works the forearm muscles all the way to their origin at the elbow. In addition to flexing the wrist, you also lift the forearm. Although machines are designed with limited functions, a little thought and imagination will allow you to get the maximum benefit from their use. For example, by reversing your grip on a Curl machine, you can perform very strict Reverse Curls.

Execution: (1) Grasp the handle on a Curl machine in an overhand grip. Place your elbows firmly on the pad. (2) Starting at full extension, lift the handle up and toward your head as far as it will go. Lower the weight again slowly and under control until you have returned to a position of full extension.

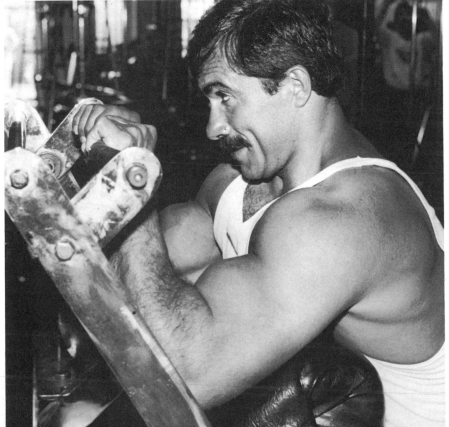

Ali Malla

One-Arm Cable Reverse Curls

Purpose of Exercise: TO ISOLATE AND DEVELOP THE FOREARM EXTENSORS.

Using one arm at a time with cables, you get constant, full-range-of-motion resistance that doesn't vary with position as much as when you use dumbbells. This makes this exercise an excellent specialized one for overcoming weak points in the forearm extensors, especially if one arm is bigger than the other.

Execution: (1) Using a floor-level pulley, grasp a handle with one hand, using a palms-down grip. (2) Concentrating on keeping your elbow completely still as a pivot point, curl the back of your hand up as far as possible toward your shoulder. At the top of the movement, lower your hand again, resisting all the way down. Finish your set with one arm, then repeat with the other.

Hammer Curls, which I have included in the biceps training program (p. 366), are also very effective for forearm training.

THE THIGHS

The Muscles of the Upper Leg

The **quadriceps** are the muscles at the front of the thigh which act as extensors of the leg. The four muscles involved are the rectus femoris, the vastus intermedium (these two muscles making up the central V-shape delineation of the middle front thigh), the vastus medialis of the inner thigh, and the vastus lateralis of the outer thigh.

     BASIC FUNCTION: To extend and straighten the leg

The **biceps femoris** and associated muscles—the thigh flexors at the rear of the leg

     BASIC FUNCTION: To curl the leg back

Other important muscles of the upper leg include the tensor fasciae latae, coming down from the hip to the outer thigh; and the sartorius, the longest muscle in the body, which weaves diagonally across the front of the thigh.

The Importance of Thigh Training

The muscles of the upper leg are the largest and most powerful in the entire body. There are few movements in sports that do not involve intense leg effort. A baseball player, golfer, discus

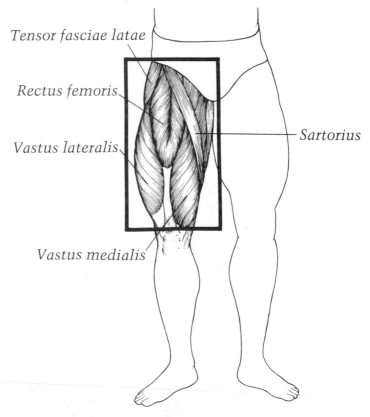

Tensor fasciae latae

Rectus femoris

Vastus lateralis

Sartorius

Vastus medialis

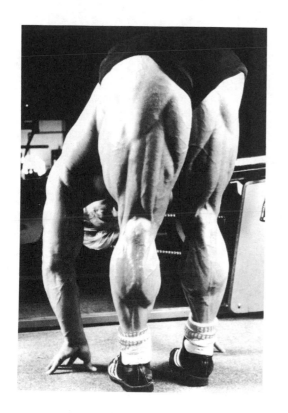

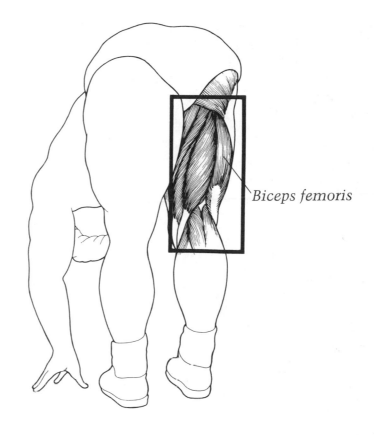

Biceps femoris

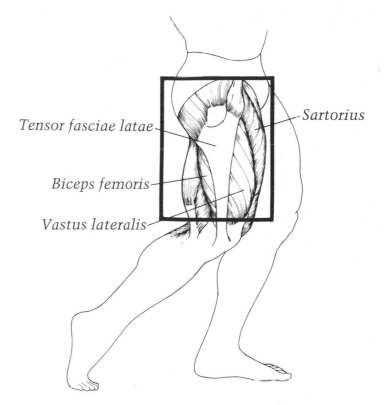

Tensor fasciae latae

Sartorius

Biceps femoris

Vastus lateralis

Sergio Oliva

thrower, shotputter, and boxer all begin their respective movements with a powerful leg drive. In weightlifting most power moves like Power Cleans, Clean and Press, and Deadlifts involve a lot of leg effort, as do the lifts used in Olympic weightlifting competition.

However, there is no sport in which thigh development is as important as it is in bodybuilding. While contest judges have the shoulders, chest, arms, back, and abs to occupy their attention above your waist, when they look at your lower body the single most compelling visual element is the thighs—the quadriceps and the leg biceps. Thighs are the most massive muscle group in the body and proportionately constitute almost half of your physique.

Can you imagine a Sergio Oliva with weak thighs? Or a Casey Viator with skinny legs? What is the point of building your arms up to 21 inches or bigger if you display them on top of a physique with thighs that hardly measure any larger?

When I was playing soccer and skiing as a teenager in Austria, the coaches urged us to do exercises like Squats, Lunges, and Calf Raises to strengthen our legs. This early training eventually led to my falling in love with the sport of bodybuilding. We were lucky in those days to have coaches who understood the need for leg strength and how to train for it. Nowadays, whenever I talk to athletic coaches around the world, virtually all of them agree that great leg strength is the foundation of athletic excellence and that weight training is the best way to develop that strength.

But the legs have another quality besides great strength—they are also capable of great endurance. Capable of moving up to a ton of weight, the legs are also designed to carry you long distances without tiring. A person in good condition can walk for weeks through rugged terrain and run for 100 miles. No other muscles of the body can deliver this dual quality of great strength and great endurance.

This is why training the legs for bodybuilding is so demanding. It isn't enough just to subject the legs to heavy overload. You have to use heavy weights *and* sufficient volume of training so that you stress the fibers involved and exhaust the endurance capacity of the leg muscles. Doing five sets of Barbell Curls for the biceps can be demanding, but doing five sets of heavy Squats with 400 or 500 pounds on your shoulders is more like running a mini-marathon, with that kind of total exhaustion squeezed into eight or nine minutes of concentrated effort.

Like many young bodybuilders, I had a tendency to train my upper body harder than my thighs. Luckily, I realized in time how important this muscle group is to a championship physique, and I began to indulge in superhuman Squats and other thigh exercises to build up this muscle mass.

An exception to the tendency of young bodybuilders to overlook leg training is Tom Platz. Tom had the opposite problem. He got heavily into leg training, and then found himself with Olympia-level legs that outclassed his upper body. Since then, he has made great strides in creating a totally proportioned body, but his unbelievable leg development has set new standards for bodybuilders to strive for.

The Demands of Leg Training

Because upper leg training is so strenuous and demanding, a lot of bodybuilders find their leg development lagging behind simply because they don't put an all-out effort into it. They look in the mirror and are disappointed in how their legs look, but they don't realize the kind of total concentration of effort it takes to make those huge muscles respond.

For many years, I did only five sets of Squats when I really should have been doing eight sets. I did not include enough Front Squats and, I now realize, I did not put enough weight on the Leg Press machine.

Once I realized my mistakes and corrected them, my thighs began to grow thick and massive. I accepted the fact that leg workouts simply have to be brutal to be effective. This involves a mental effort almost as much as a physical one. It's easy to be intimidated by 400 or 500 pounds on a Squat bar (or even 200 or 300 when you are a beginner). It is difficult to gear yourself up to loading up the Leg Press machine and grinding out rep after rep, set after set.

I remember a few years ago seeing a skinny black kid training at the weight pit on Venice Beach. I watched him doing endless sets of Squats, with very heavy weight, torturing himself with rep after rep. After a while, his thighs began to grow and soon they were huge, separated and beautifully defined. And only a year and a half later Tony Pearson entered and won the 1978 Mr. America contest.

Normal workouts are hard enough, but if thighs happen to be a weak point in your physique, you have to be prepared to push yourself even more. That means forcing yourself to break down any inhibition or barrier, blasting your thighs to create total development.

At this stage of his development, Tom Platz was considered to have too much leg mass in proportion to his upper body.

Tony Pearson's leg development is the result of a lot of hard training and use of the Priority Principle.

Many bodybuilders have trouble going to total failure in leg training. After all, going to exhaustion with 400 pounds across the back of your neck can be scary. This is why having a training partner to spot you is especially important for leg training. When you have forced out all the reps you can for your Squats, stand there holding the weight for a moment, then try for one more rep. Push your body to its limit. But make sure somebody is standing by to spot you when you do this. Also, when doing Leg Presses try to push yourself to this same degree, forcing the legs to exhaustion just the way you would any other body part.

If you want to build gigantic thighs, you must always ask yourself this question: "Is it true that I really cannot do another rep?" In my experience, whenever I challenged anyone this way, they usually could force out one more.

However, as important as hard and heavy training is for thigh development, don't make the mistake of confusing sheer effort with effective effort. As in any bodybuilding training, you have to use the correct technique if you want the maximum results. Besides going for maximum intensity in all of your thigh exercises, pay close attention to how the movement is supposed to be executed and try to master the technique involved. That way, your efforts will not be wasted and your thigh development will never lag behind.

Of course, your own physical proportions may dictate variations in your training. Certain bodybuilders with short legs, like Casey Viator, Mike Mentzer, and Franco Columbu, find Squats easy and rewarding. Their physical proportions give a mechanical and leverage advantage that makes it easier to execute Squats properly using very heavy weight. A taller bodybuilder like myself usually finds that the lower back becomes much more involved in this exercise than would be true for a shorter man. But I always did a lot of work on my lower back, so it was strong enough to enable me to squat with very heavy weight in spite of my proportions. In fact, I have often thought that Squats were my best lower back exercise. Doing Front Squats—a movement in which you must keep your back straight—in addition to regular Squats is the best way of getting the most out of your leg workouts when you have proportions like mine.

Incidentally, by trial and error I found that I was able to stay in a much better groove doing Squats by putting a low block under my heels. You can try this yourself to see if this improves your balance and the feel of the exercise. Just be careful not to use too high a block, which throws you too far onto your toes and tends to make you fall forward.

Another variation that can prove useful is doing Squats on a Smith machine, where the bar slides along a fixed track and you don't have to worry about the weight sliding off your shoulders.

My ultimate model for leg development is Tom Platz. Tom not only works as hard as any bodybuilder in the gym—to the point where he doesn't believe he has really done anything until the pain starts—but he also executes all of the exercises to perfection. You see bodybuilders all the time doing Squats by sticking out their rear ends, bending over too far, spreading their legs way out to the side—but not Tom. His form is perfect, his efforts all-out intense, and his mental concentration complete. So it is obviously more than just genes that has produced his fantastic leg development.

Building the Quadriceps

For great thighs you need mass, shape, and separation between each of the important quadriceps muscles: the rectus femoris, vastus intermedium, vastus medialis, and vastus lateralis. You need to develop the overall mass of your thighs to bring them up to where they are proportionate with your upper body. Great size only comes about by lifting heavy weight, especially with exercises like Squats and Leg Presses.

But modern bodybuilders need more than just size to win contests. They need to develop legs that show as much quality as quantity:

1. Full development and *shape* of each of the separate muscles of the quadriceps; a full and satisfying sweep of muscle on the outside of the thigh from hip to knee; the central V-shaped delineation of the middle front thigh; fullness and thickness where the quadriceps insert into the knee; and a fully developed and defined leg biceps.

2. Clear and evident *definition* in the thigh area, with striations and cross-striations standing out as if revealed in an anatomy chart.

3. Full, rounded development of the thigh as seen from the side, almost as if you were looking at a pair of parentheses ( ), with a distinct separation between the front of the thigh and the leg biceps.

The basic mass-building exercise for quadriceps is Squats—an exercise you will find in every program from Beginning to Competition and one which every great bodybuilder has learned to rely on. Squats have a complicated mechanical effect on the body.

The thighs are the most massive muscle group in the body. There are a number of exercises that produce thigh shape and separation, but for building mass there is no substitute for heavy Squats.

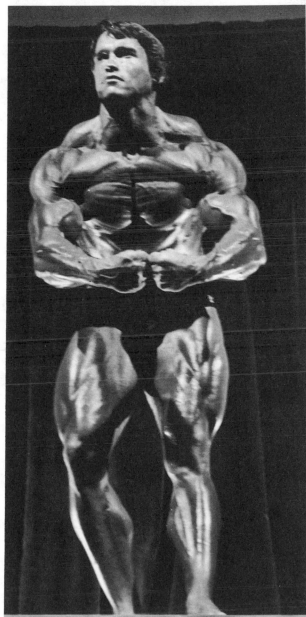

Nobody has achieved more
fullness and thickness of the
quadriceps than Tom Platz,
especially in the lower area
where the thigh muscles
insert into the knee.

Chris Dickerson did not win
the Mr. Olympia title on the
basis of mass. What Chris
had to show the judges was
pure class, great quality, and
outstanding definition,
especially in the thighs.

As you begin the Squat, the thighs bear most of the effort; the farther down you go, the more the stress is transferred to the hamstrings; at the bottom of the movement, the buttocks take up a larger proportion of the strain. However, as I explained earlier, Squats may be more or less effective depending on an individual's particular proportions. Sometimes exercises like Front Squats are also needed to more directly work the quadriceps and lessen the involvement of the lower back muscles.

Heavy Leg Presses also contribute to building massive thighs. Leg Extensions, which isolate the quadriceps themselves, are more of a shaping and defining movement.

Good muscle separation and definition obviously cannot be achieved unless you diet to severely reduce your body fat. But it takes more than just diet—you also need to isolate each individual area of the thighs with exercises like Leg Extensions, Lunges,

Bodybuilders try to develop a split between the thigh and the leg biceps—the split on Sergio Oliva's leg is so prominent that it looks as if it were achieved by the slash of a sword!

Tom Platz is rewriting the anatomy books when it comes to leg development, particularly the leg biceps. Seen from certain angles, they are so massive that his leg almost doesn't look human.

and Leg Curls. Including Hack Squats in your workouts also helps to give you ultimate hardness and definition. (Incidentally, Squats and Lunges actually work the leg biceps, too—along with the exercises described in the next section.)

The Leg Biceps

Even though there were many bodybuilders a few years ago with well-developed upper legs in both the front and the back, there wasn't all that much emphasis put on the leg biceps in competition. Now they have become enormously important thanks to bodybuilders like Tom Platz, Sergio Oliva, and Robby Robinson, who are great examples of how much this area can be developed.

Like triceps, the leg biceps play a major part in a wide variety of poses. When you do a side-chest or triceps shot, the sweep of the leg biceps is very evident. In any back shot, powerful and defined rear delts, traps, and lats will not compensate for under-developed leg biceps. Seen from the back, development of the distinct heads of the leg biceps, along with ripped and developed calves, are needed to create a balance to the muscularity of the back, shoulders, and arms displayed in poses like a rear double-biceps or rear lat spread. Also, we are seeing more and more examples of striated and even cross-striated leg biceps, something that almost didn't exist ten or fifteen years ago. And, just as in auto racing or virtually any other sport, as soon as somebody achieves something new, everybody else dives in and pursues the same achievement. So, fabulously muscular, striated, and vascular leg biceps are likely to be the norm rather than the exception in the future.

The more developed the leg biceps are, the more your legs are going to meet in the middle (see photo of Tom Platz on p. 452) and touch each other even though your legs are held some distance apart. A properly developed leg biceps leaves a distinct line separating the back of the leg from the front of the thigh when seen from the side, and is a sure indication of a bodybuilder who has really succeeded in achieving quality leg training.

The primary exercises for developing leg biceps are Leg Curls. These can be done lying down (usually using both legs at the same time) or standing (getting extra isolation using one leg at a time). But this muscle also comes into play in Squats and Lunges, especially as you work through the lower half of the range of motion.

To get a full stretch in the leg biceps, I recommend doing

Even though Tom Platz, Frank Zane, and Chris Dickerson are doing a back double-biceps shot in this photo, notice what an important part the development of the leg biceps plays in the overall effect of the pose.

Shown here at the 1974 Mr. Olympia, even though I am standing relaxed, I am consciously keeping my leg biceps tight and flexed. I was very glad that I had made an extra effort that year to really work this area hard.

Straight-Leg Deadlifts and Good Mornings, exercises that are in the Beginning Power Training program for lower back, but which also help to develop the back of the thigh.

Don't forget that leg biceps also respond extremely well to various Shocking Principles like the Stripping Method, partial and forced reps, and supersetting. The more you can shock this important muscle, the more development you can expect to see.

Beginning and Advanced Programs

In the Beginning Program, I have included just basic exercises designed to work each important area of the leg: Squats, Lunges, and Leg Curls. The first two exercises work well in combination to build up the size and strength of the thighs, and the latter is the most direct way of developing the back of the thighs.

But don't make the mistake of believing that these exercises are merely for beginners simply because they are included in the Beginning Program. No matter how advanced you become, these exercises are still vital to building and maintaining great thighs. Except for very specialized training in which you are only working on certain weak points, you will always need to rely on these basic movements.

In Advanced Training you need to do Squats in different ways. Front Squats, for example, force you to keep your back straight, which involves more of the outside thighs. In Hack Squats you go all the way down, which works the lower thighs and helps to separate the quadriceps from the leg biceps. The various kinds of Squats attack the leg from different directions; exercises for leg biceps, such as Straight-Leg Deadlifts, allow you to continue to escalate the intensity of effort you impose on these muscles.

Because leg training is so demanding, conditioning is an important factor. In the beginning, you will find the few leg exercises included to be plenty difficult enough. But after a while, when you have become stronger and more conditioned, the total efforts of the Advanced and Competition programs, as difficult as they are, will be well within your increased capabilities.

Competition Program

Once you begin to train for competition, you have to be conscious of many more aspects of leg development—full muscle shape, greater striations, cross-striations, complete muscle separation, the mass of the thighs developed in proportion to the rest of the body. To achieve this you need to demand even more from your leg training, making already difficult workouts almost impossible by using every one of the Shocking Principles you can.

Supersetting leg training, for example, can really deplete you. The thighs are the biggest muscles in the body and when you start doing two or more sets without resting you can easily drive yourself to total exhaustion unless you are in great condition. You can superset within the same muscle—Squats and Leg Extensions, for example—or back to front with Lunges and Leg Curls. But all of this intensity is for a purpose: to do everything possible to develop every part of the thigh.

At this level, you need to be extremely honest with yourself, looking at your thighs and accurately assessing where your development is merely adequate, outstanding, or simply unsatisfactory. The key to winning is to detect weak points early on and begin to correct them as soon as possible rather than waiting until it may be too late.

The Competition Program is designed to teach you total control over your own development. You will need to understand your own body structure more completely, and to fully comprehend which movements are designed to isolate the various areas of the legs—the upper or lower thighs, the inside or outside, the insertion, origin, or thickness of the leg biceps. You will need to learn to feel precisely where Squats, Front Squats, Leg Presses, and Hack Squats are having their effect, and how to alter your program to include a greater proportion of those exercises that work best for you. Knowing all this enables you to achieve the comprehensive development that it takes to win titles.

Remember, *all* the exercises detailed in these programs are important. Even if you vary the program, it is not a good idea to leave out the fundamental exercises entirely. Squats may build mass and Leg Extensions create shape and definition, but the *combination* of these two movements, plus the other important exercises, is what gives you *total* quality development.

The Competition Program is not so much a matter of doing more or different exercises as of increasing the "time intensity" of the training with a lot of supersets. For competition, it is extremely important that the thighs be superdefined, with tremendous muscle separation, and I have found that the way to achieve that look is by doing a lot of supersets: Leg Extensions and Squats, Front Squats and Leg Curls, Hack Squats and Leg Curls. Using these methods—in spite of what the scientists say about not being able to "spot reduce" areas (burn off fat in a specific area by extra muscular activity)—is the best way to achieve the desired results.

I wouldn't use the Stripping Method in thigh training all the time, but it really works well when you are preparing for competition. Years ago when I was looking for extra thigh definition, I experimented on a sliding Hack Squat machine—I put on enough weight to allow me to just do six reps, took a little off, and did six more. Eventually I did five sets this way for a total of thirty reps, which gave me a tremendous burn in the quadriceps muscles. I also found this method worked great with Leg Extensions.

Since legs have a tremendous capacity for endurance, continuing your set with the Stripping Method helps you to totally exhaust all the muscle fiber available. Some machines are very useful when you train this way because you can strip off weight quickly by just changing the pin, and can continue working your legs to total failure without fear of being unable to control the weight at the end. You can do the same thing with Squats by pulling plates off the bar, although you may find this the most grueling exercise you have ever done.

The biggest progress I made in thigh training was in 1971 when, in addition to sheer size, what I needed most was deeper definition and separation. So I began leg training with a superset of Leg Extensions followed by Squats. I hit the Leg Extensions hard, so I was very weak and tired when I got to the Squats. My thighs felt dead, and I found that I could hardly move 315 pounds. But I kept trying and soon was able to do heavy Squats immediately after Leg Extensions, and my thighs responded tremendously to this new shock. Another superset that worked well for me was Front Squats immediately followed by Leg Curls.

For isolating the thigh muscles I've always relied on Hack Squats, especially for competition training. Hack Squats produce maximum hardness, definition, and separation. I discovered the merits of this exercise through Steve Reeves, who found it really beneficial when getting his legs into competition shape.

Tom Platz has a method of exhausting the endurance capacity of the legs as well as blasting the muscles. When he is doing Leg Extensions, for example, he does as many full reps as he can. Then, as he begins to tire and cannot do full-range movements any more, he continues the set moving the weight just as far as he can—three-quarter reps, half reps, quarter reps. Finally, he is lying back on the machine, totally spent, but you can see his legs still contracting, moving the weight only inches at a time. He doesn't stop until his quadriceps quite literally fail and he is so exhausted that he cannot move the weight even a fraction of an inch. This is actually a variation of the Stripping Method, in which Tom cuts down on the range of motion rather than lightening up on the weight.

Platz demands more of his legs, which is why he gets so much more than other people. For example, he might do as many as 35 reps of Squats with 315 on the bar, another 25 reps after less than 60 seconds' rest, several sets of total-exhaustion Leg Extensions and Leg Curls, Hack Squats and Leg Presses, brutal calf work—and then go out and ride his bicycle for 20 miles to finish off his leg workout.

These are just some of the methods the champions have used to develop their thighs. Developing really top-quality legs is a matter of hard work, good knowledge of technique, and application of all the Shocking Principles to create the maximum level of training intensity—for example, forced negatives with Leg Extensions, Leg Curls, Hack Squats, or Machine Squats, all of which are done on machines, allowing the techniques to be done in safety; or staggered sets with an exercise like Squats, doing eight, ten, or even more sets over the course of a workout; or prefatiguing the quadriceps with Leg Extensions and immediately trying to do Squats with your thigh muscles screaming in pain. Pushing the legs to their ultimate development requires a mixture of courage, technique, and imagination.

The one basic need shared by all bodybuilders is of course simply the development of mass in the upper leg. I remember when I had pretty good overall development, but simply lacked size. To build up the mass I needed, I included a lot of very heavy Squats in my leg routine, especially Half Squats. Half Squats let you use an enormous amount of weight, really make the legs work intensely, but with no real danger of injury to the knees. Whenever you are trying to build mass, you need to train according to basic power principles—fewer reps and sets, more rest between sets, but with increased poundage. Full Squats, Half Squats, and Front Squats done with a barbell or on a machine are the principal power exercises. You can also do Leg Presses on a machine as a power exercise by using very heavy weight.

Flexing and Stretching

Whenever you see bodybuilders cramping up from fatigue in a contest, it is usually the leg muscles that go first. These are huge, strong muscles and it takes a lot of practice to develop the kind of endurance needed to pose the legs for hour after hour.

To build big muscles, you need to train with heavy weight. At one point, simply to put an extra inch on my thighs, I concentrated on power training, doing Squats with 500 pounds for reps.

I was perfectly happy this day to flex for photographer John Balik's camera, but I always welcome any excuse to flex during a workout. After every set, I like to stand in front of the mirror and tense the muscles I'm training. Flexing them as hard as I can brings out maximum definition, especially in the thighs.

Muscle-bound? Look at Tom Platz's incredible flexibility.

Hard posing practice and flexing the legs constantly during your workout help to create maximum muscle separation and the cross-striations that modern bodybuilders are now achieving. However, the more you contract these large muscles, the more they tend to shorten up, so it is equally important to lengthen them again with stretching movements. Virtually all the top champions use a lot of stretching in order to develop their fantastic legs. Tom Platz spends fifteen minutes stretching before he does a leg workout. Then he stretches again when he is finished.

But you can also stretch *during* a workout by including the right exercises—for example, doing Straight-Leg Deadlifts or Good Mornings to stretch the leg biceps right after you do your Leg Curls, being sure to go all the way down when doing Squats and Hack Squats, and bringing your knees all the way to your chest when doing Leg Presses.

Weak Point Training

Because the leg muscles are so large and complex, almost any bodybuilder is going to discover some weak points at some stage in his career. It is necessary to analyze what the problem is and to understand what exercises and techniques can be used to correct it.

In general, I recommend training legs according to the Priority Principle. Leg training is so demanding that, if you want to get the most out of it, you had better train them when you are fresh and strong. It is also important to have a good workout partner to push you to your limits and to be there when you need spotting.

For specific problem areas I recommend the following leg exercises:

Lower thigh development

Since the lower thigh works hardest when the knee is fully bent, I recommend the following exercises with a three-quarter movement in which you go all the way down but only come up about three-quarters of the way.
Squats, Hack Squats and Leg Presses
Leg Extensions, concentrating on letting the legs go all the way back and stretching out the thighs to the point where the lower thigh is working the hardest

When I first began competing, my legs were considered a weak point, but a lot of hard work, training my thighs according to the Priority Principle and every Shock Principle I could learn or invent, made the difference, so by the early 1970s my thigh development was no longer a problem.

Outer thigh development	Front Squats
	Hack Squats
	Any Squat or Leg Press with toes pointed straight and the feet close together
Inside thigh development	Lots of Lunges—a very valuable inside thigh exercise
	Straight-Leg Deadlifts
	Standing or Lying Leg Curls (since the leg biceps are what fill up the space between the legs when they are seen from the front)
	Any Squat or Press movement with the toes turned outward with a relatively wide foot stance
Front sweep of thighs	Hack Squats with block under the heels to further isolate the quadriceps
	Sissy Squats
Split between thighs and leg biceps	Hack Squats done a special way—go all the way down and then, as you lift up, bring your rear end forward and away from machine, almost as if you were doing Sissy Squats. This forward movement of the pelvis alters the angle of stress on the leg and helps create the desired separation between the front and back of the upper leg.

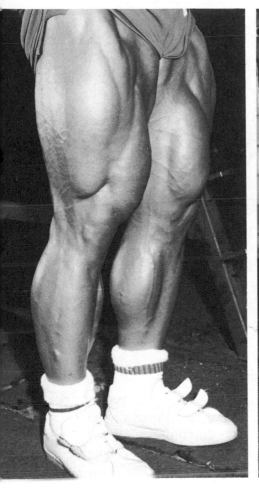

In developing the thighs, it is enormously helpful to vary your foot position when doing various Squat and Leg Press movements:

For overall development

Feet normal width apart
Toes pointed slightly out

For outer thigh (vastus lateralis) development

Feet close together
Toes pointed straight ahead

For inner thigh (abductors) and front thigh (vastus medialis) development

Feet relatively wide apart
Toes pointed out at wide angle

Squats

Purpose of Exercise: TO BUILD MASS AND STRENGTH IN THE LEGS, ESPECIALLY THE THIGHS.

Full Squats are one of the traditional mass-building exercises for the entire lower body but are primarily for developing all four heads of the quadriceps.

Execution: (1) With the barbell on a rack, step under it so that it rests across the back of your shoulders, hold on to the bar to balance it, raise up to lift it off the rack, and step away. The movement can be done with your feet flat on the floor or your heels resting on a low block for support. (2) Keeping your head up and back straight, bend your knees and lower yourself until your thighs are just lower than parallel to the floor. From this point, push yourself back up to the starting position.

It is important to go below parallel in this movement, especially when you are just learning the exercise, so that you develop strength along the entire range of motion. If you don't go low enough in the beginning, you could injure yourself later when using heavier weight. Foot position determines which

Tom Platz

area of the thighs you work the most while doing Squats: a wider stance works the inside of the thighs to a greater degree, while a narrower stance tends to work the outside more; toes turned out hits the inside of the thighs, toes turned in, the outside. The basic stance is usually feet shoulder width apart with toes turned just slightly out.

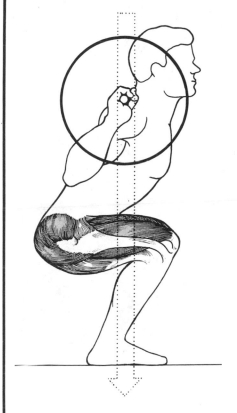

To get the most out of Squats, the bar should remain directly over your feet. As you bend your knees coming down, make sure your head is up and your back straight. This takes the lower back out of the movement and puts the stress on the leg muscles where it belongs.

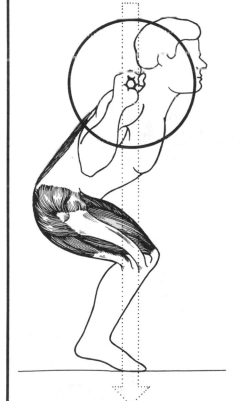

Allowing your head to lean forward, as shown here, puts additional stress on the lower back and less on the thighs, where you really want it. Bodybuilders with long legs tend to have this problem more than those with short legs.

Heavy Squats

Your Squat technique will vary a lot depending on your physical proportions. Because of my height, whenever I do heavy Squats I am forced to bend forward quite far, bringing my lower back very strongly into the exercise. Ideally, you should do Squats with your back as straight as possible. Bodybuilders like Franco Columbu and Tom Platz can do this easily with rear end and bar in about the same line when coming down with the weight, instead of the way I do it, bar way forward and rear end stuck out toward the back. This is why I always include a lot of Front Squats in my routine, in order to make certain I isolate the quadriceps.

Half Squats

Purpose of Exercise: TO DEVELOP EXTRA MASS AND POWER IN THE THIGHS.

Execution: This exercise is done the same way as regular Squats except you only go halfway down, which will enable you to use more weight.

Machine Squats

Purpose of Exercise: TO DEVELOP THE QUADRICEPS.
When you do Squats on a machine, you can work the thighs intensely while putting less strain on other areas such as the knees and lower back. There are a number of machines designed to approximate the Squat movement. They use a variety of techniques to create resistance, including weights, friction, and even air compression. Personally, I have always preferred doing Machine Squats on a Smith machine.

Execution: (1) Place your shoulders under the bar and come up to a standing position. Position your feet to obtain the desired effects from the exercise (see pp. 464–65). (2) Bend your knees and squat down until your thighs are lower than parallel, then press back up to the starting position.

Turning your toes out helps to develop the inside of the thighs. Balancing a barbell in this position could be difficult, but the machine makes it easy. Point toes in to work outer thighs. Standing with your feet moved forward helps to isolate the

468

quadriceps, especially the lower area near the knee, and minimizes strain to the lower back since you don't need to bend forward at all.

Machine Squat—toes out

Machine Squat—feet forward

Wrapping the knees when you do heavy Squats raises the hydrostatic pressure within the joint and helps to prevent joint or ligament injury.

Front Squats

Purpose of Exercise: TO WORK THE LEGS, WITH SPECIAL EMPHASIS ON THE THIGHS.
Front Squats develop the outside sweep of the quadriceps.

Execution: (1) Step up to the rack, bring your arms up under the bar, keeping the elbows high, cross your arms and grasp the bar with your hands to control it. Then lift the weight off the rack. Step back and separate your feet for balance (I find this exercise easier to do if I rest my heels on a low block to improve balance). (2) Bend your knees and, keeping your head up and your back straight, lower yourself until your thighs are below parallel to the floor. Push yourself back up to the starting position. Do this exercise slow and strict, making sure you keep your back straight. If possible, do all Squats in front of a mirror so you can check that you are keeping your back straight.

Front Half Squats are done in the same manner as Front Squats except you go only halfway down.

Sissy Squats

Purpose of Exercise: TO ISOLATE THE LOWER QUADRICEPS.
Although this movement is called a Squat it is very close to a Leg Extension in the way it affects the legs. You will feel a lot of stress right down to where the quadriceps insert into the knee.

Execution: (1) Stand upright, feet a few inches apart, holding on to a bench or something else for support. (2) Bend your knees, raise up on your toes, and slowly lower yourself toward the floor, letting your pelvis and knees go forward while your head and shoulders tilt backward. (3) Continue down as low as possible, until your buttocks practically touch your heels. Stretch the thigh muscles and hold for a moment, then straighten your legs and come back up into a standing position. Flex your thigh muscles hard at the top of the movement for maximum cuts and development.

Leg Presses

Purpose of Exercise: TO BUILD THE MASS OF THE THIGHS. If Squats have a disadvantage, it's the pressure they put on the lower back. Doing Leg Presses is a way around this that allows you to work the legs with very heavy weight.

Execution: (1) Using a Leg Press machine, position yourself under the machine and place your feet together against the crosspiece. (2) Bend your knees and lower the weight as far as possible, bringing your knees toward your shoulders. Press the weight back up again until your legs are fully extended. Don't get in the habit of pushing on your knees to help your legs press upward, or of crossing your arms across your chest and limiting your range of motion.

Leg Press Variations

There are a number of other machines on which you can do the Leg Press movement. Some of these move along an angled track, others along a horizontal. No matter which type of machine used, the exercise should be done in a similar manner, with the knees coming back as closely as possible to the shoulders.

Incline Leg Press—toes-apart position. If you want to work the inside of your thighs, use the toes-out position to get maximum development of the thigh abductors.

Hack Squats

Purpose of Exercise: TO DEVELOP THE LOWER AREA OF THE THIGH. Hack Squats are a good movement for working the lower range of the pressing motion.

Execution: (1) Depending on the design of the machine you use, either hook your shoulders under the padded bars or take hold of the handles. Your feet should be together, toes pointed slightly out. (2) Press downward with your legs and lift the mechanism, stopping when your legs are fully extended.

This keeps constant tension on the legs. Bend your knees and lower yourself all the way down. Your legs should end up bent at a much more acute angle than when you do Squats. In all your repetitions, keep working this lower range of motion by going all the way down. (3) For some of your last repetitions lower yourself in the normal way but as you press back up, arch your back and bring your hips away from the machine without locking your legs out. This will emphasize the separation between the leg biceps and the quadriceps, which makes the thighs look huge when you do a side-chest shot.

Lunges

Purpose of Exercise: TO DEVELOP THE FRONT OF THE THIGH.

Execution: (1) Holding a barbell across the back of your shoulders, stand upright with your feet together. (2) Keeping your head up, back straight, and chest thrust out, take a step forward, bend your knees, and bring your trailing knee almost to the floor. The step should be long enough so that the trailing leg is almost straight. Push yourself back up to the starting position with one strong and decisive movement, bringing your feet together, then step forward with the other foot and repeat the movement. You can do all your repetitions with one leg, then switch and repeat with the other or you can alternate legs throughout the set.

Leg Extensions

Purpose of Exercise: TO DEFINE AND SHAPE THE FRONT OF THE THIGH. Leg Extensions are great for getting really deep definition in the thighs without losing size, and especially for developing the area around the knees.

Execution: (1) Using one of the various Leg Extension machines, sit in the seat and hook your feet under the padded bar. (2) Extend your legs out to the maximum, making sure you remain sitting flat on the machine (don't let yourself lift off and cheat up the weight). Extend your legs as far as possible until they are locked out to achieve maximum contraction of the quadriceps, then lower the weight slowly until your feet are farther back than the knees and the thighs are fully stretched out. To make sure you always extend your legs fully enough, have your training partner hold out a hand on a level where your feet will kick it at the top of the extension.

Leg Curls

Purpose of Exercise: TO DEVELOP THE LEG BICEPS (REAR OF THIGH).

Execution: (1) Lie face downward on a Leg Curl machine and hook your heels under the lever mechanism. Your legs should be stretched out straight. (2) Keeping flat on the bench, curl your legs up as far as possible, until the leg biceps are fully contracted. Release and lower the weight slowly back to the starting position. Hold on to the handles or the bench itself to keep yourself from lifting up off the bench. This exercise should be done strictly and through the fullest range of motion possible. I have found that supporting myself on my elbows helps to keep the lower part of my body more firmly on the bench.

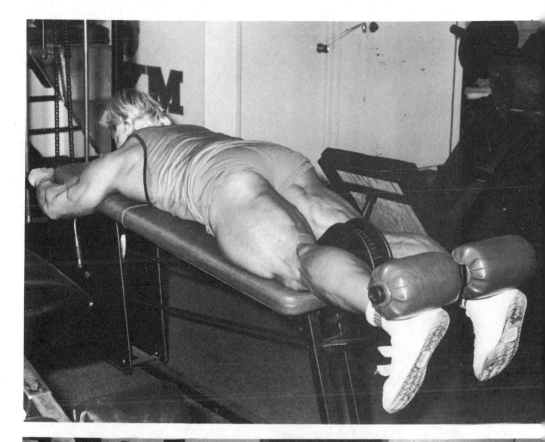

Standing Leg Curls

Purpose of Exercise: TO DEVELOP THE LEG BICEPS. Using a Standing Curl machine, you can train one leg at a time and further isolate the leg biceps.

Execution: (1) Stand against the machine and hook one leg behind the lever mechanism. (2) Hold yourself steady and curl the leg up as high as possible. Release and lower the weight back to the starting position. Do your set with one leg, then repeat the exercise using the other leg. Be certain to keep the movement slow and strict.

Straight-Leg Deadlifts

Purpose of Exercise: TO WORK THE LEG BICEPS.
This movement gives the maximum possible stretch to the leg biceps.

Execution: (1) Take hold of a barbell as for Deadlifts and come up to a standing position. (2) Keep your legs locked and bend forward from the waist, your back straight, until your torso is about parallel to the floor, the bar hanging at arm's length below you. Straighten up again, pull your shoulders back, and arch your spine to get the spinal erectors of the lower back to contract completely. Without your legs to help you as in regular Deadlifts, you will use much less weight doing this exercise. If you use Olympic weights, it is best to stand on a block or a bench so that you can lower the weight to the maximum extent without the large end plates touching the floor.

THE CALVES

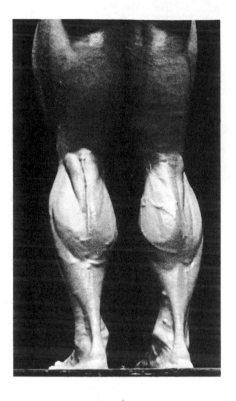

The Muscles of the Calf

The **soleus,** which is the larger and deeper of the two calf muscles and originates from both the fibula and the tibia

    BASIC FUNCTION: To flex the foot

The **gastrocnemius,** which has two heads, one originating from the lateral aspect and the other from the medial of the lower femur. Both heads join to overlay the soleus and join with it to insert into the Achilles tendon, which inserts into the heel bone.

    BASIC FUNCTION: To flex the foot

The **tibialis anterior,** which runs up the front of the lower leg alongside the shinbone

    BASIC FUNCTION: To flex the foot

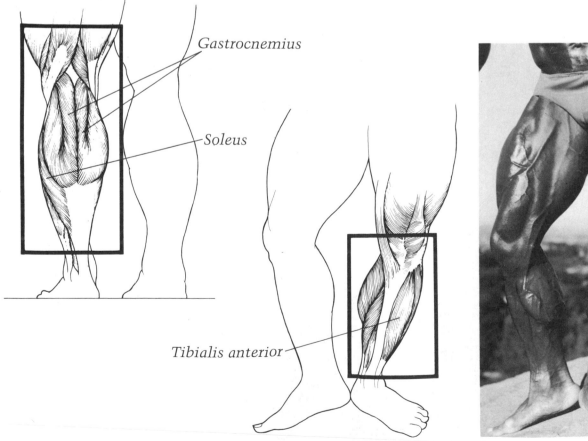

Gastrocnemius

Soleus

Tibialis anterior

Training the Calves

Calves, like the deltoids and abdominals, are a very aesthetic body part. A good pair of calves look good on the beach or tennis court as well as on stage. But, more than that, outstanding calf development has historically been associated with the ideal male physique. Huge deltoids, washboard abs, and powerful calves—these were the qualities the Greek sculptors fashioned in their classical images of warriors and athletes.

Ideally your calf development should about equal the development of your biceps. If your calves are smaller than your arms, then you need to give them extra attention. (One exception to this is Chris Dickerson, the only bodybuilder whose calves have always been naturally *larger* than his arms.)

Calves are considered the most difficult muscle group in the body to develop. But calves respond to training just like any other

Chris Dickerson and Casey Viator have impressive calf development. As great as their backs, shoulders, traps, and arms are, if nothing happened when they flexed their calves, the entire effect would be ruined.

Chris Dickerson

muscle—you just have to be aware that they need to be trained at many different angles and with extremely heavy weight.

Think about what happens when you walk and run: you turn your foot and ankle first one way, then the other; you push off, stop suddenly, turn and change direction, you climb upward, walk downhill. And with each different movement you make, the calf muscles bear your weight, raising you up on your toes, lowering you down onto your heels, twisting your feet in different directions.

Until I trained with Reg Park, I had trouble getting my calves as big as I wanted them. I was doing Calf Raises with 500 or 600 pounds, but he was using 1,000! He pointed out to me that each of my calves individually was comfortable supporting my 250 pounds of body weight, so that 500 pounds of resistance was actually a "normal" amount for them to deal with. So by training with the weight I was using, I was hardly making any impression on my calves at all!

The primary mass builder for calves is Standing Calf Raises, and here extra weight is really important. This exercise, along with Donkey Calf Raises, works both the gastrocnemius and soleus muscles of the calf. Seated Calf Raises isolate the soleus.

Many bodybuilders do their calf training as an afterthought. Before or after their regular workout they give them ten minutes or so, far less than they would for any other body part. And then they complain when their calves do not respond.

I believe in treating the calves just like every other body part. Since the calves are designed for constant work and rapid recuperation, I train them 30 to 45 minutes a day, six days a week. I also use a wide variety of exercises; not just some sets of Standing and Sitting Calf Raises, but enough movements to work every area of the calf muscles—upper and lower, inside and outside.

The calves are tough and used to a lot of hard work, so the best way to make them grow is to constantly shock them, using every high-intensity training principle possible. For example, when doing Donkey Calf Raises, I frequently started off with three 220-pound bodybuilders sitting on my back. I would continue the set until I could not do another rep, then have one of them slide off so that I could continue until my calves were screaming in agony. Finally, I would finish off the set using only my own body weight and feeling as if my calves were going to explode.

Another shock method involves doing partial reps. About one out of four of my calf workouts involved doing half and quarter movements with extremely heavy weights, which put an enormous demand on the calf muscles. Actually, you can use vir-

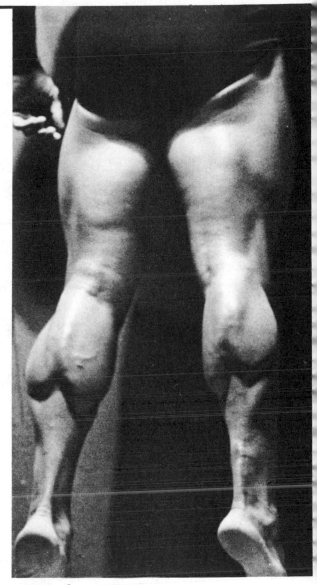

Reg Park

tually all of the Shocking Principles described in this book to develop your calves—staggered sets, rest/pause, forced reps, 21's, supersets, running the rack, and so on. The more you shock the calves, the more you subject them to unexpected stimulation, the more calf development you will see as a result.

A young bodybuilder once came over to me while I was doing Standing Calf Raises and told me how much he admired my calf development. "You can have calves just as good," I told him, "if you are willing to pay the price." He looked puzzled and asked me what I meant. "Calves like this will cost you five hundred hours," I said. "Anything less and you won't get the results."

If you analyze that 500-hour figure you get: 500 hours equals more than 660 45-minute calf workouts; 660 divided by six workouts a week equals about 110 weeks or over two years! So, unless you are genetically gifted like a Chris Dickerson and were born with magnificent calves, building them up takes a minimum of two years of brutal training.

Even with that effort, calves may not turn out to be your best body part. But I doubt there are many bodybuilders with enough physical talent to build up the rest of their bodies who will not find their calves responding well to the regimen I prescribe.

Stretching the Calves

To get a full contraction of a muscle, first you have to get a full extension. With the calves this means going all the way down when you do full-range movements, lowering your heels as far as possible before coming up all the way onto your toes to get a full contraction.

Tom Platz carries this to the ultimate by having a training partner sit on the end of a Sitting Calf Raise machine to force his heels lower and lower and stretch his calves to the extreme (something other bodybuilders ought to approach with great care if they try to copy him). What Tom is doing is using a principle that I discovered for myself many years ago: the longer the range of movement and the fuller the extension and contraction of the muscle, the more it will develop. This is especially valuable in calf training, since our normal use of the calf when we walk and run involves mostly the mid-range function.

I like to use a block for Standing Calf Raises just high enough so that my heels touch the floor at the bottom of the movement. This way I know I have lowered my heels enough to get maximum stretch from my calf muscles.

Beginning Program

When you first begin to train calves, you will probably not be able to use the amount of weight I have been talking about. The untrained calf muscle is very disproportionate in its "strength curve." Your calf muscles have carried your body weight throughout your whole life, but you rarely require them to function at the extreme ends of their range of motion—at full extension or full contraction.

Therefore, when you first start doing Calf Raises you will probably find you are enormously strong in the mid-range, but very weak at the extremes. So what you have to do the first few months of training is to bring up the strength of your calves at full contraction and full extension so that you acquire some balance throughout the strength curve. At this point you can begin to pile on the weight and develop the entire range of motion of the muscles.

Still you will find that the mid-range is disproportionately strong—due to mechanical and leverage factors—and this is why I recommend doing partial as well as full-range movements right from the beginning. In this way, you can use enormous amounts of weight to fully stress the muscle at its strongest angles.

To get you started, I have limited the calf training in the Beginning Program to 5 sets, 15 reps each of Standing Calf Raises three times a week. Concentrate on these to begin with and learn to do them correctly:

1. Get a full range of motion, full stretch at the bottom, up on your toes for a full contraction at the top.

2. Use a block high enough so that your heels can drop all the way down.

3. Use a strict movement, keeping your knees straight enough so that you are lifting the weight only with the calves, not by pressing with your legs.

4. Use a "normal" foot position, that is, with your feet pointed straight ahead, so that your entire calf is worked proportionately.

5. Do not rush through your calf training to get to something else, or simply tack on some sets for calves at the end of your workout—work your calves with as much energy and concentration as any other body part.

Advanced and Competition Programs

For Advanced and Competition Training, I recommend working calves six times a week. I have heard theories that this amount of frequency represents "overtraining," but when I look at the bodybuilders who have the best calves, I usually find they are the ones who train their calves every day.

In Advanced Training, I have included both Donkey Calf Raises and Seated Calf Raises along with the mass-building Standing Calf Raises. The Seated Raises are designed to work the soleus muscle, extending your calf lower toward your ankle, and the Donkey Raises allow you to do strict repetitions against resistance centered at the hips rather than the shoulders.

Donkey Calf Raises create a kind of deep development unlike any other calf exercise. You feel different after Donkeys—not just a pump but the feeling that you have worked the muscle right down to the bone. Another thing I like about this exercise is that the bend-over position increases the amount of stretch you can get, which gives you the longest possible range of motion.

Once you advance to the Competition Program, there will be two new exercises to learn: Front Calf Raises to develop the tibialis anterior, and One-Leg Calf Raises to further isolate the calf muscles of each leg. But beyond the exercises themselves, you'll begin to work on shaping the entire area of the calves by varying the position of your toes during the exercises.

As I said earlier, most bodybuilders whose calves refuse to grow are simply not training them hard enough or with enough weight. By the time you reach the level of Competition Training, the program will include anywhere from twelve to twenty sets of calf training, and if you do this much work correctly, with the right amount of intensity and the proper amount of weight, your calves will simply be forced to develop and grow. But there is something else you can do to help ensure this response from your calf muscles: learn to vary your program to continually surprise and stimulate the calves.

In the late 1960s and early '70s, I began changing my calf training around constantly. I would come into the gym one day and do Donkey Calf Raises, 5 sets of 10; Standing Calf Raises, 5 sets of 10; Seated Calf Raises, 5 sets of 10; Calf Raises on a pressing machine, 5 sets of 10; One-Legged Calf Raises, to bring up my weaker left calf (which only measured 19½ inches, while the other was 20 inches cold). The next day I might begin with Seated Calf Raises and then do Standing or Donkey Raises afterward—the idea being to force the calves to work in unfamiliar and unexpected ways as often as possible. Sometimes I would do 20 repetitions instead of 10, or do more sets of an exercise than just 5—maybe 40 sets total for calves one day with only 10 sets of full-range movements and the rest partial-range exercises.

In addition, I would employ every one of the Shocking Principles I could, from the Stripping Method to forced reps. I would always stretch after every single exercise, keeping the muscles working all the time and forcing them to work through the longest possible range of motion.

Doing Calf Raises with as much as 1,000 pounds might seem like an unobtainable goal if you are only up to lifting 450 pounds. But the way to reach that goal, like most other things, is by stages, a little at a time. Try increasing weight at the rate of 50 pounds per month. This gives your tendons and ligaments time to adapt and grow stronger along with your calf muscles.

Another good idea is to choose a weight that is 50 or 100 pounds higher than you can comfortably use in your regular sets and, at the end of your calf workout, try to do just three or four reps with the increased resistance. This accustoms other parts of your body—like the back, legs, and Achilles tendon—to deal with that amount of weight; but it also trains your mind to cope with the extra weight so that you will not be intimidated by it when you are ready to move up in poundage again.

Sometimes, when you are training calves for the special requirements of competition, you may find that using slightly lighter weight is actually a good idea. Working lighter with perhaps a few additional sets, and paying extra attention to contracting the muscles through the fullest range of motion, can help to finish off and fully shape the calves. Ken Waller, who has probably the biggest calves in the world, likes to use heavy weights for Standing Calf Raises, but feels he got much better development by using lighter weights (300 pounds) for Seated Calf Raises. This, of course, is not the way to build calf size in the first place, but it does show how an individual can learn to use what is best for him once he gets up to this level of development.

Advanced Training involves hitting the calves from every angle —toes-in and toes-out foot position as well as the normal one— standing and seated movements to develop both the soleus and gastrocnemius, and not neglecting the tibialis anterior at the front of the lower leg.

Give your body every advantage by being careful with technique and wearing shoes that give you strong support. Give your mind every advantage by learning to psych yourself up and increase your motiviation—by hanging a photo of a great set of calves on the calf machine, for example.

Another training technique I liked to use in calf training was supersets. For example, I would begin with a set of Seated Calf Raises, then go immediately to the Leg Press machine and do

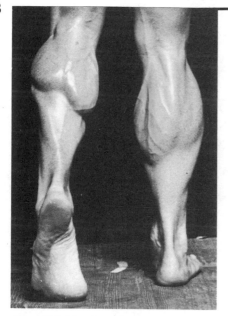

Ken Waller's calves are superior to many other top bodybuilders' because he has such good lower calf development. The gastrocnemius, which underlies the more defined soleus muscle, is full and pronounced all the way down to the ankle.

another set of Calf Raises, both movements working the lower area of the calves. I also occasionally did staggered sets—perhaps a set of Chins, then a set of Standing Calf Raises. A few exercises later, I would again do another set for calves. So by the time I was finished with the overall workout, I had already done about eight sets for calves and I could finish off my calf training with a big head start. This is great when you find yourself getting tired of calf training and not giving it all the effort you should.

Weak Point Training

You might find your calves are growing, but not proportionately; certain areas are lagging behind. The answer in calf training is the same as with any other body part—you choose specific exercises to help correct the imbalance:

Lower calves	Do additional sets of Seated Calf Raises to develop the soleus muscle of the lower calf—that "V" look in which the muscle descends down to the Achilles tendon.
	Bend the knees slightly when doing Standing Calf Raises to bring the lower calves into the movement. This works especially well if you do partial movements at the extreme bottom of the range of motion—your heels almost touching the floor.
	Calf Raises on the Leg Press machine
	Donkey Calf Raises with up to three bodybuilders piled on your back
Upper calves	Standing Calf Raises with special emphasis on the top part of the range of motion—especially when you hold yourself in a full contracted position at the top of the movement

For calves like mine you have to be willing to pay the price: at least 500 hours of intense, concentrated, and sometimes painful calf training.

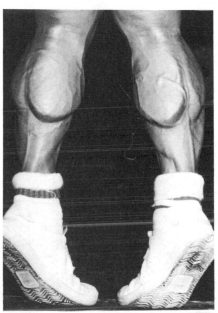

The toes-out position helps to develop the inside of the calf muscles.

Inside of the calves	Do sets of every one of the calf exercises with toes turned outward.
Outside of the calves	Calf Raises with toes turned inward
One calf too small	Add on two extra sets of One-Legged Calf Raises for the smaller calf. Your two sets could be Standing Calf Raises on one leg while holding a dumbbell in your hand, and to bring up the lower calf, Seated Calf Raises performed one-legged. In fact, any calf exercise can be adapted to a one-leg movement. Just be sure to use enough weight to really stimulate the muscle you want to bring up.
Front of the calves	Developing the tibialis anterior creates a split that makes your calves look extra wide from the front. Doing Front Calf Raises can make the calves look an inch bigger. It separates the outside from the inside and creates a wide look that sheer calf size alone cannot accomplish. Therefore, this muscle needs the same attention that the others get —a full five sets of intense training and plenty of stretching.

The toes-in position is used to hit the outside of the calf muscles.

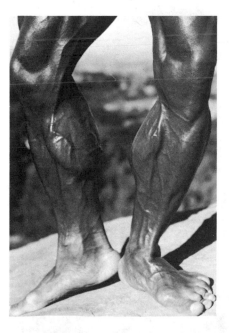

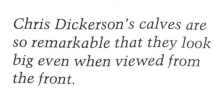

Chris Dickerson's calves are so remarkable that they look big even when viewed from the front.

One reason that bodybuilders with weak calves tend not to develop them is that they can cover them up in the gym wearing long pants so they can forget about them. I used to do this myself, but once I realized my mistake I began to make really fantastic progress in calf training.

When I was young and growing fast, getting up to 230 and then 240 pounds, I was very proud of my flaring back and powerful arms. So I loved to train wearing a tank top or no shirt at all. I would see the reflection of my muscles in the mirror and this would inspire me to train even harder so as to build greater and greater mass and quality. But one day it occurred to me that I wasn't treating the calves as seriously as the other muscles. So I made up my mind to rectify this situation.

The first thing I did was to cut off the bottoms of my training pants. Now my calves were exposed for me and everyone else to see. If they were underdeveloped—and they were—there was no hiding the fact. And the only way I could change the situation was to train my calves so hard and so intensely that the back of my legs would come to resemble huge boulders.

In the beginning my calves were a real weak point, so I did most of my early posing shots with my calves in the water!

This photo is a great example of how effective using the Priority Principle and zeroing in on your weak points can be. When I stepped on stage at a competition two years after I first began trying so hard to bring up my calves, and I turned my back to the audience, my calves were so huge that I got an ovation even before I flexed them.

At first, this was embarrassing. The other bodybuilders in the gym could see my weakness and they constantly made comments. But the plan eventually paid off. No longer able to ignore my calves, I was determined to build them into one of my best body parts. Psychologically, it was a brutal way to accomplish this, but it worked, and that is what I really cared about. Within one year my calves grew tremendously, and the comments I got in the gym were complimentary rather than critical.

If calves are your problem, use the Priority Principle to really attack them. Put calf training first in your workout, when your psychological and physical energy is at the highest. Another thing you can do is to work on your calves even when you aren't in the gym. For example, when you are walking, make an effort to go all the way up onto your toes to make the calves work through a longer range of motion. If you are on a beach, do the same thing in the sand. After a half hour of walking in the sand, digging in with your toes, you will feel a fantastic burn in your calf muscles.

Even when you are doing side poses, calf development plays an important part. When you are doing a side-chest shot, for instance, and concentrating on your upper body, a good judge will also take your calves into consideration.

Posing the Calves

In every pose you do on stage, you need to flex the calves. Bodybuilders usually learn to pose from the ground up—set the feet, flex the calves and legs, and then the upper body. But most bodybuilders don't spend time learning to flex and pose the calves by themselves. The ability to do this comes in handy when you are standing relaxed in round one and you want to hit your calves, fanning them out to impress the judges.

To learn to do this, I recommend posing and flexing the calves between each set of calf training, developing the connection between the mind and muscle so that you gain absolute control over how the calf looks. This also makes the muscle harder and more developed, since the flexing is itself a kind of isometric exercise.

You can create a stronger visual impression if you can keep your calves flexed while "standing relaxed" in the first round of competition. But you must practice flexing or you will lack the endurance to stand this way for more than a few minutes. I've seen a lot of competitors develop leg cramps because they failed to work hard enough at this.

Remember, you will want to be able to show off your calf muscles in poses in which your feet are flat on the floor as well as when you are up on your toes, so you should practice flexing in order to get the kind of muscle control you need to accomplish this. While leaning against a machine or a wall, go up on your toes as far as possible, to get maximum contraction of the calf muscle.

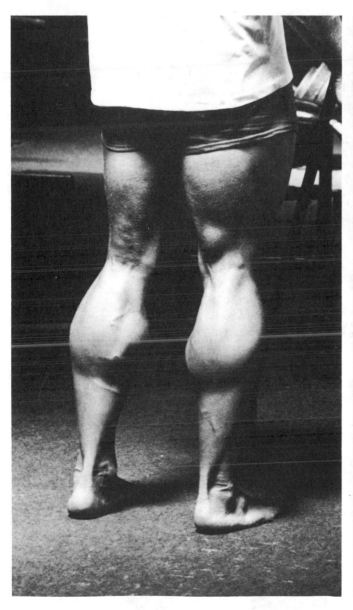

CALF EXERCISES

Standing Calf Raises

Purpose of Exercise: TO DEVELOP THE OVERALL MASS OF THE CALVES.

Execution: (1) Stand with your toes on the block of a standing Calf Raise machine, your heels extended out into space. Hook your shoulders under the pads and straighten your legs, lifting the weight clear of the support. Lower your heels as far as possible toward the floor, keeping your knees slightly bent throughout the movement in order to work the lower area of the calves as well as the upper, and feeling the calf muscles stretch to the maximum. I like a block that is high enough so that I get a full stretch when I lower my heels, but low enough that my heels touch the floor at the bottom so that I always know when I have gone far enough. (2) From the bottom of the movement, come up on your toes as far as possible. The weight should be heavy enough to exercise the calves, but not so heavy that you cannot come all the way up for most of your repetitions.

When you are too tired to do complete repetitions, finish off the set with a series of partial movements to increase the intensity of the exercise.

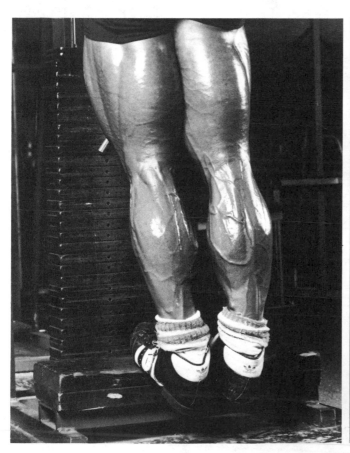
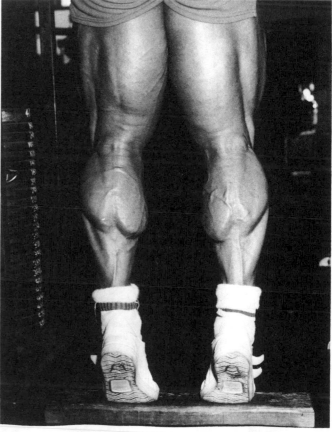

The normal position, with toes straight ahead, is best for overall calf development.

If you run into a situation in which you can't load enough weight on the calf machine, have somebody sit or stand on top of it to create more resistance with his body weight.

Calf Raises on Leg Press Machine

Purpose of Exercise: TO DEVELOP THE CALVES, ESPECIALLY THE LOWER AREA.

Execution: (1) Using one of the various types of Leg Press machines (I prefer the Vertical Leg Press for Calf Raises), position yourself as if to do a Leg Press, only push against the foot pads only with your toes, leaving your heels unsupported. Straighten your legs and press the weight up until your knees are almost locked out. Keeping your knees just slightly bent, keep your heels pressed upward but let your toes come back toward you, feeling the fullest possible stretch in the calf muscles. (2) When you can't stretch any further, press the weight upward with your toes as far as you possibly can to fully contract your calf muscles. You can't cheat at all when you do Calf Raises on a machine. Lying with your back braced against the pad, you can totally isolate the calves to give them a really intense workout.

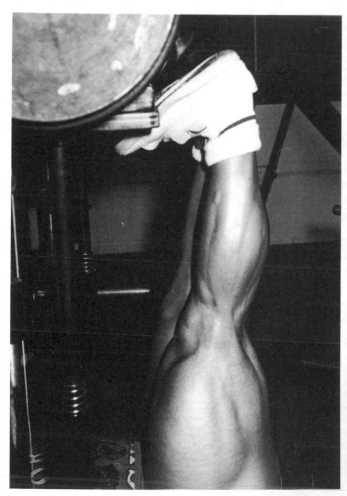
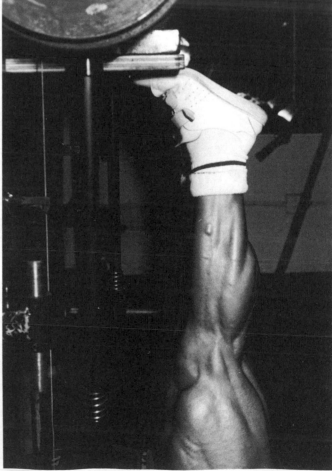

Seated Calf Raises

Purpose of Exercise: TO DEVELOP THE LOWER AND OUTER AREAS OF THE CALVES.

Execution: (1) Sit on the machine and place your toes on the bottom crosspiece, hooking your knees under the crossbar. Slowly lower your heels as far toward the ground as possible, (2) then press back up on your toes until your calves are fully contracted. Try not to rock back and forth too much but keep the calves working with a steady, rhythmic motion.

Donkey Calf Raises

Purpose of Exercise: TO DEVELOP THE THICKNESS OF THE BACK OF THE CALVES.

Donkey Calf Raises are one of my favorite exercises, and really make your calves look huge when viewed from the side.

Execution: Place your toes on a block, bend forward from the waist, and lean on a bench or a table for support. Your toes should be directly below your hips. Have a training partner add resistance by seating himself across your hips, as far back as possible to keep pressure off the lower back. With your toes turned slightly inward to give greater stimulation to the outer surfaces of the muscle, lower your heels as far as possible, and then come back up on your toes until your calves are fully contracted. If you try to cheat on this movement you end up bouncing your training partner around, so have him call this to your attention if it happens.

You can use a variation of the Stripping Method doing Donkey Calf Raises. I would frequently start with as many as three men on my back. As I got tired, I would do a few sets with just two guys, then finish off with just one. Talk about getting a burn!

One-Leg Calf Raises

Purpose of exercise: TO ISOLATE EACH SET OF CALF MUSCLES.
Doing Calf Raises one leg at a time is essential when one calf is larger than the other and you need to bring up the size of the smaller one.

Execution: (1) Stand with the toes of one leg on a block and the other leg suspended in midair behind you. Lower your heel as far as you can, (2) then come back up on your toes. Finish your set, then repeat with the other leg. If one of your calves is smaller or weaker than the other, give it some extra sets to help achieve the necessary symmetry. One-Legged Calf Raises can also be done on a Leg Press machine.

 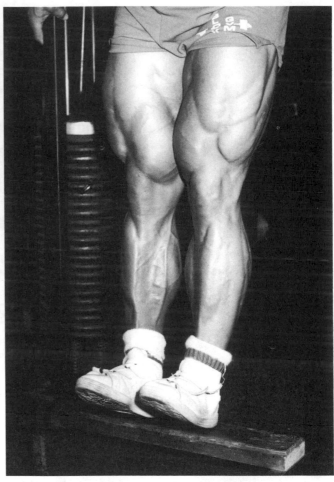

Reverse Calf Raises

Purpose of Exercise: TO DEVELOP THE FRONT OF THE LOWER LEG.
Many bodybuilders with good calves forget about developing the muscles at the front of the lower leg, primarily the tibialis anterior, which separates the inside calf from the outside calf and makes the leg seem much bigger.

Execution: (1) Stand with your heels on a block, lower your toes as far as you can, (2) then lift them up, feeling the muscles at the front of the lower leg contract as fully as possible. Do about 20 or 30 repetitions with your own body weight. As a variation, you can hook your toes under a light weight to provide extra resistance.

The Muscles of the Abdomen

The **rectus abdominis,** a long muscle extending along the length of the ventral aspect of the abdomen. It originates in the area of the pubis and inserts into the cartilage of the fifth, sixth and seventh ribs.

>   BASIC FUNCTION: to flex the spinal column and to draw the sternum toward the pelvis

The **external obliques** (obliquus externus abdominis), muscles at each side of the torso attached to the lower eight ribs and inserting at the side of the pelvis

>   BASIC FUNCTION: To flex and rotate the spinal column

The **intercostals,** two thin planes of muscular and tendon fibers occupying the spaces between the ribs

>   BASIC FUNCTION: To lift the ribs and draw them together

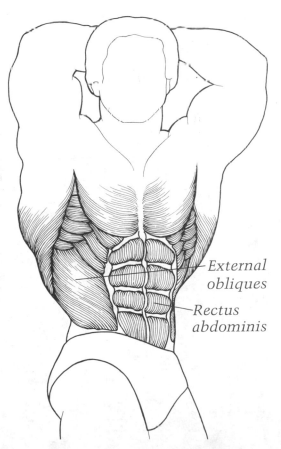

External obliques

Rectus abdominis

Training the Abdominals

The abdominal muscles have a relatively simple function. They pull the upper body (the rib cage) and the lower body (the pelvis) toward each other, and contribute to keeping your internal organs in place.

Strong abdominals are essential to maximizing performance in almost all sports. In bodybuilding, the abdominals play an extremely important role when it comes to the visible impression your physique makes on an observer. The abs are, in fact, the visual center of the body. If you superimpose an "X" on the body, with the terminal points being the shoulders and the feet, the two lines cross at the abdominals, and this is where the eyes are inevitably drawn. Men carry a disproportionate number of fat cells in the abdominal area, so well-defined abs are one sign of being in top condition—lean, hard, and strong.

A bodybuilder is likely to score points in a contest if he has wide shoulders and flaring lats that taper down to a firm, narrow waist. A small waist tends to make both your chest and your thighs appear larger, more impressive, and more aesthetic.

This traditional "V"-shaped torso is as important as sheer mass when it comes to creating a quality, championship physique. I have often seen contests in which good bodybuilders came in a few pounds overweight in order to appear bigger but found that the extra weight they were carrying at the waist spoiled the visual effect. Pierre Vandensteen, for example, competing at a body weight of only about 154 pounds, looked 30 pounds bigger on stage (allowing him to beat much more massive opponents) be-

The IFBB mandatory abdominal pose: hands behind the head, abs flexed, one leg extended.

IFBB

Well-defined abdominals are important, but so is having a small waist, which makes poses like this twist biceps shot so much more effective.

Pierre Vandensteen

cause his small, well-developed waistline made his thighs and upper body seem massive by comparison. Danny Padilla may be popularly known as the "giant killer," but Pierre was the first bodybuilder to really deserve this title, beating worthy opponents the size of Mike Katz and the quality of Kent Kuehn and Bill Grant.

If my waist had been small and hard, and with defined abs and obliques, when I came to compete in the United States in 1968, I might not have finished second to Frank Zane. But along the same lines, if Frank had gone to the 1982 Olympia in London in the kind of shape he achieved in 1979 when he beat Mike Mentzer for that title, he might well have defeated Chris Dickerson instead of having to settle for second. Frank was actually bigger than usual—more than 200 pounds—but he lacked the washboard abs that make Zane at his best so tremendously impressive. Lack of abdominal development, or failure to display the abs properly, can be very costly in competition.

How you train with your abs depends a lot on your body type. If you train the abdominal muscles with heavy weight, they get bigger and thicker. The problem is that many bodybuilders ac-

The posedown at the 1980 Mr. Olympia contest demonstrates very clearly that top bodybuilders today have to have great abs to stay in competition. As the biggest man, it was essential for me to have abs that would stand up to the likes of Mike Mentzer, Frank Zane, and Chris Dickerson.

Mohamed Makkawy

tually overdevelop the size of their abs and the muscles tend to bulge out, giving the appearance of a fat belly. Ectomorphic body-builders who have trouble building muscle mass can get away with using additional weight in their ab training. But sooner or later, even they will build the size of their abdominals and obliques to the point where more size would be detrimental.

In a close competition, abdominal development can frequently make the difference. When Mohamed Makkawy does a pose like a front double-biceps, he will get additional points for displaying

When Bill Pearl won his first contests in the early 1950s, outstanding abdominal development was not considered essential. However, by the time he had won his Mr. Universe titles, even though his body weight had actually increased, Pearl's abdominals were fantastic.

fantastic abdominal development—a technique that won him the Swedish and Belgian Grand Prix in 1982, defeating much larger and more massive opponents. If you look at old photographs of Eugene Sandow (see p. 31), the first really international physique celebrity, you'll see he had abdominals like a washboard.

In the past, it was the smaller bodybuilders who needed to worry most about abdominal development. Bigger men like Reg Park and Bill Pearl were expected to have massive chests, arms, backs, and thighs—but judges rarely asked them to do any specific ab shots, although their abs were fantastic for bodybuilders that size. Actually, Park and Pearl were the first big men to develop outstanding abs. Today, of course, nobody is going to win a Mr. Olympia, or any other top pro title, if he hasn't got good abdominals.

The most important goal of abdominal training should be definition. For the male bodybuilder, any extra body fat tends to collect around the waistline—the belly, the sides, and the lower back. Therefore, to get good ab definition, you need the combination of a strict diet and a lot of reps and sets of abdominal exercises.

"Spot" Reduction

Many bodybuilders (and I am one of them) have always believed that doing a lot of abdominal training not only hardens and develops the abdominals but also seems to help eliminate fat in the area. However, physiologists and other experts keep assuring me that "spot reduction"—that is, burning up fat in a given area by strenuous use of the adjacent muscles—just doesn't work. According to the theory, when the body needs to use fat for energy it takes it proportionately from all the areas around the body where it is stored. Therefore, doing a lot of Sit-Ups or Leg Raises will not eliminate fat in the abdominal area any more than doing any other exercise which consumes calories.

But I have to take objection to this theory. I can't say exactly what is going on physiologically during abdominal training, but I know from my own experience, and that of many other bodybuilders, that doing strenuous abdominal training does *something* to that area that makes it leaner, harder, and more defined. It may not actually be spot reduction, but it is enough *like* spot reduction so that I think a bodybuilder trying to get into contest shape would be making a serious mistake not working the abdominals to the maximum.

Burning Calories for Definition

If you go strictly by how many calories are consumed by any given exercise, it would seem that abdominal training is not a particularly good way to lose fat. Calories are consumed in proportion to the amount of total work done. When you run, for example, you move your total body weight with each step, which is quite a lot of work. When you do Sit-Ups or Leg Raises, you are lifting much less than your body weight and therefore are doing comparatively little work. Running three miles burns up more calories than most ab workouts, since the absolute amount of work done—your entire body weight times the distance—requires a lot of energy, even if it does not seem that strenuous.

But here again, the theory and the experience of most top bodybuilders are at odds. There have been weeks during which I was doing a lot of traveling and was unable to get to a gym, but I continued to run every chance I got. Yet when I got home again I would find that my abs had seemed to fade away and lose definition despite the calorie consumption of the running. I have also gone through periods when I did not train or run to any great degree, then went and took one demanding aerobics class, combined with up to a half hour of abdominal training, and suddenly my abs were as hard and defined as a washboard.

Diet and aerobic exercise will get rid of midsection fat, but the abdominals that are then revealed will not be highly developed, well shaped, or defined. For that you need a variety of exercises, many different movements that will force the abs and associated muscles to contract in as many ways as possible. As with any other muscle group, it is variety of movement that engages the maximum amount of muscle fiber and creates the best shape and definition.

The number of possible abdominal exercises is seemingly endless. In every aerobic exercise class I have attended, the teacher has shown me a few new variations of ab training. Many of these variations have a nearly identical effect on the abdominal muscles, but being able to do so many different movements makes the training that much more interesting. It would be prohibitive to list them all, but I have included a number of my favorites for each of the muscles involved.

In the beginning, the most important thing is to build up the basic strength of the abdominal area; next, you need to increase that strength, and begin to put more emphasis on the adjacent muscles; finally, for competition, the program is designed to pro-

This photograph was taken just a week before the 1980 Mr. Olympia contest; you can see how prominent and well defined my abdominal muscles were.

duce ultimate definition and quality, a full development of every necessary muscle in the abdominal region.

Once you understand how many different ways there are to pose the abdominal area, it becomes even more obvious how necessary complete abdominal development can be. Poses can feature the upper and lower abdominals, the obliques, the intercostals, and the serratus. Abs show up in a most-muscular shot, a vacuum shot, the hands-behind-head compulsory ab shot, twisting poses, and so on.

Beginning Program

Many bodybuilders who are just starting out get excited about training the chest and arms and tend to ignore the abdominals. Then, later, when they begin to think about competition, they find they have to go on extreme abdominal programs in order to catch up in this area. So I recommend training abs right from the beginning just as you do other body parts. This way, they will develop along with the rest of the body and you will never be forced to play "catch up."

Abs should be trained every day. In the Beginning Program I recommend alternating each day between five sets of Sit-Ups and five sets of Leg Raises. Both exercises work the abdominals as a whole, but the Sit-Ups tend to work the upper abdominals to a greater degree, while the Leg Raises put a greater amount of stress on the lower area.

Another practice I recommend for beginners is to start immediately working on your stomach "vacuum"—simply blowing out all your breath, sucking in your stomach as far as possible, then trying to hold this for fifteen or twenty seconds.

Simply holding in your stomach and tensing your abs as you go about your daily business is a good way of firming and strengthening them and making yourself more conscious of how to control this important area of the body. You should begin to notice right away whether your abs are likely to be a weak point in your physique so that you can take appropriate action when you move on to Advanced Training.

Advanced Program

Once you have started to develop your abdominals, you can begin to isolate and train each of the particular areas that contribute to a firm and well-defined waist. This involves doing more sets and a wider variety of exercises—like Bent-Knee Leg Raises, Bent-

Over Twists, and Crunches. These not only work the abdominals more thoroughly but also train the adjacent obliques and intercostals.

Think of all the ways you can turn and twist the torso and it becomes apparent that there a lot of angles at which you can do abdominal work in order to get a really complete workout. Twists, for example, work the obliques at one angle, and Bent-Over Twists work them at another. But you can combine the Sit-Ups you have already mastered with a twisting motion, thereby working the abs and obliques at the same time. Adding a twisting motion to Leg Raises works the obliques and intercostals as well as the lower abs. You can also get more out of the basic movements by varying them: Incline Sit-Ups and Roman Chairs; Incline Leg Raises, Vertical Leg Raises, and Hanging Leg Raises; various kinds of Crunches to get maximum contraction of both upper and lower abs simultaneously.

In Level II, I recommend beginning your workout with a warm-up session of Roman Chairs. For obliques, in addition to twisting movements, you will find exercises like Side Bends and Side Leg Raises. Again, you can't neglect any part of the midsection, and this means working the lower back as well as everything else. To develop these muscles, I have included exercises like Hyperextensions and Straight-Leg Deadlifts.

You will also find, especially in the Alternate Advanced Program, a series of exercises not traditionally done by bodybuilders. I believe in using whatever works, and in my preparation for the 1980 Mr. Olympia I worked my abdominals with a series of nonstop ab exercises I learned in aerobics class—things like Kickbacks, Rear Leg Raises, and Lying Side Scissors. These unusual exercises gave the muscles a new kind of shock and forced them to develop that much quicker.

Competition Program

When you are getting ready for competition, your aim should be to sculpt and define your total abdominal area rather than to build more size and strength. To intensify your workout, begin with ten minutes of Roman Chair Sit-Ups. I have always gotten good results starting out with Roman Chairs as have Franco Columbu, Zabo Koszewski, Ken Waller, Tom Platz and many others. They help to get you warmed up, and it is a continuous-tension exercise that keeps the abdominals working for the entire period. Also, this ten extra minutes of ab work increases the number of calories you burn.

In the Competition Program, I have included even more exercises done nonstop—aerobic-class style—than in the Advanced Program. The end product of Competition Training is total quality, and each of these exercises is designed to develop and shape a particular area of your waistline. To develop abdominals that will really impress the contest judges, you have to do exercises for the upper and lower abs, the obliques, intercostals, lower back, and every single area the judges will be scrutinizing. You should demand enormous effort from these areas in order to totally blast them into submission. Keep going, never stop for a second, and you will get the results you need.

Weak Point Training

It is just as possible to have a weak point in your abdominals as in any other body part. To help you overcome this, I have included in the abdominal training program exercises designed to work all the specific areas with which you will be concerned. Although most abdominal exercises tend to work several areas of the torso at the same time, certain movements are best for each specific area:

Serge Nubret, Mohamed Makkawy, Casey Viator, and I demonstrate four different poses in which the upper and lower abdominals, including obliques and intercostals, play a vital part.

Mohamed Makkawy

Casey Viator

Upper abs. A weak point in the upper abs is relatively rare, but if you find this is a problem try adding to your regular program any of the exercises from the Sit-Ups section, such as Incline Board Sit-Ups, Knees-in-Air Sit-Ups, Sit-Ups on the Floor, and Roman Chairs.

Lower abs. This is a more common weak point, and its cure involves doing a variety of Leg Raises, including both Straight-Leg and Bent-Knee Leg Raises, Incline Board Leg Raises, Hanging Leg Raises, Vertical Bench Leg Raises, and Alternate Leg Raises. I also like to use the Nautilus ab machine for lower abs, Seated Leg Tucks and Leg Tucks on Floor.

Obliques and intercostals. The primary exercises for obliques are Twists, Bent-Over Twists, and Side Bends, but you involve both the obliques and the intercostals when you do Sit-Ups and Leg Raises and add a twisting motion—Three-Way Roman Chairs, for example, Twisting Sit-Ups, Twisting Knees-in-Air Sit-Ups, or Alternate Twisting Knee Raises.

Lower back. I recommend Hyperextensions, Good Mornings, and Straight-Leg Deadlifts, although you will get lower back development from heavy Deadlifts as well. Twists work the lower back as well as the obliques, and movements like Kickbacks and Rear Leg Raises also help to firm up this area.

Incline Board Sit-Ups

Purpose of Exercise: FOR UPPER ABS.

Execution: (1) Lie on your back on an incline board with your head down, your knees bent to take the strain off your lower back, your feet hooked under the support strap, and your hands behind your head or on your hips. Sit up, and try to bring your chin as close to your knees as possible. (2) Lower yourself back down, but don't let your back touch the board.

The strictest way of doing this movement is with the hands behind the head. However, you can make the exercise easier—which can help you to get through a set when you are especially tired —by keeping your hands on your thighs or hips or extended out in front of you.

Dennis Tinerino

Sit-Ups can be done on various types of incline benches.

Holding a plate across your chest while doing Sit-Ups creates extra resistance for maximum abdominal strength and thickness. Only ectomorphic body types should do this exercise beyond the first two years of training.

Twisting Sit-Ups

Purpose of Exercise: FOR UPPER ABS AND INTERCOSTALS.

A variation of the normal Sit-Up involves twisting as you do the movement so that you not only involve the abdominals but the intercostals as well, giving your torso a really finished, quality look.

Execution: Position yourself on an incline board as in the preceding exercise with hands clasped behind your head. But then, as you rise up, twist to bring your right elbow to your left knee and then, on the next repetition, your left elbow to your right knee, feeling each time a "crunching" contraction of the intercostals.

Incline boards come in many varieties. This type provides support for the legs when doing Sit-Ups with bent knees.

Sit-Ups on Floor

Purpose of Exercise: FOR UPPER ABS.

Execution: (1) Lie on your back, knees bent, feet flat on the floor, your hands on the outside of your thighs. (2) Sit up and bring your head as close to your knees as possible. Lower yourself slowly back to the floor. After 20 reps you can use your arms to help you cheat a little by swinging them forward to allow you to do extra repetitions. Make sure you do this exercise very slowly and keep your chin pressed into your chest.

Knees-in-Air Sit-Ups

Purpose of Exercise: FOR UPPER AND LOWER ABS.

Execution: Lie on your back on the floor, hands clasped behind your neck. Keeping your knees bent, raise your feet in the air and cross your ankles. Keeping your knees steady, sit up and bring your head as close to your knees as possible. Really try to feel the "crunch" as the abs contract, don't just go through the motions. Lower yourself back to the floor slowly. To make the movement easier when you are fatigued, do the exercise with your arms extended in front of you instead of behind your neck.

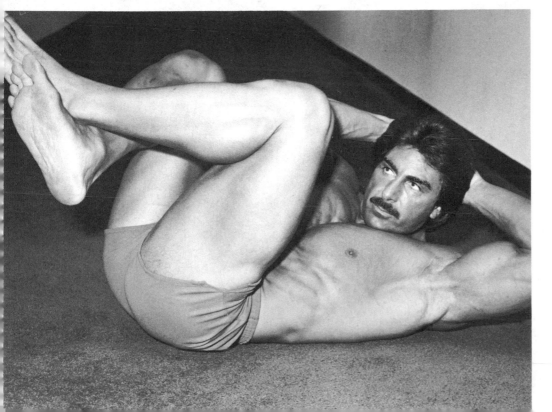

Twisting Knees-in-Air Sit-Ups

Purpose of Exercise: FOR UPPER AND LOWER ABS AND INTERCOSTALS. This twisting motion helps to work a much wider range of the abdominal area, including the obliques and intercostals.

Execution: You can also add a twist to Knee-in-Air Sit-Ups by bringing your elbow to the opposite knee as you sit up.

Roman Chair Sit-Ups

Purpose of Exercise: FOR UPPER ABS.

Execution: Sit on the Roman Chair bench, hook your feet under the support, and fold your arms in front of you. Keeping your stomach tucked in, lower yourself back to approximately a 70-degree angle, but not all the way to a 90-degree angle where your torso is parallel to the floor. Raise yourself back up and come forward as far as possible, deliberately flexing and "crunching" your abdominal muscles to increase the contraction.

I like to rest the front of the Roman Chair bench on a block of some sort, because keeping it at an incline makes the exercise that much more intense. In fact, you can vary the resistance doing Roman Chairs by starting out with the bench at a steep incline, then lowering it after ten minutes or so of effort so that you can keep going even though you are getting tired.

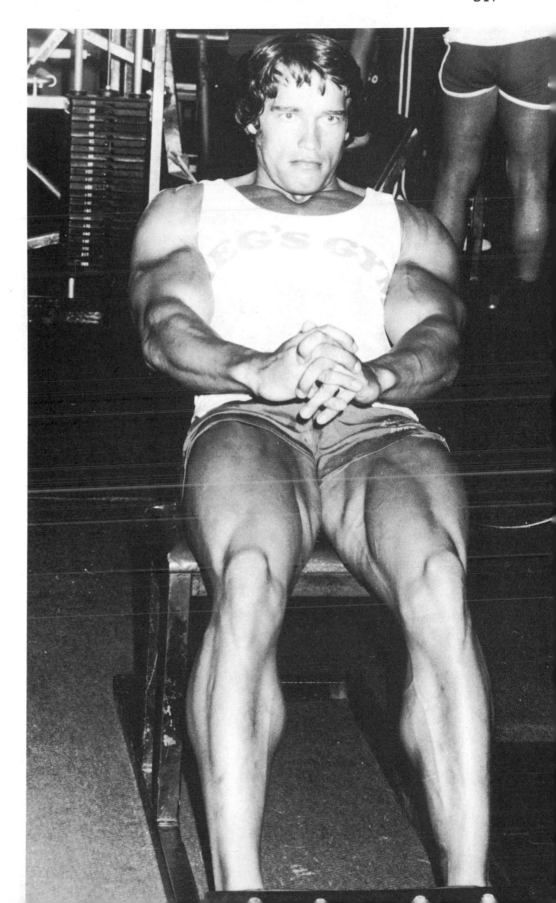

Three-Way Roman Chair Sit-Ups

Purpose of Exercise: FOR UPPER ABS, INTERCOSTALS, AND OBLIQUES.

Execution: Begin by doing a series of Roman Chair repetitions in which you lean straight back, then contract your abdominals and come straight forward. Do this for five minutes, then vary the movement by twisting to one side as you lean back, then come forward slowly so that you feel the obliques and intercostals crunch together. Do a series of repetitions in this manner for three to five minutes, then switch and twist to the other side to work the opposite set of torso muscles for three to five minutes.

Incline Board Leg Raises

Purpose of Exercise: FOR LOWER ABS.

Execution: (1) Lie on your back on an incline board, head higher than your feet. Reach back and take hold of the top of the board or some other support. (2) Keeping your legs straight and feet flexed, raise them up as high as you can, then lower them slowly, stopping just as they touch the board (don't let your heels "bounce" against the board). Breathing is important while doing Leg Raises. As you raise your legs and compress the abdominal cavity, breathe out; as you lower your legs again, inhale deeply.

NOTE: For all Leg Raise movements, it is important to tuck your chin forward into the chest in order to flex the upper abdominal area during the exercise.

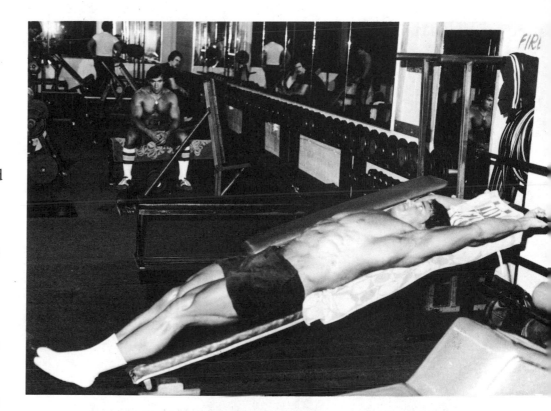

Bent-Knee Incline Board Leg Raises

Purpose of Exercise: FOR LOWER ABS.

Execution: Lie on your back on an incline board, head higher than your feet. Reach back and take hold of the top of the board or some other support.

With your *knees bent*, raise your legs as high as you can, then lower them slowly, stopping just as they touch the board. Exhale as you lift, and inhale as you lower your legs. Bending your knees rather then keeping them straight makes the movement a little easier and also helps to increase your range of motion.

Flat Bench Leg Raises

Purpose of Exercise: FOR LOWER ABS.

Execution: (1) Sit on the end of a flat bench and lie back with legs extended straight out and your hands underneath your buttocks for support.
(2) Keeping your legs straight, raise them as high as you can, then lower them slowly until they are *below* the level of the bench.

Bent-Knee Flat Bench Leg Raises

Purpose of Exercise: FOR LOWER ABS.

Execution: Start in the same position as the previous exercise. With your knees bent, raise them as high as possible toward your chest, then lower them slowly to the starting position.

Hanging Leg Raises

Purpose of Exercise: FOR LOWER ABS.

Execution: (1) Take hold of a chinning bar with an overhand grip and hang at arm's length from the bar. (2) Keeping your legs as straight as you can, lift them up in front of you as far as possible, then lower them back down toward the floor, but don't let them touch. Don't swing while doing this movement. (Since the effort of hanging from the bar is not really part of the exercise, I recommend using lifting straps to help secure your hands to the bar to prevent your fingers and hands from getting tired before you have fully exercised the abdominals.)

Bent-Knee Hanging Leg Raises

Purpose of Exercise: FOR LOWER ABS.

Execution: After you begin to tire doing Hanging Leg Raises, bending your knees will enable you to do more reps with a longer range of motion.

Take hold of a chinning bar with an overhand grip and hang at arm's length from the bar. Bend your knees, then lift your legs as high as possible. Lower them back to the starting position. Be sure not to swing while doing this exercise. (Again, I recommend you use lifting straps to help secure your grip on the bar.)

Vertical Bench Leg Raises

Purpose of Exercise: FOR LOWER ABS.

Execution: (1) Support yourself on your arms on a vertical bench. (2) Holding your upper body steady, straighten your legs and lift them up as high as you can, then lower them again slowly. Make sure not to lift your lower back off the back support.

Bent-Knee Vertical Bench Leg Raises

Purpose of Exercise: FOR LOWER ABS.
This is a great exercise to do right after the above Vertical Bench Leg Raises.

Execution: Support yourself on your arms on a vertical bench. Holding your upper body steady, bend your knees and raise them up as high as you can and flex your abs. Keeping your legs bent, lower them again to the starting position.

Vertical Bench Alternate Leg Raises

Purpose of Exercise: FOR LOWER ABS.
Any variation of an exercise tends to force the muscles to respond in new and different ways. When working the abdominals with Vertical Bench Leg Raises, try doing the movement using each leg alternately instead of raising them simultaneously. This way you create an entirely new kind of stress for the abdominals to cope with.

Execution: Support yourself on the vertical bench as before. Raise one straight leg, lower it again, then repeat with the other leg. Then do the exercise with your knee bent. For further variation, you can do Alternate Leg Raises on an incline bench, flat bench, or on the floor.

Seated Leg Tucks

Purpose of Exercise: FOR UPPER AND LOWER ABS.

Execution: (1) Sit on a bench, holding on to the sides for support. Raise your legs slightly and bend your knees. Straighten your legs, leaning backward as balance requires. (2) Lift your knees up toward your chest as you simultaneously sit up, bringing your knees and chest together and flexing your abs really hard. Throughout the movement, make certain you can feel continuous tension in the abdominal muscles. Do not let your feet touch the floor at any time during the exercise.

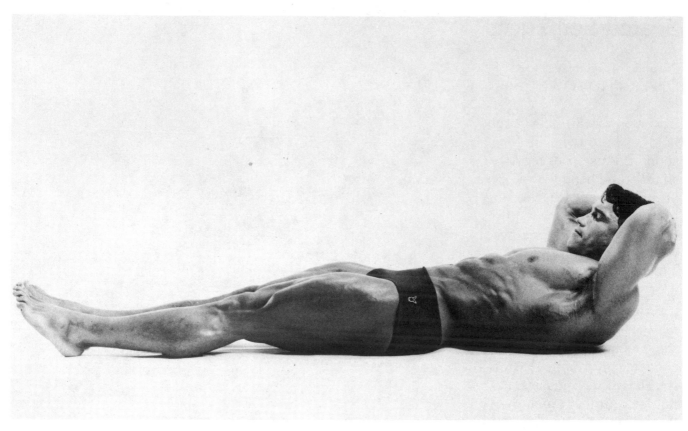

Leg Tucks on Floor

Purpose of Exercise: FOR UPPER AND LOWER ABS.

Execution: (1) Lie on the floor on your back, your hands behind your head. (2) Lift your head and shoulders up as if doing a Sit-Up and simultaneously bring your knees up as far as possible. Try to touch your elbows to your knees, then lower your upper body and legs back to the starting position. For best results, do this exercise very slowly.

Alternate Knee Raises

Purpose of Exercise: FOR LOWER ABS.

Execution: Lie back on the floor supporting yourself on your elbows, your hands under your buttocks for support. Lift both legs clear of the floor. Bring one knee up as close to your shoulder as possible. Straighten that leg and simultaneously bring the other knee up to the shoulder. Continue this movement, both legs pumping at the same time, one up and one down.

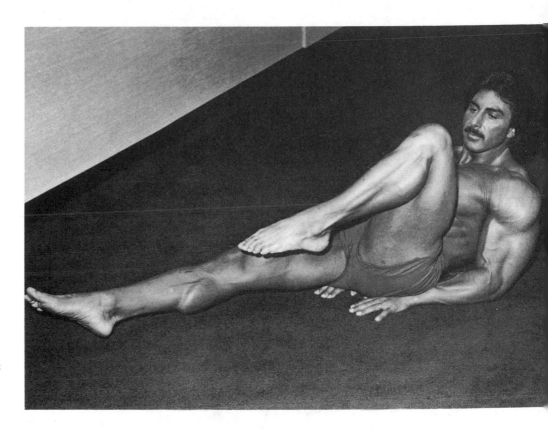

Alternate Twisting Knee Raises

Purpose of Exercise: FOR LOWER ABS, INTERCOSTALS, AND OBLIQUES.

Execution: Lie on your back on the floor, hands behind your neck, head raised. Lift both legs off the floor about 2 inches. Raise one knee toward your head and simultaneously twist and try to touch it with the opposite elbow. Return to the starting position and repeat with the other knee. The legs move as if you were riding a bicycle.

Crunches

Purpose of Exercise: FOR UPPER AND LOWER ABS. Crunches are a good way to develop a maximum definition in the abdominals.

Execution: (1) Lie on your back on the floor. With your knees bent, raise your legs and place your feet against a wall or bench for support. Place your hands behind your head. (2) Raise your head and shoulders toward your knees with a sit-up motion and simultaneously lift the pelvis and feel the contraction of the abdominals as the upper and lower body crunch together. At the top of the movement, flex the abdominals even harder to get the fullest possible contraction, then release and return to the starting position.

Toe-Touch Crunches

Purpose of Exercise: FOR UPPER AND LOWER ABS. This is a Crunch variation that requires a lot of flexibility as well as abdominal strength. It is also unique in that it forces you to keep constant tension on the lower abdominals at the same time you are flexing the upper abdominals.

Execution: (1) Lie on your back on the floor and extend your legs straight up. (2) Keeping the legs straight and up in the air, sit up by reaching upward with your hands and trying to touch your toes with your fingertips. Relax and return to the starting position. If you find yourself unable to perform this movement, try practicing by lying with your buttocks against a wall and your feet straight up, supported by the wall.

Nautilus Machine Crunches

Purpose of Exercise: FOR UPPER AND LOWER ABS.

Execution: Adjust the height of the seat to suit your proportions (the pivot point of the upper part of the machine should be about shoulder height) and choose a weight that allows you to do 8 to 12 repetitions. When using weights for resistance, you do not do as many reps as when doing Sit-Ups with your own body weight. Because this is a crunching movement it is the only abdominal exercise that can be done with weight resistance. A full movement would over-enlarge the abdomen.

(1) Sit on the machine, hook your feet behind the crosspieces, and take hold of the handles above your shoulders. (2) Curl your upper body downward, flexing the abs, while simultaneously pulling your knees upward. Crunch the upper and lower body together, bringing your knees and elbows as close together as possible. Hold this position for a moment, then slowly release, lowering the weight stack under control back to the starting position.

Seated Twists

Purpose of Exercise: FOR THE OBLIQUES.
This exercise develops the obliques at the sides of the lower torso.

Execution: Sit on the end of a bench, feet flat on the floor and comfortably apart. Take hold of a broom handle or light bar and hold it across the back of your shoulders. Keeping your head stationary, and making sure your pelvis does not shift on the bench, swing your shoulders in one direction as far as you can, feeling the oblique muscles on that side fully contract. Come back to the center, then twist as far as you can in the other direction. As you get looser and more warmed up, increase the pace, swinging energetically first in one direction, then reversing and swinging back the other way.

NOTE: Twisting exercises, in addition to working the obliques and intercostals, help develop a narrow waist.

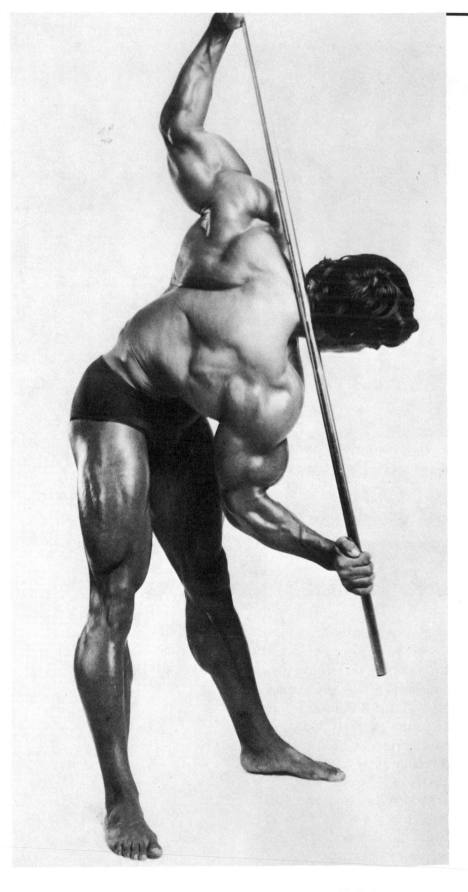

Standing Bent-Over Twists

Purpose of Exercise: FOR THE OBLIQUES.

In Bent-Over Twists you fully contract the obliques in order to develop a firm, tight waistline.

Execution: Stand upright, legs straight, feet shoulder width apart. Hold a broom handle across the back of your shoulders. Bend forward from the waist as far as comfortable. Turning from the waist but not letting your hips move at all, twist in one direction until the end of the broom handle is pointing toward the floor, then twist back the other way until the other end of the broom handle is pointing toward the floor. Continue this windmill movement, swinging energetically first in one direction, then back in the other direction, picking up speed as you become looser and warmed up.

Side Bends

Purpose of Exercise: FOR THE OBLIQUES.

The obliques not only help your body to twist, they are also primarily responsible for bending the torso side to side. Variations of Side Bends involve using dumbbells or other resistance, but I feel that firming and defining this area is preferable to developing extra mass, which tends to thicken the waistline. Therefore, I recommend doing Side Bends without weights in the following manner.

Execution: Stand upright with feet more than shoulder distance apart, toes pointed out, and clasp your hands behind your head. Bend your knees and come down into a half squat. Then bend to the right, bringing your right elbow close to your right knee. Tense and flex the obliques on that side. Come back to the starting position, then bend to the other side and repeat.

Side Leg Raises

Purpose of Exercise: FOR THE OBLIQUES AND INTERCOSTALS.
This exercise works the entire side of the torso—the intercostals as well as the obliques—and can really contribute to giving your waist a narrow look from the front.

Execution: (1) Lie on your side supporting yourself on your elbow, your lower leg bent under for support. (2) Keeping the upper leg straight, raise it slowly as high as it will go, then lower it again, but stopping short of letting it touch the floor. Finish your repetitions with this leg, then turn onto your other side and repeat the movement. Don't move your hips at all during this movement.

Bent-Knee Side Leg Raises

Purpose of Exercise: FOR THE OBLIQUES AND INTERCOSTALS.

Execution: Lie on your side supporting yourself on your elbow, your lower leg bent under for support. Bend the knee of your upper leg and raise it slowly toward your chest as high as you can, then lower it again, stopping short of letting it touch the floor. Finish the repetitions, then turn and work the opposite leg.

Front Kicks

Purpose of Exercise: FOR THE OBLIQUES AND INTERCOSTALS.
This is done exactly the same way as Side Leg Raises except to the front. These exercises are most effective when done one right after another without stopping.

Bench Kickbacks

Purpose of Exercise: FOR THE LOWER BACK.

Execution: (1) Kneel with one leg on the end of a bench. Reach forward and grip the bench with arms locked, for support. (2) Raise your other leg as high as you can, then bring it back down, not letting it quite touch the floor. Concentrate throughout the movement on flexing and contracting the buttocks. Complete your repetitions, then repeat using the other leg. The same movement can be done, with somewhat more difficulty, kneeling on the floor.

Rear Leg Scissors

Purpose of Exercise: FOR THE LOWER BACK AND BUTTOCKS.

Execution: (1) Lie on your stomach on the floor, hands under your thighs. Raise your legs off the floor as far as possible. (2) Move your feet apart a short distance, then bring them together and cross one over the other. Move them apart and then cross them again with the opposite leg on top in a continuous nonstop movement. Continue in this way until you complete your repetitions. Concentrate on feeling the contraction of the buttocks and the lower back.

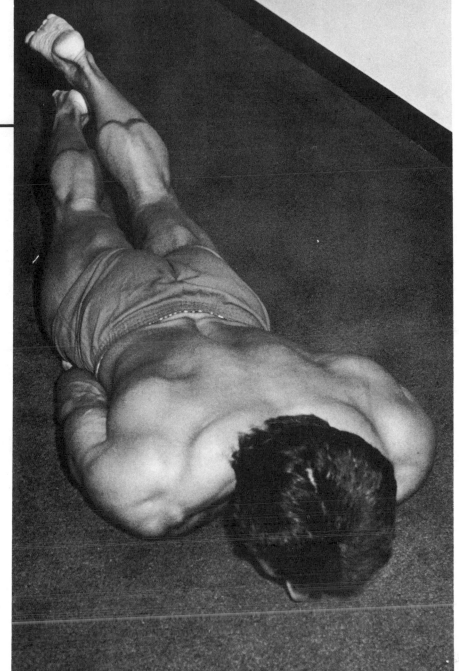

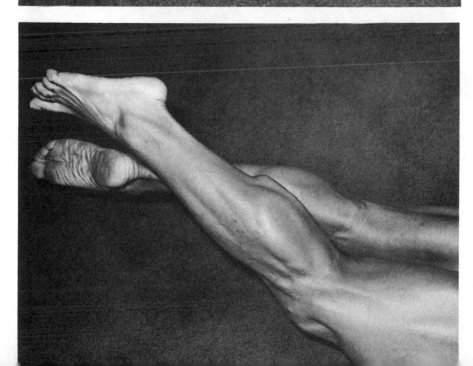

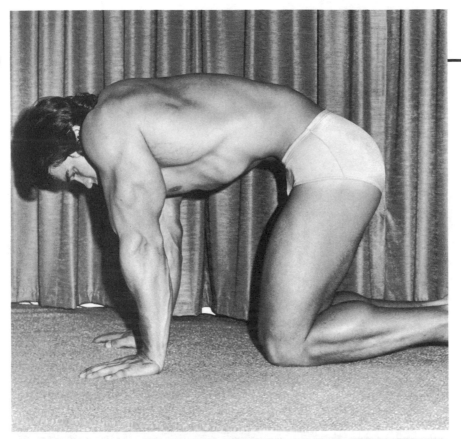

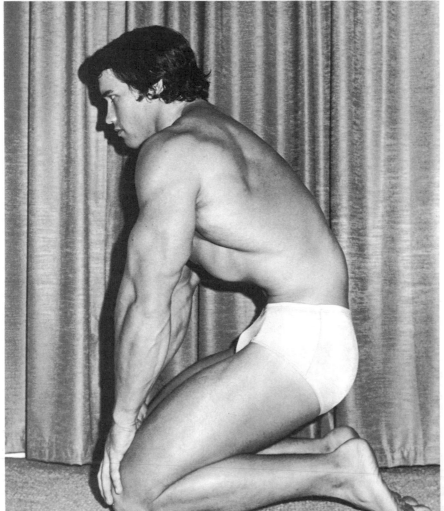

Vacuum

Being able to produce and hold a vacuum actually reduces the size of your waistline, and allows you to suck in and hold the abdominals when you are posing. But mastering the vacuum is a matter of hard, consistent practice.

Get down on your hands and knees, blow out all your breath, and suck in your abdominals as much as you can. Hold this for 20–30 seconds, relax for a few moments, then try it again two or three times.

The next step is to practice your vacuum in a kneeling position. Kneel upright with your hands on your knees and try to hold the vacuum as long as you can.

Doing a seated vacuum is more difficult still, since gravity is in opposition to your efforts. But once you can hold a vacuum in a seated position without any problem, you will be able to practice holding a vacuum while standing and doing a variety of poses.

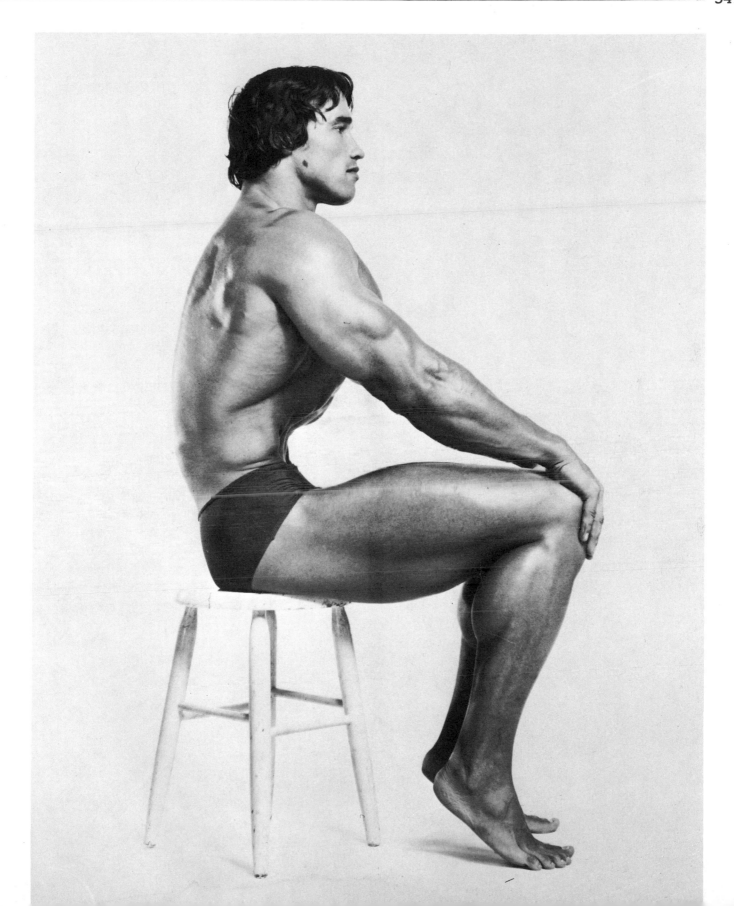

BOOK FOUR
Competition

CHAPTER 1
Posing

It may take years to build and shape your physique, as well as months of careful contest training and rigorous diet, but eventually the time will come when you find yourself ready to step out on stage and compete for a title. No matter how good your physique may be, or how cut-up and defined you are, you still have to communicate this quality to the judges and the audience. But remember, they are not just looking at your muscles and your cuts, they are looking at *you*—the total you—everything from how you stand, move, and pose, to your skin tone, haircut, and posing trunks, and whether you seem confident or anxious, a winner or a loser. Their impression of you is formed by your mastery of posing—your ability to display your physique with drama and excitement.

Actually, I had always been against excessive contest preparation, feeling that all you should have to bring to a competition is your trained body and some sort of posing routine. However, over the last decade or so the sport has become so sophisticated that a bodybuilder can't rely simply on what he has achieved in the gym and the ability to do a few simple poses. Nowadays you need to deal with every detail, every aspect of presentation, or risk losing by a narrow margin. Many a bodybuilder has lost a competition simply because his posing was not good enough, because he lost his balance doing moves he had not practiced enough or tried poses that did not really suit his physique.

The bodybuilder's physique is like a work of art; the effect of a great painting can be ruined if it is poorly displayed, if the frame, the lighting, and the setting are not designed to show it off to best advantage. So, too, the finest physique can fail to move the judges if the bodybuilder does not understand how to present himself in such a manner as to call attention to the true qualities of his physique.

Mastering the art of "standing relaxed" in round one and performing the compulsory poses in round two are essential if you want to do well in the third round of IFBB amateur or professional bodybuilding contests. The third round is a creative opportunity to pose any way you choose, to exhibit poses that bring out your strong points, minimize your weaknesses, and generally work to impress the judges.

Every top bodybuilder has certain poses for which he becomes famous, that allow him to use his outstanding body parts to rout his opponents. Sometimes these poses are quite conventional and used by virtually everyone, but which individual bodybuilders are able to make their own by virtue of some unusual ability or development. Others use highly unusual variations that they themselves may have invented.

Understanding how to vary your poses is also important, since different poses for the same body part tend to emphasize different areas or qualities of the entire body. For example, certain back poses will draw attention to mass and others to symmetry; one pose might display your triceps most effectively, another your biceps. By using the proper pose, you could force the judges to notice outstanding calves, or camouflage the fact that your calves are not as good as they should be.

One should choose poses that are creative on two levels: making them as aesthetic and dramatic as possible, almost like a form of dance; and manipulating the focus of attention of the judges, so that they notice what you want them to and ignore what you would prefer they ignore. This is not easy to learn, it takes time. But it is a valuable and virtually essential skill for any bodybuilder desiring to become a true champion.

Learning by Observing

One of the best ways of learning what's involved in becoming an effective competitor is to train with a bodybuilder who has contest experience. Not only will you pick up vital training information, but you will also have a chance to share his knowledge of posing, diet, and contest preparation.

Go to as many bodybuilding competitions as possible. Carefully watch everything that goes on: what takes place in each of the rounds, how the contest is conducted, and what sort of instructions the bodybuilders are given on stage during prejudging. Look at the competitors and try to understand why one is doing something right and another isn't. For example, what sort of expressions do they have on their faces? Does one look too mean or another as if he isn't taking the contest seriously? Take notes.

Actually, I learned more about what goes on in a competition by watching than I ever did when I was in the show and preoccupied with my own performance.

I have used the same approach in making films. When I was hired to act in *Stay Hungry*, the director sent me out to watch television shows being made all over Hollywood. This helped me to learn the vocabulary and techniques of the business—and the more I learned about movie-making, the more effective I was when it was my turn to be in front of the camera. I watched, I made notes—and I won a Golden Globe award my first time out, so I know this way of learning really works.

You can see what is happening on stage much better from the audience than you can when you are standing up there yourself. You can detect mistakes and learn how to avoid them. You can see if one competitor is using too much oil, one is too smooth, and how effective different styles of posing and presentation can be. Once you have a clear idea of what works and what doesn't, you can begin to plan your own presentation.

Posing Routine

Until about ten years ago posing meant simply "free posing"—doing your own personal routine. But today's contests are more complicated and the judges look at the body more technically, so it has become increasingly important to learn how to pose the body in all situations demanded by competition.

In IFBB contests, there are three basic kinds of posing required, with similar requirements under the rules of other organizations on both a national and international level:

Round One: Standing Relaxed

In the first round, you are judged on symmetry, proportion, and overall development. The judges observe you while you are standing in a lineup, and then individually as they ask you to stand facing them, hands at your sides, then to turn three times so that they can see you from all sides. After this, you can be called out again for a direct comparison with the other body-builders.

But this so-called "standing relaxed" involves keeping almost every muscle in your body tensed, a really tough thing to do unless you have prepared for it. When there are a large number of competitors in your class you may have to stand on stage for

"Standing relaxed"—front view. Notice that these competitors, although not hitting a pose, have every muscle flexed and under control.

"Standing relaxed"—side view

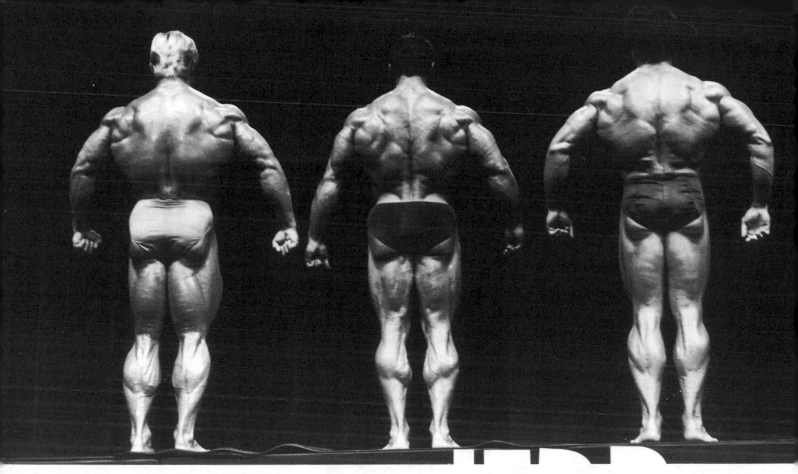

"Standing relaxed"—back view. Each of the contestants has his leg biceps, calves, and lower back totally flexed, even though this is a relaxed back-view pose.

thirty or forty minutes as all the comparisons are made, and you never know when one of the judges may be looking at you.

Round Two: Compulsory Poses

The second round is designed to show the judges your strengths and weaknesses. This is a cold, clinical look at the exact nature of your muscular development. Over the years, a certain number of compulsory poses have come to be accepted (although they are subject to periodic change), and every would-be competitive bodybuilder should learn them and practice each one, over and over:

> Front double-biceps
> Front lat spread
> Side chest
> Rear double-biceps
> Rear lat spread
> Side triceps
> Abdominal pose with hands behind head and leg
>   extended

In some cases, you may be asked to do a side chest or side triceps from either side, so you should practice these poses facing in both directions.

The compulsories are designed so that you cannot hide anything. The judges get a clear look at your strong points *and* your

Front double-biceps

Front lat spread (Samir Bannout)

Side chest shot

Rear double-biceps

Rear lat spread (Chris
Dickerson)

Side triceps (Chris Dickerson)

Abdominal pose with hands
behind head and leg extended
(Tom Platz)

Sergio Oliva, with his combination of massive muscularity and tiny waist is an awesome sight on stage.

weaknesses. This makes it extraordinarily important for you to learn to do these poses well. The judges look at each individual body part—judging for shape, balance, proportion, separation, and so forth—and you need to be able to show them what you have achieved in all those hours of training and diet.

You will be asked to go through the compulsories on your own and then later you may be called back out to pose for direct comparisons with other competitors. When this is going on, you remain on stage standing "relaxed" again for long periods of time.

Round Three: Free Posing

In round two, the judges make you show them what *they* want to look at; but round three gives you the opportunity to show the judges what *you* want them to see.

In this round you are given a certain amount of time (less than a minute in some competitions, as much as three to four minutes in top-level professional contests) to perform your own posing routine. In most contests the third round, which is the one that really counts, is conducted during prejudging and no music is allowed; the free posing that takes place to music at the evening show does not count in the scoring. In other contests the evening posing is counted as the third round, and music is sometimes permitted.

Free posing allows you to emphasize your strong points and to hide your weaknesses to some extent. However, if you avoid hitting those poses that expose your weaknesses, you can sometimes create the opposite effect and actually call the judges' attention to what you want them to overlook.

Round Four: The Posedown

In many contests, the various class winners or the top finishers free-pose together on stage while the judges take a last look at them and award one point extra to whoever they think is the best in the contest. With seven judges each giving a single point, the results of a close contest can ride on this round alone.

You don't really have the opportunity to go through your whole posing routine during this round, but should just do your best shots, being aware of what the other bodybuilders around you are doing, and trying to top them and convince the judges that you are indeed the winner.

This picture of Boyer Coe, myself, and Chris Dickerson from the 1980 Mr. Olympia was taken at the beginning of the posedown when the six finalists go through the compulsories together, giving the judges a chance to make direct comparisons.

Bertil Fox, Mohamed Makkawy, and Johnny Fuller hitting a side triceps at the 1982 Olympia.

IFBB

The most dramatic part of the posedown comes when the finalists are free to pose any way they want, to show their strong points, expose their opponents' weaknesses, and try to dominate the stage. At the 1982 Olympia in London, Frank Zane, Samir Bannout, Chris Dickerson, Albert Beckles, Tom Platz, and Casey Viator contended fiercely in this exciting and important round.

How Bodybuilding Is Scored

There have been various procedures and scoring systems used throughout the history of bodybuilding. Along with giving competitors a score based on the development of their physiques, some systems also included points for demonstrations of athletic ability—hand balancing, for example—and even for personality, with bodybuilders being scored on how they answered questions put to them by the judges.

Originally, a placement system was used in scoring, with the competitors placed in order—first, second, third, and so on. Then, in some international competitions, a point system was adopted in which competitors were given a score of from 20 (for the best) on down in each of three rounds, the bodybuilder with the highest total score being the winner, the one with the next highest finishing second, and on down through the field.

If this isn't confusing enough, the IFBB has currently abandoned the point system and gone *back* to the placement system it used originally.

There have also been other ways of organizing a competition other than with the three-round system. Some contests have used two rounds—in which the contestants are first compared hitting all the basic poses and then when free posing. In some systems, you give a score for each separate round and, in others, you simply take notes and then give one overall score at the end of the contest.

The official procedures have varied a lot, too. In the Mr. Olympia contests of the late 1960s, the judges would go off into a corner together after the contest and decide among themselves who would win the title. More recently, very strict procedures have been adopted and judges are watched carefully to ensure that they do not talk among themselves during the course of the show or share their ideas on how the contest should be scored.

So nothing is really permanent when it comes to judging procedures. I can, however, tell you what systems are in use as of this writing. In American amateur bodybuilding, sanctioned by the National Physique Committee of the U.S.A., the system used is:

1. Two rounds—comparison posing and free posing.
2. The placement system is used.
3. One score is given each competitor by each judge at the end of the contest.

In international amateur and professional competition, sanctioned by the International Federation of Bodybuilders, the system used is:

1. Three rounds—general assessment (standing relaxed), compulsory posing, free posing.
2. The top five competitors after the three rounds advance to a posedown.
3. Each judge scores each competitor for each of all three rounds and gives the top five an additional score for the posedown.
4. The placement system is used.

However, just to show you how changeable these procedures can be, the IFBB has been discussing additional changes. One is to reverse the order of rounds one and two, starting with the compulsories and following with standing relaxed, or combine rounds one and two into a single round. Another potential change is to have the judges give only a single score at the end of the contest as in NPC contests.

But no matter what scoring system is used, remember that bodybuilders are evaluated relative to each other rather than compared to some kind of hypothetical ideal. That is, the best bodybuilder in the show always gets the highest score (a 20 in the point system, first place in the placement system), and everybody else is compared to him. It doesn't matter if he has a lot of faults and is not really that good a bodybuilder. As long as he is the best in the show, he gets the 20 or first place. (Sports like gymnastics and diving don't compare the athletes to each other but to a theoretical ideal. So, using a 10-point system, a gymnast can win a contest with a 9.5 or a 9.2 so long as the others get a lower score; but if he or she scores a 10, that literally means that the performance was not just the best but was *perfect!*)

In IFBB bodybuilding competitions, if a competitor scores a "perfect" 300 using the point system (a score of 20 from each of five judges—high and low score thrown out so two judges don't count—totaling 100 per round times 3 rounds) or a 20 using the placement system (a score of 1 from five judges—high and low score thrown out so two judges don't count—in all three rounds and posedown equals $5 \times 4 = 20$), it doesn't mean he is perfect, just that all the judges agree he is the best in that particular contest.

Olympia Judging Sheets

If you know how to read judging sheets, you can figure out what really happened in a contest. For example, looking at the sheets from the 1979 Mr. Olympia, you can see that the contest was held with two weight divisions, under and over 200 pounds. Each weight class was judged separately, with the top three from each class coming together at the end in a posedown.

The IFBB was still using the point system in 1979. In the light-weight class, Frank Zane won the first two rounds with scores of 100 in each (high and low marks in each round discarded, the others added up to produce a total—in Frank's case, $5 \times 20 = 100$). In round three, Boyer Coe managed to edge Frank out by 1 point, 100 to 99.

In the over-200 pound class, Mike Mentzer got three 100 scores. Notice that every judge in every round gave him a 20. This allowed him to go into the posedown that night with a total of 300 points against Zane's 299. The problem was, however, that since the contest was held with two separate classes, Mentzer had not achieved that score in direct comparison to Zane, who was in the other class. Therefore, Mentzer was starting with an advantage over Zane that, in one sense, he hadn't earned.

But the posedown determined the final scoring. Zane's much greater competition experience prevailed, and five judges awarded him first place, with only one judge voting for Mentzer. Zane started a point behind, gained 4 points in the posedown, and finished 304 to 301, with a 3-point victory.

INTERNATIONAL FEDERATION OF BODYBUILDERS

I.F.B.B.

JUDGES ANALYSIS — Bill

Contest: "MR. OLYMPIA"

Category:

Place: Columbus

Date: 10. Oct. 1981

No.	Name	Country	Jacques Blommaert Belgium	Jim Manion USA	Winston Roberts Canada	Sven-Ole Thorsen Denmark	Franco Fassi Italy	Dominic Certo USA	Doug Evans Wales	Points	Place	Avg.
			FIRST ROUND									
1	FRANCO COLUMBU	USA	18	19	19	19	20	19	20	96		
17	CHRIS DICKERSON	USA	18	18	20	20	19	19	20	96		
4	TOM PLATZ	USA	20	19	19	19	19	20	19	96		
10	ROY CALLENDER	Canada	19	19	19	18	19	20	18	94		
2	DANNY PADILLA	USA	19	20	20	17	19	18	19	95		
7	JUSUP WILKOSZ	Germany	19	18	18	18	18	19	17	91		
15	DENNIS TINERINO	USA	16	18	18	15	18	18	18	88		
1	JOHNNY FULLER	England	17	18	18	17	17	18	18	88		
3	SAMIR BANNOUT	USA	17	17	17	15	18	18	17	86		
8	ROGER WALKER	Australia	17	17	18	16	18	18	18	88		
16	HUBERT METZ	Germany	16	16	17	14	17	18	16	82		
5	CARLOS RODRIGUEZ	USA	16	16	16	12	16	17	16	80		
9	ED CORNEY	USA	16	15	17	12	17	17	16	81		
4	STEVE DAVIS	USA	15	15	16	13	16	17	15	77		
13	MIKE KATZ	USA	16	16	16	13	14	17	15	77		
6	KEN WALLER	USA	15	16	16	13	14	17	15	76		
12	JORMA RATY	Finland	15	15	14	15	17	16	17	78		
			SECOND ROUND									
11	FRANCO COLUMBU	USA	18	20	19	20	20	20	20	99		
17	CHRIS DICKERSON	USA	18	19	20	20	19	19	19	96		
14	TOM PLATZ	USA	19	19	19	19	19	20	20	96		
10	ROY CALLENDER	Canada	20	19	20	19	19	19	19	96		
2	DANNY PADILLA	USA	19	19	19	18	19	18	19	94		
7	JUSUP WILKOSZ	Germany	18	18	18	18	18	19	17	90		
15	DENNIS TINERINO	USA	16	18	18	15	18	18	18	88		
1	JOHNNY FULLER	England	16	18	18	17	18	18	18	89		
3	SAMIR BANNOUT	USA	17	17	17	16	18	18	17	86		
8	ROGER WALKER	Australia	17	17	18	16	18	18	17	87		
16	HUBERT METZ	Germany	18	16	18	15	17	18	17	86		
5	CARLOS RODRIGUEZ	USA	17	17	16	13	17	18	17	84		
9	ED CORNEY	USA	16	15	16	13	16	17	17	80		
4	STEVE DAVIS	USA	16	16	16	14	17	17	15	80		
13	MIKE KATZ	USA	15	16	16	14	16	17	16	79		
6	KEN WALLER	USA	15	15	16	14	16	17	16	78		
12	JORMA RATY	Finland	15	15	15	15	16	16	18	77		
			THIRD ROUND									
11	FRANCO COLUMBU	USA	18	20	19	20	20	20	20	99		
17	CHRIS DICKERSON	USA	19	19	20	20	19	19	20	97		
14	TOM PLATZ	USA	19	20	18	20	18	20	19	96		
10	ROY CALLENDER	Canada	20	19	19	19	19	20	19	96		
2	DANNY PADILLA	USA	18	20	19	18	18	18	19	92		
7	JUSUP WILKOSZ	Germany	19	17	18	18	18	18	17	89		
15	DENNIS TINERINO	USA	17	18	18	15	18	18	18	89		
1	JOHNNY FULLER	England	16	17	18	17	17	18	18	87		
3	SAMIR BANNOUT	USA	18	18	19	16	19	18	18	91		
8	ROGER WALKER	Australia	17	17	18	16	17	18	17	86		
16	HUBERT METZ	Germany	17	16	17	15	17	18	17	84		
5	CARLOS RODRIGUEZ	USA	17	17	17	13	17	18	17	85		
9	ED CORNEY	USA	18	17	17	13	18	17	16	85		

INTERNATIONAL FEDERATION OF BODYBUILDERS

JUDGES ANALYSIS
Contest ..."MR. OLYMPIA"...........
Category ....

Place: Columbus.
Date: 10 Oct. 1981

No.	Name	Country	Jacques Blommaert Belgium	Jim Manion USA	Winston Roberts Canada	Sven-Ole Thorsen Denmark	Franco Fassi Italy	Dominic Certo USA	Doug Evans Wales	Points	Place	Av
4	STEVE DAVIS	USA	16	17	18	14	18	17	16	84		
13	MIKE KATZ	USA	16	16	16	14	17	17	16	81		
6	KEN WALLER	USA	16	16	17	14	16	17	16	81		
12	JORMA RATY	Finland	15	16	16	15	16	16	18	79		
		TOTALS										
11	FRANCO COLUMBU	USA	54	59	57	59	60	59	60	294	1	
17	CHRIS DICKERSON	USA	55	56	60	60	57	57	59	289	2	
14	TOM PLATZ	USA	58	58	56	58	56	60	58	288	3	
10	ROY CALLENDER	Canada	59	57	58	56	57	59	56	286	4	
2	DANNY PADILLA	USA	56	59	58	53	56	54	57	281	5	
7	JUSUP WILKOSZ	Germany	56	53	54	54	54	56	51	270	6	
15	DENNIS TINERINO	USA	49	54	54	45	54	54	54	265	7	
1	JOHNNY FULLER	England	49	53	54	51	52	54	54	264	8	
3	SAMIR BANNOUT	USA	52	52	53	47	55	54	52	263	9	
8	ROGER WALKER	Australia	51	51	54	48	53	54	52	261	10	
16	HUBERT METZ	Germany	51	48	52	44	51	54	50	252	11	
5	CARLOS RODRIGUEZ	USA	50	50	49	38	50	53	50	249	12	
9	ED CORNEY	USA	50	47	50	38	51	51	49	246	13	
4	STEVE DAVIS	USA	47	48	50	41	51	51	46	241	14	
13	MIKE KATZ	USA	47	48	48	41	47	51	47	237	15	
6	KEN WALLER	USA	46	47	49	41	46	50	47	235	16	
12	JORMA RATY	Finland	45	46	45	45	49	48	53	234	17	
		POSEDOWN										
11	FRANCO COLUMBU	USA	-	-	-	-	1	-	1	296	1	
17	CHRIS DICKERSON	USA	-	-	1	1	-	-	-	291	2	
14	TOM PLATZ	USA	1	-	-	-	-	1	-	290	3	
10	ROY CALLENDER	Canada	-	-	-	-	-	-	-	286	4	
2	DANNY PADILLA	USA	-	1	-	-	-	-	-	282	5	
7	JUSUP WILKOSZ	Germany	-	-	-	-	-	-	-	270	6	

INTERNATIONAL FEDERATION OF BODYBUILDERS

SHEET JP/3

JUDGING PANEL CHAIRMAN/SECRETARY — CATEGORY RESULTS SHEET

CONTEST ....M.R. OLYMPIA...........

PLACE ....COLUMBUS, OHIO, U.SA........................ DATE 10 Oct 1981...

CATEGORY .... OVER/UP TO .... KILOS

ROUNDS 1, 2, and 3 MARKS ADDED TOGETHER FOR CATEGORY PLACINGS

The highest and lowest score for each Competitor in each Round have been eliminated. The Three Highest Placed Competitors will compete at the public posedown for their Final Placings.

Competitors Number	Competitors Names	Country	Marks			Total Marks	Place Award
			Round 1	Round 2	Round 3		
11	FRANCO COLUMBU	USA	96	99	99	294	1
17	CHRIS DICKERSON	USA	96	96	97	289	2
14	TOM PLATZ	USA	96	96	96	288	3
10	ROY CALLENDER	Canada	94	96	96	286	4
2	DANNY PADILLA	USA	95	94	92	281	5
7	JUSUP WILKOSZ	Germany	91	90	89	270	6
15	DENNIS TINERINO	USA	88	88	89	265	7
1	JOHNNY FULLER	England	88	89	87	264	8
3	SAMIR BANNOUT	USA	86	86	91	263	9
8	ROGER WALKER	Australia	88	87	86	261	10
16	HUBERT METZ	Germany	82	86	84	252	11
5	CARLOS RODRIGUEZ	USA	80	84	85	249	12
9	ED CORNEY	USA	81	80	85	246	13
4	STEVE DAVIS	USA	77	80	84	241	14
13	MIKE KATZ	USA	77	79	81	237	15
6	KEN WALLER	USA	76	78	81	235	16
12	JORMA RATY	Finland	78	77	79	234	17
		POSEDOWN					
11	FRANCO COLUMBU	USA	294	+	2	296	1
17	CHRIS DICKERSON	USA	289	+	2	291	2
14	TOM PLATZ	USA	288	+	2	290	3
10	ROY CALLENDER	Canada	286	-	-	286	4
2	DANNY PADILLA	USA	281	+	1	282	5
7	JUSUP WILKOSZ	Germany	270		-	270	6

Signed Chairman Judging Panel .... Country ....

Signed Secretary Judging Panel ....Oscar State............... Country ....England........

Signed I.F.B.B. President .... Country ....

"MR. OLYMPIA" 200 lb Class

Columbus, Ohio, USA

7 October 1979

ROUND	N°	NAME	COUNTRY	Jacques Blommaert Belgium	Winston Roberts Canada	Malih Alaywan Lebanon	Franco Fassi Italy	Albert Busek Germany	Reg Park South Africa	Bill Pearl USA	TOTAL	PLACE
FIRST	9	FRANK ZANE	USA	20	20	20	20	20	20	19	100	
	2	BOYER COE	USA	20	19	18	17	19	17	19	92	
	5	ROBBY ROBINSON	USA	19	19	18	19	19	18	19	94	
	3	CHRIS DICKERSON	USA	19	20	19	18	19	19	20	96	
	1	DANNY PADILLA	USA	19	17	19	18	19	18	19	93	
	8	CARLOS RODRIGUEZ	USA	19	18	17	16	18	15	17	86	
	7	ALBERT BECKLES	England	19	18	17	16	18	12	18	87	
	6	TOM PLATZ	USA	19	18	18	17	18	13	18	89	
	4	ED CORNEY	USA	18	17	18	16	18	16	18	87	
	10	STEVE DAVIS	USA	17	16	16	16	17	11	16	81	
SECOND	9	FRANK ZANE	USA	20	20	20	19	20	20	20	100	
	2	BOYER COE	USA	20	20	19	19	20	17	20	98	
	5	ROBBY ROBINSON	USA	18	19	20	20	20	19	19	97	
	3	CHRIS DICKERSON	USA	18	19	19	19	19	18	19	94	
	1	DANNY PADILLA	USA	18	18	18	17	19	17	19	90	
	8	CARLOS RODRIGUEZ	USA	18	18	18	18	19	16	18	90	
	7	ALBERT BECKLES	England	19	17	18	18	19	12	18	90	
	6	TOM PLATZ	USA	18	17	19	17	18	13	18	88	
	4	ED CORNEY	USA	17	18	19	17	18	15	18	88	
	10	STEVE DAVIS	USA	17	16	16	17	16	11	16	81	
THIRD	9	FRANK ZANE	USA	20	19	20	20	20	20	19	99	
	2	BOYER COE	USA	20	20	20	19	20	20	20	100	
	5	ROBBY ROBINSON	USA	20	20	20	19	19	19	20	98	
	3	CHRIS DICKERSON	USA	18	19	20	18	19	18	19	93	
	1	DANNY PADILLA	USA	18	18	19	17	18	16	19	90	
	8	CARLOS RODRIGUEZ	USA	18	19	18	18	19	18	19	92	
	7	ALBERT BECKLES	England	19	18	18	18	18	17	19	91	
	6	TOM PLATZ	USA	18	18	18	18	18	16	18	90	
	4	ED CORNEY	USA	19	18	19	17	19	17	18	91	
	10	STEVE DAVIS	USA	17	17	17	17	16	16	17	84	
TOTALS	9	FRANK ZANE	USA	60	59	60	59	60	60	58	299	1
	2	BOYER COE	USA	60	59	57	55	59	54	59	290	2
	5	ROBBY ROBINSON	USA	57	58	58	58	58	56	58	289	3
	3	CHRIS DICKERSON	USA	55	58	58	55	57	55	58	283	4
	1	DANNY PADILLA	USA	55	53	56	53	56	51	57	273	5
	8	CARLOS RODRIGUEZ	USA	55	55	53	52	56	49	55	268	6
	7	ALBERT BECKLES	England	57	53	53	52	55	41	55	268	7
	6	TOM PLATZ	USA	55	53	55	52	54	42	54	267	8
	4	ED CORNEY	USA	54	53	56	50	55	48	54	266	9
	10	STEVE DAVIS	USA	51	49	49	50	49	38	49	246	10

"MR. OLYMPIA" Over 200 lb Class

Columbus, Ohio, USA

7 October 1979

ROUND	NO	NAME	COUNTRY	Jacques Blommaert Belgium	Winston Roberts Canada	Malik Alaywan Lebanon	Franco Fassi Italy	Albert Busek Germany	Reg Park South Africa	Bill Pearl USA	TOTAL	PLACE
FIRST	13	MIKE MENTZER	USA	20	20	20	20	20	20	20	100	
	14	DENNIS TINERINO	USA	17	19	19	19	19	19	19	95	
	11	ROGER WALKER	Australia	18	19	19	18	19	18	19	93	
	15	ROY CALLENDER	Canada	18	18	18	18	19	17	18	90	
	12	BOB BIRDSONG	USA	18	18	18	17	18	17	18	89	
SECOND	13	MIKE MENTZER	USA	20	20	20	20	20	20	20	100	
	14	DENNIS TINERINO	USA	18	18	18	18	19	19	19	92	
	11	ROGER WALKER	Australia	19	19	19	19	19	18	19	95	
	15	ROY CALLENDER	Canada	18	18	19	19	19	17	18	92	
	12	BOB BIRDSONG	USA	18	17	18	18	18	16	18	89	
THIRD	13	MIKE MENTZER	USA	20	20	20	20	20	20	20	100	
	14	DENNIS TINERINO	USA	19	20	18	19	19	19	20	97	
	11	ROGER WALKER	Australia	19	19	19	19	19	18	19	95	
	15	ROY CALLENDER	Canada	18	18	19	18	19	17	18	91	
	12	BOB BIRDSONG	USA	18	17	18	18	18	16	19	89	
TOTALS	13	MIKE MENTZER	USA	60	60	60	60	60	60	60	300	1
	14	DENNIS TINERINO	USA	54	57	55	56	57	57	58	284	2
	11	ROGER WALKER	Australia	56	31	57	56	57	54	57	283	3
	15	ROY CALLENDER	Canada	54	54	56	55	57	51	54	273	4
	12	BOB BIRDSONG	USA	54	52	54	53	54	49	55	267	5
POSEDOWN	9	FRANK ZANE	USA	1	1	2	1	1	1	3	304	1
	13	MIKE MENTZER	USA	2	3	1	2	3	3	2	301	2
	2	BOYER COE	USA	4	2	5	3	2	5	1		3
	5	ROBBY ROBINSON	USA	3	4	3	6	4	2	6		4
	14	DENNIS TINERINO	USA	6	5	4	5	5	6	5		5
	3	CHRIS DICKERSON	USA	5	6	6	4	6	4	4		6

INTERNATIONAL FEDERATION OF BODYBUILDERS

SHEET JP/3

JUDGING PANEL CHAIRMAN/SECRETARY — CATEGORY RESULTS SHEET

CONTEST ..MR. OLYMPIA....................

PLACE ..COLUMBUS, USA.................................... DATE 7 Oct 1979

CATEGORY .... OVER/UP TO 200 lb KILOS

ROUNDS 1, 2, and 3 MARKS ADDED TOGETHER FOR CATEGORY PLACINGS

The highest and lowest score for each Competitor in each Round have been eliminated. The Three Highest Placed Competitors will compete at the public posedown for their Final Placings.

Competitors Number	Competitors Names	Country	Marks			Total Marks	Place Award
			Round 1	Round 2	Round 3		
1	DANNY PADILLA	USA	93	90	90	273	5
2	BOYER COE	USA	92	98	100	290	2
3	CHRIS DICKERSON	USA	96	94	93	283	4
4	ED CORNEY	USA	87	88	91	266	9
5	ROBBY ROBINSON	USA	94	97	98	289	3
6	TOM PLATZ	USA	89	88	90	267	8
7	ALBERT BECKLES	England	87	90	91	268	7
8	CARLOS RODRIGUEZ	USA	86	90	92	268	6
9	FRANK ZANE	USA	100	100	99	299	1
10	STEVE DAVIS	USA	81	81	84	246	10
		OVER 200 lb					
11	ROGER WALKER	Australia	93	95	95	283	3
12	BOB BIRDSONG	USA	89	89	89	267	5
13	MIKE MENTZER	USA	100	100	100	300	1
14	DENNIS TINERINO	USA	95	92	97	284	2
15	ROY CALLENDER	Canada	90	92	91	273	4
		POSE - DOWN					
			First Places				
9	FRANK ZANE	USA	5			304	1
13	MIKE MENTZER	USA	1			301	2
2	BOYER COE	USA	1			291	3
5	ROBBY ROBINSON	USA				289	4
14	DENNIS TINERINO	USA				284	5
3	CHRIS DICKERSON	USA				283	6

Signed Chairman Judging Panel .... Country ....

Signed Secretary Judging Panel ..Oscar State.. Country ..England..

Signed I.F.B.B. President .... Country ....

Practicing Posing

It is never too soon to practice posing. You should begin the first day you walk into a gym. Study photos of other bodybuilders, go to contests and watch how the competitors pose, and try to emulate them. Begin by doing your poses in front of a mirror until you think you have a feel for them. Then try doing them without a mirror while a friend watches you.

Between sets, flex the muscles you are training, hit some poses, and study yourself in the mirror. This will condition you to hard, sustained contractions of the muscles and also help you to analyze the current state of your development.

Posing in front of the mirror helps you to analyze faults in your posing techniques. Here I am getting critical advice from Robby Robinson, Ken Waller, Franco Columbu, and Ed Corney. This kind of criticism is sometimes painful but really helps.

Checking out my triceps after doing twenty-five sets of triceps training

I like to do this straight-arm triceps pose after my chest or triceps training, to bring out the muscles I have just trained while they are still pumped and hard.

Even at age twenty I knew instinctively to spend time flexing and posing my biceps after a session of arm training.

Holding the muscles flexed for a few minutes after a workout helps condition you to the hard discipline needed for competition posing.

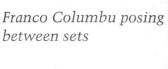

Franco Columbu posing between sets

Remember that the judges will often have you holding poses for minutes at a time, and that you might have to stay flexed for hours during a strenuous prejudging. So in your posing practice, don't just hit poses for a few seconds and then relax. Hold them until it hurts, then hold them some more—now is the time to go to failure, to get muscle cramps, to suffer so that your posing in competition will be smooth, competent, and powerful. Keep at it for at least an hour a day, maybe even more as you get closer to a contest. You will be glad you did once you find yourself standing on stage.

Another thing to remember is that bodybuilders under pressure tend to pose faster than they would in practice. So I recommend that you count slowly to 3, 4, or 5, and to use this as a measure of how long to hold your pose. This way you will avoid rushing when you get caught up in the excitement of an actual contest.

One of the most important qualities to develop in your posing is confidence: whether you are standing relaxed on stage, going through the compulsories, or doing your own routine, you need to appear confident, to radiate energy and competence. But to do this requires a lot of practice so that you can hit each shot per-

The best way to learn a pose is to ask somebody more experienced to watch you and correct your mistakes. Here I am working with Billy Graham, the wrestling superstar. This was a month before he competed, and he ended up winning the best posing award.

Here are Ed Corney, Donny Gable, Brian Abede, and I watching a mini-posedown between Robby Robinson and Ken Waller. Competing in the gym in this way will teach you timing and how to quickly counter a competitor's pose with one that makes you look better. Robby and Ken have developed into experts at posedowns.

fectly and continue to pose over and over again without showing signs of strain and fatigue.

My training partners and I have always hit poses together—had sort of mini-posedowns in the gym—so that we could compare and analyze what we had achieved and what areas we still needed to work on. If you are less experienced, it helps to train with somebody who knows a lot more than you do. When I was eighteen and had not yet competed, I trained with Kurt Manul (Mr. Austria). I would pose in front of the mirror and he would watch me and then say, "This is how you stand in the lineup," or "Make sure you flex your deltoids in this pose." I learned which muscles were most important in each pose, how to hit these poses quickly and accurately, how to stand to show off a V-shape, how long to hold a pose, and how to hold a vacuum.

In addition to your regular, concentrated practice, I also recommend that from time to time you just run through your poses very quickly, not really hitting them with full strength, but just familiarizing yourself with the feeling of going from one to the other quickly and without hesitation, smoothing out the transitions and teaching your body how to get from one pose to another without stumbling or awkwardness.

This may be called a relaxed pose, but as you can see in this photo you still have to flex everything, and you need to practice a long time to be able to stand in this position for the whole of round one.

Standing relaxed from the side—thighs flexed, abs tight, arms hanging loose

Although a head judge might call you on this, I have always found it possible to attract the attention of the judges in round one by hitting this variation of the relaxed pose every once in a while—a slight twist of the waist, arms and chest flexed hard, and up on my toes to show the calves.

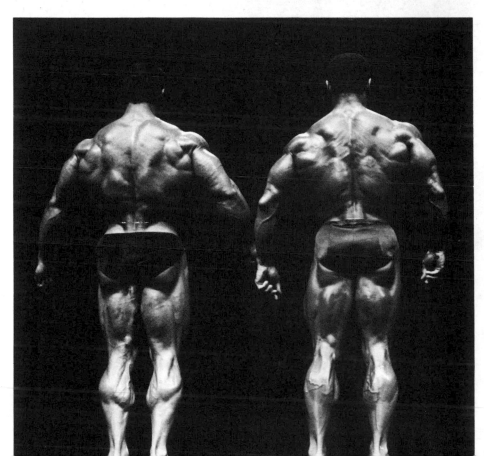

Casey Viator and Chris Dickerson demonstrate the traditional way of doing the relaxed pose from the back.

Round One Practice

The only way to condition yourself for standing with all of your muscles tensed for long periods of time is to *do* it. Stand with your thighs and abs tensed, your lats flared, your pecs massive. Don't be too obviously "posed," but let your arms hang almost naturally at your sides. Use a clock or a stopwatch and practice standing like this for one minute, then turn and stand for one minute facing each of the other three directions. Flex the calves, especially when your back is facing where the judges would be, and don't forget the leg biceps, the buttocks, the lower back, and the lats; keep the waist pulled in, be conscious of the whole body. Four minutes of this will exhaust you, but you need to keep at it until you can stand like this for half an hour or more without shaking, sweating, cramping, or looking too strained and anxious. It is best to practice this with a training partner watching to see that you keep everything flexed and warning you when you let down.

Round Two Practice

The first thing to do in mastering round two compulsories is simply to study the basic poses and learn to do them competently. However, once you have mastered the fundamentals, you should realize that there are a number of variations of the basic poses that tend to suit one type of physique better than others.

For example, when Bill Pearl and Sergio Oliva do a double-biceps pose they do it with their legs straight on. They are both huge, with great legs, so they can afford to do that. Someone with a body like Frank Zane would never do a straight-on double-biceps pose but would always add a little twist. By doing this, Frank takes what is a power pose for the other guys and turns it into a ballet-like aesthetic pose for himself.

For your own practice, study posing photos of the champions and try to duplicate them. Study yourself in the mirror, have someone take photographs of you or, if you can arrange it, make a video tape of yourself posing. It is also important to pose in front of other people—your training partner, other bodybuilders in the gym, anyone who can watch you and spot weaknesses in your presentation.

With every pose, be sure to flex your legs first and keep them flexed as you tense your abdominals and then pose your upper body. No matter what muscles the pose is supposed to show, you

Changing position in the relaxed pose from the back, as Chris Dickerson is doing here, accomplishes two things: the occasional movement helps prevent cramps, and demonstrating more muscularity may gain extra points from the judges because it attracts attention.

When you have the huge lats and arms of Sergio Oliva, tapering down to a tiny waist, you can do a front double-biceps straight on and make it look terrific.

Although Frank Zane does not have Sergio's mass, with a slight twist he turns the front double-biceps pose into an artistic tour de force, and makes the pose just as effective.

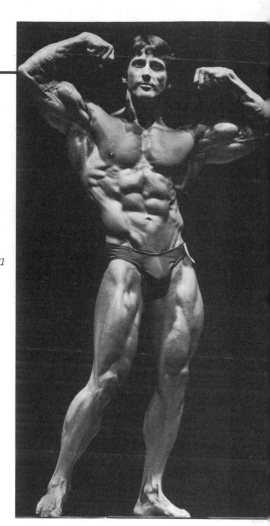

It may be called the front double-biceps pose, but more than the biceps are involved —you need to flex every muscle, from the calves and thighs to the abs, muscles of the torso, and the pecs.

There are a number of ways of doing a side-chest pose. Here I am demonstrating the pose as it is usually done.

The front double-biceps is one of the most difficult poses, because it tends to emphasize any weakness. In the compulsory round, you are not allowed any means of getting around this. However, there are certain conventional variations that are commonly used in the third round. Experienced bodybuilders like Casey Viator, Chris Dickerson, and Frank Zane have learned what variation of the front double-biceps pose suits them best.

Johnny Fuller does the side-chest pose with a slight twist, which lets him show off his abdominals and intercostals as well.

Extending the arms and holding a stomach vacuum when doing a side-chest pose lets you show off your upper pecs much more than a regular chest pose. It can be used in combination with the regular chest pose—hit this one, hold it a moment, then bring your elbow back into the conventional compulsory pose.

This is another variation of the side-chest shot, which enables you to show the definition of your inner pectorals.

Doing a rear double-biceps, Casey Viator, Samir Bannout, and Chris Dickerson are flexing every muscle—the calves, leg biceps, lower back, lats, upper back and traps, deltoids, arms, and forearms. Notice how each has turned his head to help bring out the traps.

are always posing the *entire* body. Once you have learned a pose, practice holding it for thirty seconds, then for one minute, gradually building up your endurance. Try to keep your face relaxed so that you don't look strained. After you can hold each pose for one minute, try hitting all seven poses without stopping.

Details are all-important in the compulsories. When doing a front double-biceps, hit the thighs hard and don't relax them as long as you are holding that pose, and be sure to keep your abdominals flexed as well. For a side-chest shot, pull the stomach up into a vacuum and draw the elbow back as far as you can. Try standing on the leg closest to the judges, bending the rear leg and flexing the calf, or standing on the rear leg and flexing the calf of the front leg, and decide which is the best way for you.

On any rear shot, flex the calves and the lower back. For the rear double-biceps, pull your elbows back and arch your back somewhat—the judges are looking up at you, don't forget, and you need to bend backward slightly for them to get a good view.

Many bodybuilders forget how important the chest muscles are in a front lat spread. As you spread your lats, lift the chest high and bring the shoulders forward to accentuate the pectorals. In fact, in a front double-biceps pose, if you leave your chest and shoulders in position and drop your arms down to your hips as you flare your lats, your chest will be posed just about the way you want it. Don't ever bend forward and scrunch your pecs together as if doing a most-muscular shot. Remember, too, your legs should be fully flexed.

IFBB

The pose may be the same, but each top bodybuilder does the front lat spread in a slightly different manner. Frank Zane and Samir Bannout press their fists into their waist to make it look smaller; Chris Dickerson presses in with his wrists, which makes his arms look shorter and bigger; Albert Beckles hits his abs hard and does a little twist.

For a rear lat spread, put one leg back, flex the calf, draw your shoulders together, and *slowly* open up your lats, letting the judges watch the process as these muscles unfold.

For a triceps pose, you can again choose which leg should be used to support you. Try holding the pose with your abdominals flexed or with a vacuum to see which looks better. Press your arm as hard against your lats as you can.

With an overhead abdominal pose, flex your thighs really hard, tense your abdominals and, when you are fully into the pose— cough, which will get the last of the air out of your lungs and bring out the abdominals fully.

Holding these poses for any length of time is difficult, but

You can see how Chris Dickerson keeps his thighs tense and his pectorals flexed and hard. He also makes his forearms look shorter by pressing his wrists into the waist. Because of his hand position you can't look through his lats.

When I do a front lat spread, I press in at the waist to make it look smaller and flare out my lats to get as much of a V-shape as possible. Notice how I manage to bring out pectoral striations at the same time.

Samir Bannout starting a rear lat spread. Talk about being in fantastic shape! See how far back he starts to press in his thumbs.

This side-triceps pose as done by Casey Viator is the compulsory required by the IFBB—shoulder rolled back to show both the biceps and triceps, stomach sucked in and flexed, up on one toe with both calves flexed.

Here Casey does a variation of a side-triceps pose.

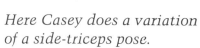

Jusup Wilkosz has the kind of tremendous triceps development that makes this triceps pose effective.

eventually you'll need to do the pose for a full minute without moving, or even breathing.

One other, more subtle thing to practice is to rotate slightly as you do each pose so that the judges on the extreme left and right get as good a view as those in the center. Learn to do this move-

Casey Viator, Samir Bannout, and Albert Beckles demonstrate how no two bodybuilders hit a pose exactly the same way. All these overhead abdominal poses are acceptable compulsories, and moving from one to another can help to keep the attention of the judges.

Samir Bannout sometimes uses this abdominal pose variation, with one hand up and the other behind the waist.

Frank Zane practically owns this vacuum pose. It shows off the serratus in the best possible way; it shows the biceps in a favorable position; it displays maximum symmetry and allows him to dwarf other bodybuilders on stage doing shots like a most-muscular. Bill Pearl is also a master of this shot, but if you don't have this type of body, it's not for you.

ment slowly and gracefully, making it part of the pose rather than a distraction from it.

Remember that these compulsories are also the basis of your free-posing routine, so you have to be good at them if you are going to look good in round three.

Round Three Practice

The idea of free posing is to present the best elements of your physique to the judges. In your early competitions, you will not yet have the total development you are training for, so there will be poses you will want to avoid until you can really bring them off. Find the poses that make you look your best and base your routine on them.

The basis for the third round free-posing routine is the compulsories from round two. In doing these poses, remember the rule I gave earlier: pose from the ground up. Plant your feet, flex your calves, thighs, and abs, and then hit the upper body. Take an inventory of each body part and make certain nothing is ignored.

As time goes on and your body improves, you can go beyond the compulsories and begin to add more poses in order to show this new development. For example, you don't need 20-inch arms to be able to do a front double-biceps pose—which is good, because you will need to do this pose during the compulsories. However, until your arms are really outstanding you should avoid a pose with your arms straight out, which will emphasize their relative lack of development. But once your arms have improved, you might choose to add a movement like one Sergio used to do, where you stand with your arms straight out and then bring them into a double-biceps, which will call attention to their size and development. If your lats are particularly outstanding, it makes sense to learn three or four new ways to show them off. If you have great abs, by all means find a way to display this strength. On the other hand, if you are especially weak in any area, work like hell in the gym to correct the imbalance, but in the meantime try not to pose in such a way as to call attention to that particular body part.

Anytime you pose, make sure that all the judges have an equal chance of seeing you, the ones at the side as well as those directly in front. It is a lot easier to remember to turn slightly when doing the compulsories; during your free posing, with so much more going on, it takes a little more effort.

Remember, free posing is drama: keep a smile or relaxed expression on your face. This projects confidence. In some poses, look out at the audience; in others, look at the muscle. Keep your routine varied and interesting.

I recommend to all beginners that they concentrate on doing a few poses well rather than a lot of them less competently. Start out with eight or ten and become the master of them. Once you can do your routine without a hitch—and you should practice it constantly, three or four times a day for at least three months before a competition—then you can begin to expand and develop it.

Have photos taken of your posing routine and study these pictures to determine what you are doing right and in which areas you still need work. If a pose doesn't look right, don't use it until it does!

When I was first learning to pose, I took a hard look at myself to determine what suited me best. I had to be a realist. I saw that it makes no sense for a guy to pose like Reg Park if he has no rib cage, calves, or abdominals. It would have been very foolish for me to attempt Steve Reeves' style of posing, the arms overhead kind of thing. Reeves had broad shoulders, a flat chest, and narrow waist, and overhead poses suited him. It wouldn't look good on me, John Grimek, or Reg Park, since all of us have a more boxy look to our physiques.

Your type of muscle structure should determine the speed and style of your posing. If you are a Zane type, you slow it down and concentrate on grace and rhythm, your routine aesthetic and smooth like a classical symphony. With my build, I have always adopted the philosophy "If you have a big gun, shoot it!" and I have gone in for a more dramatic style, faster and more dynamic, relying on my ability to blow minds with my size and muscularity.

Never forget that you are on view every moment you are on stage. If you are simply standing there waiting, the judges can still see if your abs are good or not, so keep them tight. Moving from one pose to another, the same thing applies: just because you are going through a transition rather than hitting a pose, it doesn't mean the judges can't see you. I even went a step beyond —standing and moving in such a way as to maximize the effect of my physique even when I was backstage! The other competitors are always checking you out, and if they see you looking great, you can sometimes defeat them before they ever set foot on stage.

Another thing every bodybuilder has to learn is how to pace himself when he poses. With the pressure and excitement of a contest, adrenaline flooding your body, you may have a tendency

Steve Reeves is one of the few bodybuilders to ever master this pose. You need long legs, a very symmetrical body, a V-shaped torso with a small waist, wide shoulders, and an almost flat chest (which helps to show off your lats). It also helps to have a square, flat-chested frame like that of Frank Zane, Don Howorth, or Jim Haislip, for example. A bodybuilder like Sergio Oliva would do an overhead shot like this very differently.

Samir Bannout demonstrates a variation of the arms-overhead pose with his arms only partially extended, and yet standing in such a way that it requires tremendous symmetry to make the pose work.

Frank Zane in a pose both aesthetic and original: one arm behind the neck, one arm extended, very relaxed, a twist to the waist, and thighs flexed. There is no one particular muscle featured in this pose. It is simply beautiful and good to use as a transition between one dramatic pose and another— a technique Zane is famous for.

You can't call this a triceps pose, an abdominal pose, or a chest pose. It is an in-between pose used while going from, for example, a side-chest to a twisting double-biceps, which allows me to flex the abs and triceps, show the small waist, and then go on to the next pose. This is the kind of pose you have to play around with to see if it suits you or not.

to rush your posing. Even an experienced bodybuilder like Mike Mentzer found himself doing this in the 1979 Mr. Olympia, and this contributed quite a lot to his loss to Frank Zane. I always try to pace my poses evenly. I time myself by counting slowly to three. My attitude is, if a pose is worth looking at, it's worth holding long enough to give everybody a good look.

If your method is to jiggle around a bit before settling into your pose, that's okay as long as you know it appeals to the audience. This is where experience before crowds becomes invaluable. Be alert to the reactions of the audience; the feedback they give you can be extremely helpful. Remember, a gym mirror can only tell you so much.

Take special care in setting up the pose that will knock the audience out of their seats. You see this a lot in good back shots: the bodybuilder scrunches his shoulder blades together, fists on hips, and holds this comparatively poor pose for about five seconds—then he finally, slowly, spreads out the lats and leaves the audience gasping.

Good posing is a performing art, and the art of performing is most often a matter of good timing. You should leave the stage at a high point, when anything else would be anticlimactic. Your

*Chris Dickerson's
imaginative most-muscular
pose begins with a flourish . . .*

*. . . and finishes with a
dramatic contraction of the
whole body.*

routine should build up to a crescendo, saving the major wallops for last because people like drama, and they expect to be entertained and excited by your performance.

Good posing is like a symphony: the faster movements contrast with the slower ones; the dynamics should constantly change. There are quick, dramatic movements, to be followed by slow, graceful ones. There is rhythm and there is emotion. And it is here that you will find the highest level of achievement in bodybuilding.

There is one prominent bodybuilder who advises in his seminars that bodybuilders should never make any overdramatic moves—should go from a back pose to a side pose, for example, not back pose immediately to front pose. There are certainly times when you should follow this advice, but there are others in which an unexpected move is effective—like Chris Dickerson's dramatic most-muscular shot, in which he contracts his upper body, thrusts out his leg, and appears to be no less than some mythical satyr suddenly manifesting on stage.

This twisting double-biceps pose maximizes the size of the arms while minimizing the waist.

The twisting one-arm biceps shot creates an aesthetic effect and makes your waist look small. With this pose you can show off the inside of one arm and the outside of the other simultaneously. However, if you don't have good height on your biceps, you would do better to avoid this pose. (Incidentally, keep the thumb inside the fist of your raised arm or it will stick out and cause a distraction.)

This biceps shot, with the arm behind the head, introduces an aesthetic twist that really makes it a beautiful pose. But it won't work unless you keep your thighs and calves tensed for the duration of the pose.

Another variation of the biceps shot: raised arm, wrist (not hand) into the waist to make the forearm look shorter and waist smaller, torso twisted slightly, and legs flexed really hard.

I use this arms-extended pose to show the judges just how huge my arms—forearms, biceps, and triceps—really are. At the same time, I make my waist small and flex my legs hard for maximum definition.

I use a number of
conventional twisting back
poses in my routines, which
show the development and
muscularity of my back,
minimize my waist size, and
display my arms to their best
advantage.

Sergio Oliva was able to do poses no one else could duplicate. He would use this hands-over-head back pose to show off his incomparable triceps and forearms as well as his magnificent lats, then bring his arms down into a conventional back double-biceps.

Frank Zane uses poses like this aesthetic variation of the back double-biceps not only to display his excellent muscularity, but to wield his tremendous symmetry like a weapon against other competitors.

Chris Dickerson uses variations of conventional poses to display his muscularity and symmetry. But notice that he is also saying to the judges, "Sure my back is great, but take a look at my calves! Who else can show you calves like this?"

Mohamed Makkawy is one of the smallest of the top competitors, but poses like this aesthetic back shot enabled him to win two professional Grand Prix events in 1982, beating a number of men far more massive than he was.

This three-quarters back shot is not done by many bodybuilders. By opening up my hands instead of clenching my fists I emphasize symmetry as much as muscularity. In all twisting shots, the leg away from the judges should be to the front, making the pelvis twist against the torso so that your waist looks smaller.

Frank Zane and Chris Dickerson demonstrate two ways of doing kneeling back poses. The kneeling poses are especially good for shorter bodybuilders because they make them look more massive. Sergio Oliva also used this kind of pose very effectively even though he weighed over 200 pounds.

Chris Dickerson caught midway between two back poses. Notice that Chris has made sure he still looks great even though he is in transition.

Kneeling poses are difficult, because it is hard to kneel and come up gracefully. This unique Frank Zane pose, a cross between a kneeling side-chest and a kneeling triceps shot, uses the kneeling position to make him appear more massive while still showing off his symmetry.

Albert Beckles is one of the few bodybuilders who can do this unconventional kneeling and twisting double-biceps shot. For this dramatic pose, you need a small waist and high biceps—but it is also a good way of hiding the fact that you don't have huge calves.

Dennis Tinerino gets a lot of audience response from this kneeling pose, and he is probably the only bodybuilder to make use of it. Dennis is massive in the first place, and this pose exaggerates his size and makes him look gargantuan.

The great champions have taken the trouble to invent unique and difficult poses. For example, Samir Bannout and Frank Zane both do a lunging pose, but each has an individual and identifiable approach to making it work.

Before I do a most-muscular pose, I bend down, take hold of my wrist, and really pump up the biceps. This has always been a great crowd pleaser, combining movement with a display of the outside of the biceps.

598

Franco Columbu is the master of the most-muscular pose and is able to do at least eight effective variations. This is one of his favorites, almost in standing-relaxed pose, but displaying the development of his arms, forearms, deltoids, chest, abdominals, and legs—with the promise of even more awesome muscularity to come.

IFBB

This variation of the most-muscular is one of my favorites. Holding on to my wrist, I can get the arms really pumped up, bring the veins out clearly, and show off the mass, definition, and striations of the pectorals.

I have always used the conventional most-muscular pose in my routine because it allows me to show off both my mass and outstanding definition. Bending forward like this, the pose also calls attention to trapezius development.

Casey Viator doing two
variations of his most-
muscular pose

Frank Zane has never liked to
do a conventional most-
muscular pose, feeling that
his relative lack of mass
would cause him to look
unsymmetrical. So he has
developed this variation,
placing his hands on his
thighs, that shows off his
definition—in the deltoids,
pectorals, intercostals, and
serratus as well as the
abdominals—and allows him
to make best use of his
outstanding symmetry and
proportions. Nobody else can
do this pose as effectively as
Zane.

1   2   3

Ed Corney is considered one of the great posers of all time, not just because of his mastery of each individual pose, but also because he considered each transition between poses to be as important as the poses themselves. Corney developed a free-posing routine that was both beautiful and dynamic and that was carefully constructed to emphasize his strong points and draw attention away from his less impressive body parts.

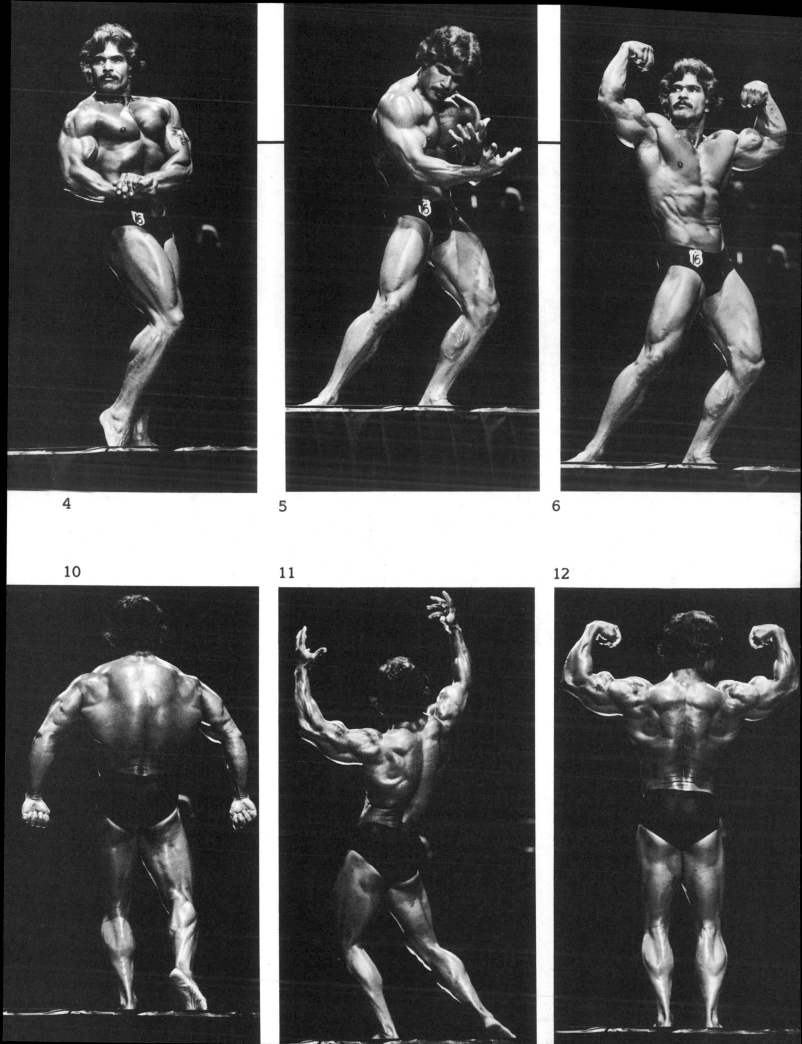

4

5

6

10

11

12

7   8   9

13   14   15

16

17

18

22

23

24

19

20

21

25

26

27

28

29

30

33

31

32

34

Choosing Posing Music (for Round Three)

In the early days of the sport, bodybuilders did not pose to specific pieces of music in competition and posing exhibitions. Often music was played, but it was simply meant to provide background. The individual posing routines were not geared to the mood, style, or rhythm of the music.

In the 1950s Reg Park was one of the first bodybuilders to pose to specific music, a piece called "The Legend of the Glass Mountains." And, of course, once other bodybuilders saw how well this worked, soon everyone was doing it.

When it comes to choosing a piece of music upon which to base your free-posing routine, the only limit is your imagination. You can use anything that works, but be sure that your selection meets the following criteria:

1. It should be the right length, long enough to allow you to create an impressive routine but not so long that the judges and audience begin to get bored. In amateur competition posing time is fixed (usually two minutes), but on the professional level you can pose for as long as you want.

2. It should have the right pace and rhythm to go with the kind of routine you want to perform. You don't want the music to force you to pose faster or slower than you would prefer or to force you to conform to an uncomfortable rhythm.

3. The mood and feel of the music should complement your posing style. A posing routine backed up by classical music will be very different from one done to rock 'n' roll.

4. If there are lyrics or sound effects in the piece, they should not distract from your posing.

5. The music should be appropriate to your individual physique. A smaller, more aesthetic bodybuilder takes risks when he poses to grandiose, fate-and-doom music better suited to a massive, Herculean physique.

Also, be careful not to use music that is too popular at the moment, or you risk subjecting the judges to their third rendition of the same piece. There was a time when every other bodybuilder seemed to be posing to "Chariots of Fire" or "Eye of the Tiger." In addition to these pieces of music, some others that have become overused include: "I Want Muscle" and the themes from *Superman, Rocky I* ("Getting Strong"), *2001 Space Odyssey, Star Wars,* and *Exodus.*

So, see to it that you choose a good match between your posing style and your music. For example, because I was usually the biggest man in the competition and could count on my size to help overwhelm my opponents, I liked to use very expressive, dramatic music like "Exodus." I kept my routine to around two minutes, hitting about twenty to twenty-two poses, showing the judges the superiority of my development and then getting off, keeping it short and sweet.

Length of music is important because when you pose for longer periods of time you risk boring the judges. But it can be done. When Franco Columbu won the 1981 Mr. Olympia contest, his free-posing routine was a full 4 minutes 15 seconds!—longer than any other competitor. He just kept making the drama build, impressing the judges and then, when they thought they had seen everything, surprising them with something new and even more interesting. As a result, he got 20's from the judges right across the board.

Sergio Oliva, on the other hand, never bothered with this kind of presentation. He came out, posed for a minute or two, hitting maybe fourteen poses, and let his awesome physique speak for itself.

At the 1982 Mr. Olympia, Casey Viator came out posing to the theme music from *Conan*, with its heavy dramatic beat, the drums pounding underneath. Casey has a physique that is Herculean enough to get away with this. A less densely muscled bodybuilder might look ridiculous trying to live up to this kind of music. In fact, one woman bodybuilder came on in round three after making the audience listen to thirty or forty seconds of "Thus Spake Zarathustra"—the theme music from *2001 Space Odyssey*—a move so pretentious as to be completely ridiculous and hardly expected to endear her to the judges.

Franco always explains at his seminars that he doesn't like to pose to rock music or selections that have distracting singing in them. Rock, to Franco, just isn't classy enough. In his second Olympia victory in 1981, he posed to Mozart's *Eine Kleine Nachtmusik*, a piece that is every bit as dramatic as it is classical.

Chris Dickerson also chose classical music when he won his Olympia title in 1982. Chris posed to a seventeenth-century composition called "Trumpet Voluntary," very slow, elegant, and dramatic. His routine lasted 2 minutes 40 seconds and included about twenty-eight poses. He agrees that routines that last much longer than two and a half to three minutes are in danger of getting boring.

One top champion who is not afraid of rock music is Frank

Zane. At the 1980 Mr. Olympia, Frank did a classic Zane posing routine, using really far-out music from Pink Floyd, positively psychedelic, while hitting a series of the aesthetic poses he is famous for.

This would not suit Ed Corney, however. Ed is a very creative, inventive poser who is capable of putting together a stylish routine of maybe thirty to thirty-five poses. If he tried to pose to overly heavy, dramatic music or powerful rock selections, he might find it difficult to sustain the aesthetic mood he is known for.

But you can go too far in trying to be imaginative. At one show I went to recently two different bodybuilders posed to the "Darth Vader" music from *Star Wars* and the sound effects mixed in with the music were much too intrusive and distracting.

After choosing your music, the next step is to make a tape of it that you can take to contests. Many beginners make their own tapes on home equipment, but when you begin to compete on the national or international level it is better to have your tapes professionally recorded, which will ensure the highest possible audio quality. And I always recommend that you have at least one extra copy of your tape with you at all competitions. Tapes sometimes break or get lost. The last thing you want is to end up with no music at the last minute and be forced to pose to music you are not familiar with.

Sometimes, you will find a piece of music that you like a lot but it will not be quite long enough or there will be boring parts mixed in. You can get around this problem by having the tape edited, cutting out the boring parts or otherwise changing the piece to suit yourself. You can even edit two musical selections together in order to have a dramatic change occur in the middle of your routine for added impact.

Round Four Practice

The posedown is not like regular posing. You don't go through a set routine—you are in *direct* competition with the other bodybuilders for the attention of the judges. Your most formidable opponents are right on stage next to you, which gives you a tremendous opportunity to convince the judges that you are the one who ought to be declared the winner. But to use posing to gain that end, you need to use your mind. Posing, at the highest levels, is almost more mental than physical, a kind of three-dimensional chess game.

This series of six photos shows "defensive posing" on my part. In this contest, after I hit a front-lat pose Franco followed suit, and he has about the best lats in the world.

612

So not to look bad next to his lat spread, I immediately went to a biceps shot, allowing me to use my height to tower over him. To counter, Franco hit a one-arm biceps shot and flexed his abs. And, although my abdominals were sharp, I was not ready to go into a direct comparison with Franco.

By the time the posedown occurs, everyone is tired—you have been posing all day in the prejudging and done your posing routine under the pressures of the evening show. It is very easy to let down at this point. I have seen bodybuilders in the middle of a posedown begin to hesitate, lose track of what they were doing, and then have to quickly hit any random pose so as not to make complete fools of themselves. Fatigue, both mental and physical, becomes the enemy at this stage. The only way to avoid burning out before the posedown is finished is to prepare for it thoroughly, to practice this kind of free posing over and over. Only constant conditioning will prepare you for the rigors of this last phase of the competition.

When preparing for a contest, I have always made it a point to know who I will be posing against and to plan accordingly. I look at films of their posing routines, study each one to see how the sequence of poses is put together and whether the sequence and style stay the same. I look for inconsistencies, which indicate to me that an opponent is not sure of his routine, that he is still looking for something better. A consistent routine, on the other hand, indicates to me that he is satisfied, and so I take what he considers to be his best poses and improve on them.

My turn to counter: to avoid direct comparison of our abdominals, I moved into a twisting three-quarter back pose to show my arms and the definition of my shoulders and back.

By doing this, it's as if I am challenging my opponent to a duel —and a top competitor will always rise to the challenge. Then I wheel in the heavy artillery, throw in a lot of big muscle, make a flank attack with a changed routine, and completely screw up the opposition. The ability to do this is important, because all of the top champions these days are very good bodybuilders and it frequently takes a superior strategy to carry the day.

In the 1975 Mr. Olympia contest in South Africa I was on stage in a posedown with Franco. He hit a lat spread—and his lat spread is truly awesome! I was too smart to go up against his strong point, so instead, I hit a front double-biceps pose—showing how much bigger I was—then a most-muscular pose—proving I was as muscular as my opponent—and then a twisting back shot—to demonstrate, in my own way, how good my back development was. I knew I had time for all three of these poses, because Franco takes a lot of time in bringing his lats out to the full, and by continually changing poses I would be attracting the eyes of the judges.

This kind of strategy is beyond the range of most beginners, but it is important to understand what posing is really all about on this level if you want to master its intricacies.

614

Franco's next move was to turn around and do a back double-biceps pose. Since I was confident that my own back was thick, muscular, and highly defined, I hit the same shot and let the judges see how good I was.

You have to learn to pace yourself in a contest. If the opposition grows weak, you lessen your own intensity so that you stay just ahead of him. When you see him hit a good pose, you hit an equal or better one. If he strikes a mediocre pose, you can warm up one of your leftovers to keep pace. You shouldn't unload all of your best poses in a row: save them for the end and then pull the cork, giving the judges all your favorites and leaving your foe in shambles.

Be very careful how you approach a confrontation. Many bodybuilders attempt to emulate the way I move around on stage and challenge individual bodybuilders, but in doing so, they actually cost themselves points. For example, in the 1981 Olympia, Danny Padilla made it a point to move over and pose next to Franco. Danny was as cut as could be imagined in that contest, but his diet had left him a little small—and standing next to Franco simply made everyone aware of this. In the same contest, Roy Callender stood next to Tom Platz, hit leg shots, and pointed at his legs as if to say, "Check my legs against Tom's." Roy looked great that night, and his overall balance was as good as anyone's, but there is probably nobody in the world who can survive a direct leg comparison with Tom Platz.

Franco and I hitting a most-muscular, each of us confident in his ability to look better than the other.

Franco also used the trick of doing kneeling shots when I tried to dominate him with height. This way the fact that he was much shorter than I did not cost him points with the judges.

By 1972 the posedown had become an institution. Notice that neither Serge Nubret, on the left, nor I was willing to go directly up against Sergio Oliva's formidable lat spread. Instead we did double-bicep back poses.

So you have to be aware of your competition. When Sergio Oliva and I went head to head in the 1970 Mr. Olympia, he seemed to completely forget I was standing next to him and only paid attention to his own posing. I was hitting three or four shots to his one, doing counterposes to what he was doing, trying to make myself look good and call attention to Sergio's weaknesses. His body was as good as mine that night on stage, but I won primarily because of how I conducted myself in the posedown.

The posedown helps the judges make their final decision, but it is also the most enjoyable part of the contest for the audience. It is like Roman gladiators in hand-to-hand combat, the only thing missing are the swords and tridents. When the top bodybuilders in the world begin to duel on a championship stage, the decibel reading in the auditorium goes right off the scale—and the more enthusiastic the cheering of the audience, the more inspired the bodybuilders become.

Many people don't realize it, but the posedown as we know it today came about because of a battle between Sergio Oliva and me at the 1970 Olympia in Columbus. Up until that time, the judges brought out the finalists and simply asked them to do certain set poses for direct comparison. This evening we were doing a double-biceps shot—one of my best poses—and Sergio looked over at me and I suppose he began to feel outclassed. So he suddenly turned one arm down into a triceps pose as if to say,

"The perfection of the arm is to have both triceps and biceps!" I knew enough not to follow him. Instead, I switched to a side-chest pose, and then he hit the same shot. We kept this up, with the audience going crazy, and nobody could stop us for fifteen minutes. The M.C. realized how exciting it was and just let us go.

The important thing to remember is that improvisation requires an absolute command of each pose, an ability to move from one to another smoothly and gracefully—and the only way to acquire this kind of skill, so that you appear just as competent and graceful during the posedown as you do performing your own routine, is by hard and constant practice.

But remember the reason for the posedown—it is your chance to garner a few extra and maybe essential points. The judges are

In a posedown, you go with your strengths. At the 1973 Mr. Olympia, Serge Nubret relied on his enormous chest, Franco Columbu on his amazing lats, and I on my superior definition with a variation of a most-muscular shot.

IFBB

Here is a great example of defensive posing: When Tom Platz hits a thigh shot, a pose in which no bodybuilder in the world can match him, Casey Viator on the right immediately turns around to do a twisting three-quarter back pose, while Albert Beckles, on the left, hits a back double-biceps, one of his best poses. At the far left, far enough away not to be concerned with Platz, Zane is doing his aesthetic biceps shot, Samir Bannout is showing off his amazing symmetry, and Chris Dickerson is displaying his great lats.

looking for the winner, the bodybuilder to whom they will each give a final point, and so it is important to act like a winner, to stand there confidently with a smile on your face, as if the whole thing was a piece of cake. The idea of competition, after all, is to win.

Tactics are all-important in a posedown. When the six top guys are standing out there together, nobody wants to be the first to hit a pose. If a double-biceps is called and you hit it first, the judges will look at you and then look at the others as they each hit the same shot. By the time the last competitor hits the pose you will be fading somewhat—you are always at your best when you hit the pose fresh—and you will suffer by comparison.

What I have done in this situation is to pretend that I am hitting the pose, making an upward move with my arms to make the others believe I am doing the pose so that they will go ahead and hit it. This way, when I actually do flex for the pose, I am the last and I have the judges' complete attention.

Another tactic is to move over in line next to the competitor you most want to beat or who you think is your toughest rival and let the judges compare you directly. I have sometimes done things like hit a biceps shot and pointed to the biceps, daring my opponent to hit the same pose.

But you can't go all out so that you tire before the end of the posedown. I have seen many bodybuilders who were doing well in the fourth round and then simply fell apart from fatigue and stopped posing. You need to pace yourself, but you also need to practice this round extensively, having posedowns in the gym with your training partners whenever you can, learning to go from one pose to another without hesitation, and being aware of what the man next to you is doing and what pose you can do to counter it.

Boxers trying to get in shape for a long fight frequently use several sparring partners in a row—two rounds with one, two rounds with the next, and then two more rounds with another fresh and rested opponent. Being that tired and boxing someone full of energy is much more difficult than going up against an opponent who is as tired as you are. To adapt this same technique to your posedown practice, try posing against a friend or training partner for five full minutes, then bring in somebody else and continue to pose against him. He'll be fresh and energetic, you'll be tired, but bodybuilding is much like other sports in that the real champions are the ones who can keep going and perform well even though they are fighting off exhaustion. And the only way to develop that capacity is by long, hard hours of practice.

Common Posing Mistakes

One common posing problem bodybuilders have is their facial expression. They believe that clenching their jaws and contorting their faces will bring out the muscles more. But you can smile, with face and neck relaxed, and still hit the poses just as hard. Funny faces simply look amateurish.

Another common mistake is flexing the muscles so hard that the bodybuilder's whole body shakes and quivers with the effort. When you practice posing, try to determine just how hard you have to flex in order to fully display your muscles, but try not to contract too hard—not only will you look peculiar standing up

The top champions have mastered the art of hitting the pose last. Although the judges have called for a back double-biceps, Casey Viator, on the left, has hit an overhead back pose and will come down eventually to the required compulsory. Samir Bannout, in the middle, has seen what Casey is doing and is hesitating. On the right, Chris Dickerson has extended his arms but he, too, is waiting to hit the shot. Notice, however, that Casey wins this battle because he is hitting an intermediate pose that looks good all on its own.

After my chest workout I always hit the side-chest pose ten times from each side to really bring out the definition of the deltoids, inner and outer pectorals, and biceps. With Franco looking on, I know he will tell me if I do the pose incorrectly.

there shaking, but you will use up energy too fast and are liable to find yourself exhausted before the end of the contest.

Loss of balance is another frequent problem. When you are tense and under pressure, it is easy to lose coordination on stage even when moving from one "relaxed" pose to another. Concentrate on going from one pose to another smoothly, with your feet planted solidly and your body balanced and under control.

There are various ways of practicing to correct posing problems. One is in the gym, posing in front of the mirror after your workout. Another is in low-level contests, facing the actual pressures of competition. There you will gain the experience you need to appear smooth, professional, and competent when the really important titles are at stake.

Remember, although you hit each of the compulsory poses individually, when you create your own posing routine you will need to be able to move smoothly from one pose to another, making the transitions appear almost effortless. To learn to do this well, you need to practice going back and forth between various poses until the movement becomes almost automatic.

Posing as Exercise

You will never be able to really refine every single muscle in the body just by training. Workouts tend to hit just the big muscle groups. But for the serratus, intercostals, and obliques, for extra chest, deltoids, thigh, and biceps definition, the finishing touches are supplied by posing.

A basic physique is developed by training, but posing adds sharpness and quality. I have noticed time after time that many bodybuilders seem to be in their best shape a day or two *after* the competition. This is due, I am sure, to all of the flexing and posing they had to do during the prejudging.

A bodybuilder who trains but never poses is like an uncut diamond—the quality is there potentially, but it cannot be seen. Just as the diamond cutter brings out the brilliance of the stone as he reveals first one facet and then another, the bodybuilder sharpens and completes his physique by long hard hours of posing practice. I learned this firsthand when I used to go over to Joe Weider's office and he would say, "Arnold, take off your shirt and let me see you pose." This annoyed me because I would start sweating, I just wasn't ready for this kind of exertion. But he would keep me posing for hours, forcing me to flex the serratus and keep the abdominals tense, until I was exhausted. He almost

622

After my biceps workout I flex the biceps as hard as I can and hold it for a minute or so, which gives them extra height and hardness. At the same time, I am tensing the chest and legs and holding in the abdomen, just the way I would do the pose on stage.

Posing for Joe always ended up giving me a terrific workout, which helped increase my endurance, muscle control, and definition.

Photo sessions force you to pose hard and long under hot lights. This picture of Joe and me was taken at Jimmy Caruso's studio just before the 1975 Mr. Olympia.

drove me out of my mind—but I would be so sore the next day that I soon realized the posing had actually been a terrific workout for parts of my body that my normal workouts apparently didn't touch.

I also made it a practice to have as many photo sessions as possible during the week before a contest. Standing under the lights, with the photographer making me hit pose after pose and holding them for long periods while he adjusted his camera and strobes ("Flex your legs," "Flex your abs," "Hold it!") was enormously tiring, and yet the next day I looked even better because of it. When I was working on *The Jayne Mansfield Story* I had to spend a full day posing in front of the cameras. I looked good in the studio, but the next day, after the hours and hours of flexing and going through my posing routine for the movie, I was absolutely cut to ribbons. In really top shape.

One of the reasons that posing (which is, after all, isometric contraction of the muscles) helps so much is that it works muscle areas that training frequently misses. You may stand in front of a mirror and flex your thighs, your pectorals, or deltoids, but how often do you consider what lies in between these larger muscle groups? What posing does is to tie those areas together and give the physique a truly finished look, the kind of polish that makes the difference between a good bodybuilder and a true champion. It exercises and stimulates all those in-between areas, the tie-ins, the minor but essential areas of the muscle structure.

So be certain, as your contest approaches, that you really hit the posing hard, not just to condition you for posing in prejudging, but to give you the ultimate definition and muscle separation that diet and training alone won't provide.

Posing for Photographs

In many respects, preparing for a photo session is much the same as getting ready for a contest: you need to master the individual poses, choose the proper posing trunks, get a good tan. However, the bodybuilder is dependent to a great deal on the skill of the photographer. Everyone will not have the benefit, as I have had, of being photographed by an Art Zeller, Jimmy Caruso, John Balik, or Albert Busek. Therefore, you are going to have to make yourself look good despite any shortcomings on the part of the person snapping the photos.

The background is extremely important as to how a bodybuilder appears in a photograph. For example, when you pose

Albert Busek lines up a photograph so that the nineteen-year-old Arnold looks huge in the foreground, dominating the "tiny" Alps in the background.

Here are two Albert Busek photos in which the camera angle is low so that the scenery in the background does not overpower my physique. This is how you can appear bigger than a mountain!

For this photo, Albert Busek and I took a boat far out on a lake so that the shoreline became distant and unobtrusive. We chose a time of day when the sun would be at about a 45-degree angle, to minimize harsh shadows.

with a huge building, a large bridge, or anything else big or confusing behind you, your body will tend to be dwarfed by the background and look smaller. By studying many photographs I discovered that a neutral background, like the sea or sky, is the most favorable. Also, having huge mountains far in the distance can make you appear enormous.

Getting the right angle is also important. If the camera is pointing down, the body will look small. But if it is at waist level or below, and shooting upward, the physique looks that much taller and more massive.

Time of day is also vital. Around noon, the sun is straight overhead, which creates harsh and unflattering shadows. Your photos will look better if your do your photo sessions when the sun is close to a 45-degree angle, at nine or ten in the morning or three or four in the afternoon, depending on the time of year. Overcast days generally are better for color shots. A really good photographer will often use fill-in flash or a reflector to get rid of the shadows under the eyes that occur even when you are shooting at the right time of day.

The way your physique comes out on film is dependent to a

This is a John Balik photo taken at "Muscle Rock," where so many great bodybuilders have been photographed. Again, the hills behind me are soft and distant and remain in the background.

The neutrality of the sky and beach make a good backdrop that does not compete for attention with my physique. The buildings in the background look small and insignificant. Notice, also, the lack of harsh shadows, since John Balik set up this session for late in the afternoon.

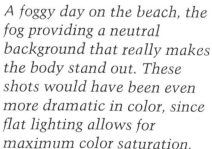

A foggy day on the beach, the fog providing a neutral background that really makes the body stand out. These shots would have been even more dramatic in color, since flat lighting allows for maximum color saturation.

large degree on the lens used. The longer the lens, the less distortion. With a wide-angle lens, you introduce curvature into the picture that can create an unpleasant effect. In 35mm photography, unless you are looking for a special effect, never use a lens shorter than 50mm, and even then the photographer must be careful not to shoot at too great an upward angle. You are much safer being photographed with a 90mm or 135mm lens (or their

If you shoot at the proper angle and the right time of day, the ocean can make a dramatic background. But when you stand in the bright sun like this, you need a deep tan to keep the light from washing out all your definition.

This is an example of how not to do it. Even though the photographer tried to leave the background out of focus, it is still so busy that it distracts from the figure in the foreground. The huge mountain also makes me look shorter and smaller than if I had been photographed against the sky.

Another example of a background that is too big, close, intrusive, and busy.

In this photo I am posing in the niche of a building to make myself look like a statue.

equivalents in other filming formats), which makes distortion virtually impossible.

Sometimes, bodybuilders pose with props or in unusual locations, like Steve Reeves holding a discus or me holding the sword I used in *Conan the Barbarian*. In doing this, care must be taken that the photo really works, that the props, buildings, or whatever in the picture make the physique look better rather than detracting from it.

Shooting in a studio is an art, and requires an experienced professional. I have had young bodybuilders send me photos that were apparently done by studio photographers, but were so poorly lit and the poses so awkward that it was evident the photographer had little knowledge of physique photography.

Russ Warner likes to shoot against a white background, which makes the body look huge and massive.

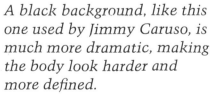

A black background, like this one used by Jimmy Caruso, is much more dramatic, making the body look harder and more defined.

There are many different approaches to studio physique photography. Russ Warner, for example, likes to shoot against a white background. With the right lighting, this can make you look huge and massive. However, the most dramatic results are achieved by using a black background—a favorite of Jimmy Caruso—which makes the muscles look even harder and more defined.

CHAPTER 2
Total Preparation

Bob Birdsong's physique looks best in low-cut posing trunks.

It is really sad to see a bodybuilder with a great physique, who has obviously paid his dues in the gym, posing beautifully on stage and then ruining the total effect because he has overlooked some detail of his presentation. The higher the level you reach in bodybuilding, the more competitive it becomes. And when a judge is comparing you to an equally good opponent and having trouble deciding to whom to award the higher score, some minor aspect of your appearance may make the difference, such as your posing trunks, skin tone, skin color, haircut, or cleanliness.

These presentation details don't usually add many points to your score. Good physical development, posing, and stage manner are what do that. But anything that takes away from your total appearance on stage can cause you to lose points, and that is something even the best bodybuilders can't afford.

Posing Trunks

It is important to choose the right posing trunks well before the competition. If you wait until just a few days before the event you are taking a chance—you may have to search quite a while to find the ones you want, to order a pair through the mail, or even to have them specially tailored for you. Evaluate the cut, color, and texture of a particular pair of posing trunks, and have photos taken wearing them so you are absolutely sure they suit you in every way.

If you are tall and have long legs, you can wear trunks that are cut a little lower on the thigh. If you have short legs and a long torso, you can cut them higher on the thigh and the waist. How full or brief your posing trunks are also depends on your build. Bob Birdsong, with his flaring back and tiny waist, looks good in

Frank Zane

Franco Columbu

very brief posing trunks. Frank Zane also wears brief trunks, because he has flaring obliques and the smaller trunks ride below these and help to slim his waist. Franco Columbu has a similar waistline, so he also looks good in relatively brief posing trunks.

For somebody with a physique like mine, much thicker and wider, brief trunks would look ridiculous. Can you imagine a bodybuilder the size and structure of Lou Ferrigno wearing delicate, Zane-like posing trunks? No, the larger, more Herculean bodybuilders require trunks cut a little fuller.

It is also important to choose the right color, and to avoid anything too fancy. In fact, trunks that are too shiny or are not a solid color are currently against the rules of the IFBB. And that is just as well: the last thing you want is posing trunks that will make more of an impression on the judges than you do!

Solid colors are the best. I always liked darker colors, because trunks that are too bright draw a lot of attention to the waistline, and I was never wasp-waisted. Ken Waller always looked good in a pale blue, and Franco has always done well wearing deep red. The right color helps to set off your physique, and should complement your skin tone, hair and eye color as well as your muscular development. So experiment, and see what works best for you.

Once you have determined the cut and color of the posing trunks you want to use, try to obtain several pairs so that you can put on fresh trunks after a long prejudging session and look your best for the evening show. It is also good to have extra trunks so that you can change for backstage photos or a picture-

Lou Ferrigno (left) and I, both of us having large, massive frames, look much better in higher-cut posing trunks. Serge Nubret (center), on the other hand, with his narrow waist, can wear trunks cut much lower at the waist and higher at the leg.

The top of my posing trunks comes to just about an inch below the obliques. Any higher, and they would make the obliques look fat. Lower, and the cut would not suit my body type.

taking session the day after a competition. I always liked to have a variety of different-color trunks available too, for photos taken against various colored backgrounds or outdoors.

Tanning

When a light-skinned bodybuilder stands under the bright lights on stage the illumination tends to wash him out and makes it difficult for the judges to see his definition and development. The way to avoid this is by getting a good, even tan.

The skin tans to protect itself from the dangerous ultraviolet rays of the sun. When the skin is exposed to these rays, the melanin (skin pigment) which has remained from your last tan, but has faded, becomes dark again; this is why you can *seem* to tan after just one day in the sun but, in fact, your body has produced no new pigment to protect you. True tanning, during which new melanin is produced, takes considerably longer, a week to ten days, so it doesn't pay to stay out in the sun for long hours at a time trying to rush a tan.

It is best to tan in stages, twenty minutes to a half hour a day in the beginning, depending on your skin type, where you live, the time of year, and the altitude (the higher up you are, the stronger the ultraviolet rays). If you are fair-skinned and burn

A good tan helps to keep your definition from disappearing under the bright stage lights. These bodybuilders are sunbathing to get dark for an upcoming contest.

638

Where I lived in Europe the sun wasn't intense enough for me to get a dark tan, whereas Dennis Tinerino had the advantage of a much hotter climate. As a result, he looks tan and defined, while I look white and appear smoother than I really was.

This photo was taken in Palm Springs in 1974. See how much more attractive, hard, and defined the physique looks with a dark tan.

easily, you must take extra caution. But remember, even the darkest skin can be burned and damaged by the sun if the exposure is long enough.

Experts advise not to sunbathe between the hours of 10 AM and 2 PM, when the rays of the sun are most intense (and can therefore do the most damage to the skin), but that is exactly the time when most people prefer to lie out in the sun. So let me just pass on the warning that excessive exposure to the sun tends to cause wrinkles and gives the skin a leathery look and that the sun's ultraviolet rays can cause skin cancer. Tanning, then, must be approached with a certain degree of moderation and care.

One way to help control the amount of exposure you get is by using a suntan oil (not just plain oil—that doesn't protect you, it just keeps you from perspiring, leading to the possibility of sunstroke). The best ones contain PABA, a protective chemical, and modern suntan oils are graded by number, according to how much protection they give, 1 being the least and the higher numbers giving more protection.

One aesthetic consideration is that you don't want your face to be darker than the rest of your body. But your face, and your nose in particular, tends to absorb a lot more sun. So take care to protect your face by wearing a hat or using a sunscreen to prevent your nose and forehead from getting burned.

Tanning Parlors and Sunlamps

Indoor tanning parlors have proliferated all over the country. You step into a room that is, in effect, a giant sunlamp and you get your exposure in short, calculated doses. Some of these parlors use "alpha" and some "beta" radiation (which simply refers to the wavelength of the ultraviolet), but it is important to realize that any rays that can tan you can also burn and damage your skin, so the same cautions apply to using suntan parlors as to lying out in the sun. Start slowly. Give your skin the time it needs to tan, and try to avoid burning and peeling, which not only makes you look bad but forces you to start all over. Home sunlamps present the same dangers. Many people have burned themselves badly, even their eyes, by remaining too long under a sunlamp.

Increasingly, gyms are installing suntan equipment right on the premises. Gold's Gym, for example, has a machine which puts out the safer "beta" radiation. As this idea spreads, bodybuilders will find it easier to keep up their tans year round, even in cold climates.

There are many products on the market that purport to speed up the tanning process. These pills, oils, or creams work by stimulating the body's ability to produce color or by making the skin extrasensitive to the rays of the sun. The problem is, many of these products have not been approved by the FDA and their sale is illegal in the United States. Several California bodybuilders I know of have gotten badly burned from using the creams and oils in too great a concentration (usually they need to be diluted) or by staying out in the sun too long. Because of the dangers involved, I can't really recommend using any of these products.

Selecting an Artificial Color

Most white bodybuilders, even when they have gotten a really good tan, like to make it look deeper on stage by using some sort of artificial color. At almost any drugstore you will find a lot of space devoted to various kinds of skin colorings. Over the last ten or twenty years, bodybuilders have tried nearly all of them. Products like ManTan, which gives you instant coloring, or Coppertone's Q-T, where the color takes some time to appear, have helped competitors darken their natural tans for an even better stage appearance than they could achieve naturally.

How you enhance your tan for competition depends to a large degree on what your natural skin coloring is. If you have a lot of pigment and can get a natural dark tan, a product like Tan-in-a-Minute or Q-T will make your tan look even deeper and more impressive. If you have light skin or you haven't had the time to get out into the sun (or into a tanning booth), these products can give you a yellowish, jaundiced look. In this case, you need some kind of "stain" that imparts a deeper color.

Ken Waller, who is very light skinned, used to get as dark a tan as he could and then begin applying Q-T the day before the show —putting on four or five layers, giving each an hour to dry before putting on the next. The next morning he would wash with lukewarm water, then apply one final coat. By using this many coats of the product, he could get dark enough to look good on stage.

One product that both light- and dark-skinned bodybuilders are using quite a bit these days is a coloring called Dy-O-Derm. If your local pharmacy is not aware of this product, they can order if from Owens Labs Division, Derma Products of Texas, P.O. Box 1959, Forth Worth, Texas 76101.

Oiling the Body

Bodybuilders use oil on stage to highlight the shape of the body and bring out the full definition of the muscles. Intense lights have a tendency to flatten you out, and a light coat of oil along with a good tan allows the judges to fully appreciate your development.

You need help to oil yourself completely—somebody to put oil on your back and tell you whether you have achieved an even application. In your early contests, you can generally find another competitor who will oil your back if you oil his. However, when you get into higher-level competition, you can never be sure that a rival won't play a trick on you, oil only half your back, or use too much or too little. So you would do well to have a friend or training partner available, someone whom you've practiced with, who knows exactly where and how much oil to apply.

The kind of oil you use is up to you—anything from baby oil to olive oil—but be aware that too much oil can be as bad as too little, making you look like a basted turkey on stage. Keep a towel handy and wipe off any excess, which is not only distracting but against the rules in IFBB contests.

Hair Style

If your hair is long and shaggy, it not only comes down over your neck and obscures your traps, but makes your head look bigger—and your body correspondingly smaller. The same applies to a really bushy afro. Very short hair, on the other hand, can make you look like a refugee from boot camp.

But there is a more practical consideration as well: if your hair is too long, during the course of the contest it will get wet and stringy with perspiration and oil, and will leave you looking like something dragged out of a swamp instead of a champion bodybuilder. So be sure your hair is short enough to keep neat.

Study your haircut in the mirror, look at photos, and decide whether you would present a better appearance with longer or shorter hair, or cut in a different style. There are even some bodybuilders who have chosen to lighten or darken their hair to improve their appearance. And above all, make sure you keep your hair looking clean and healthy by shampooing regularly and, if necessary, conditioning it.

The way your hair is cut can affect your overall look. Here Robby Robinson has an afro, and this extra mass of hair tends to make his neck, traps, and shoulders look too small.

In this shot, Robby is wearing his hair short, which helps to make his whole upper body appear even more huge than it is.

Body Hair

Another means bodybuilders use to improve their appearance is to shave off their body hair prior to a contest. This gives the skin a much smoother and cleaner appearance, and makes the muscles more visible. The simplest way to do this is just with a regular safety razor, carefully going over the chest, arms, and legs, anywhere you want to get rid of hair. It feels funny to be shaved like this, and it takes getting used to. For one thing, it always made me feel smaller and lighter, and that can be a psychological disadvantage going into a contest.

Therefore, I don't recommend you shave just before a contest. Instead, try shaving a couple of weeks prior to the competition and then giving yourself periodic touch-ups. This way, if you should cut yourself or irritate your skin, there will be plenty of time for your skin to heal and return to normal.

Franco always had an odd approach to removing body hair: he didn't like to shave, so a while before any contest he would begin pulling out body hair with his fingers! By the time he was ready to shave, there was very little hair left. This is not a method I would generally recommend.

Finishing Touches

Really good bodybuilders leave nothing to chance on stage. Many wear something on their feet backstage so that when they come out to pose, their soles will not be dirty. Others bring several changes of posing trunks and change whenever their trunks become soiled with sweat and oil.

Keeping your skin, hair, and clothing clean, your hair neatly cut, having the right tan and skin coloring, knowing what kind of posing trunks to wear—all of these are important elements in the total preparation that goes into making a bodybuilding champion.

CHAPTER 3
Competition Strategy and Tactics

This was the shape I was in when I entered my first bodybuilding contest.

When I first began competing, I had no choice but to quickly move up to contests on the level of Junior Mr. Europe, Best Built Man in Europe, Mr. Europe, and Mr. Universe. Even though I was a very fast developer, I still waited a full three years before getting into competition because there were few lower-level contests I could enter. If there had been contests like Mr. Venice Beach, for example, or Mr. Los Angeles, as well as all of the teenage and junior competitions that now exist, I would have been able to begin competing after only one year of training and would have gained that much more feedback and contest experience.

Many bodybuilders prefer to wait to compete until they think they are good enough to jump into regional or national contests and win the title, but I think this is a mistake. They may find they lack the experience to show themselves to their best advantage, while their competitors may well be much more experienced.

Getting Started

There is nothing like knowing exactly when your next contest is going to be to spur an aggressively competitive bodybuilder on to greater and greater efforts in the gym. Just the specter of standing on stage and looking bad, making a fool of yourself because you didn't train or diet hard enough, should be enough motivation to make you do those few extra sets and reps and to stay with the discipline of a strict diet. Without that fixed contest date ahead of you, you can say to yourself that it doesn't matter and, in a sense, it doesn't. So you simply don't go the limit all the time.

I recommend to bodybuilders who want to go into competition that they do so as soon as they are able. Pick the lowest-level contest you can find and enter as soon as you feel that you will not disgrace yourself. By exposing yourself this way you will find out what your weak points are. You will also know where you made your mistakes—did you forget your posing routine, neglect to make eye contact with the judges, use too much oil, wear the wrong kind of posing trunks? And, of course, what can you take pride in having done right?

Practice makes perfect. Experience is the best teacher. If you enter a contest and fail to win it, after having prepared as hard and well as you could, then so be it. You can learn from losing just as well as from winning. Try to win, but if you don't, learn why so that you can do better next time.

Advanced Competitions

Once you have gained some experience and have proved yourself a good enough bodybuilder to win small contests, you now have to begin to choose competitions on the basis of what they mean to your career.

I was very careful after winning the Amateur Mr. Universe title in London not to jump into the professional ranks until I was sure I had a good shot at winning. If I had gone against the top pros just a year too early, I might have severely curtailed the momentum of my career.

A good illustration of how this works is the experience of my friend Jusup Wilkosz. After winning the 1979 Mr. Universe title, Jusup was immediately eligible to compete in the Olympia. But he was smart enough to realize that this would not be good tactics. Instead, he entered the 1980 Professional Mr. Universe contest and won it. This made him a two-time international champion, with everyone thinking of him as a winner.

Then Wilkosz decided to give the Olympia a try, but his journey to Columbus in 1981 resulted in a disappointing sixth-place finish. And it was here, I believe, that he made a real mistake. After the Olympia, he decided to enter a European Grand Prix and was defeated by Boyer Coe, who was in phenomenal shape. My advice would have been to stay out of the Grand Prix and enter the Professional Mr. Universe contest that year in Australia, which I believe Jusup could have won, re-establishing himself as a champion. Instead, he had two international defeats which cancelled out his earlier victories.

Tom Platz is another good example. He finished third in the 1981 Olympia and impressed a lot of people. Then he decided not to continue competing but to spend his time doing seminars and exhibitions instead. But since Jusup had declined to go to Australia, Tom probably could have won that event. The winner was Dennis Tinerino, and Tom had already defeated him handily at the Olympia. With a little more thought and planning, Platz might have won another international title and furthered the momentum of his career.

Lou Ferrigno made a smart move entering the Mr. Universe contest twice (and winning). But in 1974, a year he could probably have won the Professional Mr. Universe contest, instead he entered the Mr. Olympia and lost. There is nothing wrong with losing a competition, but if you have a choice of two contests it makes sense to enter the one you can win.

In the beginning, as far as your career is concerned, it hardly matters whether you place second or last. What you need is experience, motivation, and feedback. But once you have made a reputation, you have to protect it, and that means not leaping into competitions that are way beyond you. Admitting that certain competitions are over your head is no disgrace—after my early Mr. Universe win the reason I didn't go immediately for the Professional Mr. Universe title is that I didn't think I could win it. I was being realistic. A year later I had improved, I knew who my competition was, and I believed it was worth the risk.

Sometimes, you can enhance your reputation simply by not doing very well one year in a contest and then improving your placement by a wide margin the next. Tom Platz impressed a lot of people at the 1980 Mr. Olympia contest even though he didn't place. In 1981, he placed third, earned an ovation from the crowd, and garnered two first-place votes from the judges. Obviously, he would have preferred to win the title, but his improvement in only one year was itself a kind of victory.

Once you are on your way, strategy becomes important—where you compete, when you compete, who you will be competing against, whether to enter only one contest or two in a row. Dennis Tinerino was disappointed at not placing in the 1981 Olympia, but immediately went to Australia and won the Professional Mr. Universe title. Training for the Olympia, dieting hard, and then undergoing the rigors of prejudging and the evening show left him in the best shape of his life and he took full advantage of this.

Years ago, when only one overall winner was chosen at the Mr. Universe contest, he had to be so good that he probably was ready to go on and make a try for the Olympia title. Now there are weight classes, and each winner of a weight class becomes eligible to enter the Olympia. Many who exercise their eligibility too soon end up regretting it, because they do so poorly that they lose the prestige of being a world champion and become identified as losers.

Many of these bodybuilders are quite good, just not ready for competition on that level. Yorma Raty of Finland, for example, with one of the best backs in bodybuilding, entered the Olympia the year after winning a Universe weight class and finished dead last. Jacques Neuville and Lance Dreher each won Mr. Universe titles in 1981, and then went on to finish 13th and 15th respectively at the 1982 Olympia. For these bodybuilders, entering the Olympia was not a wise career move.

I recommend that a bodybuilder who wins the Mr. America

title and goes on to win the Universe should plan on competing for a title like Mr. International or Professional Mr. Universe the following year. This way he can gain more experience against bodybuilders he has a chance of beating, start to build up a following, and begin to make the international judges take notice. For a European bodybuilder, the progression would be to win the championship of his country, then move on to the Best Built Man of Europe competition, to Mr. Europe, Mr. International, and then Mr. Universe and on up.

An American bodybuilder who wants to be a top champion should hesitate going into the Mr. America contest if it means he might finish 12th or 16th. There are lesser but very important contests that would be better for gaining experience and building a reputation until he could be sure he would place high if not win his class in the America. Why go out of your way to build a reputation as a loser?

Momentum is important in any sports career, and it plays the same role in bodybuilding. Winning can become a habit if you handle your career properly. But remember, you can't be a winner unless you are not afraid to lose. Being fearful of not doing well makes you think like a loser, it inhibits you and robs you of energy. Make a reasonable decision as to what you ought to do, and then go ahead and do it without reservation; give it your all, and let the chips fall where they may. All you can do is your best, and if that isn't enough, that's just the way it goes. But if you have an all-out, positive attitude, confidence in your own ability, and massive enthusiasm, your strategy will tend to work out far more often than if you had been tentative and fearful.

Publicity

"I can't possibly win that contest," bodybuilders are all too likely to complain. "I just haven't gotten enough publicity in the magazines."

Getting the right kind of publicity is one of the requirements of a successful bodybuilding career. The easiest way to garner that publicity is to win contests! But, making sure that the editors of the major bodybuilding magazines know who you are ensures that you have a better shot at getting good publicity.

Publicity can be a two-edged sword. If you get extensive play in the magazines, then come to a contest with everyone expecting to see King Kong and you disappoint them, you may find this can work against you. But it is also true that advance publicity

helps the judges to become familiar with the qualities of your physique. They don't have to study you for long periods on stage to know that you have, for example, good lats or fantastic calves. They already know this, so they just check you over quickly, confirm their expectations, then go on to examine others and see if they measure up to *you*.

Some people seem to generate more publicity than others without really trying. When I was training and running a gym in Munich, I did a picture story for a magazine in which I walked around the city in my posing trunks during a snowstorm and was photographed window shopping, in front of the train station, and so on. This was clearly manufactured publicity, the kind Hollywood was once famous for—a publicity stunt. But it was done for *Stern* magazine, with a readership of millions, and this was my way of bringing bodybuilding to the general public. To get into this kind of magazine, you need to so something highly unusual. Publicity in bodybuilding magazines is quite a different matter.

When I went to London for the Mr. Universe contest I had no need of such stunts. I was young, huge, and relatively unknown —the European contender who came out of nowhere. I just seemed to attract attention and publicity without even trying.

But some have gone about getting publicity in other ways. Andreas Cahling was often pictured in *Muscle & Fitness* long before he won the Mr. International contest. Certainly his blond, Nordic looks made him an ideal candidate for representing bodybuilding to the public, but he also went out of his way to maintain good relations with Joe Weider, his writers and photographers and, above all, to be available, sometimes on short notice, when the magazine needed somebody to pose for photographs.

In the 1981 Mr. Universe contest in Cairo, American Lance Dreher beat Norwegian Gunnar Rosbo, but the huge Rosbo was so physically impressive, so outgoing, friendly, and willing to interrupt what he was doing for interviews or photographs, that he ended up with more publicity than the winner.

Many bodybuilders simply wait around for the magazines to come to them, but I always took the initiative and sent articles on my training methods, stories about my feelings and ideas about bodybuilding and life in general to various publications. I never worried about getting paid for articles or a cover shot—I figured that the more the judges and people got to know and like me, to understand who I was and what I was about, the better chance I had for a successful career.

Publicity is also a great way to capitalize on victory. It used to be that the winner of the Mr. America contest would be featured all the following year in John Grimek's magazine with personality profiles and training instructions. This helped to indelibly impress the winner's name on the public's consciousness. Not every bodybuilder is aware of this possibility. I had to practically beg Jusup Wilkosz to get him to fly over to the United States to do interviews and go into the studio for professional photographs so that the bodybuilding audience could learn about him.

A lot of bodybuilders, it seems to me, have the wrong attitude. When one of the top bodybuilding photographers comes around and asks to take their picture, you hear them say, "Well, how much do you pay?" That's a good way *not* to get any publicity.

Publicity is just one factor in a bodybuilding career, but it is an important one. Publicity won't win you a contest if you aren't any good, but it could help in a close decision. And if you are contemplating going on to a professional career, publicity is a great help when it comes to booking seminars and exhibitions and selling mail-order products.

Just keep in mind that the magazines *need* interesting bodybuilders to feature in their pages. So if you are good, if you do well in contests and make yourself available, you'll get publicity. The trick then is to live up to the publicity you get, and that can be even more difficult than getting the coverage in the first place!

Politics and Public Relations

Some bodybuilders who are disappointed by poor showings in contests feel that somehow "politics" is to blame—that certain competitors are taking advantage of relationships with judges or officials to place higher than they deserve. On the one hand, this kind of feeling is totally understandable: when you are a bodybuilder, it is *you*—your own body—that is being judged, and when you don't do well the blow to your ego can be tremendous. Not only that: by the time a bodybuilder is ready for a competition he has undergone months of strenuous training and diet and then is put under the additional strain of the contest itself, at a time when he is most vulnerable emotionally. Nonetheless, as understandable as this view is, the idea that "politics" is what gets you ahead in bodybuilding, or that friendly relations between the individuals involved in the bodybuilding world is somehow bad, is just not true.

Politics is simply the way human beings get together and regulate their behavior, and the behavior of the institutions in which they are involved. Without political interaction, nothing gets done. Politics is a fact of life. And judges, contest officials, and bodybuilding federation administrators are just as human as anybody else, so there are bound to be certain political considerations in any contest, no matter how honest and ethical the officials involved may be.

There are sometimes circumstances in which one vested interest or another stands to benefit if one or the other bodybuilder wins a contest. This is always going to be true, because somebody has to pay the bills for these contests, and the money is usually going to come from people like gym owners, equipment manufacturers, and others with financial interests in the bodybuilding world.

I have been a promoter as well as a competitor, and I can tell you that the accusations of wrongdoing that come about when certain bodybuilders do badly in contests and have to salve their egos usually have little or no basis in truth. I can certainly attest firsthand to the integrity of the contests I put on with Jim Lorimer in Columbus. Nor have I seen more than an occasional problem in all the contests I have entered or been present at as a spectator. Bodybuilding is the same as any other sport: the best man should win, without regard to any outside factors. And all of us should strive to see that this rule is enforced no matter what.

I wanted to explain this to prevent any young bodybuilder from believing that (1) his chances in bodybuilding competition would be limited if he lacked certain "political" connections or that (2) attempting to develop connections could in any way take the place of hard and determined training.

Nonetheless, in the sense that politics is really just the way people in groups relate to each other, there are a lot of political considerations that do play a part in bodybuilding, falling under the heading of what I would simply call "public relations."

Judging a bodybuilding contest is a subjective, imperfect process. And when it comes down to a close decision, especially one in which the bodybuilders involved are so evenly matched that there is no way a judge can actually decide who is the better man, what he thinks of the competitors is liable to play a large, if only subconscious, part.

People are rarely neutral. Everyone has opinions, either positive or negative. The last thing you want is to face judges who have a negative reaction to you. Therefore, it makes sense to maintain friendly relations with judges and other officials, to get to know them and their families, remember their wives' names, even send them Christmas cards.

Maintaining good relations with bodybuilding judges is not a way of getting extra points, it is a way of ensuring that you won't *lose* points because of any unconscious hostility on the part of one judge or another. It's simply a way of making sure that you get all the points coming to you.

There are many bodybuilders who seem to go out of their way to damage their careers by their behavior toward the judges. Competitors have been known to throw their trophies around backstage or even come out on stage and insult the judges in public. I once saw Roger Callard get very upset about the judging and say all kinds of things on stage. An hour later he had cooled off and regretted his outburst. He sent letters of apology and tried to make up for his behavior. In the next Mr. America contest, he lost, and I believe he lost partially for that reason. So it pays to keep control of your temper, to behave like a professional, and not to attack the judges in public.

Learning to Peak for Competition

A good bodybuilder plans his competition strategy the way a successful general conducts a military campaign. You need to choose the right time and place to do battle, to be certain that your army (your physique) is well trained and ready. You need to be confident of your battle tactics, know when to attack, when to withdraw, and how to conserve ammunition (energy) so that it lasts until the end of the conflict.

But many bodybuilders with fantastic physiques, who have a thorough grasp of preparation, posing, and everything else, come up short because they fail in one area: *they are not at their absolute best on the day of the competition.*

A bodybuilding contest is about who is the best bodybuilder on that particular stage on that particular day. Who is potentially the best, or who is best most of the time, should have nothing to do with it. You may be great the day before the contest or the day after, but unless you can time your preparation so that you peak on the very day of the competition you are going to be constantly disappointed.

Peaking for a competition is a matter of experience and careful timing. Each individual has to find out exactly how to manipulate his own diet and training to be able to come into a contest in absolutely top shape. However, there are certain general techniques that are very useful. Up until 1970 I came into contests just a little off—peaking a bit too early, getting into my best shape a few days *after* the competition. But then, quite by accident, I discovered how to come in just right the day of the contest.

In the 1970 Mr. Universe contest in London, I was a little off—too smooth—but I was the best one there, so I won. Right afterward, I went to Columbus for the Mr. World contest. I had lost to Sergio in the Olympia the year before, and I was determined to avenge myself in this contest.

When I arrived in Columbus I was cut, hard, and in the best shape of my life . . . and I began to wonder why. I realized it was because of having competed such a short time before and then posing for photographs afterward, that the effort of all this posing had left me in better shape than I was before the contest. Competition, in other words, turned out to be a great way to get in shape for competition.

I beat Sergio for Mr. World in Columbus and then got ready to compete again the next week at the Mr. Olympia contest. I felt too light and skinny, so I ate a little carrot cake every day, four or five meals, and trained a little less. By the time of the competition I found I had all of the definition I had had at the Mr. World, and all of the size I had had at the Mr. Universe!

That taught me a lesson: if I got so much better a week after competition, why not aim for getting into contest shape a full week before the contest. Spend that pre-contest Saturday posing like crazy all day, hitting all sorts of shots, just as if I were per-

654

These "before and after" photos were taken about eighteen days apart, two or three months before a competition. I marked the earlier photos to pinpoint weak points I wanted to improve.
Biceps before . . .

forming in the contest. Then have photos taken all day Sunday, which means a lot more posing, and Monday to Wednesday train well (minimum of fifteen sets per body part), eat well, but not excessively, and rest on Thursday and Friday, except for continued posing practice.

Most young bodybuilders do it quite differently. They diet right up until the Friday before the contest, or even Saturday morning, and then stuff themselves full of carbohydrates just before the contest. I know from experience this doesn't work. One explanation is that muscle size depends not only on the quantity of muscle tissue present, but also on carbohydrate energy stored in the muscles in the form of glycogen (see Contest Dieting, p. 695). When the glycogen is depleted, the muscles get flat—and it takes something like three full days for your body to completely re-

. . . and after

more seperation
9.7.80

9.25.80

More
outer thighs

9.25.80

Thighs before . . .   . . . and after

Triceps before . . .   . . . and after

More triceps

stock its glycogen supply once it is exhausted (the time varies somewhat with the individual). So dieting hard right up to the contest leaves you too little time to replenish the glycogen—and eating excessive carbohydrate simply raises your blood sugar level precipitately and leads to excess water retention. How many times have you heard a bodybuilder complain about coming into a contest both flat and puffy? This may well be one explanation —and why my improvisational approach to contest preparation paid off.

Any last-minute experimentation before an important contest can be a disaster. The day before a contest, after months of discipline and preparation, what you need most is patience—and few bodybuilders have it. So they try to do something extra and get totally screwed up. This can even happen with experienced bodybuilders. At the 1981 Olympia, one competitor tried a special liquid to help him tan and ended up with burned and peeling skin; another who had been in competition fifteen years suddenly decided to try a diuretic, which he never had before, and got terrible cramps during prejudging.

I believe in simply sticking to the essentials. The more special requirements you have, the more that can go wrong and upset you. Sergio used to show up at a contest with his posing trunks under his clothes. He would just undress, oil up, and be ready to go. The only extra thing he brought along was a long white butcher's coat he wore backstage while pumping up.

For other bodybuilders a more complex approach seems to work better. Frank Zane, for example, has always paid close attention to every single detail. He checks out his dressing room to make sure it is suitable and provides enough space. He has everything he needs, including somebody to help him pump up and oil up. Frequently, that someone is his wife Christine, who has been a great asset to him throughout his career. Zane even went so far in the 1979 Olympia as to have his own trailer parked outside the auditorium, giving him a place to pump up in total privacy, which helped to psych out his opposition. In similar circumstances, I have arranged to have dumbbells available in a separate room so that I could pump up in privacy.

The Day of the Contest

On the day of the contest, you don't want any surprises. Every detail counts. For example, how are the lights set up on stage? As a producer, I know there are areas on stage with strong light and others where the light is weaker. Therefore, it pays to check out the stage lighting so you know where to stand and where not to stand during the contest. The angle at which the light hits you is also important. If the angle is steep, you have to be very careful not to bend forward too far when you do your poses or all you will do is create a giant shadow over your body.

Learn what you can about the judges. After you have been in a few contests, you will begin to understand what different judges are looking for. Some prefer size, while others give more points for definition or symmetry. You can't change your physique for the contest, but you can alter your posing routine somewhat if you know what the judges like.

It is also a good idea to introduce yourself to the master of ceremonies and make sure he has enough information to be able to give you a good introduction. I know that when I have acted as the M.C. at bodybuilding events, I was always willing to co-operate when a bodybuilder asked me to say something specific in introducing him. This can have an influence on both the judges and the audience.

You should also know exactly how you are going to spend your day. On the morning of the contest, I would generally have a good breakfast—eggs, potatoes, cottage cheese, orange juice—but not an excessive amount. Generally, prejudging starts around one o'clock, so I would have the morning to walk around and prepare my mind for the competition ahead. For those bodybuilders who have to make an earlier prejudging, nine o'clock for example, I would recommend getting up very early, maybe five o'clock, and having an early meal, so that the body has time to wake up.

Roger Callard had a good way of spending the time between breakfast and the contest—he would find someplace where he could lie in the sun to help bring out his veins and burn out excess water. He would come back looking a full 5 percent better, and after a quick pump-up he was ready to compete.

Try to avoid letting negative thoughts and feelings dominate your mind. I remember Mike Katz at one contest walking around a few hours before prejudging talking about what he would do when he lost the competition and complaining how everything was wrong and that a certain competitor should not have been allowed in the contest. As a lifelong competitive athlete and for-mer professional football player, Mike should have remembered the degree to which negative thoughts can set you up for losing, becoming in effect a self-fulfilling prophecy.

We used to spend the time leading up to a contest differently than most seem to do now. A camaraderie existed then that has now largely disappeared. I remember checking into adjoining rooms at a hotel in New York with Zabo Koszewski, Franco Columbu and Eddie Giuliani and there was protein powder all over the place, liver pills under the pillows, and Tan-in-a-Minute all over the sheets and towels. We had a lot of fun, painting each other with color, going out to eat together, and sharing a taxi to the auditorium. This was a lot more pleasurable than the hiding out in the dressing room, the don't-let-anyone-see-you kind of thing that goes on today.

Pumping up before the contest is also an important part of your strategy. I learned a trick from my friend Wag Bennett in England, something the old-time bodybuilders used to do: the day before

Doing a set of towel pulls for the lats

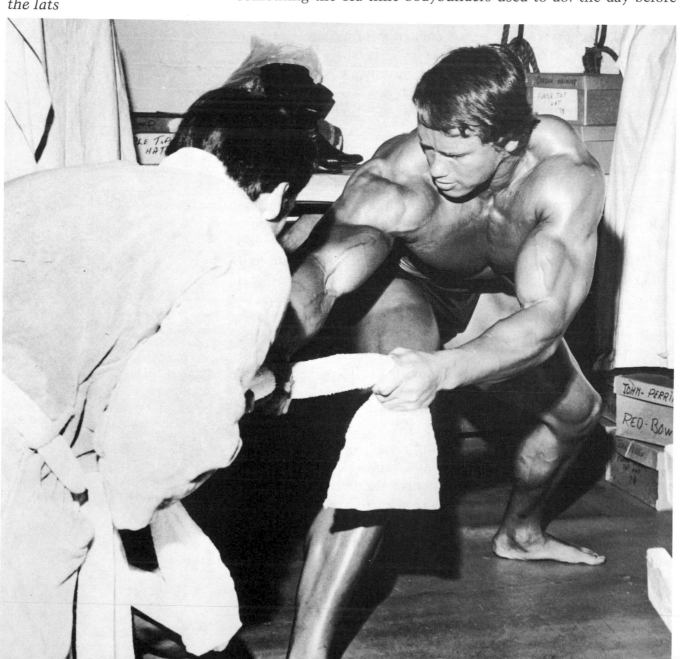

the contest, do one set to failure each hour for each of your weak points for a minimum of fourteen hours. This can theoretically increase the size of that muscle from ½ inch to a full inch the day of the contest. Maybe it stimulates glycogen retention, or just brings more fluid to the area, I don't know, but I do know it worked for me. At the Mr. Universe contest in London in 1967, I was able to pump up my calves during the last twenty-four hours before the contest from 17½ inches to well over 18 inches.

The advantage of pumping up the day before is that you don't need to pump that body part excessively during the contest itself. It is my experience that too much of a pump can destroy your definition. Of course, this depends on your body type. If you are naturally fairly smooth, when you pump up too much you will just look bloated on stage. All the more reason to come into the contest with a lower body weight to retain your definition— provided you get down to that weight early enough and keep it stable for a period of time. I believe the longer you keep your body weight at a given level, the more mature and finished your muscle structure will appear. Dropping down five pounds a week or so before the contest will not allow you to get hard and cut, and all the pumping in the world won't improve it.

I would start a half hour before the prejudging with some stretching and posing, going through my routine a few times. Then I would pump only the areas that I thought were weak— shoulders, for example, which were never as outstanding as my pectorals, or doing a set of lats. I would do a set, then do some more posing, then another pumping set. This way I would not burn myself out. After all, a prejudging that starts at one o'clock can go on until three o'clock, and it is during the last part of the prejudging that you do your own posing routine. One thing you should never do in a competition is to pump your thighs, because this will destroy the definition in that area and you will not be able to get the proper effect when you flex them.

During the beginning of this preparation, I would keep my training suit on, until I began to feel too warm. Then I would take off the top, keeping a T-shirt on. Gradually, off would come the long pants, then the T-shirt, and I would be stripped down to posing trunks just in time to oil up and go right out on stage.

The last thing I did before going out on stage was to put on a small amount of oil. Then before each round I pumped up a little more and put on more oil if I needed it. But the important thing is to keep posing, to pace yourself, and to throw in a pumping set every once in a while.

During contests, Franco and I would usually eat some home-

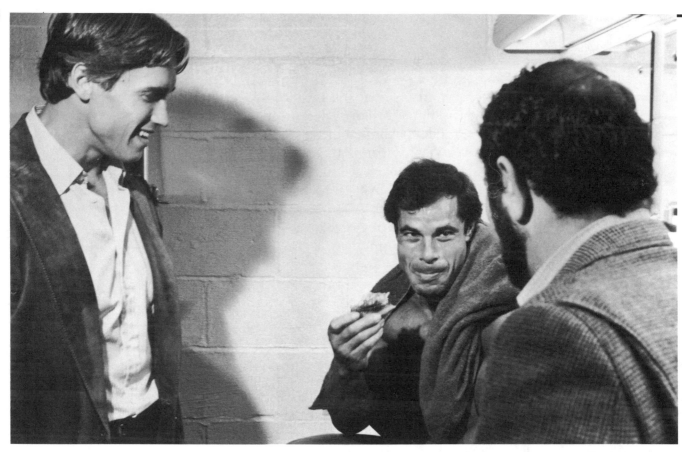

Franco eating pizza during prejudging to keep his energy level up

made carrot cake—made with very little sugar—to provide carbohydrate energy. Some bodybuilders sip wine (and, of course, others drink something stronger) but, again, don't experiment with anything at the last minute before an important contest. Experiment when it doesn't matter that much.

During prejudging, I rarely paid attention to what the other bodybuilders were doing. I just concentrated on what I was going to do, and didn't really take their presence into consideration until the posedown.

Between prejudging and the evening show, I generally walked around; ate a little something; thought through what I had done right or wrong; planned what I was going to do in the evening show; talked to people who had watched the prejudging, to get an honest evaluation of my performance; decided who among my opponents was a threat, who was not, and what tactics I could use to get the upper hand in the posedown. Above all, on stage or off, I always acted like the winner. I enjoyed the evening show and my chance to perform for the audience.

Admittedly, under the pressure of competition it is hard to keep in mind everything you ought to be doing at all times. No matter how experienced you are, it helps to have somebody with you at a contest to act as a coach. Franco and I have frequently helped each other in this way. In 1980 he came to Australia to help me win the Mr. Olympia, and in 1981 I returned the favor in Columbus, advising him on contest strategy and helping him to focus his energy on winning. Of course, not everyone is lucky enough to have a Mr. Olympia around as a contest coach, but you can usually find a friend or training partner to go to shows with you and cheer on your efforts to win.

Finally, I always kept a journal handy to write down everything I did and how I felt right up to and during the contest: Did I start to get cramps, and why? Did the audience respond more to one kind of pose than another? Anything that could help me to do better in the next competition. Franco, Frank Zane, and many other bodybuilders do the same thing. After all, there are only so many of these variables that you can keep in your head, and when you want to be a champion you can't afford to leave anything to chance.

Franco and my friend Bill Drake gave me a lot of advice and moral support at the 1980 Olympia . . .

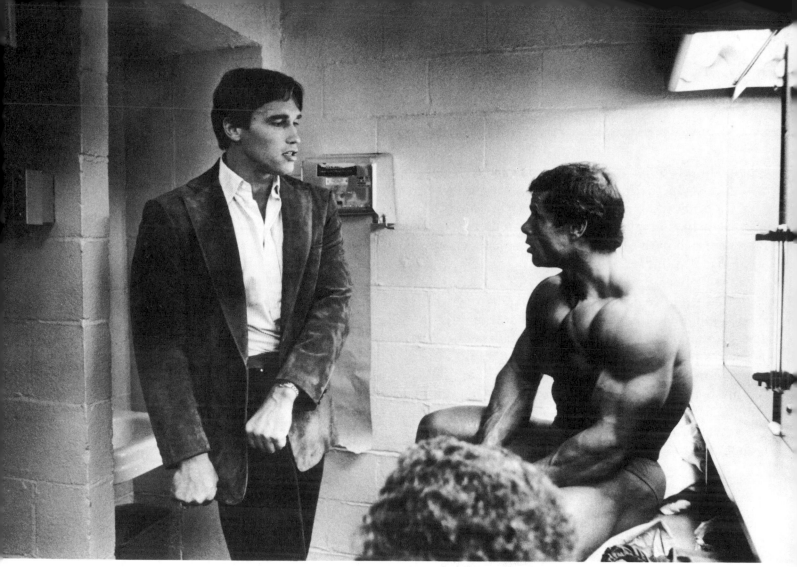

. . . and at the 1981 Olympia, I returned the favor. Here I am telling Franco not to lean too far forward because of the heavy shadows cast by the overhead lights on stage.

Psychological Warfare

There is always a psychological element in any sports competition. Athletic performance at the highest levels requires a tremendous degree of self-confidence and concentration, and anything that interferes with either will seriously threaten the athlete's chances of winning.

Psyching out your opponents or "gamesmanship" is common to all sports. Before his fight with Sonny Liston back in the 1960s, Muhammad Ali appeared at the weigh-in screaming and hysterical, apparently totally out of his mind, and really shook up the then heavyweight champion. I know of a swimmer who admits to suddenly checking his suit just before the gun sounds to start the race, knowing that one or two of his opponents will begin to wonder if their own suits are in order and look down to check just as the starting pistol fires—breaking their concentration and causing them to hesitate a fraction of a second as the race starts.

None of this is cheating. Cheating is when you break the rules, not when you take advantage of an opponent's psychological weakness. When you figure it, anyone who wishes to claim the title of champion should be the master of his own mind as well as of his sport. If he isn't, and your psyching throws him, then he has no business complaining.

One of the most famous examples of psyching in bodybuilding occurred during the 1975 Mr. Universe contest in South Africa, and is shown in the movie *Pumping Iron*. Ken Waller, more as a joke than anything else, made away with Mike Katz's T-shirt—nothing that would change the course of the contest dramatically, but just one more thing that Mike had to deal with in a situation in which the pressures were already almost overwhelming. Although the movie exaggerated how seriously Mike actually took this prank, I believe he did waste a certain amount of time and concentration looking for his T-shirt—and when you are in a competition on this level, you can't afford to waste anything.

I have to confess to having used similar tactics myself on occasion. In the 1980 Olympia I was standing on stage next to Frank Zane, and started telling him jokes. Soon he was laughing so hard he could hardly hit his poses. In another contest I repeated to Serge Nubret that one of the judges had remarked that he looked too small and probably should have been in the lighter weight category. "That's what I was afraid of," he told me, and from that moment on he was obsessed with this idea, kept asking me how he looked, and his posing was thrown way off because he was reluctant to do certain shots that he felt he was too light to bring off. In close contests like those between Serge and me, psychological factors can be decisive.

Franco had a direct way of psyching out his opponents before a contest. He would arrange for somebody to telephone him when one of his competitors was training in World Gym. Franco would hasten to the gym, do a few warm-up sets, then take off his training suit and run around the gym in just a pair of shorts. Most bodybuilders like to keep themselves covered when they're getting ready for a contest, but Franco acted as if he were totally unconcerned about his competition and was eager to show off what good shape he was in. I saw Chris Dickerson practically run out of the gym once when Franco pulled this stunt and then challenged Chris to take off his shirt too. So you can see how far in advance of a competition psychological warfare can begin.

At the 1981 Olympia, Franco saw to it that he had a lot of media coverage. With Italian television there to film him and other photographers taking all sorts of shots of him as if he were already the winner, the other competitors were made to feel like also-rans.

Nobody is immune to being psyched out. In fact, I have to

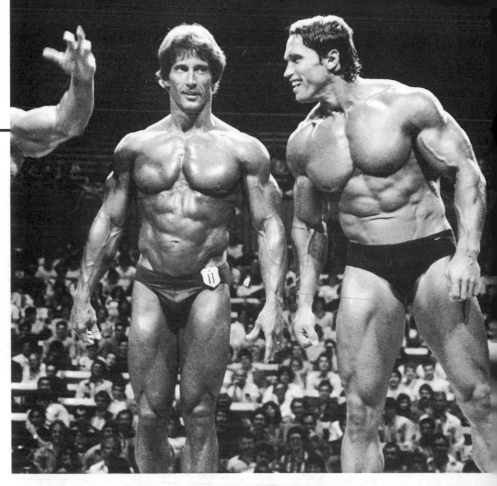

The gentle art of psychological warfare: At the 1980 Olympia, at one point I leaned over and told Frank Zane a joke . . .

. . . and, sure enough, he was laughing so hard that his concentration for his next pose was gone.

admit that I've been on the receiving end of this treatment as well as dishing it out. In 1969, Sergio Oliva pulled a trick on me, which taught me what psychological warfare is really all about. At that contest, Sergio walked around the whole time before we went on stage with his shoulders pulled in, looking very narrow, and wearing a long butcher's coat. I remember thinking that his back didn't look very big. He went into a corner to put some oil on, and I still didn't get a good look. But then he lowered the boom: as he walked out into the light on his way to the stage he said, "Take a look at this!" and he flared his lats—and the way those lats came out, I swear to you, I have never seen anything like it since. It was his way of saying, "That's it, it's all over." And it was. I was destroyed. I looked over at Franco and he tried to tell me it was just the lighting, but I knew better.

During the posing Sergio kept calling me "baby." He was totally in control and at ease—"Hey, baby, take a look at this shot!" —and I just didn't have a chance. But keep in mind, he could only accomplish this because of the genuine quality of his physique. If a lesser bodybuilder had tried any of these things I would have just laughed at him.

And that is the most potent way of psyching out your opponents: by simply being good—by having a dynamite physique and knowing how to present it. Many bodybuilders make the mistake of staying on stage posing as long as they can. But this is risky because the audience is liable to get bored. "Always leave them laughing" is the show-business axiom that applies here. I would try to work the audience up to a fever pitch and then leave the stage. This always meant I would be called back for an encore, which had a devastating effect on the other competitors and the judges as well.

Psychological warfare can be very subtle, just as it can be blatant and brutal. At the 1979 Olympia, as all the contestants were milling around waiting to be weighed, none of them willing to be the first to strip down and show the others his body, Frank Zane slipped in quietly, took off his sweats, and was weighed and gone before anyone realized what was going on. Someone had also arranged that a motel billboard near the airport carried a big welcome for "Frank Zane, Mr. Olympia," a definite psychological jolt for the arriving competitors.

If your personality is such that you prefer not to get involved in efforts like this, just be aware that you are likely to be the target of psyching at some time. Being aware of this is half the battle in keeping these maneuvers from upsetting you and throwing you off your stride.

BOOK FIVE
Health, Nutrition, Diet, and Drugs

CHAPTER 1
Nutrition and Diet

Bodybuilders are constantly concerned with diet—what and how much to eat to build mass or lose body fat. But it is a mistake to diet without first understanding the basic principles of nutrition. These principles allow you to change your body composition through diet while maintaining maximum strength, health, and energy. They help you to build and maintain maximum muscle mass. Therefore, *the basic principles of nutrition are as valuable to a bodybuilder as the basic principles of training.*

Training has been improved over the years, not revolutionized. So I believe the reason we see more and more first-rate competitors entering contests these days is due as much to increased knowledge of nutrition as it is to better methods of training. Needless to say, better nutrition will not create a champion without a lot of hard and dedicated training. I believe that the balance of factors involved is equal parts training, nutrition, and mental attitude.

In the past, bodybuilders approached diet and nutrition on an instinctive, seat-of-the-pants basis. So, at first, they were able to build size, but not get really ripped. When bodybuilders like Harold Poole came along, who were able to get totally cut-up, they tended to be smaller.

In my own early years, I ate well and grew to a tremendous size. But I found that sheer bulk would not take me to the heights I wanted to attain. So, about the time I came to live in California, I began a serious study of diet and nutrition in an attempt to develop a physique that had *everything*—size, shape, proportion, and ripped to shreds! To be a top champion, I reasoned, means you have to push your body to its limit. And the body will not be able to respond to the maximum unless it has enough of the vital nutrients on hand at the right place and the right time.

The fundamentals of nutrition are relatively simple. Learning to apply them to your own training, understanding the individual needs of your own body, how it responds to various kinds of weight-loss or weight-gain diets, is something else again. Like any other aspect of training, ultimately you are forced to fall back on the Instinct Principle.

First learn the fundamentals, isolating the variables that play such an important part in the production of energy and the building and maintenance of muscle tissue. Understanding nutrition is more than just knowing what the various nutrients are and how the body uses them; you have to learn to apply this information to your own needs and your own individual body type.

The Special Requirements of Bodybuilding

Bodybuilders are virtually unique in the demands they place upon their bodies. They require simultaneously maximum muscle mass and minimum body fat, which is an extremely difficult state to attain. Athletes like gymnasts, boxers, and wrestlers, who need to become very lean, follow a training regimen that burns up so many calories that they rarely have to diet to reduce body fat. Nor do they usually attempt, as competition bodybuilders must, to get down to a relative body fat of 3–5 percent for men and 7–9 percent for women. Most strength athletes such as football players work to maximize the size and strength of the muscles with only minor attention to reducing body fat.

Bodybuilders have little margin for error. They have to eat enough to grow, then be able to reduce body fat without sacrificing muscle mass. They can use aerobic exercise to burn up extra calories, but not to the point where their gym workouts suffer. They need to control calories, but get sufficient protein to build and maintain their muscle tissue.

Nutrition is a complex and ever-expanding science, and nutritionists are giving us new information almost daily. However, certain basic principles of nutrition are well established, and mastering these fundamentals is essential for the bodybuilder who wants to achieve his total genetic potential for growth and physical development.

The Basic Nutrients

There are certain basic nutrients which are necessary for the body to achieve maximum growth and energy production. They are:

1. Protein
2. Carbohydrates
3. Fats
4. Vitamins
5. Minerals
6. Water

It is important to know which foods to eat and in what quantity in order to ensure that you get the necessary supply of each of these nutrients. Beyond this, you also have to be concerned with the relative *balance* of each of the nutrients—how much of one you need in relation to how much of the others. No matter what kind of metabolism or body type you possess, the biochemistry of the body requires that certain nutrients be present in specific combinations if you want to maximize the processes of building muscle, burning fat, and creating energy.

Protein

Protein is used by the body to build, repair, and maintain muscle tissue. Protein is made up of a number of amino acids, and the body cannot use the protein you ingest unless all of the necessary amino acids are present. However, the body itself can only produce some of these amino acids. The others, called the essential amino acids, have to be obtained from the foods you eat.

Some foods contain what is called *complete protein*, that is, they provide all the amino acids necessary to produce usable protein. Examples of these foods would be milk, eggs, meat, fish, and various vegetable products, such as soybeans. But even these foods contain differing amounts of usable protein per weight:

Food	% Protein by Weight	% Net Protein Utilization
Soybean flour	42	61
Cheese	22–36	70
Meat and fowl	19–31	68
Fish	18–25	80
Eggs	12	94
Brown rice	8	70
Milk	4	82

This chart tells us, for example, that an egg contains only 12 percent protein by weight. Yet, because of the specific amino acids present in that protein, 94 percent of it can be used by your body. In contrast, 42 percent of soybean flour is protein, but the makeup of that protein is such that your body is able to use only 61 percent of it. So there is a big difference between how much protein a food contains and how much of that protein you can actually use to build muscle.

Eggs are such a good source of quality protein that they are used as a basis of comparison in rating the protein quality of other foods, with eggs given an arbitrary value of 100:

Food	Protein Rating
Eggs	100
Fish	70
Cow's milk	60
Lean beef	69
Soybeans	47
Dry beans	34
Peanuts	43
Whole-grain wheat	44
Brown rice	57
White rice	56
White potato	34

As you can see from this list, foods like rice, potatoes, and beans give you considerably less *usable* protein than eggs or fish. Because these foods lack one or more of the essential amino acids, they cannot satisfy the body's protein needs. You can, however combine two or more sources of this low-quality protein (incomplete protein) to obtain high-quality, complete protein. Combining protein in this way is useful to bodybuilders because it usually involves eating foods that are very low in fat, and thus contain fewer calories than most complete protein sources. When you are trying to build maximum muscle mass with as little body fat as possible, this can be a great advantage.

Since each of the sources of incomplete protein lacks certain of the essential amino acids, you need to be very specific in your food combinations in order to end up with complete protein. In *Diet for a Small Planet* by Frances Moore Lappé (Ballantine Books, 1974), the following combinations are recommended:

Grains plus Seeds

Breads with added seed meals
Breads with sesame or sunflower seed spread
Rice with sesame seeds

Grains plus Milk Products

Cereal with milk
Pasta with milk or cheese
Bread with milk or cheese

Grains plus Legumes

Rice and beans
Wheat bread and baked beans
Corn soy or wheat-soy bread
Legume soup with bread

You could consult a nutritional guide to find out exactly which of the eight essential amino acids are missing in any particular food, but this is actually unnecessary. If you simply remember the food groups as listed above, you will be able to combine your foods correctly to maximize usable protein.

Carbohydrates

Carbohydrates are made up of atoms of carbon, hydrogen, and oxygen synthesized by plants through photosynthesis. The basic carbohydrates are:

Monosaccharides

Glucose (blood sugar)
Fructose (fruit sugar)
Galactose (a kind of milk sugar)

Oliosaccharides

Sucrose (table sugar)
Lactose (milk sugar)
Maltose (malt sugar)

Polysaccharides

Plant polysaccharides (starch and cellulose)
Animal polysaccharides (glycogen)

Simple carbohydrates, such as those found in fruits and processed sugar, metabolize very quickly in the body. *Complex carbohydrates,* starch and cellulose primarily, are found, respectively, in foods like potatoes and rice and in a wide variety of vegetables. Complex carbohydrates take longer to metabolize and therefore have a kind of "time-release" effect in providing energy to the body.

Carbohydrates are the easiest form of food for the body to convert into energy. Once ingested, carbohydrates are turned into *glucose,* which circulates in the bloodstream and fuels muscular contraction, and *glycogen,* which is stored in the muscles and the liver for future use. Adequate supplies of carbohydrate are essential for the serious bodybuilder for a number of reasons:

1. Carbohydrate is a primary form of energy. The carbohydrate stored in the muscles as glycogen is what allows you to do heavy and intense weight training.

2. Muscle size is increased when the body stores glycogen and water in the individual muscle cells.

3. Carbohydrate in the body has a "protein-sparing" effect, keeping the body from burning up excessive protein for energy. (More about this later.)

4. Carbohydrate is the main source of energy that fuels the functioning of the brain, and deprivation can have severe effects on mood, personality, and mental ability.

Fats

Fats are made up of the same elements as carbohydrates—carbon, hydrogen, and oxygen—but the way the atoms are linked together is different. Fats can be found in both plants and animals and are insoluble in water. They are grouped in three categories: *simple fats* (triglycerides), *compound fats* (phospholipides, glucolipids, lipoproteins), and *derived fats* (cholesterol).

Fats in the body serve three basic functions: (1) They provide the major source of stored energy; (2) they serve to cushion and protect the major organs; and (3) they act as an insulator, preserving body heat and protecting against excessive cold.

Fat is the most calorie-dense of any nutrient. A pound of fat contains about 3,500 calories, as opposed to 1,600 calories stored in a pound of protein or carbohydrate.

When you exercise, assuming you stay within your aerobic capacity (don't get out of breath), the body uses fats and carbohydrates for energy on about a 50–50 basis. But the longer you continue to exercise, the higher the percentage of fat used. After three hours or so, the body may derive as much as 80 percent of its energy from fat.

Fat molecules differ biochemically in their composition, being either *saturated, unsaturated,* or *polyunsaturated.* (These terms simply refer to the number of hydrogen atoms that attach to the molecule.) In addition to other factors, diets high in saturated fat tend to raise the cholesterol level of the blood. Therefore, health experts recommend that something like two-thirds of your fat intake be polyunsaturated fats.

Saturated fats are found in foods such as:

Beef
Lamb
Pork
Chicken
Shellfish
Egg yolks
Cream
Milk
Cheese
Butter
Chocolate
Lard
Vegetable shortening

Unsaturated fats are found in:

Avocadoes
Cashews
Olives and olive oil
Peanuts, peanut oil, peanut butter

Polyunsaturated fats are found in:

Almonds
Cottonseed oil
Margarine (usually)
Pecans
Sunflower oil
Corn oil
Fish
Mayonnaise
Safflower oil
Soybean oil
Walnuts

Vitamins

Vitamins are organic substances that the body needs in minute amounts and that we ingest with our foods. Vitamins do not supply energy, nor do they contribute substantially to the mass of the body; rather, they act as catalysts, substances that help to trigger other reactions in the body.

There are two basic categories of vitamins: water-soluble and fat-soluble. The water-soluble vitamins are not stored in the body, and any excess amounts are flushed out in the urine. The fat-soluble vitamins are dissolved and stored in the fatty tissues of the body. It is necessary to take in water-soluble vitamins on a daily basis, but the fat-soluble vitamins can be ingested less often.

Water-Soluble Vitamins

B_6 (pyridoxine)
B_1 (thiamine)
B_2 (riboflavin)
Niacin
Pantothenic acid
Biotin
Choline
Folacin (folic acid)
B_{12} (cyanocobalamin)
Vitamin C (ascorbic acid)

Fat-Soluble Vitamins

Vitamin A
Vitamin D
Vitamin E
Vitamin K

Minerals

Minerals are inorganic substances that the body needs in very small quantities. There are twenty-two metallic elements in the body, which make up about 4 percent of total body weight.

Minerals are found abundantly in the soil and water of the planet and eventually are taken in by the root systems of plants. Human beings obtain minerals by eating the plants or by eating the animals that eat the plants. If you eat a variety of meats and vegetables in your diet, you can usually depend on getting a sufficiency of minerals.

The minerals in the body play a part in a variety of metabolic processes, and contribute to the synthesis of such elements as glycogen, protein, and fats.

Water

Water is often overlooked as a vital nutrient. Water is a major component of the body. It acts as a means of transportation for the various chemicals in the system and the medium in which the various biochemical reactions among the basic nutrients take place.

The body is made up of 40 to 60 percent water. Muscle is composed of 72 percent water by weight, while fat weight is only 20 to 25 percent water. This means that diets or other activities that result in excessive fluid loss have a significant effect on muscle size.

Calories and Energy

A calorie is a measurement of the amount of energy contained in food. By weight different kinds of foods contain different amounts of calories. Proteins and carbohydrates contain approximately 4 calories per gram, and fats 9 calories. Fats are obviously the most efficient fuel when it comes to caloric density, but this also makes them undesirable if you are on a low-calorie program for weight control or reduction.

If you take in more calories than the body can burn off, the excess is stored in the form of fat (adipose cells) distributed throughout the body. It doesn't matter whether the excess is in the form of protein, carbohydrate, or fat—the body breaks it down and stores it against a time when the body will require more energy than provided by food intake. At this point, the fat in the adipose cells will be retrieved and metabolized to make up the difference.

If your body has all of the nutrients it needs to function optimally, and if you are eating at least the minimum quantity of the various foods required at any given time by your digestive and energy-producing systems, fat gain and fat loss is a matter of simple arithmetic:

Eating 3,500 calories more than you need = 1 pound of fat gained
Eating 3,500 calories less than you need = 1 pound of fat lost

But most diets unfortunately do not take these factors into consideration, and therefore a number of undesirable things can happen:

1. The body can begin to metabolize muscle tissue.
2. The body's ability to metabolize fat can be impaired.
3. Various vitamin or mineral deficiencies can occur.
4. The energy output of the body can be impaired.
5. A number of physical and pyschological symptoms can be experienced.

Because of the possibility that these problems can occur, any diet regimen (whether for weight gain or weight loss) has to take into account the body's need for certain nutritional minimums and for a relative balance of various foods in the daily food intake. The latter is usually referred to as a "balanced diet."

Exercise and Energy Expenditure

Your body burns up calories in two basic ways: in basal metabolism, the energy it takes to maintain life over a period of time; and in physical activity. Your basal metabolism, or resting metabolic rate (RMR), is related to how much muscle mass you have. The more lean your body mass, the higher your RMR. The formula to calculate this is:

$$\text{Lean body mass pounds} \div 2.205 \times 30.4$$

By this reckoning, a person with a lean body mass of 150 pounds would have an RMR of about 2,100 calories, while a 250-pound individual would burn up about 3,500 calories, irrespective of vigorous exercise. Obviously, this means that the larger person has to eat a lot more to maintain body weight and can lose weight on a diet that would be fattening for the smaller one.

The amount of calories you burn when exercising depends on the kind of activity you are engaged in. The more weight you move—whether your own body weight or a barbell—the more energy it takes. Here are examples of the energy expenditure of various types of exercise:

Activity	Calories Burned per Hour
Sitting	72–84
Walking (3 mph)	240–300
Calisthenics	300–360
Cycling (10 mph)	360–420
Jogging (5 mph)	420–480
Skiing	420–480
Running (5.5 mph)	600–660

The energy expenditure of bodybuilding is largely determined on how intense the training is. When you lift heavy weights and take long rest periods between sets, you burn relatively few calories. When you train continuously, going from one set to another, one exercise to another, with very little rest, you burn considerable calories over the one and a half or two hours of your workout. When you train on a split schedule, with two workouts a day, you burn up that much more energy—which is why I always trained in this fashion to get cut-up and ready for a contest. (Exactly how many calories are consumed in this kind of workout is hard to say. But an expert once estimated that Franco Columbu and I each burned up close to 2,000 calories total in our two daily competition workouts.)

However, it is also obvious from the above table that aerobic exercise such as running is the most efficient for burning up calories and speeding up the process of metabolizing body fat. Running for a half hour every day will result in loss of about a pound of fat every ten days in addition to the weight loss obtained by dieting and other kinds of training.

Nutritional Minimums

Depriving the body of calories is one thing (the body has calories stored in the form of fat that it can use to make up for this deprivation), but depriving it of essential nutrients is something else. Bodybuilders put a great strain on the body as they strive to get it to respond to its maximum. Therefore any nutritional deprivation can be much more serious for the bodybuilder than for someone leading a less physically demanding life.

There is some disagreement over what actually constitutes nutritional minimums for both athletes and nonathletes, but the following guidelines represent a reasonable approach.

Protein. The generally recommended amount of protein in the average diet is **1 gram per kilo (2.2 pounds) of body weight.** A few experts believe that even hard-training bodybuilders do not require any more protein than this, that, in fact, the need for protein in the diet is highly overrated. However, the majority of bodybuilders prefer to take in larger amounts of protein, recommending about **1 gram per pound of body weight.**

When a bodybuilder is trying to get in shape for a contest, his goals have to include both maximum muscle mass and minimum body fat, which means eating enough protein to build and maintain lean body tissue but no more than necessary—because the excess will simply be turned into body fat. So, for most individuals, no more than 1 gram of protein for each pound of body weight is recommended.

Carbohydrates. The need for carbohydrates in the diet varies a great deal depending on your level of activity. The body requires about **60 grams of carbohydrate** simply to carry on the basic processes of the nervous system (the brain, for example, is fueled almost entirely by carbohydrate).

Carbohydrate is also an important fuel for muscular activity. If your diet is too low in carbohydrates, your workouts will suffer. Many bodybuilders attempt to lose weight by overly restricting carbohydrates and increasing ingestion of protein, but, as we have seen, carbohydrate, on a gram-for-gram basis, is not more fattening than protein and is the food from which the body most easily obtains energy.

The general rule of thumb is to eat enough carbohydrate to get you through your workouts and to keep you out of a state of "ketosis" (see p. 683). However, when you are trying to get cut-up for a contest the kind of carbohydrate you include in your diet becomes extremely important. Complex carbohydrates found in vegetables, rice, and potatoes provide energy and nutrition with minimum calories. The simple carbohydrates in fruits are a good short-term energy source. But foods containing processed sugar—cakes, candy, soft drinks, processed foods with sugar added—are virtually "empty calories," adding tremendously to your caloric intake while providing very little in the way of nutrition.

Fats. Getting enough fats is seldom a problem in the American diet. Eggs, red meats, dairy products, and oils are all very high in fat. It is common to see diets that contain as much as 50 percent fats. For health reasons, the normal recommendation is to keep fats below 30 percent. Bodybuilders will find it easier to get cut-up by keeping fats even lower than this, 20 percent being a reasonable figure. (See Balanced Diet, p. 681.)

Vitamins and minerals. The debate on what our actual vitamin and mineral requirements might be is never-ending. Many nutritionists feel that a balanced diet of properly prepared, nonprocessed foods provides an adequate supply of vitamins and minerals, even for serious athletes. Nonetheless, most bodybuilders prefer taking a variety of vitamin and mineral supplements to be certain they are getting enough. There is no clear evidence that it is necessary for most athletes to take supplements, but bodybuilders are a special case—they are virtually the only group of athletes who work toward building maximum muscle mass while at the same time attempting to reduce body fat to such extremes.

It is quite probable that the combination of intense training and strict dieting causes bodybuilders to experience some nutrient deprivation. So it makes sense for bodybuilders to take vitamin and mineral supplements to optimize their training and physical development. But ingesting "megadoses" of these supplements—100 to 1,000 times the U.S. government Recommended Daily Allowance (RDA)—is probably just a waste of money. Excess amounts of the water-soluble vitamins (such as vitamin C) are simply eliminated from the body in the urine. Megadoses of the fat-soluble vitamins as well as certain minerals can actually be dangerous to your health.

Some health experts assert that the only vitamins you should ingest are those from "natural" sources. However, the action in the body of natural vitamins extracted from foods and synthetic vitamins, created in the laboratory, seems to be identical. Most nutritionists agree that the body cannot tell the difference between the natural vitamin and its synthesized form. (An exception to this is vitamin E, because the natural form is slightly different and more effective than the synthesized variety.)

When bodybuilders train very hard they lose excessive amounts of mineral salts such as sodium and potassium chloride through perspiration. These minerals, along with chlorine, are called "electrolytes" because they exist in the body as electrically charged particles. One of the functions of electrolytes is to control the exchange of fluids between various parts of the body, maintaining a constant flow of nutrients and eliminating waste products. So if you lose excessive amounts of water through perspiration your capacity for training can be severely limited, as well as your tolerance for heat. This can lead to cramps or, in more severe cases, heat exhaustion or heat stroke.

Usually, this loss can be replaced by drinking water and taking in small amounts of salt. The potassium levels can be replenished by eating a balanced diet. However, many bodybuilders preparing for competition will use diuretics (which I do not recommend), which also contribute to mineral loss. Some users of diuretics have found that a potassium supplement helped them to avoid cramps. However, at a recent Mr. Universe contest one young amateur bodybuilder took too much potassium and ended up with violent nausea that almost caused him to withdraw from the competition. So, remember, too much can be as harmful as too little.

The "Supersaturation" Theory

Experts are often heard decrying the ingestion of excess protein, vitamins, and minerals by bodybuilders on the grounds that the body is only capable of using small amounts of the various nutrients at any one time. They say it is useless to eat more than 60 grams of protein at any one meal because the body cannot use more than that at any given time. Other nutritionists have done studies in which they measured the elimination of water-soluble vitamins in the urine and concluded that the body was simply excreting almost all of the supplementation.

Bodybuilders and many other athletes, however, do not accept most of these theories. Their experience tells them that extra protein and vitamin and mineral supplements do make a difference. One idea that might explain why they could be correct is something called the "supersaturation" theory.

You've heard the cliché that there is never a cop around when you need one. Suppose there are a hundred violent crimes committed on the streets in a given city each night, and that city employs a police force of five hundred men. There are certainly enough police to take care of each of these crimes—*provided they are in the vicinity of the crime when it occurs.* If they are across town, or even two blocks away, they can't be of much help to the victim. Some nutritionists apply that theory to the question of what to eat for maximum growth.

If the body is supersaturated with nutrients whenever an important reaction begins to occur—protein synthesis, for example, or the creation of creatine phosphate for energy—*the nutrients required are right there on the spot.* Therefore the body is able to work and grow in ways that would not be possible if you accepted lower nutritional minimums.

This theory accounts for why bodybuilders have traditionally attempted to "build up"—allowing themselves to put on a little fat while trying to build maximum muscle mass—and then "cut up" by dieting strenuously and trying to keep what muscle they have without creating any significant amount of new mass. First they supersaturate, then they try to hold what they have in a state of nutritional deprivation.

Balanced Diet

The body works best when you ingest foods in certain combinations. The required dietary "balance" is pretty much the same for the bodybuilder as for anyone else. The currently recommended balance, according to the McGovern Select Committee on Nutrition and Human Needs, is approximately: protein, 12 percent; carbohydrate, 58 percent; and fats, 30 percent.

In my own career, I usually found myself eating a diet balanced quite differently: protein, 40 percent; carbohydrate, 40 percent; and fats, 20 percent. It should be remembered, however, that I was 240 pounds and training very hard. My 40 percent of carbohydrate represented more actual food than the average person's 58 percent—so I was certainly getting all of the nutrients my body needed.

However, there are bodybuilders who go much too far in their pursuit of protein, eating as much as 70 percent protein in their diets. Others believe protein is not that important, and eat as little as 10 or 12 percent. I believe that neither of these approaches is likely to be very successful.

There are also bodybuilders who eat only a few foods for months on end—tuna, chicken, fruit, and salads, for example. This may help them to cut down on body fat, but it also prevents them from taking in all the nutrients they need for maximum energy and growth. Cutting way down on any of the general food groups leaves you open to developing vitamin and mineral deficiencies. Eating a lot of fruit (as in the "Beverly Hills Diet") makes it difficult to obtain sufficient protein and a wide enough variety of vitamins and minerals. Vegetarian and super-high-carbohydrate diets might not provide enough protein for a bodybuilder attempting to build maximum muscle mass. Diets too high in protein can put an unhealthy strain on your kidneys and liver, cause your body to lose calcium, and make you fat.

I remember Ken Waller sitting down to three high-protein portions at each meal, thinking his body could use all of this at one time. The result was that Ken usually had to lose a lot of body fat prior to a contest in order to get in shape.

Bodybuilders who go to extremes in diet usually opt for the high-protein approach. They feel this maximizes muscle growth and minimizes body fat at the same time. However, in addition to the problems listed above, a diet too high in protein and too low in carbohydrates can cause you to lose muscle mass rather than gain it, due to the loss of the "protein-sparing" effect of the carbohydrate.

The "Protein-Sparing" Effect

Carbohydrate not only supplies the body with energy but has a "protein-sparing" effect as well. As long as your body can use carbohydrates for energy, it will spare the protein you eat to be used for building and maintaining your muscle structure. In the absence of carbohydrate, your body will attempt to use the available protein to supply energy, metabolizing the protein in the muscle structure you have worked so hard to build.

Too little carbohydrate in the body also affects how you look —your muscles shrink as they lose glycogen and you end up with a drawn, pinched look. As good a bodybuilder as he is, Frank Zane often has this look on stage instead of looking healthy and full of energy. Danny Padilla also developed this look at the 1981 Olympia due to a very low-carbohydrate diet.

The Importance of Glycogen

Much of the muscle size that bodybuilders create comes from the enhancement of the "support systems" in the muscles rather than simple growth of the muscle itself. One such support system is the increase in blood supply to the muscles that accompanies intense weight training. Another is the ability of the body to store more glycogen in well-trained muscles.

Glycogen is simply carbohydrate stored in the muscle, ready to be turned into energy for muscular contraction. The trained muscle increases its ability to store glycogen, and since glycogen is bound together with water (2.7 grams of water for each gram of glycogen), this extra bulk in the muscles causes them to swell up and appear larger.

I have described the state of being "in shape" for bodybuilding as having maximum muscle mass and minimum body fat at the same time. Actually, I should add one more element to this: seeing to it that your muscles are as packed full of glycogen as possible to increase your apparent mass and size to the maximum.

Ketosis

In the absence of adequate carbohydrate, the body has difficulty metabolizing body fat. The process of fat breakdown requires the presence of both fat and carbohydrate. If your body lacks the necessary carbohydrate, the process cannot be completed and you end up with incompletely metabolized fat molecules in your system. These are called "ketone bodies," and being in this state is called "ketosis."

The high-protein, low-carb diet for weight loss was first popular in the United States as early as 1860. The concept returns to favor every few decades because it does *seem* to work. Especially for bodybuilders. When you follow this kind of diet:

1. You get to eat a lot of high-protein foods, so you do not feel deprived. Eggs are usually recommended on this diet, as are chicken, fish, meats and even milk, cheese, and butter, all of which contain little or no carbs but lots of fat.

2. You lose a significant amount of body weight within the first week.

3. Your appetite tends to diminish. This is due to the changed biochemistry of the body on a low-carb diet.

But, as I said above, this kind of diet only *seems* to work. Actually, what is happening is that:

1. Because these high-protein foods contain a lot of fat, you end up with more calories than you need.

2. The weight loss you experience is not all fat. As the carbohydrate level in your system declines you begin to dehydrate and lose a lot of water weight (much of it from the muscle cells). Then, in the absence of carbohydrate, your body will metabolize as much muscle tissue as body fat. So for every two pounds of weight loss after the initial dehydration, about one pound is muscle. Hardly a good trade-off for a bodybuilder.

3. Your appetite diminishes because of the presence of fatty ketone bodies in the bloodstream, owing to the body's inability to completely metabolize fat without the presence of carbohydrates. So your energy diminishes along with your appetite, and you also are liable to develop dizziness, nausea, and a whole host of other symptoms.

4. When you exercise, you will quickly use up the carbohydrate stored as glycogen in the muscles and will run out of energy; and the depletion of glycogen will make your muscles shrink and look smaller.

In sum, dieting by starving yourself of carbohydrate is not a good idea, either for the average person or for the competition bodybuilder. The disadvantages of following this regimen far outweigh any advantages.

Eating and Training

Many young bodybuilders ask me for advice about what and when they should eat in relation to their training program. The muscles require an ample supply of blood during training, since a lot of the "pump" you experience is from blood swelling up your muscles. But if the digestive system is also using excess amounts of blood to digest a big meal, there won't be enough to go around and your muscles will suffer for it. When you eat too heavily before training, you are setting up a conflict in the body, a demand for excess blood in too many places at once. This is why parents are right when they tell children not to go swimming right after a big meal; lack of adequate blood supply to the muscles used in swimming can lead to problems like severe cramps.

Training with a full stomach can be a very unpleasant experience. You feel bloated, sluggish, and slow, and a really hard set can make you feel nauseated.

The body metabolizes food at different rates. It takes from two to six hours for the stomach to empty its contents. Foods rich in carbohydrates digest first, followed by protein foods; fatty foods are the last to leave.

When you wake up in the morning and haven't eaten anything for eight to twelve hours, your body is depleted of carbohydrate. Since carbohydrate is needed to produce the glycogen the muscles need for intense contraction, it makes sense to eat a high-carbohydrate breakfast before going to the gym to train in the morning.

A light meal of fruit, fruit juice, or toast can be eaten before you train and will give you energy without slowing you down. However, a breakfast that includes eggs, meat, or cheese—all high in both protein and fats—will take longer to digest, so you would do better not to eat things like this before you train.

It is not a good idea to eat a big meal immediately after a workout either. You put your body under great stress when you train and you need to give your system time to return to normal, for the blood to leave the muscles and the stress reaction to diminish. This way your digestive system will function as it was designed to, turning your food into energy and masses of new muscle tissue. Wait awhile, then eat a well-balanced meal.

CHAPTER 2

How to Gain or Lose Weight

Being really skinny and having trouble putting on any appreciable amount of weight is most likely to be a problem for those who are highly ectomorphic in body type, but it can happen to anyone who takes in too few calories to allow the body to put on weight.

Obviously, you are better off adding muscle weight to your frame than fat. However, until you increase your caloric intake, you will have trouble building muscle no matter how hard you train. Individuals who are especially skinny usually don't eat enough to provide the body with the raw materials it needs for growth. So, along with their training, they need to relearn their eating habits.

How to Gain Weight

I have outlined a sample diet plan for gaining weight. Since I don't think you ought to suddenly introduce large quantities of food into your system that your body will not be able to handle, the program is constructed on three levels, to be followed in this order:

1. Begin eating according to Level I, and continue on this level until you stop gaining weight, then go on to Level II.

2. If after three weeks you are not gaining weight on the Level I diet, go on to Level II.

3. Once eating the Level II diet, continue on it as long as you continue to gain weight. When the weight gains cease, go on to Level III.

4. If after three weeks on Level II you don't experience any gain in weight, go on to Level III.

To eat more, you have to eat more often—at least five meals a day. However, instead of sitting down to five separate meals, a good alternative is to eat three good meals and supplement your food intake with high-calorie, high-protein drinks. This is exactly what I did when I was fifteen years old and desperate to gain weight, and I found that drinking protein drinks not only satisfied my extra need for calories and protein, but it cost a lot less than other protein foods.

Weight-Gain Menu Plan

The primary need of the ectomorph is for extra calories to provide the energy and nutrients to promote growth, but *not* empty calories—white flour, sugar, soft drinks, and other nonfoods that take up space in your stomach without supplying you with sufficient vital nutrients.

Those who are already heavy eaters may be surprised at the following weight-gain recommendations, but ectomorphs are generally very lean precisely because they are not big eaters. However, if you are an ectomorphic type and yet find that the Level I diet or even that of Level II is actually *less* than you normally eat, obviously you are going to have to increase your food intake even further and go right on to a higher level. Just make sure that the food you eat is wholesome and nutritious.

If you eat according to the menu plans detailed below and supplement your meals with the recommended protein drinks, you will be getting more than enough protein and shouldn't give it another thought. For ectomorphs, who have a great deal of problems adding body weight, the key is hard training and *a lot more calories*, not any lack of protein. To demonstrate this, I have included the approximate protein content of each of the suggested meals.

Level I

BREAKFAST

2 eggs, preferably poached, but any style O.K.
¼ pound meat, fish, or fowl
8 ounces milk
1 slice of whole-grain toast with butter
(protein = approx. 52 grams)

LUNCH

¼ pound meat, fish, fowl, or cheese
1 or 2 slices of whole-grain bread
8 ounces milk or fresh juice
(protein = approx. 43 grams)

DINNER

½ pound meat, fish, or fowl
Baked potato with butter or sour cream
Large raw salad
8 ounces milk

(protein = approx. 48 grams)

Level II

BREAKFAST

3 eggs, poached or any style
¼ pound meat, fish, fowl, or cheese
8 ounces milk
1 or 2 slices whole-grain toast with butter

(protein = approx. 61 grams)

LUNCH

½ pound meat, fish, fowl, or cheese (or any combination)
2 slices whole-grain bread with butter or mayonnaise
8 ounces milk
1 piece fresh fruit

(protein = approx. 71 grams)

DINNER

½ pound meat, fish, fowl, or cheese (or any combination)
Baked or boiled white or sweet potato
Large raw salad

(protein = approx. 59 grams)

Level III

BREAKFAST

4 eggs, poached or any style
8 ounces milk
1 or 2 slices whole-grain bread with butter
1 piece fresh fruit

Or hot oatmeal, bran cereal, or other cooked cereal in place of fruit and bread, sweetened only with fructose; use with half-and-half or heavy cream if desired.

(protein = approx. 72 grams)

LUNCH

½ pound meat, fish, fowl, or cheese
1 or 2 slices of whole-grain bread with butter or mayonnaise
8–16 ounces of milk
1 piece fresh fruit (with cottage cheese if desired)

(protein = approx. 74 grams)

DINNER

½ pound to 1 pound of meat, fish, fowl, or cheese (or any combination)
Baked or steamed potato, or baked or boiled beans
Lightly steamed fresh vegetable
Large raw salad
1 piece fresh fruit
8 ounces milk

(protein = approx. 112 grams)

High-Protein, High-Calorie Drinks

The trick in making protein and calories work best for you is to keep the food energy in your body available throughout the day, not just at normal meal times. The ideal way to do this is by supplementing your regular meals with special high-protein, high-calorie drinks.

There are many commercial products on the market advertised as "weight gain" aids, but I prefer to rely on creating my own drinks, since that way I know precisely what goes into them and what kind of nutritional benefit I am getting.

I began mixing my own protein drinks right from the start, but when I was fifteen years old I didn't have access to the kind of protein powder you can buy today. Instead, I put together a drink combining things like skim-milk powder, eggs, and honey, put it in a thermos bottle, and took it with me to school or work. That way I could drink half of it around ten in the morning, between breakfast and lunch, and the other half around three o'clock. The habit of having a protein drink with me proved even more valuable when I was in the army and couldn't always depend on getting three good meals a day. Sometimes my container of protein drink was the only dependable supply of protein my body would get all day.

As I learned more about nutrition, I developed protein-drink formulas that were even more effective and nutritious than those

I invented back in Austria. But the purpose remained the same: to supersaturate the body with protein, making the necessary amino acids available for maximum muscle building, and to supply the necessary calories to fuel training and growth.

The best protein powders are those that derive their amino acids from *milk and egg* sources. Most of these do not mix easily with juice or milk, so use a blender if you have one. Always check the label of any protein powder you are considering purchasing. For example, a typical milk-and-egg protein powder would have a nutritional content something like the following:

Serving size 1 ounce (about ½ cup)
Calories 110
Protein per serving 26 grams
Carbohydrate per serving 0 grams
Fat per serving 0 grams

Each of the drinks below is made in sufficient quantity for *three servings a day: preferably to be drunk between breakfast and lunch, between lunch and dinner, and an hour or so before you go to bed.* However, because protein takes a long time to digest, be sure to have the protein drink at least one and a half hours before a workout.

Level I
(protein = approx. 50 grams)

In a blender place 20 ounces milk or juice, 4 ounces whipping cream, 2 raw eggs, and 2 teaspoons of lecithin granules; blend for an instant. Wait several minutes for the lecithin granules to dissolve, then add ¼ cup of good-quality milk-and-egg protein powder and blend until mixed. If you wish, you can substitute 1 ounce of safflower oil and 3 ounces of water for cream. For flavor, use your imagination: a very ripe banana, vanilla extract, any other fruit or flavoring. To make the drink sweeter, add a tablespoon or less of fructose—do not use high-sucrose foods like ice cream or chocolate syrup. This drink will yield approximately 40 ounces of liquid.

Level II
(protein = approx. 72 grams)

In a blender place 16 ounces milk or juice, 6 ounces whipping cream, 4 raw eggs, and 4 teaspoons of lecithin granules. Blend for an instant. Wait several minutes for lecithin granules to completely dissolve. Add ½ cup of milk-and-egg protein and blend until mixed. Substitute 2 ounces of safflower oil and 5 ounces of water for cream if desired. Try alternating the cream one day with oil and water the next. Flavor as above, except that you can use as much as 2 tablespoons of fructose for sweetness.

Level III
(protein = approx. 98 grams)

Place in blender 16 ounces milk or juice, 8 ounces whipping cream, 6 raw eggs, and 6 teaspoons of lecithin and blend for an instant. Wait several minutes for the lecithin granules to totally dissolve. Add ¾ cup of milk-and-egg protein and blend until mixed. Substitute 3 ounces safflower oil and 6 ounces of water for cream if desired. Flavor as desired.

If you find your weight gain is not as large as you would like, even at Level III, here is an even more potent drink you can add to your diet (protein = approx. 96 grams): Place in blender 12 ounces milk or juice, 12 ounces whipping cream, 6 raw eggs, and 6 teaspoons of lecithin granules. Blend for an instant. Wait several minutes for lecithin granules to completely dissolve and add ¾ cup milk-and-egg protein. Blend until mixed. Substitute 4 ounces of safflower oil and 8 ounces water for cream if desired. Flavor as desired.

While vitamin and mineral supplements are not specifically fundamental to gaining weight, making sure you have no nutrient deficiencies is essential to making optimum progress in bodybuilding, whether your short-term goals are weight gain or weight loss.

How to Lose Weight

Many bodybuilders have no trouble gaining muscle mass but are constantly fighting to stay lean. This is most often the case with endomorphic body types, but can be a problem for anyone who has a tendency to overeat and affects almost anyone as they get older since the metabolism tends to slow down with advancing age, causing the body to use fewer calories. Endomorphic types develop muscle, but have a built-in resistance to developing lean muscularity. About 20 percent of endomorphs suffer from low thyroid, resulting in excessive storage of fat; low thyroid can be diagnosed and treated by a physician.

Getting rid of excess fat is a matter of simple mathematics—take in fewer calories than you expend, and your body will have to burn fat to make up the energy difference. But cutting down your food intake too drastically can have unfortunate side effects. If you don't absorb enough nutrients, you will not have the energy to train intensely and your body will not be able to build quality muscle.

Fasting would seem to be the fastest way to lose fat. But the proportion of muscle mass loss to fat loss when you fast is 60 percent to 40 percent. You actually lose more muscle than fat.

The answer is a balanced, low-calorie diet that provides sufficient protein for muscle growth and carbohydrates for energy, yet still requires the body to metabolize stored body fat. This means making every calorie count—never eating anything that does not satisfy your nutritional needs and trying to get your nutrition in foods containing the fewest possible calories.

The worst way to try to lose fat is in a hurry. Instead of trying to lose weight over a period of a month or two, give yourself six months or even a year. Two years, if that's what it takes. The slower it comes off, the easier it will be to keep it off.

When you are trying to lose fat and keep it off, assuming you are sensible enough not to be eating high-sugar soft drinks and desserts, your best bet is to restrict your intake of foods high in fats and oils (see lists on p. 693).

Although you may wish to limit your intake of carbohydrates as one way of cutting back on calories, remember that carbohydrate is necessary for energy and to provide a number of necessary nutrients. However, carbohydrate comes in different forms: the complex carbohydrates of vegetables and the simple sugars in fruit are far superior nutritionally than anything that contains processed sugar. The body copes with sugar in the system by releasing quantities of insulin to help metabolize it. Processed sugar comes in such a concentrated form, one that nature did not design, that it fools the body into thinking there is more food in the system than there really is. It then releases too much insulin, which lowers the blood sugar level below acceptable levels, leaving you in a temporary hypoglycemic state—hungry, depressed, and irritable. Remember that most fast foods, canned foods, and highly processed foods have a lot of extra sugar in them.

Use the lists below as a guide to the protein and carbohydrate you may want to include (or exclude) in your weight-loss plan.

Protein

Fish (any low-fat source; some fish and shellfish are relatively high in fat; shrimp contains high amounts of cholesterol; when in doubt, check a food guide)

Fowl (chicken, turkey; remove skin, which is high in fat; some fowl, such as duck, are higher in fat)

Eggs

Canned tuna (packed in water, not oil)

Non-fat milk (not "low-fat")

Milk-and-egg protein powder

TO BE EATEN WITH CARE: The following protein foods are nutritious but tend to be high in fat.

Beef (stick to lean cuts only; a regular 3-ounce sirloin steak gives you about 330 calories, with 20 grams protein, 27 grams fat; by comparison, a very lean cut of the same size might contain 220 calories, with 24 grams protein and only 13 grams fat)

Pork (lean cuts only; pork includes ham, sausage, and bacon, as well)

Lamb (lamb chops are higher in fat than pork chops)

Cheese (some cheeses are higher in fat than others; if you are a cheese lover, check a food guide for lower-fat kinds)

Whole milk (and other dairy products like butter, cream, and sour cream)

Carbohydrates

Vegetables (green vegetables especially—broccoli, asparagus, brussels sprouts, peas, etc.; whenever possible, eat vegetables either raw or lightly steamed)

Beans (not out of a can, too high in sugar; beans are not a complete protein, so need to be eaten in combination with meat, rice, or some other complementary food)

Salads (go easy on the dressing)

Fruits (fresh, not canned)

Whole wheat or rye bread

Baked potatoes (a medium potato contains only about 100 calories; pass up the butter or sour cream)

Rice (not white, processed rice or Minute Rice)

Avoid butter, sour cream, and such oily condiments as ketchup and mayonnaise. Bake, broil, or steam your food—don't fry or boil. Go light on salad dressings: a tablespoon of oil contains 100 calories, the same as a pat of butter. Cut down on your use of salt. A few other useful rules:

1. As recommended above, give yourself time to lose the fat—if you are losing more than two pounds a week you are probably losing muscle as well as fat.

2. Lower your caloric intake until you begin to notice weight loss. Stay at this level as long as you continue to lose weight. If a diet is successful, don't make it more severe.

3. Take vitamin and mineral supplements to ensure you are getting adequate nutrition.

4. Eat fresh food whenever you can. Canned, frozen, or otherwise processed foods are less nutritious and are generally loaded with sugar, salt, and chemical additives.

5. Learn to count calories. Otherwise, it is easy to think you are eating less than you really are. Keep track of your eating habits in your training diary.

Contest Dieting

There are a few fortunate individuals who find themselves at or below their contest weight as a competition approaches without making any special effort. Franco has always been like that—while I was looking for ways to eliminate body fat, he was laughing at me and eating pasta.

Obviously, bodybuilders who are close to their contest weight or below it are not going to have to worry about spending weeks dieting, though even they may have to go on an immediate precontest diet to eliminate those last few vestiges of subcutaneous fat still remaining. Several months before a competition these lean bodybuilders may actually need to increase their caloric intake in order to keep their body weight up. Certainly, for a bodybuilder who is already ripped to spend months dieting is bound to be detrimental to the quality of his physique.

But for those of us who do want to burn off excessive fat in the months prior to competition, there are two levels of dieting to be considered:

1. A gradual cutting back on caloric intake eight to twelve weeks before a contest (depending on how much fat you have to lose). The aim of this stage of the diet is to lose not more than two pounds of fat a week.

2. If necessary, a superstrict diet beginning three to six weeks before the contest to give you maximum definition and muscularity. This stage is designed to rid the body of as much fat and excess fluid as possible.

Obviously, if you are way overweight to start with and have twenty-five or thirty pounds to lose, it is going to take twelve to fifteen weeks to get rid of the excess fat at a rate of two pounds a week. For forty pounds, you are looking at twenty weeks. You can lose as much as you want if you just give yourself enough time.

Some bodybuilders, Ken Waller for example, actually prefer getting very heavy, then coming way down to get into contest shape. But this takes a top professional who has learned everything he needs to know about how to handle his own body. With dieting, as with competition training, it is important to understand your body type, to learn how your body reacts to dieting and vary your diet program accordingly.

The Basics of Contest Dieting

The best way to simplify your dieting is not to allow yourself to get too far overweight in the first place. For a middle- or lightweight bodybuilder, ten to fifteen pounds over contest weight should be considered maximum in most cases; for a heavyweight, fifteen to twenty pounds is the most I would recommend. In my own career, I always lowered my body weight gradually, cutting out fattening foods in my diet and subjecting myself to lots of hard, calorie-consuming training and exercise. As you gradually reduce your calorie intake and begin to burn up additional calories through exercise, the fat will start to melt away.

As you go along, gradually make your diet stricter. Cut back and watch to see if weight loss occurs. If it does not, cut back further. As long as you are losing fat, stay at that dietary level.

Remember, though, a too restricted diet for too long can cost you lean body mass as well as fat. Also, when you try to function for long periods of time on 1,200 or 1,500 calories, your metabolism tends to slow down and use up less energy. It is a good idea, however, to cut way down every few days—maybe to as low as 900 to 1,200 calories—just to "shock" the body a little with this unfamiliar demand.

There are certain other minimums which ought to be observed: (1) Do not take in less than 1 gram of protein for every kilo (2.2 pounds) of body weight; and (2) include a minimum of 60 to 80 grams of complex carbohydrate in your diet, adding more carbohydrate as necessary to fuel your workouts.

When you are preparing for a contest, and are not concerned with building a lot of additional muscle mass, you don't need to eat excessive amounts of protein. At this point, *quality* becomes more important than quantity.

But you still need *adequate* amounts of protein even the day before the contest. Just because you are not primarily concerned with packing on mass doesn't mean that you treat your body as if you expected it to shrink. To keep as much lean body mass as possible, you must supply your muscles with the amino acids they require to maintain their size.

By "adequate" I mean just that. I can remember Ken Waller sitting down to a meal consisting of entire chickens and bragging that he could outeat anybody in the restaurant. Ken became Mr. Universe with those habits, but I wouldn't suggest anyone imitate him. I recommend taking in small amounts of protein at frequent intervals—only about 40 grams at a time—so that your body has sufficient protein available at all times.

I always dealt with the need for quality protein by making sure I ate a variety of different protein foods. For breakfast, I would have scrambled eggs and a hamburger; after my morning workout, I ate some chicken salad, then went to the beach to work on my tan; after the beach, I would have lunch—chicken or fish, and sometimes another hamburger; following my afternoon workout, I'd have a plate of tuna salad; and for dinner, more fish, eggs, or lean meat.

By eating this way I knew my body would be getting all the amino acids it needed. But I was also careful to eat low-fat sources of protein. Remember, any protein you eat in addition to what your body needs is simply treated by the body as extra calories, and extra calories are the last thing you need when you are working so hard to get cut-up and superdefined.

The easiest way to cut back on calories is to cut back on fat. Fat contains 3,500 calories per pound, while protein and carbs have only about 600. If you consult the chapter on nutrition (beginning p. 668) you will see that certain meats are high in fat (beef, pork, and lamb, for example), as are eggs, whole milk, cheese, and other dairy products.

The competition diet should include carbohydrates in the form of fresh fruits, vegetables, and grains. Some bodybuilders avoid bread, but whole-wheat bread is high in fiber and nutrition and relatively low in calories—as long as you leave off the butter. Potatoes are a wonderful source of vitamins and minerals, and a medium-size potato without butter or sour cream contains only about 100 calories.

Calorie Counting

As you probably have noticed, I have not tried to tell you exactly how many calories you should consume in order to get cut-up. This is not because calories don't count—they do. I just don't believe in counting them.

Instead, I prefer to look at results. For example, when I was preparing for the 1980 Mr. Olympia contest in Australia I had

Franco shoot photos of me once a week so I could see what effect my training and dieting was having. Those pictures told me all I needed to know. If I thought the results were coming too slow, I made changes in my program. If I liked what I saw, I kept doing the same thing.

Dieting, like training, should be done intelligently. Check your results as you go along and make any changes you think are necessary to further your progress. Since your metabolism can vary from season to season, year to year, and since one individual varies so much from the next, no arbitrary number is going to be a sufficient guide for you when it comes to designing a diet.

There are plenty of foods you can cut back on without hurting your nutritional balance. In the months prior to a contest, I found that cutting out sweets and desserts, doing without bread and butter, and eliminating wine with dinner, in combination with intense twice-a-day training, got me hard and defined with relative ease. Keep track of what you are eating in your training diary; you might find to your surprise that you are actually eating more than you thought.

If your fat loss is slower than you would like, cutting back on calories is not always the answer; instead, try combining a reasonable diet with increased aerobic exercises—running, bicycle riding, and the like. This way you burn off fat without the danger of undernourishing your body. Remember that fat is basically stored energy. It is fuel waiting to be used. The most natural way of getting rid of it is by burning it up through increased activity.

Ketone/Carbohydrate Balance

Even though ketosis is not itself a desirable state, it can be used to your advantage when you are trying to establish a competition diet involving the minimum amounts of various foods. You can test for ketosis by using Ketostix, which are available at most drugstores. When there are ketone bodies in your system, the test sticks will turn purple when they come in contact with your urine.)

To help guide you in determining the minimum amount of carbohydrate you should have in your diet, gradually cut down on carbs and test occasionally for ketosis. When you finally see the sticks start to turn purple, increase the amount of carbs in your diet until the ketone reaction ceases. At this point, you will be near ketosis, but not in it. You will be eating just enough carbohydrate to keep you healthy. To maintain this level, occasionally reduce your carbohydrate intake and repeat the testing process.

Keep in mind that the harder you train, the more carbohydrate you will need to keep you out of ketosis. And there is no way to get in shape, no matter how strictly you diet, without very hard training.

Nonetheless, despite my warnings, I know that there are body-builders who will insist on following some form of zero-carbo-hydrate diet. Therefore, to minimize the damage done by depriving yourself of carbohydrate, I recommend:

1. Do not follow such a severely restricted diet for more than four weeks—otherwise you will lose too much muscle tissue. Besides, there are certain dangers involved. For example, the heart is composed of muscle tissue, which can be attacked by the body under the stress of excessive carbohydrate loss.

2. Get off the diet at least a week before the contest and begin eating carbohydrate in moderate amounts until the glycogen supply in the muscles is fully restored.

Glycogen Replenishment

Many bodybuilders diet right up to the night before the contest, then stuff themselves with potatoes, bread, and lots of other carbs on the morning of the show. Unfortunately, this doesn't work very well.

It takes about three days for glycogen-starved muscles to fully replenish themselves. And since the body can only absorb a certain amount at any one time, you need to ingest your carbohydrate in a number of small meals rather than a few really big ones to give your body time to convert it into stored glycogen in the muscles. Therefore, for a Saturday contest, you must be sure your body has an adequate supply of carbohydrate starting about Wednesday. If you wait until the last minute, you will simply overload your body with carbohydrate that it can't metabolize. This will send your blood-sugar rate skyrocketing, which will tend to cause your body to retain a lot of water—and yet your muscles will still be flat.

In the early days of my career, I didn't know much about this glycogen-storage mechanism, but I did find out by trial and error that I ended up looking much better if I got down to contest weight a week *before* the competition and then spent the next week training, posing, and eating. What I was doing was giving my body the carbohydrate it needed to create new glycogen supplies and the time to get it done. However, even though I have explained this many times in seminars and articles, I still see bodybuilders dieting right up until the day before a contest and then stuffing themselves full of carbs at the last minute.

I can't tell you how many times I've heard bodybuilders complain about coming into a contest both flat and puffy. In many cases, the cause is simply improper understanding of diet and the role of carbohydrate in producing maximum muscle size and definition.

Losing Water

Another problem that plagues bodybuilders is having to get rid of as much of the body's water as possible so that they will look hard and defined. Many resort to the use of diuretics, which is not only unnecessary but can be dangerous.

There is more water in your body than any other element. Muscle is mostly water. Fat, on the other hand, contains very little water. When your body turns carbohydrate into stored glycogen, the glycogen binds with water—almost three times as much water as glycogen, which represents quite a bit of mass. So getting rid of water the wrong way will simply mean that you cause your muscles to shrink, which is not a good way to set about winning a championship.

There are other, better, and more natural ways to control the water in your body. For example:

1. Avoid foods that cause excess water retention in the body, such as salt (sodium), saccharin (found in many diet foods including diet sodas), and coffee.

2. Limit your fluid intake as the contest approaches. You don't have to cut out fluids entirely, just don't drink a lot. (Bottled water is superior to tap water; grapefruit juice gives you some carbs without being too sweet.)

3. Keep your blood-sugar level steady. Don't let yourself get too hungry, and don't stuff yourself right before a contest. Too much food raises your blood-sugar level and makes your body retain water.

4. Let your body sweat normally through exercise. Training gets rid of a lot of water. So does aerobic exercise like running and bicycle riding. Posing is an especially good way to squeeze water out of the body and harden you up.

5. Don't develop an overreliance on the steam room or sauna to lose water. You can lose water this way, but you also tend to

deplete the body if you overdo it. Remember, sweat is not just water—you also sweat away a lot of minerals. So be sure to use a mineral supplement (but no salt!) to replenish the body after using the steam room or sauna.

6. Before you take any drug or chemical, check to see what its side effects are. For example, anabolic steroids cause your body to retain excess water. So do many prescription and over-the-counter medicines. Just before one Olympia I took a cortisone shot for a shoulder injury. I didn't know that this would cause me to retain excess water. I was so puffy that I had to pose all day before the contest and most of the night in order to get my body hard again.

7. Include as many outdoor workouts in your training as you can, to let the sun help to bake any excess water out of your system.

Establishing Your Timetable

To repeat, the way to get rid of all the fat you need to is to start early enough and to give yourself plenty of time. If you aim for two pounds of fat loss a week, you will come out about right. However, you should not time your diet so that you end up at contest weight the day of the competition. Instead, do what I do and time your diet so that you are at the right weight one week before the contest. This gives you three advantages:

1. You have time to make adjustments if your timing is not perfect.

2. You are able to replenish your body's stock of glycogen during the last week to create maximum muscularity.

3. You come into the contest well fed and full of the energy it takes to pose and compete for hours on end.

CHAPTER 4

Common Injuries and How to Treat Them*

To become successful at bodybuilding, you must constantly try to push beyond your physical limits. But there is always a chance that you will exceed the ability of your physical structure to endure the strain. This can result in injury.

Some injuries are so slight and so common that we barely take notice of them. Others are more serious and require the attention of a physician. Progress for a bodybuilder is dependent on good physical health, and an injury can lead to a serious setback. Therefore, it is important to understand the types of injuries that might occur, how to prevent them, how to work around them, and what can be done to treat and rehabilitate them.

The body is a highly complex physical and biochemical mechanism which is subject to a variety of injuries, and each individual is more susceptible to certain types of injury. Injuries usually occur at the weakest place along a given structure: in the muscle, at the muscle/tendon juncture; along a tendon, at the tendon/bone attachment; in a ligament, at a joint; and so on. Sometimes injuries occur over a period of time because of overuse, sometimes because of an acute episode, such as mishandling a very heavy weight.

In dealing with the subject of injuries, it is important to be technically and medically accurate. The medical concepts and vocabulary may be difficult for the layman to absorb; but it is important that the dedicated bodybuilder have access to the information he needs to help prevent, treat, and avoid recurrence of

* The authors would like to give special thanks to orthopedic surgeon Barry L. Burton, M.D., of Los Angeles and Inglewood, California, for his invaluable contributions to this chapter on training injuries and their treatment.

physical injuries. Therefore, I have divided this section into two basic parts:

Technical information—a clinical examination of how the muscle/tendon and the joint/ligament structures of the body can incur injury, and what can be done to prevent and rehabilitate the various kinds of strains and sprains that can accompany intense physical training.

Practical information—a specific look, body part by body part, at those injuries which are most likely to affect the competition bodybuilder and how to deal with them.

Muscle and Tendon

Tendons connect skeletal (voluntary) muscle to bone. Tendinous connective tissue is found at both ends of a muscle (tendons of origin and tendons of insertion).

Injuries to the muscle or tendon can occur in several ways. One way is by direct trauma, such as a blow from a blunt or sharp object, causing a contusion (bruise) or a laceration (cut).

Another way is from strain caused by overworking these structures or by a single violent episode, such as a sudden stretching force applied to a muscle that is in the act of vigorous contraction when the force applied is stronger than the structure's ability to withstand tearing. The tear may be complete or partial and can occur at the musculotendinous junction, in the tendon or where the tendon attaches to bone.

Sometimes a small piece of bone is pulled off and left attached to the end of the tendon. This is known as an avulsion fracture. In a sense, the muscle or tendon is overpowered by the amount of resistance it is working against and the area of the least resistance is the site of injury. The degree of injury, whether mild or severe, would depend on the force of the contraction and the amount of resistance. A few fibers may be torn or the entire structure may be disrupted.

In most cases the strain is mild—simply an overstretching of the muscles, with no appreciable tearing. This would result in pain and discomfort with movement, and a subsequent muscle spasm. In more severe injuries with actual tearing of some fibers, symptoms are increased. Pain and discomfort are more severe and there is swelling and limitation of movement.

Initial Treatment

Initial treatment for all these injuries is rest, and the injured area must be protected against further injury. "Working through" or "working out" the injury can only make it worse.

For a mild strain, rest and avoid the activity that caused the injury in the first place. This may be the only treatment necessary until the extremity has recovered.

In a more severe injury to the leg, for example, crutches may be required for complete or partial limitation of weight on the injured extremity, or bed rest may be required for elevation of the leg, compression (pressure) dressing, splinting and application of ice packs. If the injury occurs in a non—weight-bearing extremity the same logical thinking should follow.

In very severe muscle and tendon injuries, with complete rupture of any of the components, the integrity of these components must be restored and surgical repair may be required. Even in these severe cases, the first-aid principles are the same as described above: rest (to promote healing), elevation (to aid blood flow out of the injured area), ice packs (to cause vasoconstriction and reduce hemorrhaging), compression (again, to reduce hemorrhaging and swelling), and immobilization (to prevent further injury).

Spasms and Cramps

Muscle spasm is another sign of strain. It is a sudden, often violent contraction of muscle, which is a protective reflex that in a sense, is guarding that area against further motion until there has been time for recovery. The spasm may last for an extended period of time, causing a great deal of pain, or it can be of shorter duration, such as the muscle cramping that is the result of overuse and fatigue. Rest and protection against further injury may be all that is required.

Tendinitis

Overuse may result in tenosynovitis, an inflammatory condition of the synovium which lines a tendon sheath and surrounds the tendon. One of the most common examples would be bicepital tenosynovitis, which involves the tendon of the long head of the biceps brachii, in the bicepital groove of the shoulder. The early symptom is shoulder pain, which may be present only with motion as the tendon passes back and forth in its sheath, or may be constant and occur even at rest.

In the early stages, treatment is the same as for muscle strain: rest, moist heat and protection against further injury. In the very acute stage, injection of coricosteroid may also be required. In advanced stages, the complications are serious and surgery may be required.

Pain

Pain when you're training is a warning sign that tells you an area has been injured. By letting the pain be your guide, you can practice preventive medicine. First avoid the activity that caused the pain and allow the area involved to recover. After an adequate period of rest you can gradually resume the activity that caused the injury.

Once you have regained full range of motion of the injured extremity and there is no associated pain, you have healed enough to increase the resistance to that movement on a gradual, progressive basis.

If you begin to feel pain, *you have gone too far.* Healing takes place by degrees over a period of time, and pain is an indicator of how far along you are. To progress too much too soon and not stay within the boundaries described—freedom from pain—risks reinjury, more severe injury and chronic injury.

Bodybuilders often become frustrated with prolonged or even short recuperation periods because of the resultant loss of conditioning, the setbacks, the "shrinking" (muscular atrophy and loss of muscle volume), and the mental and emotional anguish of not being able to train. However, the ability to deal competently with injury and to have the discipline to allow healing to take place is essential to a successful bodybuilding career. To do otherwise could further delay or completely prevent you from achieving your goals.

Therapy

If there is no bleeding or swelling, moist heat should be applied in some form of hot pack rather than a heat lamp, which just tends to warm the skin. A steam bath, a Jacuzzi, and even a nice hot bath are all good therapy. There is no evidence that soaking in Epsom salts has any positive benefits, and the various commercial preparations advertised as soothing "muscle soreness" only stimulate the surface of the skin and have no real therapeutic value.

In cases where muscle strain has been severe enough to cause actual rupture of fibers, with the associated bleeding and swelling of tissue, heat should *not* be used, since it would promote vasodilation (an increase in the diameter of the blood vessels), which would increase blood supply to the part involved and induce swelling. Here, ice packs should be used to promote vasoconstriction (a decrease in the diameter of the blood vessels), reducing the flow of blood to the area. Compression, elevation, and immobilization are all recommended treatments in the event of swelling.

Bleeding into tissues can be localized, as in a bruise or contusion, collected in a local pool (hematoma) or extravasate and, with seepage, discolor a large part of an extremity distant from the site of injury (ecchymosis).

The common *black-and-blue mark* is a local hemorrhage into the skin and subcutaneous tissue from rupture of minor vessels (capillaries), probably the result of a direct blow. Most bodybuilders just take such common bumps and bruises for granted. However, ice packs and compression can be used to reduce the swelling.

Gravity can work for you as well as against you. Elevating the swollen extremity allows gravity to escalate the return of blood to the heart through the venous system and helps to reduce swelling. Think of it as having water run downhill rather than having to pump it uphill. Compression in the form of a pressure dressing is also useful in limiting the amount of bleeding into the tissues of an injured extremity.

Also, be aware that self-treatment of minor muscle pulls is fine, but for more serious injuries you should seek medical treatment. A severe injury left untreated can get worse and cause you an extended setback. However, it is also true that not every doctor is equally experienced in sportsmedicine or in dealing with the particular needs and abilities of athletes. In the event you need medical help, seek out the services of a doctor or, more specifically, an orthopedist qualified to help you with your particular problem.

Preventing Injury

"An ounce of prevention is worth a pound of cure" should be the rule of every bodybuilder. There is a fine line between overuse and chronic strain due to heavy workouts. Intense workouts are bound to lead to occasional residual muscular soreness or soreness of the muscle/tendon complex. This kind of overuse is not exactly an injury, and most bodybuilders take it as a sign that they have actually trained hard enough. However, if you are so sore that you can hardly move and the intensity of your subsequent workouts is diminished, you have probably gone too far.

Muscles that are tight, tired and sore are more vulnerable to injury. If you insist on working out even under these conditions, there is a good chance that you will "pull" or tear some part of the muscle/tendon complex. The best preventive under these circumstances is gradual stretching, warm-ups, or, when the condition is severe, *keeping the workout light*. Stretching involves the entire muscle/tendon complex, lengthening it so that the chance of an exercise movement's suddenly stretching these structures past their limits and causing damage is reduced. Warming up pumps blood and oxygen to the area and literally raises the temperature of the muscles involved, allowing them to contract with greater force.

The best way to avoid training injuries is by taking care to stretch and warm up before working out and by observing proper technique when training with heavy weights. Remember, the stronger you are, the more strain you are able to put on your muscles and tendons, but often the muscles gain strength at a faster rate than the tendons, thus creating an imbalance that can cause problems. You must allow yourself to progress at a reasonable rate, and not attempt to train too intensely or with too much weight without proper preparation.

Joints and Ligaments

Movement occurs at a joint where two bones come together. The articulating parts of the joint, the parts that come in contact with each other, are composed of *hyaline cartilage*, a very smooth, gristlelike substance. It allows for the smooth gliding or motion of one part of the joint on the other.

"Chondromalacia" is a condition involving the softening or fraying of this smooth joint surface. This is often the first step in a long chain of events leading to degenerative arthritis, the degeneration of the bone and cartilage of a joint, which is a very painful and chronically disabling condition. Degenerative joint disease may also be initiated by chondral (cartilage) and osteochondral (bone-and-cartilage) fractures.

The *joint capsule* is a thick, fibrous envelope enclosing the joint and is intimately associated with the ligaments. *Ligaments* are tough, fibrous bands which connect two bones together. They help to stabilize the joint and prevent abnormal joint motion, while allowing motion to proceed in the normal functional direction.

The capsule and ligaments are the passive stabilizers of the joint, as opposed to the muscle/tendon group, which has an active stabilizing effect. In addition to its motor function, the muscle/tendon group on one side of a joint can actively stabilize the joint when it combines with the opposing muscle/tendon group on the other side to prevent motion. You can think of this as something like two tug-of-war teams so equal in strength that no matter how hard they try, they stay right where they are as if glued to the ground.

Injuries to the Capsule and Ligaments

Injuries can involve the capsule and ligaments as well as the osteocartilaginous (bone-and-cartilage) structures of the joint. Injuries to a ligament can occur from a direct blow by a blunt object, resulting in a contusion (bruise), or by a sharp object, resulting in a laceration (cut).

Ligamentous injury can also occur from overstress, resulting in damage to the substance of the ligament or to the site of its attachment. Injury to a ligament in this manner is commonly called a "sprain." It is a stretch injury to a passive, restraining structure—as opposed to a "strain," which occurs to the active structure, the muscle/tendon complex.

Often a violent external force causes the joint to move in an abnormal direction, stressing the ligament or ligaments beyond their ability to withstand tearing. The area of least resistance becomes the site of injury.

A ligament stretched too far will tear. The tear may be partial or complete. It can occur anywhere within the substance of the ligament or at the site of bony attachment, in which case a small piece of bone may be pulled off and left attached to the end of the ligament—an "avulsion fracture" of bone occurs, and treatment is often the same as for a severe sprain.

The degree of injury, whether mild or severe, would depend upon the amount of force applied and the inherent strength of the structures involved. Only a few ligament fibers may be torn, or the ligament may be partially or completely disrupted. Usually, if you experience little pain and few symptoms, the damage is minor; if pain, swelling, and discomfort are more noticeable, the injury is more severe.

Treatment of Sprains

In cases of mild sprain, where only a few fibers of a ligament have been torn, there may be little hemorrhage (bleeding) and swelling and only slight loss of joint function. Here treatment depends on the degree of pain and swelling, and many of the same general principles discussed in the treatment of strains apply.

Treatment may include one or more of the following: rest and limitation of the appropriate activities; elevation of the injured extremity; compression (pressure) dressing; application of ice packs; and splinting. Certainly, you should avoid any training movements that cause any discomfort to the injured area. This is another case where trying to "work through" an injury simply makes it worse.

In more severe sprain (partial ligament tear), there are more extensive tearing of the ligament fibers, more bleeding and swelling, more pain with motion, and more loss of joint function. Here the joint definitely should be protected to permit proper healing.

For example, suppose you have sustained a moderately severe ankle sprain in which there are significant bleeding into the tissues, swelling (edema) of the ankle and foot, throbbing pain when the foot is "dependent" (below heart level, so that gravity is working against you), pain with motion and with weight bearing, and limitation of joint motion. In this case, treatment by a doctor is recommended to be certain there are no broken bones and no clinically detectable instability (complete ligament rupture). The latter is often a difficult diagnosis, and stress X-rays—X-rays taken while the joint is subjected to a specific stress—may be warranted to rule out complete ligamentous rupture.

The ankle joint should be protected to allow for proper healing. Remember, we are talking about *partial tears*. In other words, part of the ligament still remains in continuity, and therefore there is no wide retraction, or gapping, of the torn portion. *Rest* the injured area. Since the ankle is part of a weight-bearing extremity, that means no walking on the leg involved.

Crutches can help you get around, but their use should be kept to a minimum, since part of the treatment involves elevation of the injured area. A bulky compression (pressure) dressing helps to limit the amount of bleeding and swelling. Application of ice packs to the injured area for 48 hours or so is useful, since this promotes vasoconstriction, which decreases blood flow to the area. Immobilization by splint or cast provides the most protection, since it prevents motion, decreases pain, and allows for optimum healing. When the swelling goes down you can apply heat. Heat applied immediately, however, can increase swelling, so it is recommended that heat treatment and warm soaks be delayed until recovery is well under way and range-of-motion exercises are being undertaken. Also, keep in mind that these are first-aid treatments only, and in any severe injury further treatment should be carried out by an orthopedic surgeon.

When the torn ends of the ligament are no longer in good apposition (touching or contacting) and a wide gap exists, reapposition is important. This allows ligament end to heal to ligament end, rather than having a large interposed scar formation, an elongated, lax ligament, chronic instability, and ultimately degenerative joint disease (degenerative arthritis).

Joint Dislocation

Joint dislocation and subluxation (partial dislocation) are conditions in which the opposing surfaces or articulating ends of the bones comprising a joint are no longer in normal relationship to each other. Instead, they are displaced, in the chronic condition because of ligamentous and capsular laxity (lack of tension) or in the acute condition because of tearing.

In severe sprain with ligament rupture, the joint subluxates—that is, it moves in an abnormal direction. This may be only momentary and relocation may occur spontaneously. If the force is violent enough, the entire joint may be disrupted and there may be complete dislocation.

Every effort has been made to be certain that the preceding material is medically and clinically accurate. However, since a medical education is not one of the prerequisites to a career in competition bodybuilding, and since the anatomy of the various parts of the body can be extremely complex, the following section deals with how you can go about applying this knowledge to your own injuries and competitive goals.

The Calves

The calf muscles, especially when you include very heavy calf raises in your workout, are subject to overstress and tearing. With too much weight, the muscle/tendon structure can tear at its weakest point—either at the point of insertion or origin of the tendon, at a tendon/muscle juncture, or within the body of the muscle itself.

One very good way to help prevent this kind of strain is by stretching the calves thoroughly before doing Calf Raises and in between each set and the next. In addition, be certain to use lighter weights to warm up in your first few sets before using heavier resistance.

Calf injury can also result from *overuse.* Constant overtraining may lead to progressively greater pain and soreness which will be alleviated only by resting the area.

This pain and soreness may be localized or may extend all the way down to the Achilles tendon. In cases of minor strain, stop training calves right away and rest the area until the pain goes away. If there is any swelling, the basic treatment is that described earlier—including ice, elevation, and compression. In more serious injuries, it is recommended you consult a physician.

The Knee

In bodybuilding injuries to the knee usually occur as the result of doing exercises like heavy Squats, in which the knee is subjected to heavy stress while in a bent position. The injury may be to the ligamentous structures, to the patella (kneecap), to the internal structures of the knee, or to the muscles and tendon that attach to the knee.

The patella is covered by a layer of tendinous material that is part of the tendon structure by which the quadriceps muscles attach below the knee and allow the leg to extend. Overstressing the knee may result in some degree of tearing anywhere within this area.

In knee *sprains*, some damage is done to the ligamentous structure of the knee joint itself. This most often happens when it is at its weakest, most acute angle, as in a full Squat. Also any twisting motion, expecially in lifting a heavy weight, could result in knee sprain.

The *meniscus* is the cartilaginous structure inside the knee, and any twisting of the joint in an exercise like a full Squat could result in a tearing of the meniscus, which might then require orthopedic surgery.

To avoid overstressing the knee, it is important to engage in a full warm-up before putting it under any great stress. You should also be very much aware of the need to concentrate on proper exercise technique—for example, in a Squat, you should go down fully under control—no "bouncing" at the bottom—and stop when you are just below parallel. There is no need to go all the way down to the bottom, but "half Squats" will keep you from strengthening the lower range of motion of the movement.

Wrapping the knees or using an elastic brace will help to support the area during very heavy lifts.

Treatment for knee injuries involves the normal prescription of rest, ice, etc. for mild strain or sprain and a physician's care for more serious injuries. Except for other conditions that are not directly injury-related, cortisone injections are not normally indicated for knee injuries.

For bodybuilders with knee problems who need to work around the injury prior to a contest, sometimes it is possible to do Squats on a Smith machine, positioning your feet well forward to isolate the quadriceps and take stress off the knee. If knee problems are too severe for this method, I recommend using Leg Extensions—partial range if necessary, or high-rep, low-weight movements—but not when excessive pain is present.

The Upper Leg

The *vastus medialis* is the long muscle of the quadriceps that attaches at the inside of the knee. When you fully extend the leg and lock it out, stress is placed specifically at this attachment and strain can occur. This may be felt in the area of the knee but is actually an upper-leg problem.

Injuries to the back of the leg often occur because the leg biceps have not been stretched enough. Along with stretching exercises to lengthen the muscle/tendon structure, you can also include Straight-Leg Deadlifts in your routine, which have a stretching effect.

The Groin

"Groin pulls" can occur when the area is overstretched during movements such as Lunges, and are among the most difficult problems to overcome because the area is in constant use, always being stretched, whenever you are active. The basic treatment usually involves a lot of absolute rest to allow the injury to heal itself.

Lower Abdomen

Males have a congenital weakness in the lower abdominal area. Sometimes when abdominal pressure is raised too high, a tear in the abdominal wall can occur. This can happen during any heavy lift in which you hold your breath.

A tear in the abdominal wall is called a *hernia*, and it may allow parts of the viscera to extrude through the opening. Serious cases may require surgery.

One way to help prevent hernias is to gradually expel your breath during heavy lifts. This keeps the abdominal pressure high enough to help stabilize you during the movement, but not so high that it can injure the abdominal wall.

It is also possible to strain the abdominal muscles and tendons, just as you can any other muscle/tendon structure, and treatment for strains in this area is the same as for any other muscle strain.

Lower Back

It is possible to strain the spinal erectors or other lower-back muscles by overstressing the area, especially when you do a movement that hyperextends the lower back—like Deadlifts, or bench exercises such as Bench Presses or Leg Raises, in which the lower back is lifted clear of the bench and hyperextended. A certain amount of curvature of the lower back is normal, but bending it too far under stress can cause problems.

When you strain the lower back, you may feel pain radiating down into the hips or upward toward the middle back. Sometimes these muscles will go into spasm to prevent further injury.

You can also have a sprain in the lower back when there is an injury to the ligaments in the area. It may often be difficult for you to tell whether you have incurred a strain or a sprain, but in any event, the treatment is virtually identical.

Another lower-back injury you can incur is a ruptured disc. The discs are situated in between the vertebrae, and when they rupture, the pulpy material inside the disc can extrude and press upon adjacent nerves. You may feel pain anywhere along the back or even down into the legs, but it is this specific pressure which causes the pain, and treatment involves alleviating that pressure.

One specific type of nerve problem is "sciatica." The sciatic nerve is the largest nerve of the body, extending from the back all the way down the leg, and when pressure is put on this nerve the pain is severe and disabling.

Another cause of lower-back problems can be abdominal work such as Straight-Leg Sit-Ups and Straight-Leg Raises, which both put a lot of stress on the lower back. Bodybuilders who have been able to do heavy Deadlifts or Good Mornings with no difficulty have sometimes been surprised to find themselves incurring back injuries while doing abdominal training.

Upper Back

Any of the upper-back muscles may be subjected to strain—the trapezius, levator scapuli, teres major, latissimus dorsi, and so on. Neck strains, for example, are fairly common. Often it is difficult to say which particular muscle has been overstressed. You may feel pain when you turn your head, lift your shoulder or bend your back. Frank Zane, for example, strained an upper-back muscle simply by tensing the area to stabilize himself while he did Preacher Bench Curls.

Often you will both contract these muscles and pull on them at the same time, which may lead to overstress and some degree of muscle tear. If the injury is not too severe, it is not necessary to know precisely which muscle is affected. Simply rest the area and use the appropriate treatment.

The Shoulders

Shoulder injuries are relatively common among bodybuilders. Heavy Bench Presses, Dumbbell Presses, and Shoulder Presses put a particularly high degree of stress on the shoulders.

Heavy stress can cause partial tearing of the "rotator cuff" (the tendons of the rotator muscles for the internal and external rotators). It is also possible to overstress any part of the three heads of the deltoids or their tendons of insertion or origin.

Another possible problem in the shoulder area is "subdeltoid bursitis." A bursa provides a lubricated surface where a tendon glides directly over the periosteum of a bone. Bursitis is a condition in which, through wear or other conditions, the bursa is not able to do its job and movement in the area causes pain and difficulty. Frank Zane suffered from shoulder bursitis and was able to overcome it with extensive vitamin supplementation, treatment by a chiropractor and subjecting the area to only light training until it healed.

"Biceptial tendinitis" is another common shoulder problem in which the biceps tendon working back and forth gets inflamed because of stress and friction. Medications such as cortisone are frequently indicated in treatment of shoulder injuries such as this.

In the event of shoulder injury, it is sometimes possible to do shoulder exercises at different angles—Bent-Over Laterals instead of Front Presses, for example, to work the rear head instead of the front—or to simply use the Flushing Method and hold heavy dumbbells out to the side, which will keep the deltoids toned and firm prior to a contest.

The Pectorals

Strains in the chest muscles most often occur where the pectorals insert into the humerus (upper arm). Since many bodybuilders like to bench as heavy as they can, this strain is often associated with overstress due to handling too heavy a weight—as well as failing to warm up properly.

Poor technique also accounts for a high proportion of chest injuries. Dropping the weight down too quickly while doing a Bench Press can cause a very heavy and sudden jerk to the whole pectoral structure. Similarly, dropping the weights too quickly when executing Dumbbell Flys can also overstress the pectorals —especially if the muscles are tight and have not been warmed up and stretched before the workout.

The Biceps

Biceps tears can occur at either end of the muscle—the origin, at the scapula, or the insertion into the radius—or anywhere along the muscle itself. Stress to the biceps can be acute, or it may be cumulative.

The biceps are relatively small muscles and are easily over-trained because they are involved in a wide range of exercises. Besides the exercises for biceps and back training, any kind of pulling motion—from Seated Rows to Wide-Grip Chins—also works the biceps. This makes it difficult to "work around" a biceps injury, since the muscles are needed for so many different movements. Nonetheless, the only way a biceps strain will get better is through rest.

In cases of very severe injury, where there is a complete tear of the biceps, surgery would probably be necessary to repair the structure.

The Triceps

Triceps are subject to the same sorts of strains as the biceps and other muscles. Another common triceps injury is "olecranon bursitis" (the olecranon is the point of the elbow). When you do extension movements like Triceps Extensions or French Presses, you pull on the insertion of the triceps, at the elbow. This overlies a bursa, which can become irritated when a lot of stress is put on the area and produce a burning sensation.

Triceps can also be strained by overtraining or by sudden stress due to poor training technique. In cases of a complete tear of the triceps, surgery would be required to repair the structure.

The Elbows

The elbows are subjected to constant stress whenever you do pressing movements. In addition to the acute problems that can result from overstressing the joint by using heavy weights or sloppy technique, there is also a certain amount of cumulative damage that occurs over months and years of heavy training, sometimes resulting in degenerative arthritis.

This kind of degenerative problem can occur in other joints such as the shoulder or knees and is difficult to detect in the early stages since it can come on too slowly to be immediately noticeable. Gradually increasing degrees of pain can be one symptom; an increasing limitation of range of motion is another. Either of these indicates some damage to the internal structure of the elbow which, if left untreated, may eventually become irreversible.

In case of sudden strain of the elbow area, the same principles of treatment apply: rest, ice, elevation, and compression.

To stabilize the elbow joint for very heavy lifts, you can wrap the area or use an elastic brace.

The Forearms

Since in most exercises you rely on your wrists and forearms to help you grip the weight, you are frequently both contracting and stretching these muscles at the same time. This can often lead to muscle or tendon strain.

Pulling or curl motions with your palms turned forward, such as Chins, Power Cleans, or Reverse Curls, put the forearms in a position of leverage disadvantage in which they are weaker and can be more easily strained. Often the injury is to the origin of the forearm extensor muscles, near the elbow; this is also known as "tennis elbow." However, this kind of movement can lead to muscle strain anywhere along the muscles at the top of the forearm.

Because of the frequency of forearm injuries from doing Reverse Curls, Dr. Franco Columbu recommends avoiding this movement and instead using only Reverse Wrist Curls to build the top of the forearms.

Forearm injuries can become chronic because you need to grip hard during so many different exercises. Therefore, it is difficult to rest the forearm muscles once they have been strained.

In addition to resting the forearms to treat strain, I have found that acupuncture can help to speed up healing.

Training Around Injuries

While it is absolutely necessary to rest an injured area in order for it to heal, bodybuilders training for competition cannot simply stop every time they experience a minor strain or sprain. They need to find a way to continue training and yet avoid making an injury worse.

There is no one, clear-cut way of doing this. It takes experience to find which movements aggravate a condition and which do not. Training for the 1980 Olympia, I injured my shoulder shortly before the contest. I was unable to do conventional Shoulder Presses without experiencing pain. However, I found I could do Presses using a narrow grip with my palms facing, and so I was able to continue training shoulders without making the injury worse. There is also the isometriclike Flushing Method with dumbbells I mentioned earlier.

One bodybuilder who had strained a forearm so that he could not do Barbell Curls or Machine Curls found by trial and error that he could do Hammer Curls with dumbbells, with his forearms turned at a certain angle. This allowed him to train without pain while the injury was healing. You can sometimes work around a forearm or biceps injury by doing E-Z Bar Curls to change the position of your hands.

Triceps injuries make most kinds of Presses and Triceps Extensions difficult. One exercise that is often still possible despite triceps strain is Triceps Kickbacks, because there is very little stress on the triceps until the very end of the movement.

Often, in the case of mild strain, you can still train the injured area if you take a lot of extra time to warm up and stretch before you work against any significant degree of resistance.

Sometimes it is possible to train around an injury, and sometimes it isn't. Certainly, in the event of a very serious injury it is probably impossible to continue your workouts as before.

Just remember—a contest is only a contest. A career is much more. And trying to train through an injury and making it worse can lead to permanent and disabling problems which will remain with you the rest of your life.

Cold-Weather Training

Training in cold weather necessitates taking certain additional precautions to avoid injury. In cold temperatures it takes longer for the body to warm up, so you need to delegate more time to warm-up and stretching before your workout. Additionally, it is a good idea to dress warmly in the gym so that your muscles don't cool off between sets.

A Quick Summary

- Most injuries in bodybuilding are *strains*, overstressing or overstretching muscles and/or tendons. Proper warm-up, prestretching, and proper lifting technique help to prevent strain. Once a strain occurs, you need to rest the area. Other aids to healing may include the use of ice to keep down swelling, elevation to promote venous return of blood, and compression. Later in the healing process, heat can be used, including ultrasound.
- In cases of light or moderate strain, it is often unnecessary to pinpoint exactly where in a complex structure the strain has occurred. You can feel which general area is involved, you can

tell which movements aggravate the damage and so you can avoid working that area.

- Strain can occur in areas that you are not actually working but simply contracting for leverage.
- Most joint injuries that occur in bodybuilders are a result of years of wear and tear on the body. These problems build up slowly. Younger bodybuilders train very hard and don't notice any problems, but in later years they can pay the price of this physical abuse.
- Younger bodybuilders have greater recuperative powers and can bounce back from injuries faster than older bodybuilders. As you grow older and continue to train, there are things you can't get away with, training methods that would not have resulted in injury in your youth but will once you are older and your body has suffered from years of strain. This may involve a change in training style (which may work fine, since you probably have the size already that young bodybuilders are still trying to achieve).

Anabolic Steroids and Ergogenic Aids

No book on modern bodybuilding would be complete without a discussion of anabolic steroids. Steroid use has become prevalent in all sports, and bodybuilding is no exception. However, no matter how widespread the use of these drugs might be, they are still the subject of deep controversy.

Are steroids dangerous? To what degree do they really enhance strength, size, training ability, and muscular performance? We still do not have precise answers to these questions. Far more effort seems to be devoted to attempting to ban the drugs rather than finding the answers to these questions. One thing we do know: they do seem to help some individuals in some cases, and the majority of bodybuilders are convinced that using steroids is necessary in order to scale the heights of international bodybuilding competition.

Actually, there are two problems connected with steroids: one is their use, the other their misuse. Whatever long-term problems may be caused by using these drugs, if you misuse them—take too much, over too long a period, or in the wrong combinations —you can expect immediate, serious, and possibly fatal results.

I have prepared this discussion of steroids in consultation with Dr. James E. Wright, a noted authority on the subject. But I want to make it clear that this does not constitute an endorsement on my part of steroid use. Of all the great bodybuilders I have known and competed against, I don't know of one who used steroids as anything more than a last-minute, finishing touch to an already superb physique. The top champions frequently resort to such aids because they are aware that their competitors are using them, and they don't want to give away an edge. However, there is a move on within the IFBB to ban steroids completely because there is a definite threat to the individual's health and welfare when these drugs are used.

And I also firmly believe that if steroids had never been discovered, the same bodybuilders would have inevitably emerged as the winners. Success in bodybuilding is more dependent on hard work and good genes than on use of any drug.

What Are Anabolic Steroids?

Anabolic steroids are a group of powerful synthetic chemical compounds that resemble the natural male sex hormones. Hormones are chemical regulators in the body which influence or control a wide range of processes such as growth, development and specialization of tissues, the reproductive cycle, and many aspects of behavior.

Cells are primarily made up of protein. Therefore one of the most important factors in making growth possible is the production or synthesis of new protein. The hormones that make it possible for the cells to produce new protein are primarily the androgens—the male hormone testosterone and its chemical relatives. Testosterone is present in both males and females to differing degrees.

Male hormones actually have two different kinds of effects in the body: an *anabolic* effect, which stimulates growth; and an *androgenic* effect, which increases male sexual characteristics. Anabolic steroids are synthesized in such a way as to maximize the anabolic effect and minimize the androgenic one. Although the various kinds of steroids differ in the degree to which they accomplish this, all of them are designed to produce growth with minimal effect on sexual characteristics.

Steroids are complex molecules carried in the bloodstream and acting as messengers. There are thousands of tiny steroid receptor sites in the cells, and the steroid molecules deliver many messages, among the most important being to increase protein synthesis, and to increase creatine phosphate (CP) synthesis. Depending on the type of steroid, either one or both of these messages are delivered in various ratios.

Creatine phosphate is a short-term energy restorer which allows you to contract your muscles for more than just a few seconds. The more CP available, the more muscular work you can do. The more work you can do, the harder you can train and the more muscle you can grow.

Steroids and Bodybuilding

By the late 1940s, bodybuilders had discovered the effects of testosterone and were using it to stimulate muscle growth and to make themselves train with more intensity and aggression. The first synthetic anabolic was developed in 1953, having a strength-building effect three to five times higher than testosterone and a level of androgenicity about one-third that of testosterone. Throughout the 1960s, additional types of anabolic steroids were developed and their use by bodybuilders and other athletes continued to increase, despite a number of scientific studies that called into question their effectiveness in building strength and muscle tissue.

A large number of athletes from a variety of sports were interviewed about their drug use at the 1972 Olympics, and a total of 68 percent admitted to using anabolic steroids. Dr. Wright estimates that more than 90 percent of athletes in strength-related sports are using these drugs today.

Most competition bodybuilders use or have used anabolic steroids. They believe that steroids help them to get bigger and stronger. And they like the feeling of aggression they get while using these drugs because it helps them to train harder. And, not to be overlooked, they take them because they know their competition is taking them and they don't want to give away an advantage.

The Need to Plateau

There are many beginner and intermediate bodybuilders who, hearing that the champions are using steroids, believe that they too can make enormous gains by taking these drugs. But studies done on the effect of steroids do not bear this out.

Steroids have their greatest effect on size and strength only when the bodybuilder has "plateaued"—that is, made about as much gain as possible without the use of drugs. Trained individuals respond to steroids much better than untrained ones. Gains are also maximized if you continue to train very hard during the period you are using steroids.

Steroids allow you to train more intensely, but this is not all that significant for a bodybuilder who is not training as hard as he could be in the first place and doesn't need steroids to increase intensity, or who has not developed as far as he can without the use of steroids. But the health risks are the same in either case, which means that the less-developed bodybuilder is taking the same risks as the more-developed but stands to gain a lot less. This makes for a very poor risk/benefit ratio.

Steroids and the Liver

The liver is the largest and one of the most important organs in the body. One of its functions is the inactivation, detoxification, and elimination of a whole range of substances, including anabolic steroids. However, depending on the particular chemical structure of individual steroids, they will be processed by the liver at varying speeds. Some steroids are totally eliminated in twenty-four hours—which puts great demands on the liver and can lead to liver problems—while others can last in the body for days or weeks.

Anabolic steroids are administered in two basic forms, orally or by injection. Oral steroids (such as Dianabol) are quickly destroyed by the liver. Since they are eliminated so quickly, you need to take very large doses of the orals to get the desired effect. This, in turn, increases the toxic effect on the liver.

Injectable steroids go directly into the bloodstream, bypassing the liver, which means that you can take smaller effective doses and there is much less of a toxic effect. Injectables are generally given in an oil base. Since these take about three days to take effect, the liver does not have to work so hard in dealing with them. Injectables are therefore considered much safer.

However, although both orals and injectables stimulate protein synthesis, orals generally tend to stimulate creatine phosphate synthesis while injectables do not.

Once the steroid molecules interact with the steroid sites of the cells they float back into the bloodstream to be used over and over until destroyed by the liver. Therefore, if you have 200 mg of an injectable in your system, and it is chemically constructed to have a lifetime of 17 days, your body is not simply using 12 mg a day—it is using 200 mg the first day, about 188 mg the second, 176 the third, 164 the next, and so on until the entire amount has been eliminated. Having to destroy such a relatively small amount of the steroid each day means that the liver has a fairly easy job of it.

With oral steroids like Dianabol, which have such short life spans, when you take a 200 mg dose the liver destroys the entire 200 mg in one day, which puts a tremendous strain on your liver function.

Injectables also come in aqueous (water) base, which are much faster to affect the system.

When an anabolic steroid enters your system, the body changes some of the drug into estrogen, a female hormone. When this begins to happen, you need higher and higher dosages to retain the effect. So, in addition to possible liver problems, the higher estrogen levels in the body may lead to side effects like increased body fat, greater water retention, and occasionally, gynecomastia —the development of breastlike tissue in males.

Steroids and Teenagers

Teenagers should never take anabolic steroids in an attempt to build up the size and strength of their muscle structure. During the teenage years, young males are already in their most anabolic state, with testosterone flooding the system. Adding synthetic anabolics at this point is totally unnecessary.

It is also true that, except in rare cases, a teenager will not have developed far enough to have plateaued. And I was no exception. Although I won the Mr. Universe title at age twenty, I improved considerably after that, showing that I was nowhere near my peak.

Additionally, steroids tend to close over the ends of growing bones. A teenager who has not yet achieved his total growth may find that steroids prevent him from growing to his full height— and this effect is totally irreversible.

Medical Considerations

Anabolic steroids are not simply used by bodybuilders and other athletes. They have many therapeutic applications, being commonly used in medicine as replacement therapy for people with low hormone production, for malnutrition and underweight conditions, in the treatment of skeletal disorders, in a variety of surgical situations to improve a patient's physical condition beforehand and to help him or her in recovery, and to stimulate growth in specific circumstances in pediatric cases.

Absolute contraindications to steroid use are pregnancy or the presence of prostate or male breast cancer.

Anabolic steroids have a wide-ranging effect on a number of other important physical functions. The possible medical complications associated with steroid use include:

Altering of liver functions. A great deal of stress is placed on the liver when you introduce steroids into your body. With prolonged use of high dosages there can be progressive cholestatis and jaundice, peliosis hepatitis, hemorrhaging, and even the possibility of liver cancer. There have been fatalities among patients subjected to this kind of therapy. As we have already seen, injectables appear not to stress the detoxifying function of the liver to the same extent as the orals.

Altering of cardiovascular function. The use of steroids can lead to changes in the clotting mechanism of the blood, in the metabolism of glucose, and in triglyceride and cholesterol levels in the blood. To offset this tendency, a low-fat diet is recommended. The use of oral steroids can lead to hyperinsulinism, reduced glucose levels, and to a reduction in both oral and intravenous glucose tolerance, associated with a marked insulin resistance. Steroids raise the risk of atherosclerosis (which can be offset by intense aerobic training) and increase the level of cortisol, the body's major stress hormone.

Increases in nervous tension and/or blood pressure. This can lead to hypertension, as well as radical changes in the body's fluid/electrolyte balance.

Depression of normal testosterone production. The body has mechanisms that monitor the amount of testosterone in the system and alert the endocrine system to increase or decrease hormone production. When steroids are taken, the body registers the increase as excessive and tends to lower or shut down the production of testosterone. This can lead to changes in libido and many other physical functions related to hormone levels, such as aggression and fat metabolism.

Androgenic effects. The occurrence of androgenic effects may be more a factor of duration rather than dose. Some of these include increased facial and body hair; increased sebaceous secretions (oily skin), which can cause acne; priapism (persistent, often painful erection); thinning of scalp hair; prostatic hypertrophy; and premature epiphyseal closure (the closing off of the ends of bones prior to full maturity).

Common Symptoms

While most of the above effects of taking anabolic steroids are rarely reported, the following are fairly common:

Gastrointestinal disorders (with the oral steroids), including loss of appetite, burning of the tongue, gagging, vomiting, diarrhea, constipation, intestinal irritation, and a bloated feeling—in 1 to 2 percent of those taking orals

Muscle cramps and spasms

Increased or decreased feelings of aggression
Headaches
Nose bleeds
Dizziness, faintness, drowsiness, or lethargy
Skin rash or local reactions at the site of injection
Sore nipples
Gynecomastia (development of breastlike tissue in males)
Alteration of thyroid function

Ergogenic Aids

Ergogenic aids are anything that helps you raise your performance above the expected level. Some are psychological, as we have covered in discussing the mental side of training. But some are physical and can have a definite effect on how much progress you make in the gym.

Enhancing performance is valuable at any stage of your training, but will be especially important when you are training for competition and trying to get the ultimate from your body. At this level, even a slight change in intensity over a period of time can make the difference between winning and losing.

Bodybuilders and other athletes are always looking for an edge, some way of taking their performance past established limits. There are a number of substances which are believed to be extremely helpful to performance, and some that are thought to help but whose efficacy is much more doubtful. Dr. Lawrence Golding has compiled a partial list of those drugs and hormones thought to be most ergogenic:

Adrenaline   Coramine (nikethamide)
Alcohol   Lecithin
Alkalis   Metrazol (pentylenetetrazol)
Amphetamines   Noradrenaline
Caffeine   Steroids
Cocaine   Sulfa drugs

Most bodybuilders are concerned with only a few of these substances. Following are my recommendations, both pro and con.

Pro

Caffeine. Taken in limited quantities such as in a few cups of coffee, caffeine has a mildly stimulating effect. Caffeine in larger doses, however, can be harmful. In fact, the International Olympic Committee is now testing for excessive levels of caffeine, which will constitute grounds for an athlete's disqualification.

Glycogen. Glycogen is the form in which carbohydrate is stored in the muscles. When your body is low on glycogen, your energy level suffers. Therefore, a bodybuilder who attempts a low- or zero-carbohydrate diet for any prolonged period cannot train with any intensity. Incidentally, your glucose (blood carbohydrate) and glycogen levels are generally lowest when you wake up in the morning, since it is normally eight hours or more since you have eaten. Therefore, for maximum energy, eating some fruit or other carbohydrate an hour prior to training in the gym can make you feel much more energetic.

Vitamins. Contrary to what many people believe, vitamins do not create energy. They are catalysts and merely help other reactions to occur. Nevertheless, a vitamin deficiency can interfere with the release of energy, so it pays to take vitamin supplements to make sure your system is not deficient in some way, especially if you are dieting.

Oxygen. Trying to train really hard for competition, I noticed that I tended to fail aerobically before my muscles would fail. I simply couldn't get enough oxygen into my system. To counteract this, I tried taking breaths of pure oxygen from time to time, and this increased my aerobic endurance considerably. Other bodybuilders confirmed that it works. Anyone who has watched professional football games on television is familiar with the athlete sitting on the sidelines taking oxygen, and this is for the same reason.

Minerals. If your body is deficient in any of the important minerals (which it probably isn't, unless you are dieting), you are going to notice a falloff in energy production. To ensure that your training intensity stays at maximum, you can take supplements of calcium, potassium, manganese, magnesium, kelp (for iodine), and alfalfa. A good, inexpensive source of potassium, by the way, is Lite Salt.

Thyroid. Thyroid is a necessary and valuable aid to training—for those who have a thyroid deficiency. If your thyroid is not working properly, you will lack energy and have trouble building muscle. However, that determination should be made by a physician. If you take thyroid in the absence of a thyroid deficiency, you can harm your thyroid gland, throw off your entire endocrine system, and actually make it difficult for the body to acquire muscle mass.

Con

Amphetamines. Any form of powerful, artificial stimulant like amphetamines, excess caffeine, or cocaine will ultimately be more harmful than helpful to your training. It is well known that many athletes in contact sports take amphetamines to help kill the pain of a physical injury; but the last thing you want when you are trying to concentrate awareness on various muscles is to kill the sensation. You certainly don't want to become over-stimulated, work a muscle too hard, and injure it without knowing it—but that can happen with amphetamines and other superstimulants. Amphetamines are also very bad for your health in a number of ways, regardless of their effect on your training.

Aspirin. You will occasionally find bodybuilders who advocate using aspirin to help them get a really hard workout. Here again, anything that dulls sensation to the muscles means you can't really feel them, can't train them with ultimate intensity, and may not know it if you incur an injury.

Alcohol and marijuana. I don't think I have to go any further here than to state the fact that you can't train hard when you are stoned. Bodybuilders who come to the gym high on booze or grass are simply not going to make the kind of progress they ought to.

Miracle pills. Not only is there a sucker born every minute, but most of them seem to be buying various health concoctions "guaranteed" to help you feel better, get stronger, lose weight, and so forth. Be aware that most of these things do not work. If you want to spend your money on miracle pills, it's your money —but don't expect to make progress in bodybuilding without real dedication and hard work. No miracle pill can do it for you.

Photo Credits

Photo by permission CHARLES ATLAS LTD., N.Y.: 37. JOHN BALIK: 61, 62, 88, 127, 128, 129, 130, 131, 132, 133, 134, 135, 136, 137, 143 (right), 144, 213, 220, 233, 238 (right), 239, 240 (right), 246, 247, 248, 249, 256 (top), 257, 261, 265, 290 (bottom), 291 (right), 345 (top), 348, 374 (top), 393 (top), 400, 403, 404, 405, 413, 414, 415, 416, 424, 425, 427, 435, 436, 438, 439, 440, 442, 443, 444, 445, 447, 455 (top), 460, 463, 464, 466 (bottom), 467, 468, 470, 471, 472, 473, 474, 475, 476, 477, 478, 480 (top), 489 (top, center), 494, 496, 497, 499, 500, 501, 502, 504, 513 (top), 514, 515, 516 (bottom), 518, 522, 523, 525, 526, 529, 531, 532, 535, 536, 537, 538, 539, 548, 549 (bottom), 551, 553, 554, 570 (bottom), 571, 573 (right), 574 (top), 575, 576, 577, 582, 584, 587 (top), 588 (right), 591 (left), 592, 593, 594, 595, 596 (top), 600 (top), 601–7, 618, 619, 620, 622, 628, 654, 655. RAHEO BLAIR: 141 (right). J. BESTER: 315, 323 (bottom). ALBERT BUSEK: 55 (bottom), 57 (bottom), 89, 90, 91, 123 (top), 148, 206 (bottom), 224 (right), 260, 267, 289 (top), 297, 302, 303, 312 (top), 333 (left), 346 (bottom), 347, 349, 354 (bottom), 360 (left), 361 (right), 377 (top), 384, 387 (bottom), 393 (bottom), 401 (bottom), 402, 407, 418, 420, 421, 434, 455 (bottom), 459, 469, 490, 491, 492 (right), 493, 495 (right), 498, 517, 519, 530, 564 (bottom), 565 (bottom), 569 (left), 578 (bottom), 588 (left), 616, 626, 627, 629, 630 (top, bottom right), 631, 638. CARUSO: 4, 29, 45 (bottom), 46 (left), 47 (left, top right), 53, 58, 59 (left), 60 (left), 64, 143 (left), 219, 224 (left), 226 (top), 231, 238 (left), 269, 285, 293, 317 (right), 323 (top), 332 (center), 355, 358 (center), 359, 361 (bottom left), 365, 377 (bottom), 379, 380, 382 (bottom), 448, 451, 454, 488, 492 (left), 503 (left), 505, 506, 511 (right), 549 (top), 550, 552, 569 (right), 570 (top), 572 (top right), 573 (left), 574 (bottom right), 589, 590 (left), 598 (right), 612, 614, 624, 632 (right), 636, 642. DUDLEY CARVER: 141 (left). ANITA COLUMBU: 316, 318. COURTESY FRANCO COLUMBU: 566. BENNO DAHMAN: 45 (top), 54 (right), 55 (top), 100, 290 (top), 326. MAGDA DE VELASCO: 48 (bottom). BILL DOBBINS: 236, 289 (bottom), 334, 335, 336, 337, 338, 572 (bottom), 579 (top). F. C. ARCHIVE: 226 (right). ROBERT GARDNER: 237 (bottom), 245, 251, 259, 294, 298, 309, 332 (bottom), 340, 342, 344, 352, 375, 396, 408, 409, 411 (bottom), 412, 423, 428, 429, 430, 431, 432, 437, 441, 446, 461, 479, 512, 516 (top), 520, 521, 527, 528, 534, 541. GEORGE GREENWOOD/EDWARD HANKEY: 48 (top), 49, 50, 51, 52 (bottom), 279, 581, 658. KENNEDY: 43 (right). KENNEDY/JOSEPH WEIDER: 483. TONY LANZA: 222. LON: 43 (left). CHRIS LUND: 225 (right), 321 (left), 323 (center), 386, 449, 452 (left), 596 (bottom). GEORGE MAGEE: 362 (right). ROBERT NAILON: 587 (bottom). MICHAEL NEVEUX: 221, 223 (left), 243, 244, 252, 253, 255, 263, 266, 267, 284, 299, 301, 304, 305, 308, 311 (bottom), 355 (top), 389 (right), 511 (left), 547 (top), 579 (bottom). NEAL NORDLINGER: 274 (left), 320 (left), 327, 543, 660, 661, 662, 664. RAYMOND L. PAYNE: 214, 215. STEPHEN RENZ: 547 (bottom). © 1982 UNIVERSAL CITY STUDIOS, INC.: 208. © UNIVERSAL CITY STUDIOS, INC.: 209. RUSS WARNER: 142 (bottom right), 226 (bottom right), 632 (left). RUSS WARNER/JOSEPH WEIDER: 292 (bottom). JOSEPH WEIDER ARCHIVES, courtesy of *Muscle and Fitness* magazine: 31, 32, 33, 34, 35, 36, 38, 39, 40, 41, 42, 46 (bottom right), 47 (bottom right), 52 (top), 54 (left), 60 (right), 75, 142 (top right, left), 143 (top left), 145, 146, 149, 217, 221, 223 (right), 225 (left), 226 (left), 234, 237 (top), 268, 272 (left), 274 (right), 275, 276 (right), 291 (left), 292 (top), 300, 307, 319, 321 (right), 328, 332 (top), 355 (bottom), 356, 363, 364 (bottom), 378, 381, 382 (top), 383, 385, 389 (left), 392, 395, 410, 422, 450, 452 (right), 480 (bottom), 481, 482, 489 (bottom), 510 (right), 533, 564 (top), 572 (top left), 578 (top, center), 580, 583, 590 (right), 591 (right), 598 (left), 600 (bottom), 611, 613, 615, 633, 634, 644. DOUGLAS WHITE/JOSEPH WEIDER: 228. ART ZELLER: 56, 57 (top), 59 (right), 86, 87, 113, 121, 123 (center, bottom), 200, 206 (top), 207, 226 (bottom left), 240 (left), 241, 242, 250, 254, 256 (bottom), 258, 264, 270, 271, 272 (right), 273, 276 (left), 282, 286, 295, 296, 303, 306, 310, 311 (top), 312 (bottom), 313, 314, 317 (left), 320 (right), 322, 331, 333 (top), 339, 341, 343, 345 (bottom), 346 (top), 350, 354 (top), 357, 358 (top, bottom), 360 (right), 361 (top left), 362 (left), 364 (top), 373, 374 (bottom), 376, 387 (top), 388, 399, 401 (top), 406, 407, 411 (top), 417, 419, 433, 453, 466, 495 (left), 503 (right), 508, 510 (left), 513 (bottom), 524, 540, 563, 565 (top), 567, 568, 574 (bottom left), 585, 586, 597, 599, 617, 623, 630 (left), 637.

COLOR SECTION CREDITS

JOHN BALIK: Frank Zane, Albert Beckles, Chris Dickerson, Bertil Fox, Tom Platz, Samir Bannout. COLUMBU ARCHIVES: Franco Columbu. TONY LANZA: Steve Reeves. JACK MATSUMOTO: John Grimek. MICHAEL NEVEUX: Sergio Oliva, Lee Haney. LEO STERN: Bill Pearl. WEIDER ARCHIVES: Reg Park, Larry Scott, Lou Ferrigno. ART ZELLER: Dave Draper.

Several of the photos taken from the Weider Archives that appear in this book had no indication of the photographer who took the photo. We regret that the photographer could not be credited in the proper way in those cases.

Drawings by Bruce Algra.

Drawing on page 103 by Lynn Marks.